A New Guide to **Kansas Mushrooms**

A New Guide to **Kansas**

Mushrooms

Sherry Kay, Benjamin Sikes, and Caleb Morse

University Press of Kansas

Published by the University Press of Kansas (Lawrence, Kansas 66045), which was organized by the Kansas Board of Regents and is operated and funded by Emporia State University, Fort Hays State University, Kansas State University, Pittsburg State University, the University of Kansas, and Wichita State University.

This book is an introduction and identification guide to many of the wild mushrooms found in Kansas. Information about edibility is included, but this book is not intended to allow individuals to select mushrooms to eat based only on these descriptions. Wild mushrooms may be poisonous, and some can be fatal if consumed. The authors and publisher strongly advise anyone gathering mushrooms for eating to seek the help of an experienced mycologist. Never eat any mushroom unless you are 100 percent certain of its identity. The authors and publisher accept no responsibility for readers who do not follow this advice and disclaim any and all liability in connection with the collection and consumption of any wild mushrooms or other fungi or plants, whether described in this book or not.

Library of Congress Cataloging-in-Publication Data

Names: Kay, Sherry, author. | Sikes, Benjamin, author. | Morse, Caleb, author.
Title: A new guide to Kansas mushrooms / Sherry Kay, Benjamin Sikes, Caleb Morse.
Description: Lawrence : University Press of Kansas, 2022. | Serves as a second edition and update to A Guide to Kansas Mushrooms (1993) by Horn, Kay, and Abel. | Includes bibliographical references and index.
Identifiers: LCCN 2021038316
ISBN 9780700633067 (paperback)
ISBN 9780700633074 (ebook)
Subjects: LCSH: Mushrooms—Kansas—Identification. | Mycology—Kansas.
Classification: LCC QK617 .K379 2022 | DDC 579.609781—dc23
LC record available at https://lccn.loc.gov/2021038316.
British Library Cataloguing-in-Publication Data is available.

Printed in the United States of America

10 9 8 7 6 5 4 3 2 1

The paper used in this publication is acid-free and meets the minimum requirements of the American National Standard for Permanence of Paper for Printed Library Materials Z39.48-1992.

To Richard “Skip” Kay

and

Robert Lichtwardt

Contents

More on Mushrooms

Preface

This book is about Kansas mushrooms. Although several of the photographs show mushrooms from other states, the same species have been seen here in Kansas. Representative specimens of most, if not all, are deposited in the McGregor Herbarium at the University of Kansas.

The first edition of this book, published in 1993, was successful for several reasons, perhaps mainly because it provided a depth of material addressed to both the beginner and those who wanted a better understanding of the fungal kingdom. The mushroom illustrations were of high quality, but the description for each species also offered a detailed evaluation of the photo, including how individuals of this species might vary, and noted other species similar to the one under discussion. The supporting essays were just that, important to the topic, and feedback about those pieces has been good; readers did want to know about mycological Latin, the history of Kansas mushrooming, and mushroom habitats. All in all, it was an innovative book, and the second edition intends to continue as the first began.

Two main concerns prompted this revision. First, the revolution in DNA sequencing and genetic analysis has improved our knowledge of the relationships among mushrooms, driving changes in individual mushroom names and revisions in major groupings within the fungal kingdom. These changes are based on comparing representative parts of DNA from individual mushroom specimens and using genetic data to retrace the common ancestors among many different fungi. Now we know, for example, that the cap-and-stalk-shaped Russulales (nos. 80–88) are related to the huge, shelving *Bondarzewia berkeleyi* (no. 115). The scientific names have been changed to better reflect our improved understanding of these relationships among mushrooms. It is likely that additional names will change in the future as additional genetic information is analyzed, but the nomenclature of this book can be viewed as an accurate snapshot of our knowledge at this time. Updated names for mushrooms in this book were vetted primarily through Index Fungorum, with additional clarifications from "Mycobank," the tenth edition of *Dictionary of the Fungi*, and Michael Kuo's excellent, well-researched website mushroomexpert.com.

The second reason for revision is the number of new mushrooms that have been found since the advent of the first edition. When the first book was written, 727 different species had been recorded in Kansas. Now, over 1,200 have been seen! Perhaps the hardest part of this revision was deciding which of these additional species should be added to the 150 in the first edition. We decided that fifty more would be appropriate without adding too much to the bulk of the book. First to be considered were species, genera, or representatives of families that occur frequently but were not in the first edition, such as the species *Pseudosperma rimosum* (no. 56) of the family Inocybaceae. There are many members of the Inocybaceae in Kansas, and while as a group they are easy to recognize, they are small, not showy, hard to identify to the species level, and often poisonous. We believe knowledge of this family is important (even if knowing every species is not). Second to be added were common lawn mushrooms, included for the casual observer and the frantic parent of mycophilic offspring—though such parents should always consult an expert. A third group added was unusual mushrooms, rarely found in other books and/or not expected to be seen in Kansas, such as the species *Pseudocraterellus pseudoclavatus* (no. 143).

Mushrooms can be beautiful. Luckily, Carla Wick and Hank Guarisco, gifted photographers and good friends to mycology, supplied many exceptional photos for the new edition. But in the end, another factor for inclusion was whether we had good enough photos of the additional species. Many important mushrooms have still been left out, though some are mentioned without an accompanying picture. As noted in the first edition, Kansas, being centrally located in the United States, "offers a unique crossroads of mushroom possibilities": northern mushrooms are found with southern species, as eastern and western kinds also appear here, and some may mix to produce mushrooms particular to Kansas. Certainly, many more species from this region need to be identified and named.

In order to get the most out of this book, the reader should start with "How to Identify a Mushroom." Additional aids and supplementary materials are provided to enable the user to recognize and understand many of the mushrooms found in Kansas. The main body of the book, the Anthology, contains photos of two hundred species accompanied by written descriptions that discuss characteristics visible in the photo, variations in coloration and appearance based on different conditions, variations seen in Kansas; using the dichotomous keys, readers can identify 120 additional species.

Much of the supplementary material from the first edition has been retained, including essays on history, mycological Latin, habitats, and edibility, although modified and updated as needed. Essays new to this edition cover how to grow mushrooms, the revolution in taxonomy, and online resources. This last section can help the reader continue to navigate the dynamic mushroom world, both as taxonomy changes and as smartphones and other digital devices inspire new ways to discover this mostly hidden world. Another key addition to the book is phylogenetic trees (i.e., cladograms; see Appendices A and B), which show the evolutionary relationships among the species listed as they are currently understood. As outlined for the names above, our understanding of these relationships has improved remarkably. While information about fungal relationships continues to be revealed, those presented here are based on the best knowledge available at the time of writing.

Like the first book, this edition aims to satisfy both the beginner and those well acquainted with mycology. A beginner does not have to follow the systematic classification—arranged loosely from phylum to class, order, family, genus, and species—to identify a mushroom. Technical terms in the Anthology that aid in identifying a species are both defined in the glossary and explained in the text to assist beginners. Readers interested in the relationships among mushrooms should consult the trees here and online resources such as Mycobank and Index Fungorum to track future changes. Like mushrooms themselves, our knowledge about relationships within the fungal kingdom will continue to evolve. Nevertheless, we believe this book will be useful and entertaining (even in its imperfections) to all interested readers. Enjoy!

Bibliography

Crous, P. W., W. Gams, J. A. Stalpers, V. Robert, and G. Stegehuis. 2004. "Mycobank: An Online Initiative to Launch Mycology into the 21st Century." *Studies in Mycology* 50: 19–22.

Kirk, Paul M., Paul E. Cannon, David W. Mintneer, and Stalpers A. Joost. *Ainsworth and Bisby's Dictionary of the Fungi.* 10th ed. Wallingford, UK: CABinternational, 2008.

Kuo, Michael. Mushroomexpert.com. 2021. http://www.mushroomexpert.com.

Robert, V., G. Stegehuis, and J. Stalpers. 2005. The Mycobank Engine and Related Databases. http://www.mycobank.org/.

Royal Botanical Gardens Kew, Landcare Research–NZ, and Institute of Microbiology, Chinese Academy of Sciences. Index Fungorum, accessed December 2021, http://www.indexfungorum.org.

Acknowledgments

We first must thank Kaw Valley Mycological Society members, including George Sayers, Fadra Mitchell, Katy Willson, Patti Adams, and Will Fraundorfer, for their outstanding contributions. We especially thank Carla Wick, Ron Meyers, Terry Shister, Hans-Peter Schulte, and Hank Guarisco for their book-specific contributions. We thank Bruce Horn and Dean Abel for allowing us to use their contributions from the first edition. Rosanne Healy provided much-appreciated truffle identification and terminology. László Nagy provided much-needed advice to pare down the phylogeny of Agaricomycotina from more than five thousand species (which he and his collaborators built) to those represented in the book. Many thanks to Dana Peterson and the Kansas Applied Remote Sensing group (KARS) for digitizing and improving the land-cover map used in the Kansas Habitats section. We are also most indebted to Candace Dettbarn for digitizing the text of the first edition of the book.

SK: My husband, Richard "Skip" Kay, the center of my life for forty-four years, died in the summer of 2018. Nevertheless, he helped me plan this book even in the emergency room while waiting for medical attention. Robert Lichtwardt, the mycologist at the University of Kansas for many years, always supported amateur mycology. Skip and Robert were the two kindest and most intelligent people I have had the good fortune to have in my life. Additionally, I want to personally thank my living family, Lawrence Kay, Jennifer Kaufman, Sophie Tyler Kaufman Kay, Sally Kay, Nathan Creamer, and Gail Thursz, for their support, as well as my three dogs, Trudy, Caleb, and Chip, and two horses, Merlyon and BeyBey, for getting me up in the morning to continue the arduous journey to complete this book. Further, many thanks to my co-authors, Ben and Caleb, for substantially improving this book.

BS: I would first like to thank my wife, April, and my sons, Liam, Thomas, Asher, and Daniel, for the time that they willingly donated so this work could be completed. Their patience and (convincing) enthusiasm for my diatribes on mushrooms and cladograms really helped keep me engaged. My mother, Monique Lewis, also visited multiple times during the writing and helped all around. We all should thank our mothers if we write a book! The late Robert Lichtwardt helped me immensely when I first arrived at the University of Kansas, provided excellent mentorship and resources on mycology, and generally was one of the most knowledgeable and kindest people I have met. He is missed. Finally, I would like to thank my coauthors, Sherry and Caleb. They have been extremely patient with me, helped me numerous times in teaching mycology at the University of Kansas, and are good friends.

CM: I thank my parents, Jane and Warner Morse, who instilled in me an interest in nature and allowed me the freedom to explore it as a child, and my wife, Katherine, and our children, Helen and Lydia, for their unending patience and loving support, their own enthusiasm for natural history, and many happy walks in the woods. I'm grateful to my coauthors, Sherry and Ben, for involving me in this project and for cultivating in many others a passion for mycology.

A New Guide to **Kansas Mushrooms**

Read This First!

How to Identify a Mushroom

Sherry Kay and Benjamin Sikes

Scientists call them fungi, but most of us just call them mushrooms. Because mushrooms differ greatly from other forms of life, their anatomy is not familiar to us. Instead of thinking in terms of legs or leaves, we must learn a new vocabulary that adequately describes mushrooms. The overall study of mushrooms is called mycology, but in this book we aim to keep scientific jargon to a minimum to allow readers to learn simple identification skills. We have appended a glossary of unavoidable technical terms for reference (p. 369) and will define most technical terms in the text. One major clarification must be made from the beginning. This book deals only with two primary subdivisions of the mushroom kingdom, namely, the phyla Basidiomycota and Ascomycota (see the Glossary). It should also be noted that none of the members included are species that are lichenized, that is, associated with a photosynthesizing organism in a mutualism to form a lichen. As one works to identify a mushroom, it is important to remember that many will have a common name (or names), such as yellow morel, as well as a scientific name, such as *Morchella americana* (no. 181). Whenever possible, we have provided both names. The next section describes the principal features found among these mushrooms. It should also be said at the outset that "toadstool" is a popular rather than a scientific term; broadly, it denotes a mushroom with a cap on top of a stalk, and it often has negative connotations.

Visible Features for Identifying Mushrooms

A mushroom develops from a nodule, or pinhead, that forms within the **mycelium** (plural mycelia) (Fig. 1), the mass of threadlike **hyphae** that make up the mushroom organism (Fig. 10, p. 293). This development is likely true of both Basidiomycota and Ascomycota. In the gilled section of Basidiomycota (those looking most like the ordinary grocery-store mushroom), the nodule grows into a mushroom "egg" (Fig. 2A). The egg sometimes has an outer layer of tissue, the **universal veil** that surrounds the developing fruiting body. As the egg expands, the universal veil ruptures (Fig. 2B and C), and remnants may remain as a cup, or **volva**, at the base of the stalk or as warts or volval patches on the cap (Fig. 2D). Many mushrooms lack a universal veil and therefore do not have either a volva or volval patches. Sometimes there is a second layer of tissue, the **partial veil** (Fig. 2C), covering the bladelike **gills** that bear spores (Fig. 2D). Remnants of the partial veil may remain as a ring, or **annulus**, circling the stalk (Fig. 2D) or as fragments hanging from the margin of the cap. The ring may be skirtlike, as in some species of *Amanita*; collar-like, as in many species of *Macrolepiota*; or merely the faint remains of a **cortina** (a partial veil composed of filaments resembling a spiderweb), as is typical of the genus *Cortinarius*. Naturally, mushrooms that do not form a partial veil also lack an annulus.

Figure 1. Strands of fungal mycelium—the feeding state, or spawn, of a mushroom—growing on a rotting log.

The **stalk** may be central and support the cap in the middle, or it may be off center and/or lateral, as in species of *Panus* and *Pleurotus*. In other mushrooms, a stalk may be totally lacking, as in the shelving polypores, some of which have what appear to be gills. However, there are many more nongilled than gilled mushrooms. Puffballs lack a proper stalk but may have a supporting base. Other mushrooms—truffles, jellies, earthstars, and bird's nest fungi—usually do not have stalks, and a specialized mycological vocabulary exists to describe their parts.

The manner in which the gills attach to the top of the stalk is another important feature. Mushrooms in the genera *Agaricus*, *Amanita*, and *Pluteus*, among others, have **free** gills that do not extend to the top of the stalk (Fig. 3A). Others have **decurrent** gills that extend down the stalk (Fig. 3B), as in the genera *Omphalotus* and *Pleurotus*. There are a great number of variations between the extremes of free and decurrent, which in this book are simply called **attached** gills (Fig. 3C–E).

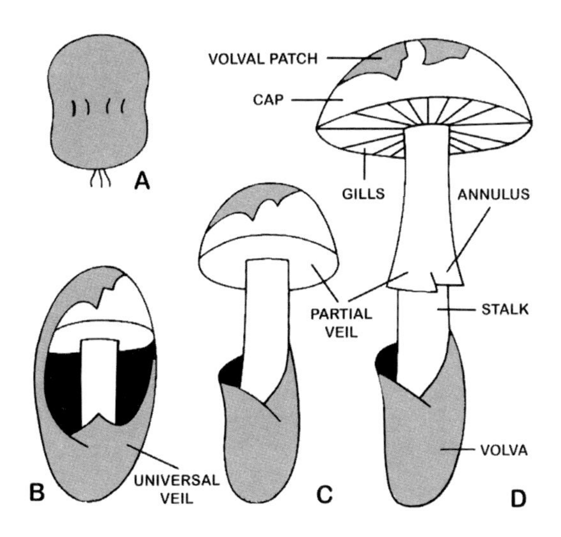

Figure 2. Mushroom anatomy. Developing mushroom:
A. Mushroom egg, sometimes called the button stage.
B. Rupture of the universal veil.
C. Partial veil still covers the gills.
D. Gills are exposed as the partial veil collapses and forms an annulus on the stalk. Remnants of the universal veil form a volva at the base of the stalk and volval patches on the cap.

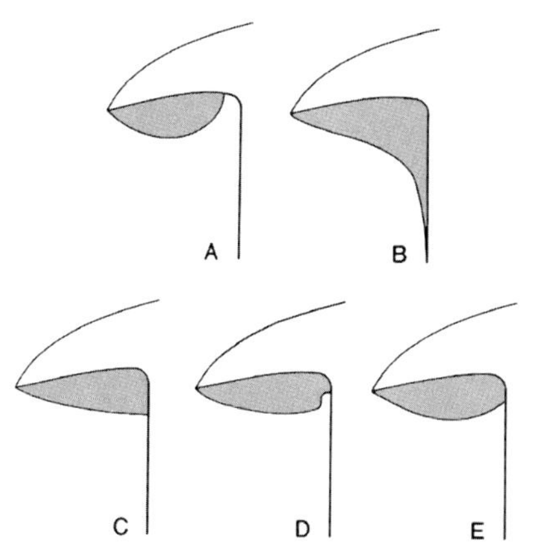

Figure 3. Gill attachment.
A. Free—gills do not extend to top of stalk.
B. Decurrent—gills descend down stalk.
C. Attached (adnate)—gills abut squarely to stalk.
D. Attached (notched)—gills are notched where they join the stalk.
E. Attached (adnexed)—gills curve upward toward the stalk.

The gills are where the spores are produced in the conventional grocery-store mushrooms, but everyone knows there are different mushroom shapes, and the spore-bearing surfaces will also look different. Therefore, it is important to determine where a mushroom produces its spores (this location is called the **hymenium** [plural hymenia]) and what it looks like. Figure 4 shows some different spore-producing surfaces in Basidiomycota. Ascomycota, like morels, have smooth, pitted, wrinkled, and sometimes finely pimpled hymenia, though these features are not defining and could be similar to the features of Basidiomycota hymenia. Taken together, the presence or absence of these features helps to tell you what mushroom you have.

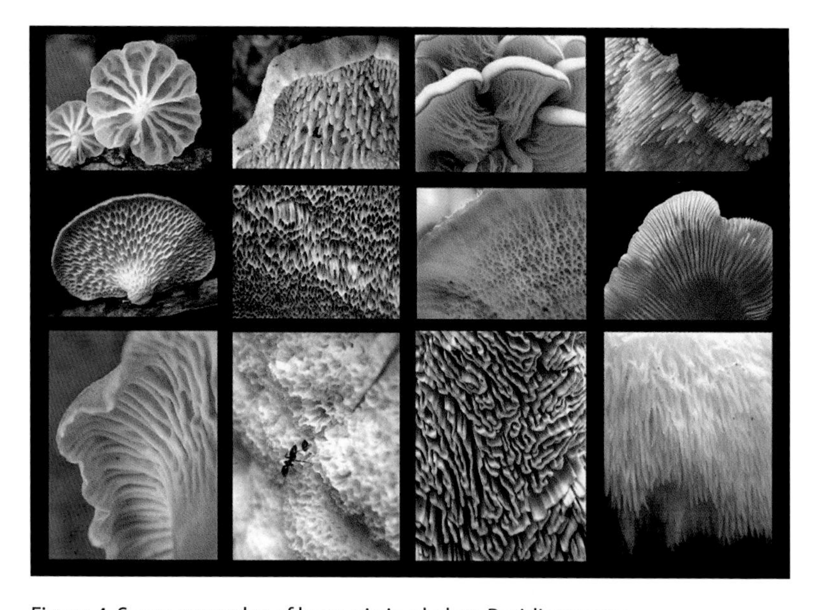

Figure 4. Some examples of hymenia in phylum Basidiomycota.

Top row (*left to right*): *Marasmius* species with veining between wide-spaced gills; *Hydnum repandum* with teeth; *Pleurotus* species with gills running down the stalk (decurrent) and cross-gills; toothed resupinate (lying flat on the substrate) species.

Middle row (*left to right*): *Neofavolus alveolaris* with angular pores; irregular pores of different heights; elongate irregular pores; closely spaced gills with shorter gills interspersed (lamellulae).

Lower row (*left to right*): *Cantharellus* species with blunt ridges (not gills); ragged pores; coarse mazelike pores; *Hericium* species with teeth of uneven length.

Location, substrate, and other elements important to identification

Beyond physical features, the location where the mushroom is growing and what it is growing on are also often critical to identification. Distinct kinds of mushrooms have different habitats, from woods to pastures to lawns. The growth habits of mushrooms—that is, do they grow in a cluster (**caespitose**), singly or in arcs or rings? (Fig. 5)—may be a clue to their identity. Some mushrooms may be found only in wet areas or immediately after a rain, and these are important features to note. To aid in your search and identification, specific Kansas mushroom habitats are detailed in "Kansas Habitats" (p. 297). The substance on which the mushroom grows, called the **substrate**, is also a key to identity. Mushrooms lack chlorophyll and cannot make their own food, so like us, they must obtain their food from organic sources. Mushrooms may be found growing on different types of wood—living, rotten, or in between—as well as on the ground—bare, hard, or covered in leaf litter. The strategy by which a mushroom obtains its food is a key feature of its ecology and can help with identification. Many mushrooms obtain their food by decomposing wood, leaves, or other organic matter. These are considered **saprotrophic**, that is, free-living decomposers. Mushrooms can also be **parasitic**, damaging or killing living organisms that they live on or inside. These include exotic mushrooms such as *Cordyceps*, which are key insect parasites, as well as more common ones that attack living trees and other plants. However, it is now recognized that many mushrooms have a **mutualistic** relationship with plants, meaning a mutually beneficial partnership. Most vascular plants (ferns, trees, shrubs, and flowering plants) have a fungal mycelium growing in or on their roots, and some of these produce mushrooms. This intimate relationship is called a **mycorrhizal** association. Recent research has indicated more complex and evolving relationships between living plants and fungi, termed **biotrophic** and generally meaning ranging from parasitic through mutualistic; these newly discovered life modes may include interactions between fungi and almost all green plants, even mosses, ferns, and grasses. Among other functions, the fungus increases the root's ability to take up mineral nutrients from the soil; in return, the plant provides sugars and other necessary substances to the fungus. Mycorrhizae are one of the most widespread mutualisms on Earth and have been found in fossils from the earliest land plants, more than 400 million years old, where they may have aided plant colonization of land. Recent fossil findings even suggest that fungal structures occurred an amazing one billion years ago! Because different mycorrhizal, parasitic, and even saprotrophic mushrooms can have prefer-

Figure 5. A fairy ring of *Chlorophyllum molybdites* (no. 79) in a typical configuration.

ences for certain types of trees, knowing what trees are nearby may also help tell you what mushroom you have.

It is well known that some mushrooms are deadly to eat (not to touch or smell), hence the importance of identification if you plan to eat a mushroom you have picked. But you should also consider contamination in the substrate and/or habitat where that mushroom was growing. Mushrooms readily suck up poisons such as pesticides and even lead left over from leaded gas. Indeed, the common oyster mushroom, *Pleurotus ostreatus* (no. 38), can consume diesel, oil, and even plastic and thus may play an important role in "bioremediation." However edible a mushroom species appears to be, if it is growing in a contaminated area, it could poison you. You should not be fooled into thinking a mushroom is safe to eat because there are bites taken out of it or it contains larvae. There are insects that specialize in poisonous mushrooms, and even some other mammals tolerate particular poisons better than humans.

All of the above should be carefully observed in the field. You cannot rely on analysis only after the specimen has been collected. A deadly *Amanita*'s fragile cup at the stalk base can easily disappear if hastily picked; a slimy *Hygrophorus* cap may dry out; a purple *Cortinarius* may fade to grey in your basket; and a milky *Lactarius* may dry out and not make milk at home. It is also a good idea to look at all stages of development. If you can find young and old stages of your specimen in the field, you may find that age can make a dramatic difference in color, shape, smell, and so on. Finding a number of specimens is also desirable because the environment may distort individuals. One mushroom may have lost its ring to insect predation, been stepped on by a raccoon and grown lopsided, been drowned by high water (more likely blasted by drought here), or been affected by any of countless circumstances, but if you have several similar mushrooms, you will gain a better idea of what characteristics are truly representative or even whether your finds are the same species. Close observation is the key. A note about seasonality: we have included times of the year when each species is expected, but mushrooms are opportunists and will fruit when they feel the time is right. I have seen oysters during a January thaw. Climate change is also a factor, so consider what the weather has been like in identifying your mushroom.

The color of the spores is almost always an important clue to identity, so as soon as possible, you should obtain a spore print (Fig. 6) to determine spore color. To do so, place the cap of the mushroom on a piece of paper, aluminum foil, or a microscope slide and invert a glass or cup over it. The mushroom should be placed with the hymenium down, as this is where the spores are produced. The cup keeps the humidity high and contains any bugs that reside in the mushroom. In thirty minutes, the mushroom may expel enough spores to make a powdery deposit thick enough to determine the color, but leaving the setup overnight will likely result in a more satisfactorily heavy deposit of spores the next day. A moistened bit of cotton or paper towel on top of the

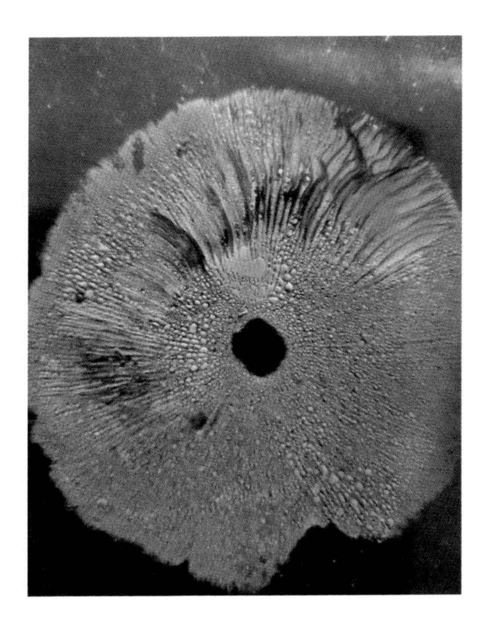

Figure 6. The pink spore print of *Pluteus cervinus* (no. 45).

cap will aid the process by keeping it from drying out. It is a good idea to make the spore print on both white and black paper to ensure a contrast with spore color. Do not refrigerate your specimen before trying to get a spore print; mushrooms often won't drop their spores after a chill and sometimes won't furnish spores for other reasons. The color of the spores should help you determine generally what group your find belongs to and sometimes is defining. For instance, a circle of big, meaty, mostly white mushrooms appears on your lawn. They look a lot like the edible *Macrolepiota procera* (no. 78, though those usually occur in the woods and not in a ring—there are many other clues you should attend to). If you get a spore print from this lawn species, it almost certainly will be a dusty green, not the white that would identify it as *M. procera*, and that will tell you that the mushroom is *Chlorophyllum molybdites* (no. 79), the most common poisoner in Kansas. Spore color is always a good way to help you on the road to identification.

Identification of mushrooms increasingly relies on the use of advanced tools, including microscopes and DNA sequencing. Stains and microscopes have been consistent and excellent mycological identification aids for years. Advances in deciphering DNA sequences have, in many ways, revolutionized our understanding of fungal evolution and how species are related. However, as of the writing of this book, many of these methods and materials are not widely available to the amateur (or even many experienced mycologists). Later parts of the book (see "Sex, Lies and the Truth about Mushrooms," for instance, p. 287) contain more information on how to proceed with what might be available to the keen amateur. Gene sequencing has informed and of course updated our species names to reflect current nomenclature and taxonomy, but even without your own DNA sequencer, noting the physical features, habitat, substrate, and other features outlined above will help you match a mushroom to those included in this book. The entries in the Anthology appear in two parts; first the informal description, which often notes particular features of the accompanying photo and mentions and describes other comparable species, and at the end a more technical "*Description*." The latter includes details that may benefit readers with access to more advanced tools, specifically the microscopic dimensions of spores and chemical responses to reagents such as **Melzer's solution**. Melzer's is an iodine-based reagent that is somewhat difficult to obtain but useful. It is most often used on white spores, and when a drop is applied to the spores of the specimen, there is sometimes a color change that can help with identification. A color change to dark blue is called **amyloid**, while if spores change to a reddish-brown darker than the original solution, the spore response is called **dextrinoid**. If there is no change, the term **nonamyloid** will be employed.

Bibliography

Bessette, Alan E., Arleen R. Bessette, and David W. Fischer. *Mushrooms of Northeastern North America*. Syracuse, NY: Syracuse University Press, 1997.

Bessette, Alan E., William C. Roody, and Arleen R. Bessette. *North American Boletes: A Color Guide to the Fleshy Pored Mushrooms*. Syracuse, NY: Syracuse University Press, 2000.

Beug, Michael W., Alan E. Bessette, and Arleen R. Bessette. *Ascomycete Fungi of North America: A Mushroom Reference Guide*. 1st ed. Austin: University of Texas Press, 2014.

Binion, Denise, Steve Stephenson, William Roody, Harold H. Burdsall, Jr., Orson K. Miller, Jr., and Larissa Vasilyeva. *Macrofungi Associated with Oaks of Eastern North America*. Morgantown: West Virginia University Press, 2008.

Bunyard, Britt A., and Jay Justice. *Amanitas of North America*. Batavia, IL: Fungi Press, 2020.

Gilbertson, R. L., and L. Ryvarden. *North American Polypores*. 2 volumes. Oslo: Fungiflora Oslo A/S Norway, 1986.

Jennings, D. H., and G. Lysek. *Fungal Biology: Understanding the Fungal Lifestyle*. Oxford, UK: Bios Scientific Publishers, 1996.

Kaufman, C. H. *The Gilled Mushrooms (Agaricaceae) of Michigan and the Great Lakes Regions*. 2 volumes. Toronto, Ontario, Canada: Dover Publications, 1971 (1918).

Kuo, Michael. *Morels*. Ann Arbor: University of Michigan Press, 2005.

Kuo, Michael, and Andrew S. Methven. *Mushrooms of the Midwest*. Urbana, Chicago, and Springfield: University of Illinois Press, 2014.

Long, Litt Woon. *The Way through the Woods*. Translated by Barbara J. Haveland. New York: Spiegel & Grau (Random House), 2019.

Loron, C. C., C. François, R. H. Rainbird, E. C. Turner, S. Borensztajn, and E. J. Javaux. "Early Fungi from the Proterozoic Era in Arctic Canada." *Nature* 570, no. 7760 (June 2019): 232–235.

McKnight, Kent H., and Vera B. McKnight. *A Field Guide to Mushrooms: North America*. 1st ed. Boston: Houghton Mifflin Company, 1987.

Phillips, Roger. *Mushrooms of North America*. Boston: Little, Brown and Company, 1991.

Smith, Alexander. "New and Unusual Cortnarii from Michigan with a Key to the North American Species of Subgenus *Bulbopodium*." *Bulletin of the Torey Botanical Club* 69, no. 1 (January 1942): 44–64.

Taylor, T. N., W. Remy, H. Hass, and H. Kerp. "Fossil Arbuscular Mycorrhizae from the Early Devonian." *Mycologia* 87, no. 4 (July 1, 1995): 560–573.

The Edibility Issue: Poisons and Individual Reactions

Dean Abel

Poisonous mushrooms are often tasty and attractive and do not discourage predators, human or otherwise, with a bad taste. Some species of insects choose poisonous mushrooms in which to lay their eggs, and their larvae seem to thrive. So you must become knowledgeable and cautious if you plan to eat wild mushrooms. A well-worn myco-aphorism states, "There are old mushroom hunters, and there are bold mushroom hunters, but there are no old, bold mushroom hunters." The mushroom you are trying to identify may key out close to a similar species, or it may closely resemble a picture in a guidebook, but mycology is not horseshoes, and close does not count. If one is eating mushrooms, close can kill.

Even mushrooms that are well-established choice edibles—for example, chanterelles (nos. 134–135) or morels (nos. 181–182)—sometimes make people sick. Such idiosyncratic reactions may be due to an individual's allergic sensitivity to particular species. Poisoning by edible mushrooms may also be due to the eating of spoiled or uncooked mushrooms, or it may be a mycophobe's psychosomatic reaction to eating something weird, for sometimes merely the notion that one has eaten a wild mushroom, and not the mushroom itself, causes symptoms akin to poisoning. If you suspect that you have eaten a poisonous mushroom, a panic reaction may occur, and sure enough, you will get sick. Jonathan Ott reported a survey of nine accidental and nine intentional diners upon *Amanita muscaria* (see no. 2). The accidental users experienced nausea, muscle spasms, fear of dying, and severe drowsiness (five lost consciousness). The intentional users experienced nausea, drowsiness without loss of consciousness, and hallucinations. Ott ascribes the diverse experiences of the poisoning victims to the setting of their mushroom encounter and to their different expectations.

Often cases of mushroom poisoning involve the ingestion of mixed species, either through carelessly confusing them during collection or celebrating a good day's foray by eating a number of different mushrooms. Generally, I do not like to combine my woodland culinary finds. I recommend eating only one kind of mushroom at a time, especially if it is one you have not eaten before. Also I do not eat quantities of wild mushrooms more than two or three days in a row. Pigging out for a week on oyster mushrooms (*Pleurotus ostreatus*, no. 38) or yellow chanterelles (no. 134) can make some people sick. The phenomenon may indicate a cumulative poisoning by unknown toxins or it may simply be that chitin and butter are not the most digestible combination.

There is growing evidence that mushrooms take up and concentrate heavy metals and other toxic substances from the soil, and though this may benefit the environment at large, it makes mushrooms less desirable as food. I would rather not be the final link in the food chain to remove mercury and lead from our spoiled lands. Therefore, I am hesitant to eat mushrooms growing on the well-manicured lawns of parks or cemeteries, on farmlands, or along roadways because of possible contamination by pesticides, herbicides, or automotive wastes.

When sampling a new species of mushroom, I always eat just a little bit, usually sautéed in butter or oil—never more than two or three bites—and wait. If I do not get sick, I prepare a heartier meal of them the next day. I always set aside a few uneaten ones just in case I might require a professional identification if either I or someone else who ate them should become ill. In every case of suspected mushroom poisoning, it is imperative to identify the mushroom involved because different poisons require different treatments. It is easier to do this by looking at a specimen that was kept in a paper bag in the refrigerator than by looking for spores in vomit at the hospital.

Even if you do not eat mushrooms, remember that mushrooms release billions of spores and that some people suffer an allergic reaction to these airborne irritants. A friend and I were making spore prints and examining mushrooms in my room when he was overcome by a fit of sneezing. He recovered when he left the room. In another instance, as he was extracting a large specimen of *Discina caroliniana* (no. 178) from a sack, out came a cloud of spores, and he suffered a similar attack of sneezing.

You cannot get sick merely from handling a poisonous mushroom. If you are a taster—and many mushrooms are identified in part by their taste or odor—do not swallow the nibble that you chew. Spit it out, and rinse your mouth out afterward.

I have eaten over fifty kinds of wild mushrooms, including species of *Amanita*, but even on occasions when I may not know exactly what species I am eating, I am always 100 percent positive that I am not eating a deadly poisonous mushroom. Only once, after eating some small white shelves that I took to be young *Pleurotus ostreatus*, did I experience explosive diarrhea the next morning. I recall that the mushrooms smelled of coconut, lacking the fishy odor I now recognize, so perhaps I should have hesitated.

Mushroom poisons are classified by the symptoms they provoke in the victim. Because the treatment for one type of poisoning may compound the effects of other toxins, it is of the utmost importance to determine the cause of the poisoning accurately. For example, atropine may aggravate the symptoms of muscimol/ibotenic-acid poisoning but will alleviate those of severe muscarine poisoning. Although both types of toxins are present in *Amanita muscaria*, muscimol and ibotenic acid are the predominant ones, so the administration of atropine is inappropriate and may prolong the victim's suffering.

The Deadly Poisons

There are poisonous mushrooms that will kill you if you eat them, but not right away. The insidious thing about these mushrooms is that the symptoms of their poisoning are typically delayed, so by the time the victim gets sick, the mushroom has already been digested and the toxins absorbed into the body. The most deadly toxins are the cyclopeptides called "amatoxins," which cause acute liver and kidney dysfunction. They are found primarily in mushrooms in the genus *Amanita* but also in a number of small species of *Leucoagaricus* (no. 76), in *Leucocoprinus* (no. 77; also possibly other lepiotoid mushrooms, see p. 117), and in *Galerina marginata* (no. 58), a little brown mushroom (LBM) common on logs in Kansas.

Amatoxin poisoning proceeds through characteristic stages. The first symptoms are delayed six to twenty-four hours after ingestion and consist of abdominal pain, nausea, vomiting, and diarrhea. Next, there is a period of

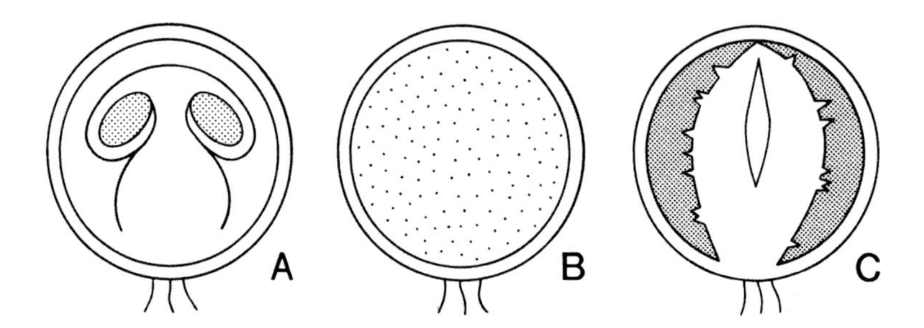

Figure 7. Cross-section of mushroom eggs.
A. Deadly poisonous *Amanita* button enveloped by a universal veil.
B. Puffball, which is spongy and homogeneous inside.
C. Stinkhorn (*Phallus hadriani*, no. 155) with an unexpanded stalk surrounded by dark spore slime.

remission in which the symptoms recede for a day, but then they reappear, leading to liver and kidney failure, convulsions, coma, and death in four to seven days. Despite a mortality rate of 50 percent in untreated cases, supportive medical treatments involving liver transplants and new drug therapies promise a 95 percent chance of survival. The deadly white *Amanita* most often found in Kansas is *A. bisporigera* (no. 3), the two-spored variety of the destroying angel. Care must be taken not to mistake a poisonous *Amanita* egg for an edible puffball (Fig. 7). I have found eggs of *A. bisporigera* that required a hand lens to determine the outline of the developing mushroom inside.

Amatoxins inhibit an enzyme in liver cells called "RNA polymerase B," which copies the genetic code of DNA into messenger RNA molecules. The ensuing disruption of liver cell metabolism accounts for the severe liver dysfunction caused by amatoxins. Amatoxins also lead to kidney failure because as the kidneys attempt to filter out the poison, it damages the convoluted tubules of the kidneys and reenters the blood to recirculate and cause another round of destruction.

Orellanine is another deadly poison that is found in some species of the genus *Cortinarius* (nos. 48–54). Orellanine is a bipyridine, as is the herbicide paraquat, and inhibits the activity of the enzyme alkaline phosphatase in kidney cells. Many of the symptoms of orellanine poisoning are similar to those induced by amatoxins, but the muscular pain, excessive thirst, and painful urination, which may appear after thirty-six hours, can be delayed as long as one to two weeks after ingestion. Orellanine destroys the kidney tubules, and in severe cases, treatment may require blood dialysis or a kidney transplant. Fatalities occur, and orellanine poisoning should be considered in cases of kidney failure from unknown origin. In addition to orellanine, toxic cyclopeptides called "cortinarins" may be present and play a role in *Cortinarius* poisonings. There are more species of *Cortinarius* in North America than of any other genus, and all of them should be excluded from the dining table.

Gyromitrin, a toxin present in species of *Discina* and *Gyromitra* (nos. 178–179)—the false morels—causes similar but less severe liver and kidney dysfunction. During cooking and in the acid environment of the stomach, gyromitrin is broken down into various toxic hydrazines, including monomethylhydrazine (MMH), which is used as a fuel to propel rockets. Symptoms generally appear within six to eight hours and consist of nausea, headache, delirium, and convulsions, although vomiting may be the only obvious reaction. MMH is a water-soluble compound that may be partially removed from the mushrooms by boiling and discarding the water. However, there are reports of gourmet cooks who were poisoned simply by inhaling the aromatic but MMH-laden vapor from the boiling stew pot. In the spring, many Kansans collect and eat these false morels, which they call beefsteaks, elephant ears, or simply the red ones. Though neither *Discina fastigiata* nor *D. caroliniana*, the two most common species in Kansas, have been conclusively shown to contain gyromitrin, I would never eat them.

The Hallucinogenic Poisons

Some mushrooms contain the powerful mood-altering chemicals psilocybin and psilocin. The most notorious are the *Psilocybe* mushrooms, which have only occasionally been reported in Kansas, but their toxins may also be present in other species, such as *Panaeolina foenisecii* (no. 62), an LBM that is common on Kansas lawns. The state's recorded species of *Psilocybe* (see no. 57) are not known to be hallucinogenic. The onset of symptoms is usually rapid and may include abdominal cramps, nausea, and vomiting in addition to mood changes ranging from anxiety to euphoria accompanied by hallucinations. The cramping and nausea can be minimized by ingesting these hallucinogenic toxins in a tea that has been brewed from the dried mushrooms. Intoxication lasts five to six hours, and recovery normally requires no medical intervention. Reports of seizures in children who have ingested these mushrooms indicate that such species are a potential danger to young people. Although *Psilocybe* mushrooms typically bruise a bluish color, this indicator can be misleading because many other mushrooms, including the edible *Boletinellus merulioides* (no. 101) and the questionable *Hortiboletus campestris* (no. 91), do as well. I have eaten *Psilocybe cubensis* cultivated in Kansas. Because I find recitations of psychedelic experiences boring, I will not bother to relate any anecdotes of my mushroom intoxications other than to say that I experienced nausea, cramps, and vivid hallucinations.

Two other types of toxins, one of which is sometimes hallucinogenic, are often confused. Muscimol and ibotenic acid, which are closely related, produce symptoms of drowsiness, confusion, euphoria, muscle spasms, visual disturbances, dilated pupils, and deep sleep or coma within thirty minutes to two hours, with recovery following within six to twenty-four hours. In contrast, muscarine causes profuse sweating, salivation, tearing, blurred vision, constricted pupils, cramps, labored breathing, and watery stools. These symptoms begin to appear fifteen to thirty minutes after consumption, while recovery can be expected within six to twenty-four hours. Both muscimol/ibotenic acid and muscarine are present in *Amanita muscaria* (see no. 2) and *A. multisquamosa* (no. 6), but muscarine only in minute amounts. Muscarine, the "sweating poison," is also present in many species of *Clitocybe* (no. 29) and members of the family Inocybaceae (no. 56).

The Alcohol Poisons

Edible species of the inky caps are generally innocuous and bland, and anyone can easily learn to recognize them as inkys. Caution must be exercised with at least one species, however, for *Coprinopsis atramentaria* (no. 66, and possibly *C. variegata* [no. 65]) contains coprine, a chemical that becomes poisonous when consumed with alcohol. Individuals may be sensitive to alcohol for up to five days after eating these mushrooms, thus one of its common names, tippler's bane. Symptoms usually appear within thirty minutes but vary with the amount and time of alcohol intake. The reaction is similar to the disulfiram syndrome in adverse alcoholism therapy and involves flushing of the face and neck, sensations of tingling and throbbing, irregular heartbeat, a metallic taste in the mouth, nausea, vomiting, and sweating. The poisoning is of short duration, for recovery occurs within two to four hours. I have eaten *C. variegata* and consumed alcohol and did not get sick, but a friend was not so fortunate, although he waited until the next day to have a drink with dinner.

The Other Poisons

The majority of mushroom poisonings involve unknown toxins that are of great variety and found in many diverse species. Poisoning is indicated by headache, cramps, nausea, vomiting, and diarrhea; these symptoms can appear at any time from thirty minutes to three hours after the mushroom meal. In some cases the symptoms may be severe, as in poisoning by *Omphalotus illudens* (no. 13) and *Chlorophyllum molybdites* (no. 79). The latter species is probably the most common cause of mushroom poisoning in Kansas due to its resemblance to edible species of *Agaricus* and lepiotoid mushrooms (*Leucoagaricus* [no. 76], *Leucocoprinus* [no. 77], *Lepiota* [nos. 75–76], and a few others found in the Conventional Agaricales section). Ansel Stubbs reported that a small piece of *Chlorophyllum* eaten raw made him ill, but on another occasion a well-cooked one caused him no upset, even though several other people who shared the meal did become violently ill. Recovery varies with the severity of the poisoning, but dehydration is generally the greatest danger. Drink plenty of liquid and get a second opinion on the identification of the mushroom you have eaten.

Bibliography

Ammirati, Joseph F., James A. Traquair, and Paul A. Horgen. *Poisonous Mushrooms of the Northern United States and Canada*. Minneapolis: University of Minnesota Press, 1985.

Benjamin, Denis R. *Mushrooms, Poisons, and Panaceas: A Handbook for Naturalists, Mycologists, and Physicians*. New York: W. H. Freeman and Company, 1995.

Lincoff, Gary, and Duane H. Mitchel. *Toxic and Hallucinogenic Mushroom Poisoning: A Handbook for Physicians and Mushroom Hunters*. New York: Van Nostrand Reinhold, 1977.

Litten, Walter. "The Most Poisonous Mushrooms." *Scientific American* 232, no. 3 (1975): 90–101.

Ott, J. "Psycho-Mycological Studies of Amanita—from Ancient Sacrament to Modern Phobia." *Journal of Psychedelic Drugs* 8 (1976): 27–35.

An Anthology of Kansas Mushrooms

Bruce Horn and Sherry Kay

Identifying an unknown mushroom is the primary goal of most users of this book. Following are descriptions and color photographs of two hundred species of mushrooms (which we sometimes call fruiting bodies and other times fungi)—many common, others rare—that have been reported from Kansas. Each of the entries is numbered; after the number is the scientific name that was current for that mushroom when this was written. In a couple of instances, we use names that have not been formally published following the rules of botanical nomenclature but that nonetheless are the best name for our species; to indicate this, we have placed these names in quotation marks. Below this name there may be one or more additional scientific or common names that are sometimes used for the species under discussion. If a scientific name is preceded by "Syn.," it is a synonym, that is, a name that is now considered obsolete by taxonomists. If a synonym is followed by "(Ed. 1)," then that name was used in the first edition. Occasionally, a scientific name will be followed by "(Ed. 1, misapplied)," which means either that the species was merely misidentified in the first edition or that species delineations have changed in the years since the original publication, and the Kansas species now has a different name. (In most instances, this annotation has been applied to species that were once believed to have very broad geographic ranges—for instance, Europe and North America—and are now known to be more limited in their distribution.) If there is a common name for the species, it is listed below all of these scientific names. The species are described in detail using macroscopic features, and for those mushroomers who wish to be more exact in their identifications, spore characteristics are given. Preceding each formal description is a general discussion on the seasonality, habitat, biology, and edibility of the fungus. Here, major characteristics useful in its identification are also discussed with reference to the color photograph; moreover, both typical and aberrant features of the specimen illustrated are noted. In addition, similar or related species are briefly mentioned in the discussion and are included in the keys along with the main entries. A species that is fully described elsewhere in this book is indicated by its species account number.

How to Use the Keys

Writers of keys are often discouraged by the way many mushroomers skip the keys and leaf through the photographs to identify their finds. Sometimes this approach is fruitful, particularly when the identity of the mushroom is further verified by carefully studying the written description. Often, however, the specimen is either not pictured or looks different from the photograph. Then it is time to turn to the keys. The species keys in this book are a dichotomous sort—that is, they consist of numbered couplets, each comprising a pair ("a" and "b") of leads from which you select the one of two mutually exclusive choices that best describes your specimen. At the end of each lead, the key will direct you in what to do, letting you know that you have arrived at the one best choice in the book (and sending you to a numbered species account) or directing you to another couplet, which in turn will pose two more mutually exclusive leads. For instance, assume you find a pure white *Amanita* fruiting in the woods. It has a smooth, dry cap; a membranous annulus; and a sac-like volva. Starting with the key for the family Amanitaceae, you are first confronted with two choices:

1a) Cap and stalk covered with thick slime; membrane enclosing the stalk from base (volva) absent *Zhuliangomyces illinitus* (no. 9)

1b) Cap and stalk dry or at most sticky (viscid); volva present, although sometimes inconspicuous go to **2**

Naturally, the second choice in the couplet is the correct route. This will lead you directly to couplet **2**, which then leads to **3** then **4** as follows:

2a) Volva not fused to the stalk, membranous, sac-like go to **3**

2b) Volva fully fused to the stalk, with uppermost edge (margin) slightly free, or consisting of flakes or scales that may be inconspicuous go to **7**

3a) Ring encircling the stalk (annulus) present go to **4**

3b) Annulus absent go to **5**

4a) Fruiting body entirely white; cap smooth at margin; basal bulb present *Amanita bisporigera* (no. 3)

4b) Fruiting body with pale gray to dark grayish-brown cap, contrasting with white stalk; cap striate at margin (with furrows radiating from the edge); basal bulb absent *Amanita spreta* (no. 5)

Sometimes both entries of the couplet give a species. If either is what you are looking for, you are in luck; if not, go back and check to see if you understood the earlier couplets, or possibly your find is not in this book, as it presents only a subset of the macrofungi in Kansas. Sometimes neither couplet gives a species, but both direct you to go on. In any case, the salient features will be stated in all couplets.

When the key has led you to a particular species, you should next turn to the entry for that species—for example, proceed to *Amanita bisporigera* (no. 3 in the Anthology). After examining the photograph and carefully reading the description, you find that the specimen matches well. From the discussion, you also note that it is deadly poisonous, and therefore, you respectfully only admire its beauty.

If you do not initially recognize it as an *Amanita*, start with the Key to Orders (pp. 21–25). In the case of *Amanita*, which belongs to family Amanitaceae in the Conventional Order Agaricales (which is in turn well represented in this guide by many different families of fungi), you will proceed next to the Key to Families of the Conventional Order Agaricales (pp. 26–30). This extra key is included only for the families of "conventional" Agaricales (as formerly defined, those families producing mushrooms with a cap and gills). This extra key to Agaricales was made necessary by the taxonomic shake-up brought about by DNA sequencing. It may be a bit difficult to use at first, as many distantly related species in the order bear a superficial resemblance to one another. But, based on careful observation of your specimen, the key will direct you to family Amanitaceae, where you will find a key to the species of *Amanita*. Luckily, for the other orders and composites of orders included in this book, the Key to Orders takes you directly to the Key to Species. With practice, you will learn to recognize the various mushroom groups, and keys to order and family can then be bypassed, as in the example above.

If you enter a couplet and you cannot decide between the two leads, note that number and proceed in one direction. If you then end up with an obviously incorrect species, try the other alternative. If you again reach an entry that does not match, the species is most likely not in the book. Even for species you think you recognize, it is often instructive to run them through the keys as a double check, since the keys tend to emphasize the important characteristics.

Genetic analyses have revealed close relationships between mushrooms that do not look alike and only distant relationships between mushrooms that do look alike. The reason is that over time, similar characteristics have evolved multiple times in different fungal lineages. While this is extraordinary, it makes it harder for mushroomers who are trying to visually identify their find. In an attempt to keep together fungi that are similar in appearance (in hopes that this book will be easier to use), different orders are sometimes grouped together in the sections of the Anthology. For instance, "Orders Cantharellales, Gomphales, Thelephorales and some atypical members of other orders" includes some groupings of fungi with unusual but soft hymenia made up of spines, branches, or smooth to rumpled surfaces. The book and the Key to Orders also include a term of convenience, "Conventional Class Gasteromycetes," the gasteroid fungi, which are all in phylum Basidiomycota but are now known to include mushrooms from several different orders. The gasteroid fungi resemble each other in that their spores are enclosed in a fungal tissue sack (like those of the puffballs) and are not discharged forcibly, as are the spores of most other Basidiomycota.

Additionally, the designation "conventional" precedes three orders in the key. This means that the order heading "Conventional Order Agaricales" contains species found in the Agaricales, as defined by common visible characteristics (having caps and gills). "Conventional Order Boletales" then contain species with tubes under a cap, and members of "Conventional Order Russulales" have brittle caps and stalks (and often brittle gills), defining visual characteristics for each of these groups without using genetic data.

This key to fungal orders begins with unusual characteristics. There are such diverse characteristics among the species included in this book that most of the class, order, and family groupings included here appear more than once in this key. In the interest of brevity, the referent will be the first word in the heading as found in the table of contents and the body of the Anthology: so, Boliniales, Leotiales, and Xylariales will be represented by "Boliniales, etc." In the Key to Orders we have sometimes included genera or individual species that stand out as having particular characters of these orders; if the line refers to a subset of the section, the words "in part" will occur.

Key to Orders

(with reference to classes, families, genera, and species, where necessary)

1a) Fruiting body arising directly from parasitized insects, truffle-like fungi, or other mushrooms or infecting corn (*Zea mays*), especially the ears go to **2**

1b) Fruiting body not parasitizing insects, truffle-like fungi, corn, or mushrooms (although sometimes parasitizing other living plants) go to **4**

2a) Fruiting body infecting corn (*Zea mays*)
Ustilago maydis (no. 175 in Gasteromycetes)

2b) Fruiting body arising from parasitized insects, truffle-like fungi, or other mushrooms go to **3**

3a) Fruiting body parasitizing the caps of mushrooms of the family Russulaceae *Asterophora lycoperdoides* (no. 37 in Tricholomataceae, etc.)

3b) Fruiting body arising from buried insects or truffle-like fungi or mold-like and coating gilled mushrooms or boletes completely
go to Boliniales, etc.
(p. 273: *Cordyceps*, *Hypomyces*, *Ophiocordyceps*, *Tolypocladium*)

4a) Fruiting body covered in minute pimple-like projections, often gray or black (one species bright coral-orange), hard at maturity, either lying flat on substrate (resupinate) or more three-dimensional in shape (spherical, club-shaped, or branched)
go to Boliniales, etc.
(p. 273: *Biscogniauxia*, *Daldinia*, *Kretzschmaria*, *Nectria*, *Xylaria*)

4b) Fruiting body not covered in minute pimple-like projections, hard or soft at maturity; color and form various go to **5**

5a) Fruiting body arising from an "egg" consisting of a membranous exterior, gelatinous layer, and embryonic fungus; at maturity covered in foul-smelling slime go to Phallales (p. 226)

5b) Fruiting body never covered in foul-smelling slime (unless rotten) go to **6**

6a) Fruiting body gelatinous throughout or with a sticky surface, at least when moist go to **7**

6b) Entire fruiting body not gelatinous when moist; if top exterior is sticky or slimy when moist, then contents tough go to **8**

7a) Fruiting body round to convoluted and filled with liquid, bright yellow to olive-yellow **or** black, cushion- or top-shaped, and sticky, covered in minute pimple-like projections go to Boliniales, etc. (p. 273: *Camarops*, *Entonaema*)

7b) Fruiting body horn, petal, or leaf-shaped, not filled with liquid or black, top-shaped, and sticky, and not covered in pimple-like projections go to Tremellales, etc. (p. 218)

8a) Fruiting body enclosing a spore mass that at maturity becomes powdery; spores shed as exterior wall breaks down or ejected through an apical pore of the spore case go to Gasteromycetes (p. 232: *Apioperdon*, *Bovistella*, *Calvatia*, *Geastrum*, *Lycoperdon*, *Pisolithus*, *Scleroderma*, *Tulostoma*)

8b) Fruiting body not enclosing a spore mass that becomes powdery at maturity go to **9**

9a) Fruiting body cup-shaped, with spore-bearing region (hymenium) on inner surface of cup or with spores borne (on basidia) within several pale to dark egg-like structures go to **10**

9b) Fruiting body not cup-shaped (although sometime vase-shaped, then with hymenium on exterior of vase) go to **11**

10a) Cup filled with several pale to dark egg-like structures enclosing spores go to Gasteromycetes (p. 232: *Crucibulum*, *Cyathus*)

10b) Cup not bearing egg-like structures; hymenium on inner surface of cup go to Helotiales, etc. (p. 254: *Aleuria*, *Bulgaria*, *Calycina*, *Galiella*, *Helvella* in part, *Humaria*, *Hymenoscyphus*, *Microstoma*, *Paragalactinia*, *Peziza*, *Sarcoscypha*, *Scutellinia*, *Urnula*)

11a) Fruiting body remaining entirely underground, solid and roundish, with a marbled interior; stalk absent (sessile) go to Helotiales, etc. (p. 254: *Tuber*)

11b) Fruiting body not remaining underground; stalk present or absent go to **12**

12a) Fruiting body highly branched and coral-like, club or finger-shaped, or made up in part or entirely of soft spines; hymenium always soft go to Cantharellales, etc. (p. 200: *Artomyces*, *Clavariadelphus*, *Clavulina*, *Clavulinopsis*, *Hericium*, *Ramaria*, *Sebacina*, *Thelephora*)

12b) Fruiting body with a distinct cap and/or resupinate, sometimes toothed but not highly branched and coral-like or club- or finger-shaped, often hard, tough, or cartilaginous go to **13**

13a) Hymenium composed of fragile, flexible, wavy, or stiff gills or gill-like structures **or** ridges, without cross-walls (making them appear mazelike); stalk usually present go to **14**

13b) Hymenium without gills: smooth, creased, wrinkled, deeply wrinkled and brain-like, deeply pitted, **or** composed of plates, teeth, or tubes with pore-like openings, these sometimes elongate or mazelike (and appearing like gills with regular or irregular cross-walls); stalk present or absent

go to **21**

14a) Hymenium of blunt ridges; fruiting body (cap, hymenium, and stalk) yellow or orange, vase-shaped

go to Cantharellales, etc. (p. 200: *Cantharellus* in part)

14b) Hymenium of gills or gill-like structures; fruiting body various colors or shapes go to **15**

15a) Hymenium of bright yellow gill-like structures, these often forked, sometimes bruising blue; cap red to dark reddish brown, velvety; spore print olive-brown; stalk yellow to reddish brown

Phylloporus rhodoxanthus group (no. 89 in Boletales)

15b) Fruiting body without the combination of bright yellow hymenium; red, velvety cap; olive-brown spore print; and yellow to reddish-brown stalk

go to **16**

16a) Caps tough, hairy, zoned white, gray, and brown; gills white, tough; stalk absent *Lenzites betulinus* (see no. 104 in Hymenochaetales, etc.)

16b) Fruiting body without the combination of tough, hairy caps zoned white, gray, and brown and tough white gills; stalk present or absent

go to **17**

17a) Cap dark-colored, rather rubbery, finely fuzzy or with gelatinous spines; stalk absent go to Hymenochaetales, etc. (p. 162: *Hohenbuehelia*)

17b) Fruiting body without the combination of dark-colored cap, rubbery texture, and being finely fuzzy or with gelatinous spines; stalk present or absent go to **18**

18a) Cap funnel-shaped, initially violet, maturing tan, fuzzy; gills running down stalk (decurrent); stalk present

Panus conchatus (no. 103 in Hymenochaetales, etc.)

18b) Fruiting body without the combination of funnel-shaped violet to tan hairy cap and decurrent gills; stalk present or absent go to **19**

19a) Cap pale to cinnamon-brown, hairy; gills with ragged edges; stalk absent

Lentinellus ursinus (see no. 109 in Hymenochaetales, etc.)

19b) Fruiting body without the combination of pale to cinnamon-brown hairy caps and gills with ragged edges; stalk present or absent go to **20**

20a) Fruiting body, especially stalk, very brittle with stalk breaking like chalk, and in some species (of genera *Lactarius* and *Lactifluus*) exuding a milky latex (sometimes slowly changing color) when injured; remnants of universal veil (volva) or ring around stalk (annulus) absent; spore print always white to yellow (or, in some species not included in this book, orange)

go to Russulales (p. 132)

20b) Fruiting body not brittle, very rarely exuding a thin liquid when injured; volva and/or annulus sometimes present; spore print variable in color, including white, various pastel shades, pink, green, rust, brown, or black

go to Key to Families of Conventional Order Agaricales (p. 26)

21a) Hymenium composed of teeth, concentric plates, or tubes with pore-like openings or the openings sometimes elongate or mazelike (and appearing like gills with regular or irregular cross-walls) go to **22**

21b) Hymenium smooth, creased, deeply wrinkled and brain-like, or deeply pitted but without teeth or pores go to **25**

22a) Hymenium composed of teeth, at least at maturity go to **23**

22b) Hymenium composed of concentric plates or tubes with pore-like openings or the openings sometimes elongate or mazelike (and appearing like gills with regular or irregular cross-walls) go to **24**

23a) Fruiting body shelving or partially to entirely resupinate; stalks absent

go to Hymenochaetales, etc. (p. 162: *Hydnophlebia, Hydnoporia, Irpex, Irpiciporus, Trichaptum*)

23b) Fruiting body with cap and stalk, sometimes with several caps fused together

go to Cantharellales, etc. (p. 200: *Hydnum, Hydnellum, Phellodon, Sarcodon*)

24a) Fruiting body with cap and stalk, soft at maturity and not exceeding 12 inches broad; hymenium composed of tubes with pore-like openings (sometimes elongate), easily removed from cap; cap and hymenium often of bright, contrasting colors go to Boletales

(p. 144: *Aureoboletus, Boletinellus, Boletus, Gyroporus, Hortiboletus, Leccinellum, Porphyrellus Strobilomyces, Suillus, Tylopilus, Xerocomus*)

24b) Fruiting body with cap and stalk **or** stalk absent, sometimes globular, shelflike, compound and rosette-like (of many caps joined to a common stalk) **or** partially to entirely resupinate, sometimes tough at maturity, and occasionally very large; hymenium composed of concentric plates **or** tubes with pore-like openings (sometimes elongate or mazelike) but not easily removed from cap; cap and hymenium of contrasting colors or concolorous go to Hymenochaetales, etc.

(p. 162: *Abortiporus, Bondarzwia, Brunneoporus, Coltricia, Coriolopsis, Daedaleopsis, Fistulina, Fuscoporia, Ganoderma, Grifola, Ishnoderma, Laetiporus, Lentinus, Meripilus, Neofavolus, Perenniporia, Phellinus, Picipes, Polyporus, Poronidulus, Pseudoinonotus, Pyncnoporus, Trametes, Vitreoporus*)

25a) Hymenium on upper surface (outside) of cap, deeply wrinkled and brain-like or deeply pitted; stalk present

go to Helotiales, etc. (p. 254: *Discina* in part, *Gyromitra, Morchella*)

25b) Hymenium on upper or lower surface of cap, smooth, creased, or wrinkled but not brain-like or deeply pitted; stalk present or absent go to **26**

26a) Fruiting body cap-like or shelflike, tough; stalk absent

go to Hymenochaetales, etc. (p. 162: *Byssomerulius, Chondostereum, Stereum*)

26b) Fruiting body with cap and stalk (although stalk sometimes very short) go to **27**

27a) Fruiting body with bell-shaped, saddle-shaped, or lobed cap or with round to flattened greenish-yellow cap

go to Helotiales, etc. (p. 254: *Leotia, Helvella, Verpa*)

27b) Fruiting body vase-shaped or with flat purple cap go to **28**

28a) Fruiting body white to light brown, tough

Cotylidia diaphana (no. 132 in Hymenochaetales, etc.)

28b) Fruiting body yellow, purple, gray, or black, soft

go to Cantharellales, etc.

(p. 200: *Cantharellus* in part, *Craterellus, Pseudocraterellus*)

Phylum Basidiomycota

This phylum is divided into subphyla, which are in turn divided into classes, which again are divided into orders, which, other than the conventional class Gasteromycetes, is the highest level dealt with directly in the body of this work. To understand these higher relationships, consult the cladogram in the appendix.

The phylum Basidiomycota constitutes the bulk of the mostly fleshy mushrooms in this book. Included are the gilled mushrooms, boletes, polypores, parchment types, chanterelles, corals, spine mushrooms, jelly fungi, puffballs, earthstars, earthballs, bird's nest fungi, mushrooms, and stinkhorns. These diverse forms are tied together by their formation of spores on the ends of microscopic, mostly club-shaped cells called **basidia** (Fig. 8C, p. 290). Most of these shoot off their spores. However, those fungi whose basidia are enclosed in a membrane and do not discharge their spores but depend on an outside agent to act on the fruiting body to release them are grouped here under the useful if archaic name "Gasteromycetes," whose members will be presented in the latter portion of the Basidiomycota section.

Conventional Order Agaricales: Some of the Gilled Mushrooms

The order Agaricales certainly comprises the most universally recognized mushrooms. Their fruiting bodies display gills on the undersurface of their caps, which may or may not be supported by a stalk. Representatives of twenty-two families of Agaricales are presented here. Recent genetic evidence has even placed some fungi that lack conventional cap, gills, and stalk in the Agaricales. However, these species are treated with others of unconventional shape in other sections. Families often contain species with a wide diversity of features; thus, individual features are not diagnostic for whole families. For convenience, families with similar attributes are presented together. The key below is meant to provide some direction to groups of characteristics that will help you identify the appropriate family. In order to successfully use this key, you must be familiar with the figures included in "How to Identify a Mushroom"; the characteristics shown there will be used to help you choose the correct family for the species you are trying to identify.

Key to Families

1a) Fruiting body parasitizing the caps of other mushrooms of the family Russulaceae *Asterophora lycoperdoides* (no. 37 in Tricholomataceae, etc.)

1b) Fruiting body not parasitizing other mushrooms go to **2**

2a) Spore print white to pale pink, pale lilac, or pale yellow go to **3**

2b) Spore print pink (see Fig. 6), green, rusty, brown, or black go to **19**

3a) Gills free and clearly not touching the top of the stalk (with a clearly discernible space immediately adjacent to the point of attachment between the stalk and cap), at least at maturity; stalk present go to **4**

3b) Gills slightly attached at top of stalk to fully attached or running down stalk (decurrent), or stalk absent (sessile) go to **6**

4a) Fruiting body covered in thick slime

Zhuliangomyces illinitus (no. 9 in Amanitaceae)

4b) Fruiting body not covered in thick slime go to **5**

5a) Universal veil present; remnants of universal veil present as a volva at base of stalk, sometimes manifest as a bulb only at maturity or occasionally as a flap of tissue at the top of the bulb and/or warts on the cap (separate from the cap cuticle [surface tissue of the cap]); partial veil sometimes also present, manifest as a ring around the stalk (annulus)

go to Amanitaceae (p. 31: *Amanita*)

5b) Universal veil and volva absent; cap smooth or sometimes apparently warted and scaly (if apparently warted, then warts part of the cap cuticle and not easily removed); partial veil always present, manifest as an annulus (sometimes fragile, so may be lost) or a veil sticking to edge (margin) of cap in fragments as cap expands

go to Agaricaceae (p. 117: *Chlorophyllum* in part, *Echinoderma*, *Lepiota*, *Leucoagaricus*, *Leucocroprinus*, *Macrolepiota*)

6a) Stalk absent (sessile); cap fuzzy or smooth; always on wood

go to Tricholomataceae, etc. (p. 65: *Schizophyllum*, *Phyllotopsis*, *Pleurotus* in part)

6b) Stalk present; cap smooth, slimy or sticky (viscid) when moist or rarely fuzzy; on woody debris, nuts, or soil go to **7**

7a) Annulus present; fruiting bodies occurring in clusters (caespitose)

Armillaria mellea group (no. 24 in Physalacriaceae)

7b) Annulus absent; fruiting bodies occurring singly or in small groups

go to **8**

8a) Gills widely spaced, thick, and with a waxy feel when rubbed between fingers go to **9**

8b) Gills closely or widely spaced but not thick and waxy go to **10**

9a) Fruiting body (typically the cap) slimy or viscid when moist; gills white, yellow, orange, or olive (sometimes bruising black); spore print white go to Hygrophoraceae (p. 43)

9b) Fruiting body dry; cap smooth or scaly; gills pale pink, pinkish brown, or purple; spore print white, pale pink, or pale purple go to Tricholomataceae, etc. (p. 65: *Laccaria*)

10a) Fruiting on nuts, including acorns (sometimes buried); cap yellow, less than 0.75 inches broad *Mycena luteopallens* (no. 23 in Marasmiaceae, etc.)

10b) Fruiting in soil or on woody debris but not nuts; cap not both yellow and less than 0.75 inches broad go to **11**

11a) Stalks thin, wiry, not exceeding 1/10 inch (2 mm) thick go to Marasmiaceae, etc. (p. 47: *Marasmius*, *Tetrapyrgos*)

11b) Stalks not thin and wiry, typically more than 2 mm thick go to **12**

12a) Growing in soil go to **13**

12b) Growing on wood (sometimes deeply buried) go to **14**

13a) Gills widely spaced; spore print white; fruiting in open, grassy areas and in lawns, often forming fairy rings *Marasmius oreades* (no. 16 in Marasmiaceae, etc.)

13b) Gills crowded; spore print white, pinkish cream, or pale pink; fruiting in woodlands or, if in grassy openings, then caespitose go to Tricholomataceae, etc. (p. 65: *Clitocybe*, *Infundibulicybe*, *Lepista*, *Leucopaxillus*, *Lyophyllum*, *Trichloma*)

14a) Cap bright coral-pink, with a ridged network; spore print pale yellowish pink *Rhodotus palmatus* (no. 27 in Physalacriaceae)

14b) Cap without a ridged network; spore print white, cream, or pale purple go to **15**

15a) Fruiting bodies caespitose; spore print white or cream go to **16**

15b) Fruiting bodies occurring singly or in small groups; spore print white, cream, or pale purple go to **17**

16a) Caps either with fine brown hairs **or** viscid when moist, convex, becoming flat or with a central depression at maturity; gills merely attached or barely running down stalk (decurrent); spore print white
go to Physalacriaceae (p. 59: *Desarmillaria*, *Flammulina*)

16b) Caps smooth **or** striate but not hairy or viscid, with a central knob (umbo) **or** central depression at maturity; gills attached **or** strongly decurrent; spore print white or cream, one member bright orange
go to Marasmiaceae, etc. (p. 47: *Mycena* in part, *Omphalotus*, *Xeromphalmina*)

17a) Growing on buried wood; stalk ending with a long, tapering root
Hymenopellis radicata group (no. 28 in Physalacriaceae)

17b) Growing on wood, buried or not, but stalk not ending with a root
go to **18**

18a) Caps 0.2–2.75 inches broad, reddish or yellowish brown, tan, or lilac; gills merely attached; stalk central; spore print white or cream
go to Marasmiaceae, etc. (p. 47: *Mycena* in part, *Gymnopus*)

18b) Caps 1.5–16 inches broad at maturity, white, grayish brown, tan, or dark brown; stalk central, off-center, **or** lateral; gills attached **or** decurrent; spore print white or pale purple
go to Tricholomataceae, etc. (p. 65: *Hypsizygus*, *Lentinus*, *Megacollybia*, *Pleurotus* in part)

19a) Gills (and sometimes entire cap) dissolving into inky substance (deliquescing) when mature; spore print black
go to **20**

19b) Gills and cap not deliquescing; spore print pink, green, rusty, brown, or black
go to **21**

20a) Cap cylindrical at first, 1.5–7 inches tall, white with white to light brown scales, shaggy
Coprinus comatus (no. 70 in Agaricaceae)

20b) Cap oval, bell-shaped, or cone-shaped, less than 2.5 inches tall, gray to brown, striate **or** with fine scales or hairs
go to Hymenogastraceae, etc. (p. 101: *Coprinellus*, *Coprinopsis*)

21a) Spore print pink (see Fig. 6, p. 7)
go to Bolbitiaceae, etc. (p. 80: *Entoloma*, *Pluteus*, *Volvariella*)

21b) Spore print green, rusty, brown, or black
go to **22**

22a) Gills free and clearly not touching the top of the stalk (with a clearly discernible space immediately adjacent to the point of attachment between stalk and cap), at least at maturity; stalk present; spore print dull green or chocolate-brown (but not rusty)
go to Agaricaceae (p. 117: *Agaricus*, *Chlorophyllum* in part)

22b) Gills attached, at least at top of stalk, or stalk absent; spore print rusty brown, medium brown, purplish brown, or very dark brown go to **23**

23a) Stalk absent go to Cortinariaceae, etc. (p. 90: *Crepidotus*)

23b) Stalk present go to **24**

24a) Spore print rusty brown (with distinctly reddish tones) go to **25**

24b) Spore print brown to purplish brown or very dark brown go to **27**

25a) Partial veil and annulus absent
go to Bolbitiaceae, etc. (p. 80: *Bolbitius*, *Conocybe*)

25b) Partial veil present, although often visible only in immature fruiting bodies, manifest either as an annulus or cobweb-like (cortina) go to **26**

26a) Cortina present; growing in soil
go to Cortinariaceae, etc. (p. 90: *Cortinarius*)

26b) Annulus present, often disappearing; growing on rotting wood
Galerina marginata (no. 58 in Hymenogastraceae, etc.)

27a) Growing on wood (sometimes buried) or wood chips; spore print brown to purplish brown or dark brown
go to Hymenogastraceae, etc. (p. 101: *Agrocybe*, *Pholiota*, *Psathyrella*)

27b) Growing in soil or manure go to **28**

28a) Cap fibrous, sometimes finely so; spore print dull brown; annulus absent go to Cortinariaceae, etc. (p. 90: *Inocybe*, *Inosperma*, *Pseudosperma*)

28b) Cap smooth or hairy but not fibrous; spore print purplish brown or blackish brown; annulus sometimes present (sometimes consisting of a hairy ring around stalk)
go to Hymenogastraceae, etc. (p. 101: *Lacrymaria*, *Panaeolina*, *Protostropharia*, *Psilocybe*, *Stropharia*)

Family Amanitaceae

The family Amanitaceae is a favorite among mushroom devotees and a fitting start to a book on Kansas mushrooms. It includes mushrooms of striking contrasts, ranging from the drab to the brilliantly colored as well as from the deadly to the eminently edible. The most important genus, *Amanita*, is characterized by the presence of a volva (a membrane that surrounds the base of the stalk), white gills, and a white spore print; the gill attachment is free or nearly so. (There are some species with narrowly attached gills, but they are not included in this book.) A universal veil is a membrane that surrounds the developing mushroom (Fig. 2A). As the fruiting body expands, the universal veil is ruptured and remains behind as a volva at the base of the stalk (Fig. 2D). The volva may be membranous and sac-like, may be fused to the stalk in various manners, or may consist of fragile remnants that adhere to the soil. Many species show little, if any, trace of a volva. Specimens should always be carefully dug up to preserve the volva as an aid for identification. Part of the universal veil may also be carried with the cap as "volval remnants." These remnants either remain intact as a volval patch (Fig. 2D) or break into warts during the expansion of the cap. A partial veil typically covers the gills early in development and remains behind as an annulus, a ring that encircles the stalk, although some species do not form a partial veil (or an annulus). *Leucoagraricus*, *Leucocoprinus*, and *Macrolepiota* are white-spored genera (plural of genus) of the family Agaricaceae that have a ring and can be easily confused with amanitas but do not have a universal veil and therefore lack a volva and volval remnants; other differences are microscopic. Species of *Volvariella* and *Volvopluteus* (family Pluteaceae), with a sac-like volva, have a pink spore print.

A considerable mystique surrounds the genus *Amanita*, centered primarily around the fly agaric, *A. muscaria*, the archetypical red warty mushroom that contains poisonous/hallucinogenic muscimol and ibotenic acid. The genus is equally famous for deadly amatoxin-containing species, which account for most mushroom poisoning fatalities. Though several species are choice edibles, all but the most sophisticated mushroomer should avoid the genus.

Amanitas are predominantly mycorrhizal (mostly forming a symbiotic relationship with trees) and therefore commonly fruit near trees. However, several Kansas species that occur in open grassy areas do not form mycorrhizae (e.g., *Saproamanita theirsii* [no. 8]). Over two dozen amanitas have been reported from the state; some of the more common species, including at least one that is deadly poisonous, are described here. Important in Kansas mycological history is *A. populiphila*, named to science by Elizabeth Moses with the help of amanitologist Rod Tulloss. Also described is a single representative of *Zhuliangomyces* formerly considered a *Limacella*, an obscure genus characterized by a slimy universal veil that remains behind as thick slime on the cap and stalk.

Key to species

1a) Cap and stalk covered with thick slime; membrane enclosing the stalk from base (volva) absent — *Zhuliangomyces illinitus* (no. 9)

1b) Cap and stalk dry or at most sticky (viscid); volva present, although sometimes inconspicuous — go to **2**

2a) Volva not fused to the stalk, membranous, sac-like — go to **3**

2b) Volva fused to the stalk, with uppermost edge (margin) slightly free, or consisting of flakes or scales that may be inconspicuous — go to **7**

3a) Ring encircling the stalk (annulus) present — go to **4**

3b) Annulus absent — go to **5**

4a) Fruiting body entirely white; cap smooth at margin; basal bulb present — *Amanita bisporigera* (no. 3)

4b) Fruiting body with pale gray to dark grayish-brown cap, contrasting with white stalk; cap striate at margin (with furrows radiating from the edge); basal bulb absent — *Amanita spreta* (no. 5)

5a) Cap distinctly tan to orange-brown — *Amanita fulva* (no. 4)

5b) Cap whitish to pale gray (or if whitish to tan, then fruiting under cottonwoods) — go to **6**

6a) Cap gray; typically fruiting under hardwoods — *Amanita vaginata* (see no. 4)

6b) Cap whitish to tan; fruiting under cottonwood — *Amanita populiphila* (no. 1)

7a) Fruiting body and cap entirely white, covered with sticky, shaggy material; annulus and volva inconspicuous; fruiting in grassy areas [Note: if cap white *and* warty, see discussion of *Amanita muscaria* under no. 2.] — *Saproamanita thiersii* (no. 8)

7b) Fruiting body or cap not white, often with warts; annulus well developed; fruiting under trees — go to **8**

8a) Volva prominent, fused to bulbous base of stalk, with upper margin free and either inrolled or sheathing; annulus funnel-shaped; cap striate at margin *Amanita multisquamosa* (no. 6)

8b) Volva not prominent, without a well-developed upper margin; annulus not funnel-shaped; cap smooth at margin go to **9**

9a) Cap or stalk slowly bruising reddish brown; stalk gradually enlarging to club-shaped base go to **10**

9b) Cap and stalk not bruising; stalk abruptly enlarging to bulbous base go to **11**

10a) Cap yellowish with yellow warts; lower stalk bruising *Amanita flavorubescens* (see no. 7)

10b) Cap bronze to reddish brown with tan warts; both cap and stalk bruising *Amanita "amerirubescens"* (no. 7)

11a) Volva fully fused to base of stalk and forming prominent, concentric ridges of white just above bulb; cap varying from bright yellow to bright red (rarely white) *Amanita muscaria* (see no. 2)

11b) Volva partially fused to base of stalk but not forming concentric rings above bulb; cap orange-yellow with yellow warts *Amanita flavoconia* group (no. 2)

1. *Amanita populiphila* Edible with caution

This is a medium-sized, whitish to tan (usually when older) ringless mushroom that has striations on the cap edge. The smallest, button-like specimen is just emerging from the universal veil. As *A. populiphila* matures, the remnants of the universal veil become a cup-like volva enclosing the base of the stalk. The volva is membranous but thin and fragile. Sometimes thick warts are found on the cap, which are also remains of the universal veil. The typical striations on the edge of the cap (margin) are well illustrated here. Occasionally the fruiting body overall or in parts has hints of creamy, very pale orange. *Amanita populiphila* has been found in Kansas exclusively under cottonwood trees, often in grassy riparian areas (habitats along a waterway). A founding member of the Kaw Valley Mycological Society, Elizabeth Moses, named this species with the kind help of Rod Tulloss.

Description: **Cap**: 3–10 cm broad, oval, becoming flat, sometimes with a darker elevated center, basically white to tan, striate at margin, sometimes with volval remnants. **Gills**: white, free. **Stalk**: 8–16 cm long, 0.5–2 cm thick, white to tan, above occasionally pale cream or orange; annulus absent, portions of partial veil adhering to stalk above volva; volva cup-like, with lobes at margin. **Spore print**: white. **Spores**: 9–12 × 8.5–11.5 µm, roundish, nonamyloid. **Season**: summer. **Ecology**: mycorrhizal.

1. *Amanita populiphila*

2. *Amanita flavoconia* group

Edibility unknown

Yellow patches

This spectacular amanita fruits in the deciduous forests of eastern Kansas following soaking summer rains. In addition to its orangish-yellow cap, *A. flavoconia* is best identified by its fragile yellow volva that crumbles easily when soil is removed from around the base of the stalk, as was done in the photograph. Yellow warts are also present on the cap, but these often wash off in the rain. The fruiting bodies are usually solitary, and the cluster shown here is not typical. The ring on the stalk of the largest fruiting body has torn away from the stalk during expansion of the cap. As indicated by the "group" designation, *Amanita flavoconia* may actually be a complex of several different related species. The fly agaric, *A. muscaria*, is sometimes similar in color but also has forms that vary from shades of bright yellow through orange and on to bright red. It is also larger and has a volva in the form of concentric

2. *Amanita flavoconia* group

rings. A pure white form has been found in Kansas.

Description: **Cap**: 3–10 cm broad, oval becoming convex or flat, orangish yellow, often covered with yellow warts. **Gills**: white, free. **Stalk**: 5–12 cm long, 0.5–1.5 cm thick, white to pale yellow, smooth or slightly scaly, bulbous; annulus white to yellow, membranous; volva yellow, fragile. **Spore print**: white. **Spores**: 7.5–9 × 5–6.5 μm, elliptical, smooth, amyloid. **Season**: summer. **Ecology**: mycorrhizal.

3. *Amanita bisporigera* — Deadly poisonous

Destroying angel

Thorough familiarity with the deadly destroying angel, *Amanita bisporigera*, is a prerequisite for collecting edible mushrooms in Kansas since it is clearly one of the most dangerous mushrooms in the state. Only two spores rather than the usual four are produced on the microscopic basidia of this species, hence the name (verified by the microscope in this specimen). *Amanita bisporigera* and related species are also known by other colorful names: angel of death, deadly amanita, and white death cap. Their fruiting bodies contain amatoxins, which destroy liver and kidney tissue; initial symptoms may be delayed six to twenty-four hours following ingestion. *Amanita bisporigera* fruits in Kansas during the summer under hardwoods, where it can be locally abundant. The cap, stalk, and gills are stark white. The specimens in the photograph were lined up to illustrate the important features during development: a sac-like volva, a bulbous base, and a skirtlike ring. The partial veil covering the gills on the two young specimens has not yet ruptured to form an annulus. In the button stage, fruiting bodies are enveloped by a universal veil and resemble puffballs (Fig. 7), so puffball hunters, beware—always slice your prey in half from top to bottom! Other equally dangerous white species of amanita in Kansas can be distinguished from *A. bisporigera* only with a microscope.

3. *Amanita bisporigera*

Description: **Cap**: 3–10 cm broad, oval becoming broadly convex, white, smooth, viscid when wet. **Gills**: white, free. **Stalk**: 6–14 cm long, 0.5–2 cm thick, white, smooth to slightly scaly, bulbous; annulus white, membranous; volva white, sac-like, membranous, with lobed margin. **Spore print**: white. **Spores**: 7–10 µm, round, smooth, amyloid, 2 per basidium. **Season**: summer. **Ecology**: mycorrhizal.

4. *Amanita fulva*

Edible with caution

This delicate amanita fruits in hardwood forests during summer and fall in Kansas. The fruiting bodies lack an annulus. The specimens in the photograph also illustrate the sac-like volva at the stalk base and striate cap edge. Cap color, ranging from tan to orange-brown, is variable, as is the size, so this may actually be a complex of related species. *Amanita fulva* is edible but always a risk since its volva type is identical to that of deadly amanitas, and the ring of the deadlies may have been destroyed and therefore not be in evidence. Another Kansas species, *A. vaginata* (the grisette), is similar except for its pale gray cap.

4. *Amanita fulva*

Description: **Cap**: 5–10 cm broad, oval becoming flat, sometimes with central knob, tan to orange-brown, smooth, striate at margin; volval patches rarely present. **Gills**: white, free. **Stalk**: 8–16 cm long, 0.4–1.5 cm thick, white or pale brown, smooth to slightly scaly with bits of the partial veil, nonbulbous; annulus absent; volva white to tan, sac-like, membranous, lobed at margin. **Spore print**: white. **Spores**: 8–10 µm in diameter, round, smooth, nonamyloid. **Season**: summer–fall. **Ecology**: mycorrhizal.

5. *Amanita spreta* — Edibility unknown

Amanita spreta has been collected under hardwoods in eastern Kansas during the summer. It favors sandy soils. The specimens in the photograph illustrate the important features of this mushroom, namely, its sac-like volva, nonbulbous base, and membranous ring. The cap color ranges from pale to dark brown; these specimens fall at the extreme light end of the range, and the striations on the cap margin are not very evident in the picture. The volval patches on the caps of these young fruiting bodies are often not present, nor do fruitings always occur in clusters. Since the edibility of this species is questionable, experimentation is unwise. The deadly *A. bisporigera* (no. 3) is white overall and has a bulbous base.

5. *Amanita spreta*

Description: **Cap**: 5–12 cm broad, oval becoming flat, sometimes with central knob, pale to dark grayish brown, smooth, sticky, striate at margin; volval patches occasionally present. **Gills**: white, free. **Stalk**: 6–12 cm long, 1–2 cm thick, whitish, smooth to slightly hairy, without basal bulb; annulus white, membranous, volva white, sac-like, membranous, lobed at margin. **Spore print**: white. **Spores**: 10.5–13.5 × 6–8 µm, elliptical, smooth, nonamyloid. **Season**: summer. **Ecology**: mycorrhizal.

6. *Amanita multisquamosa* — Poisonous

Amanita pantherina var. *velatipes* (Ed. 1, misapplied)

In first edition of this book, this specimen was labeled *Amanita pantherina* var. *velatipes*. Amanitologist Rod Tulloss looked at the mushroom pictured and called it *A. multisquamosa*. According to him, *A. pantherina* is a European species with different field characteristics, although *A. multisquamosa* is certainly a member of the *A. pantherina* group. This elegant yet dangerously poisonous amanita fruits following summer rains in the deciduous forests of Kansas.

The handsome pair of fruiting bodies illustrated here are in their prime. Note (especially on the larger specimen) the sticky pale brown cap with concentrically arranged warts, the unusual funnel-shaped ring, and the prominently bulbous base. Rain often removes the warts while the volva is fused to the basal bulb and only its upper margin is free. As the cap expands, its margin fades to yellow; in fact, some older specimen caps can be all pale yellow (usually darker in the center). The *A. pantherina* group contains potent levels of muscimol and ibotenic acid, and *A. multisquamosa*

6. *Amanita multisquamosa*

is probably no exception. Although deaths from eating these mushrooms are rare, poisoning can be severe. Do not confuse *A. multisquamosa* or any other of the *A. pantherina* group with the edible blusher *A. "amerirubescens"* (no. 7), which has a bronze-colored cap and an inconspicuous volva/base; its fruiting body bruises reddish brown.

Description: **Cap**: 7–18 cm broad, nearly round, then convex or flat, brown becoming yellow or tan at margin, viscid when moist, striate at margin; white warts usually present, often in concentric rings. **Gills**: white, free. **Stalk**: 8–20 cm long, 0.8–2 cm thick, whitish, scaly, bulbous; annulus white, membranous; volva white, fused to bulb, with upper margin free and inrolled or sheathing. **Spore print**: white. **Spores**: 8–13 × 6–8 µm, broadly elliptical, smooth, nonamyloid. **Season**: summer. **Ecology**: mycorrhizal.

7. *Amanita "amerirubescens"* — Edible with caution

Amanita rubescens (Ed. 1)
Blusher

Amanita "amerirubescens" (a species name that has yet to be formally published) is abundant in Kansas, where it fruits during summer and fall under hardwoods. Its common name, the blusher, refers to the reddish-brown bruising of all parts of the fruiting body. Reddish-brown stains are evident on the young specimens illustrated here, particularly at the bases of their stalks and on the larger cap. The color change is too slow for the patience of most mushroomers, so larval tunnels and slug bites are usually relied upon, as they were with these specimens. In addition, note the bronze-colored cap with tan warts (which may wash off in the rain) and the stalk enlarging downward to a basal bulb

7. *Amanita "amerirubescens"*

that tapers into the earth. The volva is inconspicuous, and the membranous ring is scarcely showing beneath the smaller cap. *Hypomyces hyalinus* (see no. 195) often parasitizes the fruiting bodies, turning them into club-shaped masses that are white to pink. The blusher is a world-renowned edible with a rich, delectable flavor. One of the authors can attest to this after having eaten the specimens illustrated and survived. Only mushroom hunters with a sound knowledge of amanita species—edible, poisonous, and benign—should consider dining on the blusher. A similar but poisonous species in Kansas, *A. flavorubescens*, bruises reddish brown primarily on its lower stalk; it has a yellowish cap with yellow warts.

Description: **Cap**: 4–20 cm broad, oval becoming convex to flat, sometimes with umbo, bronze to reddish brown with tan warts, slowly bruising reddish brown. **Gills**: white, free. **Stalk**: 7–24 cm long, 0.7–4 cm thick, white to tan, smooth to slightly hairy, gradually enlarging to bulb, lower portion of bulb tapers into the earth, bruising reddish brown; annulus white to tan, skirtlike, often torn; volva inconspicuous. **Spore print**: white. **Spores**: 7–9 × 5–7 µm, elliptical, smooth, amyloid. **Season**: summer–fall. **Ecology**: mycorrhizal.

8. *Saproamanita thiersii* — Edibility unknown

Syn. = *Amanita thiersii* (Ed. 1)
The sticky lace amanita

Saproamanita thiersii (an unusual saprotrophic amanita whose habit has led to the name change) was originally described from Texas and has since been collected in Kansas and neighboring states; its range continues to widen. Large fairy rings frequently appear in lawns, pastures, and even prairies during hot, wet summer weather. This stately white amanita is recognized by the sticky, shaggy material that coats its cap and stalk. When fruiting bodies are collected, this material readily sticks to one's hands and clothing—note the thumbprint on the stalk of the overturned specimen in the photograph. The shaggy coating has also stuck to the surrounding grass while arranging the specimens. The fruiting bodies lose their stickiness with age. Other features illustrated include the membranous ring and the slightly bulbous base that lacks a conspicuous volva. *Saproamanita thiersii* is of questionable edibility since other closely related species are reportedly poisonous. After a hard rain, all the sticky lace is often washed off, leaving a very different-looking mushroom, quite bare. *Chlorophyllum molybdites* (no. 79) also grows in fairy rings in the same habitats (sometimes on the same lawn) but has a smooth cap when young, and scales that develop later are not sticky. The robust ring of *C. molybdites* is detachable (movable on the stalk), and its gills eventually turn greenish. Deadly white amanitas, such as *A. bisporigera* (no. 3), have smooth caps and a sac-like volva and fruit under trees.

Description: **Cap**: 7–20 cm broad, oval becoming convex, white, covered with sticky, shaggy material, especially when young. **Gills**: white to pale yellow, free. **Stalk**: 8–20 cm long, 1–2.5 cm thick, white, shaggy, sticky, slightly bulbous; annulus white, membranous; volva inconspicuous. **Spore print**: white. **Spores**: 7.5–9.5 × 7–9 µm, round to broadly elliptical, amyloid. **Season**: summer. **Ecology**: saprotrophic.

8. *Saproamanita thiersii*

9. *Zhuliangomyces illinitus* — Edibility unknown

Syn. = *Limacella illinita* var. *argillacea* (Ed. 1)

This uncommon mushroom has been collected in the deciduous forests of eastern Kansas during the summer. It may hold the distinction of being the slimiest mushroom in the state. The photograph shows the thick, clear slime that envelops both the cap and stalk; slime also hangs from the cap margin. In addition, fruiting bodies lack a volva and an obvious ring. Kansas populations of *Zhuliangomyces illinitus* have a whitish cap with a brown center, whereas an entirely white form of the species is often found elsewhere. Species of *Hygrophorus* may be nearly as slimy, but they generally have thick, waxy gills that are attached to decurrent rather than free, as in amanitas.

Description: **Cap**: 3–7 cm broad, oval becoming convex with broad umbo, whitish with brown center, coated with thick, clear slime that often hangs from margin. **Gills**: white, free. **Stalk**: 5–9 cm long, 3–8 mm thick, tan, slimy over lower portion, often curved; slimy partial veil not leaving annulus; volva absent. **Spore print**: white. **Spores**: 5–6 × 4–4.5 µm, broadly elliptical, smooth, nonamyloid. **Season**: summer. **Ecology**: mycorrhizal.

9. *Zhuliangomyces illinitus*

Family Hygrophoraceae

Neophyte mushroomers are often puzzled by the family Hygrophoraceae, commonly called **waxgills**. The major feature of these mushrooms, their "waxy" gills, is difficult to imagine at first and can lead to hours of consternation in the woods. However, with some practice, most members of this family can be readily recognized. The waxiness is best detected by rubbing a piece of gill between two fingers. Even the thick and translucent appearance of the gills suggests waxiness. Not unexpectedly, this characteristic is far from foolproof, since other mushrooms (for example, species of *Laccaria*) also have waxy gills. Hygrophori, members of this family, are mostly small to medium-sized mushrooms that are terrestrial under trees. Some are probably saprotrophic, but recent evidence indicates that other members of the family, including *Hygrocybe conica*, are likely mycorrhizal. Their caps are dry to slimy (though often some part of the specimen is sticky [viscid] when moist) and range in color from brilliant scarlet to bran browns and off-whites. The gills are usually attached and widely spaced, and the spore print is white.

Recent studies of the Hygrophoraceae have revealed a diversity of ecological lifestyles. Originally all were considered saprotrophic, but now most are thought to be biotrophic, that is, either parasites or mutualists (or somewhere in between). *Hygrophorus* species are clearly ectomycorrhizal, meaning they coat root tips (but do not enter them) and help their host uptake soil nutrients. Other members of the family Hygrophoraceae have not been shown to actively associate or exchange with plants, even though the body chemistry of some resembles that of the ectomycorrhizal fungi. Some may even partner with ferns, mosses, and grasses, and some are clearly still saprotrophic. More research is needed, and the study of other fungal groups is beginning to indicate more complexity in how fungi obtain their food and in the relationships in which they engage.

Although some hygrophori can be found during hot weather in Kansas, most are cool-weather fruiters that come into glory during late fall after the leaves have dropped. With the possible exception of *Hygrocybe conica*, no poisonous species are known. However, because they tend to be slimy when cooked, few mycophagists have ever praised them. Numerous other species have been cited from Kansas, but most reports need further documentation.

Key to species

1a) Fruiting body bruising black; cap conical	*Hygrocybe conica* (no. 11)
1b) Fruiting body not bruising black; cap convex to hemispheric	go to **2**

2a) Cap and stalk olive-green, fading orange to yellow (note that stalk retains green color longer than cap); gills yellow *Gliophorus psittacinus* (no. 10)

2b) Cap orange or pinkish to pale tan; stalk white; gills white, pink, or orange go to **3**

3a) Cap pinkish cinnamon to pale tan; gills white *Hygrophorus roseobrunneus* (no. 12)

3b) Cap orange to tannish orange; gills pink to pale orange *Hygrophorus subsalmonius* (see no. 12)

10. *Gliophorus psittacinus* Edible
Syn. = *Hygrophorus psittacinus*
Parrot cap

This colorful little species begins with a bright olive sticky cap that fades to dull orange or yellow. The gills remain deep yellow. The stalk is also slimy and, when young, green. It retains the green color longer than the cap but eventually also turns orange to yellow. *Gliophorus psittacinus* is infrequent in Kansas, found in summer to fall in hardwood forests (and sometimes even under eastern redcedar). It is probably not mycorrhizal, but it may be moving in that direction, so we have labeled it biotrophic. Though said to be edible, *G. psittacinus* is so small and slimy, it probably is not worth eating.

10. *Gliophorus psittacinus*

Description: **Cap**: 1–3 cm broad, semihemispheric, dark to bright olive and slimy turning to orange to yellow. **Gills**: dark yellow. **Stalk**: 3–7 cm long, 2–5 mm thick, slimy, initially green, then yellow or orange. **Spore print**: white. **Spores**: 6.5–10 × 4–6 μm elliptical, smooth, nonamyloid. **Season**: summer–fall. **Ecology**: biotrophic.

11. *Hygrocybe conica* — Edible with caution

Syn. = *Hygrophorus conicus* (Ed. 1)
Witch's hat

Hygrocybe conica fruits under hardwoods and eastern redcedar during late summer (rarely spring) in Kansas. The common name—witch's hat—refers to its distinctly conical orange cap. Even more diagnostic is the manner in which all parts of the fruiting body bruise black with handling or age. Black stains can be seen on the stalks and caps in the photograph. The witch's hat was once considered poisonous but may in fact be edible; such uncertainty suggests that it is best left uneaten.

Description: **Cap**: 2–7 cm broad, sharply conical, red or orange, often with yellow or olive tints, lighter at margin, bruising black, smooth, sticky when young, then dry. **Gills**: white, becoming pale yellow or olive, bruising black, waxy, free to slightly attached. **Stalk**: 6–11 cm long, 0.3–1 cm thick, colored as cap or lighter, white at base, bruising black, smooth or slightly hairy,

11. *Hygrocybe conica*

often striate, hollow. **Spore print**: white. **Spores**: 9–12 × 5.5–6.5 μm, elliptical, smooth, nonamyloid. **Season**: summer. **Ecology**: biotrophic.

12. *Hygrophorus roseobrunneus* Edible

Most mushroom hunters have hung up their collecting baskets by the time *Hygrophorus roseobrunneus* fruits in late fall. It occurs under hardwoods, particularly oak, in eastern Kansas. This mushroom can be recognized by its sticky, pinkish-cinnamon cap, as seen in the photograph. More mature caps develop upturned margins and often fade to tan with little hint of their original pinkness. The overturned fruiting body shows the thick and waxy white gills. These fruiting bodies were collected in December; they were part of a collection of several dozen specimens, all of which were concealed beneath a thick layer of fallen oak leaves. The meal they provided was tasteless and somewhat slimy. *Hygrophorus subsalmonius* has a slimy orange to tannish-orange cap and thick, waxy gills that are pink or pale orange; it also fruits in the fall but is less common.

Description: **Cap**: 2–9 cm broad, convex becoming flat with upturned margin, pinkish cinnamon fading to tan, lighter toward margin, sticky when wet. **Gills**: white, thick, waxy, attached to decurrent. **Stalk**: 3–9 cm long, 0.4–2 cm thick, white, upper portion with patches of short hairs. **Spore print**: white. **Spores**: 7–8 × 3.5–5 μm, elliptical, smooth, nonamyloid. **Season**: fall. **Ecology**: mycorrhizal.

12. *Hygrophorus roseobrunneus*

Families Marasmiaceae, Mycenaceae, and Omphalotaceae

Both Marasmiaceae and Mycenaceae are composed of mostly small mushrooms. Almost all are saprotrophs (growing on wood or other plant debris). However, recent research suggests that some may be transitional between saprotrophic and mycorrhizal modes of nutrition. Some grow in large clusters, and all have pale spores. These species make up the bulk of what many call little brown mushrooms (LBMs) and little white jobs (LWJs). There are hundreds of species in each family, some of which are poisonous. However, although beautiful to observe, most are too small to bother with in the kitchen.

Marasmiaceae typically have wiry stems and when dried can be completely revived after soaking in water, to the point of making spores anew. Nearly all have white spores. Here we also present two fairly common larger mushrooms, the bioluminescent jack-o'-lantern (*Omphalotus illudens*) and members of the genus *Gymnopus* (species formerly included in *Collybia*) that were historically grouped with Marasmicaeae but have now been placed in the family Omphalotaceae.

Mushrooms in the family Mycenaceae are usually more fragile, with stems that break easily. Some can be identified by the substrate in which they grow and key visible characteristics, but many more often require microscopic spore examination. Both Marasmiaceae and Mycenaceae have odoriferous members. This group and the following family, Physalacriaceae, once belonged to family Tricholomataceae.

Key to species

1a) Growing in grassy areas, frequently in rings or arcs — *Marasmius oreades* (no. 16)

1b) Growing on wood, woody debris, or nuts or in leaf litter on the forest floor — go to **2**

2a) Fruiting bodies densely clustered (caespitose) — go to **3**

2b) Fruiting bodies growing singly in groups of a few — go to **7**

3a) Caps orange or tan, with a central depression; gills running down the stalk (decurrent) — go to **4**

3b) Caps gray, grayish brown, brown, pink, or wine-colored, with a central knob (umbo); gills attached but not decurrent — go to **5**

4a) Caps orange, 2–8 inches broad — *Omphalotus illudens* (no. 13)

4b) Caps tan, less than 1 inch broad *Xeromphalina kauffmanii* (no. 20)

5a) Fruiting body pale reddish brown to pinkish, bleeding a thin red liquid when injured *Mycena haematopus* (see no. 22)

5b) Fruiting body gray, grayish brown, or brown; not bleeding when injured go to **6**

6a) Fruiting body gray or pale brown; smelling of bleach especially when pinched *Mycena alcalina* (see no. 22)

6b) Fruiting body grayish brown to brown; with a mealy smell when pinched *Mycena inclinata* (no. 22)

7a) Growing on nuts, including acorns (possibly buried); cap yellow *Mycena luteopallens* (no. 23)

7b) Growing on leaf litter or woody debris (also possibly buried); cap white, yellowish brown, tan, reddish, or lilac go to **8**

8a) Stalks breaking easily, to ¼ inch (7 mm) thick go to **9**

8b) Stalks tough, wiry, not exceeding 1/10 of an inch (2 mm) thick go to **13**

9a) Cap (and stalk) some shade of lilac, often mixed with other pastel colors, sometimes with radish-like odor *Mycena pura* (no. 21)

9b) Cap tan, reddish brown, or yellowish brown go to **10**

10a) Cap tan; stalk at least partially covered with rust-colored hairs go to **11**

10b) Cap reddish brown to yellowish brown; stalk smooth go to **12**

11a) Stalk hairy over lower 1/3 of length; fruiting in spring *Gymnopus semihirtipes* (no. 15)

11b) Stalk hairy over entire length; fruiting in summer and fall *Gymnopus spongiosus* (see no. 15)

12a) Gills white *Gymnopus dryophilus* (no. 14)

12b) Gills yellow *Gymnopus subsulphureus* (see no. 14)

13a) Cap white; stem blackish brown go to **14**

13b) Cap orange to reddish brown go to **15**

14a) Cap grooved *Marasmius rotula* (no. 17)

14b) Cap ungrooved *Tetrapyrgos nigripes* (see no. 17)

15a) Cap grooved; stem smooth *Marasmius siccus* (no. 18)

15b) Cap ungrooved; lower part of stem with shaggy white hairs *Marasmius sullivantii* (no. 19)

13. *Omphalotus illudens* Poisonous

Syn. = *Clitocybe illudens*
Jack-o'-lantern

The jack-o'-lantern, *Omphalotus illudens*, never ceases to amaze mushroomers with its brilliant orange fruiting bodies during the day and its bioluminescent gills at night. It fruits at the bases of trees and stumps during the late summer and fall in Kansas. The diagnostic features of this mushroom are shown in the photograph: clustered growth habit, overall orange color, and strongly decurrent gills, running far down the stalk. The strange greenish glow of its gills is best seen in total darkness by slipping into a closet (preferably unobserved) with a cluster of young fruiting bodies. Allow ten minutes for your eyes to adjust. If the gills do not luminesce, wrap the fruiting bodies in a paper bag and try again after several hours. The jack-o'-lantern causes mild to severe gastrointestinal poisoning. It is sometimes mistaken for the edible yellow chanterelle, *Cantharellus* "*cibarius*" group (no. 134), which has blunt gill-like ridges and fruits singly in soil. *Desarmillaria tabescens* (no. 25) fruits in clusters on wood but is browner and has slightly decurrent whitish gills.

13. *Omphalotus illudens*

Description: **Cap**: 5–20 cm broad, convex with inrolled margin, becoming flat to broadly depressed, orange, smooth, clustered. **Gills**: orange, bioluminescent, crowded, decurrent. **Stalk**: 7–25 cm long, 0.5–2.5 cm thick, orange, smooth, narrowing at base. **Spore print**: cream. **Spores**: 3–5 µm, round to broadly elliptical, smooth, nonamyloid. **Season**: late summer–fall. **Ecology**: saprotrophic.

14. *Gymnopus dryophilus*

Edible with caution

Syn. = *Collybia dryophila*
Oak-loving collybia

The oak-loving collybia, as the name suggests, prefers hardwood forests, though not always oak. It fruits during late spring and summer in Kansas on logs, buried wood, and soil. The fruiting bodies typically have a clean, waxy appearance. Young caps are dark reddish brown, as shown in the photograph, and fade to yellow-brown with age; the gills are shallow and extremely crowded. The fruiting bodies are sometimes parasitized by the collybia jelly, *Syzygospora mycetophila*, which forms convoluted jellylike masses on the cap and stalk. The oak-loving collybia is a delicious edible for many people, but caution is advised since some suffer gastrointestinal distress from eating it. Another species, *Gymnopus subsulphureus* (syn. = *Collybia subsulphurea* [Ed. 1]), is a native Kansan, being first described from the state. Except for its yellow gills, *G. subsulphureus* is nearly identical to *G. dryophilus*.

14. *Gymnopus dryophilus*

Description: **Cap**: 2–7 cm broad, convex with incurved margin, becoming flat with margin upturned and wavy, deep reddish brown fading to yellow-brown, often lighter at margin, smooth, slightly greasy. **Gills**: white, extremely crowded, shallow, attached. **Stalk**: 3–7 cm long, 2–7 mm thick, white to yellow-brown or reddish brown, smooth, hollow; base with white mycelial cords.

Spore print: white. **Spores**: 5–7 × 2–3.5 μm, elliptical, smooth, nonamyloid. **Season**: late spring–summer. **Ecology**: saprotrophic.

15. *Gymnopus semihirtipes* Edibility unknown

Syn. = *Collybia semihirtipes*

The illustration makes this quite small and occasionally abundant little mushroom look imposing. The important identifying characteristic is the fuzzy lower part of the rust-colored stalk, which is often bent, as can be observed at the bottom of the picture. The hygrophanous (darker when moist) cap is tan and sometimes shallowly wrinkled. The gills can be slightly attached to fully attached and are always pale. *Gymnopus semihirtipes* grows in the woods on rich woody humus mostly in the spring. A second species, *G. spongiosus*, differs in having rust-colored hairs extend over the entire stalk and in fruiting during summer and fall.

15. *Gymnopus semihirtipes*

Description: **Cap**: 0.5–2.5 cm broad, tan, slightly sulcate, convex. **Gills**: pale, with uneven edges (look carefully at the picture). **Stalk**: 2–8 cm tall, 5 mm thick, with an even column (pictured stalk is foreshortened), bright rusty brown, lighter at top, lower part fuzzy. **Spore print**: cream. **Spores**: 7.5–10 × 3–5 μm. **Season**: spring. **Ecology**: saprotrophic.

16. *Marasmius oreades* Edible

Fairy ring

Scotch bonnet

The world-renowned fairy-ring mushroom, *Marasmius oreades*, is a frequent sight in lawns, pastures, and prairies in Kansas from spring through fall. As

16. *Marasmius oreades*

the common name suggests, *M. oreades* often forms fairy rings (as some other lawn mushrooms do), and rings sixty feet in diameter have been reported in Kansas. Even in the absence of fruiting bodies, rings of lush green grass may be apparent where the actively growing ring of mycelium has released nutrients. When fruiting, this drab mushroom can be easily overlooked for lack of outstanding characteristics, however. The most important features—the tan cap and the widely spaced white gills—are shown in the photograph. In addition, the fruiting bodies readily rehydrate after drying out, which makes this edible easy to store and revive. The fairy-ring mushroom is a scourge to lawn manicurists, but those who savor its exceptionally rich flavor prefer to encourage its growth. Beware of other little brown lawn-dwelling mushrooms; many of these, such as the poisonous *Panaeolina foenisecii* (no. 62), can be distinguished from *M. oreades* by their dark gills and dark spore print or by their closely spaced gills.

Description: **Cap**: 1–5 cm broad, bell-shaped with incurved margin, becoming flat with central knob and uplifted margin, brown to yellow-brown or whitish, smooth. **Gills**: white to pale yellow, widely spaced, attached becoming free. **Stalk**: 2–7 cm long, 3–7 mm thick, yellow-brown to reddish brown, velvety over lower portion. **Spore print**: white. **Spores**: 7–10 × 3–6 µm, elliptical, smooth, nonamyloid. **Season**: spring–fall. **Ecology**: saprotrophic.

17. *Marasmius rotula* — Edibility unknown

Marasmius rotula is one of the most abundant mushrooms in the deciduous forests of Kansas. It fruits in troops on woody debris during the summer. The dried-up fruiting bodies quickly revive with moisture; hence, the seemingly explosive appearance of this mushroom after each rain may be somewhat deceptive. *Marasmius rotula* is easily identified by its small, prominently grooved white cap and its dark, wiry stalk. Even more diagnostic is the small collar that surrounds the stalk at the point where the gills attach. A similar species, *Tetrapyrgos nigripes* (syn. = *Marasmiellus nigripes* [Ed. 1]), has an ungrooved white cap and gills that are attached directly to the stalk; its black stalk is coated with fine white hairs.

Description: **Cap**: 1–1.5 cm broad, bell-shaped with central depression, white to pale yellow, brown in center, radially grooved. **Gills**: white to pale yellow, widely spaced, joined to collar that surrounds stalk; collar free or attached to stalk. **Stalk**: 1.5–8 cm long, 1–2 mm thick, blackish brown, white near cap, smooth, shiny, wiry, hollow. **Spore print**: white. **Spores**: 6.5–9 × 3–4.5 µm, oval, elliptical, smooth, nonamyloid. **Season**: summer. **Ecology**: saprotrophic.

17. *Marasmius rotula*

18. ***Marasmius siccus*** Edibility unknown

Of the nearly two dozen species of *Marasmius* reported from Kansas, *M. siccus*, with its orange cap, is perhaps the most striking. During the summer, it commonly carpets the forest floor, where it grows on leaf litter. The fruiting bodies revive repeatedly with rainfall, and as a consequence, the caps gradually fade in color over time. The fine cluster in the photograph illustrates the radially grooved cap and the shiny dark stalk; the gills are widely spaced. *Marasmius sullivantii* (no. 19) is often similar in color but has an ungrooved cap and crowded gills.

18. *Marasmius siccus*

Description: **Cap**: 0.5–3 cm broad, bell-shaped, often with central depression or knob, orange to orange-brown, radially grooved. **Gills**: white to pale yellow, widely spaced, attached becoming free. **Stalk**: 2–6 cm long, 0.2–1 mm thick, pale yellow becoming reddish brown, darker toward base, smooth, shiny, wiry, hollow. **Spore print**: white. **Spores**: 16–21 × 3–4.5 μm, elliptical, smooth, nonamyloid. **Season**: summer. **Ecology**: saprotrophic.

19. ***Marasmius sullivantii*** Edibility unknown

Kansas may represent the most westerly extension of *Marasmius sullivantii*. The fruiting bodies pictured here were found on hardwood debris during June in the eastern part of the state. The cap color is variable in this species, ranging from the bright orange of these specimens to reddish orange or even red. In addition, the cap lacks prominent grooves, and its gills are crowded. Before these specimens were photographed, leaves were removed from around the fruiting bodies to reveal the shaggy white hairs at the base of the stalk. Another orange species, *M. siccus* (no. 18), has a radially grooved cap and widely spaced gills.

Description: **Cap**: 0.6–2.5 cm broad, convex becoming flat, bright orange to reddish orange or red, velvety. **Gills**: whitish, crowded, free. **Stalk**: 0.5–2.5 cm long, 1–2 mm thick, reddish brown, initially with faint bloom; base with shaggy white hairs. **Spore print**: white. **Spores**: 7–9 × 3–3.5 µm, elliptical, smooth, nonamyloid. **Season**: late spring–early summer. **Ecology**: saprotrophic.

19. *Marasmius sullivantii*

20. *Xeromphalina kauffmanii* — Not edible

Blanketing rotten hardwood stumps and logs in dense troops, this lovely little mushroom occurs in Kansas from late spring to early fall. Individually,

20. *Xeromphalina kauffmanii*

each mushroom is a luminous golden tan, with a slender stalk, darker and smaller at the bottom and lightening toward the top. The caps have a dimple in the center and faint lines following the gills. The gills run down the stalk (decurrent) and are approximately the color of the cap.

Description: **Cap**: 0.5–2 cm convex, flattening in age, central depression, tiny striations, bright tan. **Gills**: colored as cap, decurrent. **Stalk**: 1–2.5 cm long, 2–4 mm thick, tapered and darker toward the base. **Spore print**: white. **Spores**: 3–6 × 2–3 µm elliptical, smooth, amyloid. **Season**: late spring–early fall. **Ecology**: saprotrophic.

21. *Mycena pura* — Edible with caution

Lilac mycena

While *Mycena pura*, probably one of a species complex, usually displays some shade of lilac, there are often other colors involved, such as pale blues, greens, or yellows. This species' general stature is as pictured when moist, almost translucent, with small lines (striations) above the gills, and there is a small hump (umbo) in the center of the cap. When dry, the fruiting bodies are opaque. Sometimes this species has a radish-like odor. This is an unusual mushroom in Kansas, seen in wet summer woods.

21. *Mycena pura*

Description: **Cap**: 2–5 cm broad, with edges rounded to sometimes uplifted, with small central umbo, lilac or other pastel color; translucent and striate when wet, opaque when dry. **Gills**: variably attached, colored as cap but paler. **Stalk**: 3–7 cm tall, 3–7 mm thick, equal along its length, colored as cap but paler. **Spore print**: white. **Spores**: 5–9 × 3–4 µm, elliptical, smooth, amyloid. **Season**: summer. **Ecology**: mycorrhizal.

22. *Mycena inclinata* Edibility unknown

Of the nearly dozen species of *Mycena* reported from Kansas, *M. inclinata* is perhaps the most conspicuous. It fruits in loose clusters on dead deciduous wood during spring (especially) and fall. The cluster in the photograph was discovered on a log in late April. The pale bell-shaped caps, with striations following the gills, have a broad central knob, often brown. In age they open and become flatter. *Mycena inclinata* resembles countless other LBMs, most of which are either poisonous or have dubious reputations as edibles. This mushroom is therefore best left to the slugs, whose robust stomachs need not be so discriminating. Another species, *M. haematopus*, also grows in clusters on wood. It has a pale reddish-brown cap with a toothed or scalloped margin and exudes blood-red liquid when cut. *Mycena alcalina* is paler and has a similar growth habit but smells of bleach, especially if bruised.

Description: **Cap**: 1–3 cm broad, conical becoming bell-shaped, with uplifted margin and broad umbo, grayish brown to brown, fading with age, often darker at center. **Gills**: white to pale gray, attached. **Stalk**: 5–10 cm long, 1–3 mm thick, pale gray, becoming rusty brown over lower half, covered with whitish flecks on lower portion at first, then smooth, hollow; base densely hairy. **Spore print**: white. **Spores**: 7–9 × 5–6.5 µm, oval, elliptical, smooth, amyloid. **Season**: spring and fall. **Ecology**: saprotrophic.

22. *Mycena inclinata*

23. *Mycena luteopallens*

Edibility unknown

Syn. = *Mycena crocea*

Walnut mycena

This delicate yellow *Mycena* fruits during late summer and early fall in Kansas. It can be readily identified by its occurrence on buried walnuts, hickory nuts, and probably acorns. Careful digging is required to reveal its attachment to nutshells. The fruiting bodies illustrated here were among dozens of clusters spotted under a black walnut tree. As seen in the photograph, most of the nuts had first been eaten by squirrels. *Mycena luteopallens* is usually found in the summer, often abundantly.

Description: **Cap**: 1–1.5 cm broad, conical becoming flat, sometimes with broad central umbo, orange-yellow fading to pale yellow, smooth. **Gills**: white to yellow, widely spaced, attached. **Stalk**: 5–10 cm long, 1–2 mm thick, yellow, translucent, smooth, hairy at base, hollow. **Spore print**: white. **Spores**: 7–9 × 4–5.5 µm, elliptical, smooth or slightly roughened, amyloid. **Season**: late summer–early fall. **Ecology**: saprotrophic.

23. *Mycena luteopallens*

Family Physalacriaceae

As a group, members of this family share attached gills and white spores; many are wood rotters or parasites on plants. *Armillaria solidipes*, considered to be the largest organism in the world, is a family member. Several *Armillaria* species occur in Kansas. As a group, these are called "honey mushrooms" and are sometimes hard to distinguish from one another. Honey mushrooms are generally good edibles, though a few can cause stomach upset. *Flammulina* and *Hymenopellis* species are also edibles found in Kansas. *Rhodotus palmatus* is an extraordinarily beautiful mushroom that appears to occur more often in Kansas than almost anywhere else. The Tricholomataceae previously claimed this family.

Key to species

1a) Growing in soil, singly or only a few together; stalk ending with a single long, tapering root — *Hymenopellis radicata* group (no. 28)

1b) Growing on wood (sometimes buried), either singly or in clusters; tapering root absent — go to **2**

2a) Fruiting bodies growing singly or a few together, bright coral-pink, with raised pale network of ridges — *Rhodotus palmatus* (no. 27)

2b) Fruiting bodies growing in a cluster (caespitose), yellow-brown, reddish brown, or yellowish orange — go to **3**

3a) Ring (annulus) present on stalk — *Armillaria mellea* group (no. 24)

3b) Annulus absent — go to **4**

4a) Cap dry, yellow-brown to reddish brown with fine brown hairs — *Desarmillaria tabescens* (no. 25)

4b) Cap sticky (viscid), yellow-orange to orange-brown, without hairs — *Flammulina velutipes* (no. 26)

24. *Armillaria mellea* group — Edible with caution

Honey mushroom

The honey mushroom, ubiquitous in many regions of North America, is infrequently collected in Kansas except during extremely wet seasons. It fruits at the bases of living hardwoods, where it acts as a virulent parasite, but also grows on dead wood. The fruiting bodies usually appear during mid- to late fall (especially November) but have been found as early as late summer. *Armillaria mellea* actually comprises a complex of species that are still being sorted out. The enormous cluster pictured here, which was growing from the base of a dead tree, illustrates a form found in Kansas. Note the long stalk and prominent white ring. The cap ranges in color from yellow-brown to brown (these bleached specimens are atypical), and fine dark hairs are usually present near the center; the gills are whitish. The honey mushroom spreads by means of black straplike rhizomorphs, which are readily seen by peeling back the dead bark. Actively growing rhizomorphs bioluminesce and are responsible for the glowing wood colloquially called "foxfire." The honey mushroom is a cherished edible for many people, but caution is advised since gastrointestinal upsets have been reported. A similar species, *Desarmillaria tabescens* (no. 25), lacks a ring.

Description: **Cap**: 2.5–6.5 cm broad, round becoming convex or flat with broad umbo, yellow-brown to brown with fine brown hairs, especially near center, sometimes striate along margin, often caespitose. **Gills**: white to light brown, attached to slightly decurrent. **Stalk**: 5–15 cm long, 0.5–1.5 cm thick, colored as cap or paler, striate, often scaly; base with black rootlike rhizomorphs; annulus white to pale yellow, membranous. **Spore print**: white. **Spores**: 7–10 × 5–6.5 µm, elliptical, smooth, nonamyloid. **Season**: late summer–fall. **Ecology**: parasitic and saprotrophic.

24. *Armillaria mellea group*

25. *Desarmillaria tabescens*

25. *Desarmillaria tabescens* Edible with caution
Syn. = *Armillariella tabescens* (Ed. 1)
Ringless honey

Enormous clusters of *Desarmillaria tabescens* fruit at the bases of dead trees and stumps during late summer and early fall in Kansas. The cluster illustrated here was collected near a buried stump beside a city street. The caps are brownish and often have darker hairs near the center; the gills are whitish. The long stalk, which is well depicted in the photograph, lacks an annulus. It is often found in town, apparently on the ground but truly on buried wood. *Desarmillaria tabescens* is a delicious edible, but first-time tasters should be cautious since some unfortunate people suffer gastric upsets from eating it. The honey mushroom, *Armillaria mellea* group (no. 24), has a ring but is otherwise very similar. The poisonous jack-o'-lantern, *Omphalotus illudens* (no. 13), also fruits in clusters and lacks an annulus but has strongly decurrent orange gills.

Description: **Cap**: 2–10 cm broad, convex becoming flat or depressed, yellow-brown to reddish brown with fine brown hairs, especially near center, caespitose. **Gills**: white to pinkish brown, sometimes straining brown, slightly decurrent. **Stalk**: 8–20 cm long, 0.5–1.5 cm thick, white to brown, streaked, often scaly; base with black rootlike rhizomorphs; annulus lacking. **Spore print**: white. **Spores**: 6–10 × 5–67 µm, elliptical, smooth, nonamyloid. **Season**: late summer–fall. **Ecology**: saprotrophic.

26. *Flammulina velutipes*

26. *Flammulina velutipes* Edible

Velvet foot

Winter mushroom

Flammulina velutipes is a stalwart survivor on dead or dying hardwoods in Kansas. During warm spells in midwinter, clusters of frozen fruiting bodies often thaw and resume growth after other mushrooms have long vanished. The fruiting bodies may also be found during spring and fall. The specimens in the photograph appear terrestrial but are actually arising from buried roots at the base of a dead elm. The important features illustrated include the velvety dark brown stalk and the sticky yellow-orange cap with white gills. They often have much longer stalks, unlike those pictured. The velvet foot is a good edible, though some object to its slippery consistency. It is widely cultivated in Japan, where it is known as enokitake. When cultivated in darkness, the fruiting bodies of this species develop smooth, elongated stalks and minute caps. Care should be taken not to confuse the velvet foot with other wood-dwelling LBMs, particularly the deadly *Galerina marginata* (no. 58), which has a ring and a brown spore print.

Description: **Cap**: 1.5–6 cm broad, convex with inrolled margin becoming flat, yellow-orange to orange-brown, lighter at margin, smooth, sticky, caespitose. **Gills**: white to pale yellow, attached. **Stalk**: 2–7 cm long, 3–7 mm thick, pale yellow when young, later velvety with dark brown hairs. **Spore print**: white.

Spores: 6.5–9 × 2.5–4 µm, elliptical, smooth, nonamyloid. **Season**: fall, winter, and spring. **Ecology**: saprotrophic and probably parasitic.

27. *Rhodotus palmatus* — Edibility unknown

The beautiful *Rhodotus palmatus*, though listed as rare in most mushroom books, is infrequent but not rare in eastern Kansas during late spring or early fall. It fruits singly or in small groups on hardwood logs. The ridges on the cap form a distinctive network that makes this species unmistakable. The specimen illustrated here shows a variation in color and the interesting rosy droplets that sometimes accompany *R. palmatus*. Examples as striking as this are not always seen, as older specimens can be quite drab; look for the ridges. The shared stalk in this picture is unusual. Though tempting, this mushroom is of uncertain edibility.

Description: **Cap**: 3–8 cm broad, convex with incurved margin, pink to salmon, covered with network of ridges, tough. **Gills**: pink to salmon, attached. **Stalk**: 2–5 cm long, 3–6 mm thick, pink, slightly hairy, off center, curved. **Spore print**: pale yellowish pink. **Spores**: 5–8 × 4.5–6.5 µm, broadly faintly warted, nonamyloid. **Season**: late spring and early fall. **Ecology**: saprotrophic.

27. *Rhodotus palmatus*

28. *Hymenopellis radicata* group Edible

Syn. = *Oudemansiella radicata* group (Ed. 1)

Syn. = *Xerula radicata* group

Rooting collybia

The rooting collybia, so called because of its former placement in the genus *Collybia*, is a common mushroom under trees and in lawns in Kansas from late spring through fall. A member of the *Hymenopellis radicata* group is pictured here. *Hymenopellis* encompasses several species that can be distinguished only microscopically. A fruiting body in the photograph was dug up to illustrate the tapering rootlike base that is attached to dead roots and may extend down one foot into the soil. The brownish cap is sticky or slimy and often wrinkled. There is wide variation in fruiting body size, which may initially confuse mushroom hunters, and colors range from white to brown, but all have a single rootlike appendage extending into the soil from the base. *Hymenopellis* are known to be saprophytes. The fibrous stalk is usually discarded when preparing specimens for the table.

Description: **Cap**: 2–12 cm broad, bell-shaped with inrolled margin, becoming flat with low umbo, white to yellow-brown or darker, radially streaked, often wrinkled, sticky to slimy when wet. **Gills**: white, widely spaced, thick, attached. **Stalk**: 6–20 cm long, 0.4–1 cm thick, white to grayish brown, smooth or finely scaly, striate, twisted, brittle; base deeply rooting. **Spore print**: white. **Spores**: 12–18 × 9–12 μm or sometimes larger in closely related species, broadly elliptical, smooth, nonamyloid. **Season**: late spring–fall. **Ecology**: saprotrophic.

28. *Hymenopellis radicata group*

Families Tricholomataceae and some former Tricholomataceae: Hydnangiaceae, Lyophyllaceae, Phyllotopsidaceae, Pleurotaceae, and Schizophyllaceae

The family Tricholomataceae was previously a catchall for gilled mushrooms that lacked characteristics clearly linking them to other known families. With DNA analyses, many of these former trichs (short for Tricholomataceae, considered the "tricky trichs" since they are hard to identify) have been put into their own families. In the strict sense, the family Tricholomataceae is represented here only by members of the genera *Leucopaxillus* and *Tricholoma*. However, we also include several species more recently segregated into the families Pleurotaceae (represented here by members of the genus *Pleurotus*, including the eminently edible oyster mushroom), Schizophyllaceae (*Schizophyllum*), Hydnangiaceae (*Laccaria*), Lyophyllaceae (*Asterophora*, *Hypsizygus*, *Lyophyllum*), and Phyllotopsidaceae (*Phyllotopsis*) (these families were chosen because they contain only a few genera) as well as several genera currently unassigned to a family (*Clitocybe*, *Lepista*, and *Megacollybia*). It's important to keep in mind that even though some of these species are superficially similar to one another, the families to which they belong may not be any more closely related to one another than they are to other families of mushrooms treated in this book. It's also illustrative of the state of our knowledge of the evolutionary relationships among fungi that several genera treated here are not well enough known even to assign them to family. It is perhaps not surprising, therefore, that these species vary widely in shape, edibility, and growth form.

Despite recent disruption of the broader taxonomy, from an identification perspective, the classical methods will still avail the reader. Pale spores are common to all in the group. Most have gills attached to the stalk, unlike members of the families Agaricaceae and Amanitaceae. Several other characteristics can help eliminate similar species, despite not being unifying characteristics across the group. Members of the family Hygrophoraceae, which also produce pale spores, differ from most trichs in typically having slimy caps and/or stalks and thick, waxy gills. Although species of *Laccaria* also have waxy gills, their caps or stalks are never slimy, unless rotten, perhaps. The Physalacriaceae, detailed just before this section, were formerly included in the Tricholomataceae and have pale spores and attached gills, too. The species of Physalacriaceae in this book each differ from the trichs in having a ring (*Armillaria*), a long, tapering root (*Hymenopellis*), raised ridges on the cap (*Rhodotus*) or a clustered growth form in combination with a hairy cap (*Desarmillaria*) or a sticky one (*Flammulina*). Species of the family

Russulaceae that have a cap and stalk also have attached gills and white to orange spores but have very brittle flesh.

Key to species

1a) Parasitic on old fruiting bodies of other mushrooms
Asterophora lycoperdoides (no. 37)

1b) Not parasitic on mushrooms go to **2**

2a) Growing on wood or immediately adjacent to wood go to **3**

2b) Not growing on wood go to **9**

3a) Cap thin-fleshed and tough, shell-shaped with edges curling under at maturity and covered in fuzzy hairs, up to 3 inches broad; stalk absent (sessile) go to **4**

3b) Cap fleshy, neither shell-shaped nor particularly tough, with edges usually flat at maturity, usually smooth, but if hairy then 4–15 inches broad and stalk present go to **5**

4a) Cap and gills white to gray, up to 1.5 inches broad
Schizophyllum commune (no. 39)

4b) Cap and gills orange-yellow, up to 3 inches broad
Phyllotopsis nidulans (no. 33)

5a) Cap and stalk covered with stiff hairs; gills running down stalk (decurrent) *Lentinus levis* (see no. 38)

5b) Cap and stalk (if present) smooth; gills decurrent or merely attached
go to **6**

6a) Fruiting bodies clustered (caespitose), often with joined, off-center stalks; gills decurrent although stalks occasionally absent go to **7**

6b) Fruiting bodies occurring singly or a few together; gills attached but not decurrent go to **8**

7a) Spore print white; growing in cool weather *Pleurotus ostreatus* (no. 38)

7b) Spore print pale to light purple; growing in warm weather
Pleurotus pulmonarius (see no. 38)

8a) Cap grayish brown to dark brown, radially streaked; typically growing immediately adjacent to wood *Megacollybia rodmanii* (no. 32)

8b) Cap white to tan, without radial streaking; growing from wounds in box elder or elm *Hypsizygus ulmarius* (see no. 38)

9a) Growing in open, grassy areas; fruiting bodies clustered (caespitose) *Lyophyllum decastes* group (no. 36)

9b) Growing in dense or open woodlands go to **10**

10a) Cap pale reddish brown, in center gills white bruising reddish; growing in sandy soil under cottonwoods, often forming arcs or fairy rings *Tricholoma populinum* (see no. 32)

10b) Cap whitish, pinkish, bluish, brown, or purple; gills variously colored but not bruising reddish; typically in oak-hickory woods, growing singly or in small groups but not ring forming go to **11**

11a) Gills readily peeling from cap; stalks arising from a pale, dense mycelial mat go to **12**

11b) Gills difficult to peel from cap; stalks not arising from dense mycelial mat go to **13**

12a) Cap pinkish buff; gills yellowish; stalk swollen at base *Leucopaxillus tricolor* (no. 31)

12b) Cap and gills both whitish; stalk narrowing at base *Leucopaxillus albissimus* (see no. 31)

13a) Gills white to light tan go to **14**

13b) Gills some shade of pinkish gray, pink, or purple go to **15**

14a) Cap initially bluish green fading to tan at maturity, initially convex to flat or slightly depressed at maturity, smelling of anise (especially when crushed); spore print pinkish cream *Clitocybe odora* (no. 29)

14b) Cap yellowish brown, initially flat to distinctly funnel-shaped, with a deep central depression at maturity, without strong odor; spore print white *Infundibulicybe gibba* (see no. 29)

15a) Gills crowded, not waxy; spore print pale pink go to **16**

15b) Gills widely spaced and slightly waxy (when rubbed); spore print white or light purple go to **17**

16a) Stalk bulbous, about 0.5–1.5 inches thick *Lepista nuda* (see no. 30)

16b) Stalk without bulb, less than 0.5 inches thick *Lepista tarda* (no. 30)

17a) Cap and stalk initially pinkish brown; gills pale pink to pinkish brown; spore print white *Laccaria laccata* (no. 34)

17b) Cap initially purple or purplish brown; gills distinctly purple; spore print white to pale purple go to **18**

18a) Cap and stalk initially purplish brown, becoming whitish at maturity, about 2–6 inches broad *Laccaria ochropurpurea* (no. 35)

18b) Cap and stalk distinctly purple, about 0.5–2 inches broad *Laccaria amethystina* (see no. 35)

29. *Clitocybe odora* Edible

Clitocybe odora is frequently collected under hardwoods during summer and early fall in Kansas. Few mushrooms change as dramatically in appearance with age, and unless all stages are observed within the same troop, as in the photograph, they might easily be mistaken for different species. When young, the caps are convex and strikingly bluish green. Eventually the caps flatten, fade to tan, and develop wavy, irregular margins. Another important feature of this mushroom is its anise odor, which is most pronounced in mature fruiting bodies and may be enhanced by crushing the flesh. Approximately a dozen species of *Clitocybe,* as well as species formerly included in the genus, have been reported from Kansas. One particularly abundant species,

29. *Clitocybe odora*

Infundibulicybe gibba (syn. = *Clitocybe gibba* [Ed. 1]), has a yellow-brown, markedly funnel-shaped cap.

Description: **Cap**: 3–9 cm broad, convex with inrolled margin, becoming flat or slightly depressed with margin wavy, bluish green fading to tan, silky, with odor of anise. **Gills**: white to light tan, crowded, attached to decurrent. **Stalk**: 2–6 cm long, 0.4–1 cm thick, white to pale yellow-brown, often streaked, smooth. **Spore print**: pinkish cream. **Spores**: 6–8 × 3.5–5 µm, elliptical, smooth, nonamyloid. **Season**: summer–early fall. **Ecology**: saprotrophic.

30. *Lepista tarda*

Edibility unknown

Syn. = *Clitocybe tarda* (Ed. 1)

Lepista tarda commonly fruits during late spring and summer in the hardwood forests of Kansas. To identify this mushroom of many disguises is a lesson in coping with frustration. When young, the cap is light purple with brown overtones, but with age it becomes progressively browner until little purple is visible, as in the mature specimens illustrated here. The gill color is also variable but is generally some shade of light purple or pink. The esteemed edible *L. nuda* (syn. = *Clitocybe nuda* [Ed. 1]), or the blewit, is also exceedingly variable in the purple coloration of its cap and gills. It can be identified by its more robust stature, thicker stalk (1–3 cm broad), and bulbous base. Both species might be confused with

30. *Lepista tarda*

purple-gilled species of *Cortinarius* (nos. 48–50, 52). However, corts have rusty-brown spores and a cobweb-like veil (cortina).

Description: **Cap**: 2–7 cm broad, convex with inrolled margin, becoming flat to slightly depressed, light purple, browner with age, smooth. **Gills**: light purple to pinkish gray, crowded, attached. **Stalk**: 2–8 cm long, 3–8 mm thick, slender, purple-brown, streaked whitish. **Spore print**: pale pink. **Spores**: 6–7 × 3.5–5 µm, elliptical, roughened, nonamyloid. **Season**: late spring–summer. **Ecology**: saprotrophic.

31. *Leucopaxillus tricolor* — Edibility unknown

Unprepossessing but long lasting and not uncommon, this species is robust and rather tough throughout, especially the stalk. The characteristic most helpful in identifying this rather ordinary-looking mushroom is that the gills can be readily peeled away from the cap. Initially the margin of the dry, pinkish-buff cap is incurved, as seen in the upturned one in the picture; later it flattens. The gills are yellowish, crowded, and attached to nearly attached to the stalk. The stalk is thick, white, and club-shaped. The smaller fruiting body in the illustration shows the thicker stalk base. What does not appear in the picture is the dense mat of mycelium always present at the bottom of the stalk, permeating the substrate. *Leucopaxillus albissimus*, also found

31. *Leucopaxillus tricolor*

in Kansas, is paler overall, and the stalk (sometimes swollen in the middle) narrows at the base, but otherwise it is very similar to *L. tricolor*. Both are found in Kansas under oaks during the summer.

Description: **Cap**: 8–20 cm, broad, convex with an inrolled margin at first, then flattening, pinkish buff. **Gills**: yellowish, crowded, attached, although sometimes only slightly. **Stalk**: 4–10 cm long, 1–2.5 cm thick, club-shaped, arising from a dense mycelial mat. **Spore print**: white. **Spores**: 6–8 × 4–5.5 µm, ovoid, amyloid. **Season**: summer. **Ecology**: saprotrophic.

32. *Megacollybia rodmanii* — Edible with caution

Syn. = *Collybia platyphylla*
Syn. = *Tricholomopsis platyphylla* (Ed. 1)

Megacollybia rodmanii is an infrequent mushroom in Kansas forests during the summer. It typically fruits alongside logs or from buried wood. If the fruiting body is carefully dug up, numerous white mycelial cords that lead to wood can often be seen arising from its base. The caps are radially streaked and range from grayish brown to the dark brown of those illustrated here; the gills are widely spaced. The fruiting bodies in the photograph, though young, are beginning to dry out in the changeable Kansas weather. *Megacollybia rodmanii* is often listed as edible or nonpoisonous, but reports of gastrointestinal

32. *Megacollybia rodmanii*

poisonings make its edibility suspect. Species of *Tricholoma* may be similar in appearance. For example, the edible *T. populinum*, which fruits in sandy soil under cottonwoods, often in large arcs or fairy rings, has a cap that is pale reddish brown in the center and white gills that stain reddish brown.

Description: **Cap**: 5–15 cm broad, convex with inrolled margin becoming flat, grayish brown to dark brown, radially streaked. **Gills**: white to gray, widely spaced, attached. **Stalk**: 6–12 cm long, 1–3 cm thick, white to gray, streaked, smooth; base with white mycelial cords. **Spore print**: white. **Spores**: 7–10 × 4.5–6 μm, oval, smooth, nonamyloid. **Season**: summer. **Ecology**: saprotrophic.

33. *Phyllotopsis nidulans* — Not edible

Syn. = *Claudopus nidulans*

Phyllotopsis nidulans fruits clustered on hardwood logs from late spring through fall in Kansas. Its stalkless orange-yellow, thin-fleshed caps and gills are distinctive. The caps in the photograph appear bleached because of their characteristic coating of white hairs. The mushroom hunter who mistakes *P. nidulans* for the edible white-gilled oyster mushroom, *Pleurotus ostreatus* (no. 38), will not be poisoned, but the bad taste will discourage a second helping.

33. *Phyllotopsis nidulans*

Description: **Cap**: 2–8 cm broad, fan-shaped with inrolled margin, orange-yellow, covered with cottony white hairs, often caespitose. **Gills**: pale to bright orange-yellow, closely spaced. **Stalk**: absent. **Spore print**: pale pinkish. **Spores**: 6–8 × 3.5–4 µm, sausage-shaped, smooth, nonamyloid. **Season**: spring–late fall. **Ecology**: saprotrophic.

34. *Laccaria laccata* — Edible

Lackluster laccaria

Laccaria laccata is an unspectacular summer and fall mushroom in the hardwood forests of Kansas. It has many color disguises, but most often its cap, gills, and stalk are pinkish to brownish. They are not always clustered, as pictured here, nor as pristine. These are quite young and will open up further as they age. As with all species of *Laccaria*, the gills feel slightly waxy when rubbed and are fairly widely spaced. Reports on the edibility of this species vary from mediocre to superb, which tells us more about the cooking talents and palates of mushroom hunters than about the palatability of the fungi they collect. *Laccaria ochropurpurea* (no. 35) is larger and has purple gills.

Description: **Cap**: 1.5–4 cm broad, round becoming depressed in center with uplifted margin, pinkish brown, fading with moisture loss, smooth to faintly

34. *Laccaria laccata*

scaly. **Gills**: pale pink to pinkish brown, widely spaced, thick, slightly waxy, attached to decurrent. **Stalk**: 2–6 cm long, 2–6 mm thick, pinkish brown, streaked, often twisted, tough. **Spore print**: white. **Spores**: 7.5–10 × 7–8.5 µm, round to broadly elliptical, spiny, nonamyloid. **Season**: summer and fall **Ecology**: mycorrhizal.

35. *Laccaria ochropurpurea* Edible

This robust purple-gilled *Laccaria* fruits abundantly in open deciduous woods of Kansas during summer and early fall. Like most species of *Laccaria*, it has thick, widely spaced gills. The cap and stalk are brownish very early on but then become whitish, as illustrated in the largest specimen. One Kansan collects this species regularly on his farm and swears by it as an edible. Care should be taken not to confuse *L. ochropurpurea* with purple-gilled species of *Cortinarius* (nos. 48–50, 52), which have a cobweb-like veil (cortina) and a rusty-brown spore print. *Laccaria. amethystina* has a smaller, funnel-shaped cap (1–5 cm broad) and is purple overall.

35. *Laccaria ochropurpurea*

Description: **Cap**: 4–15 cm broad, round with incurved margin becoming flat, often with central depression, purple-brown to tan, fading whitish, smooth or faintly scaly. **Gills**: purple, widely separated, thick, slightly waxy, attached. **Stalk**: 6–15 cm long, 1–3 cm thick, colored as cap, streaked, tough. **Spore print**: white to pale purple. **Spores**: 6–8 µm, round, spiny, nonamyloid. **Season**: summer–early fall. **Ecology**: mycorrhizal.

36. *Lyophyllum decastes* group

36. *Lyophyllum decastes* group Edible
Fried chicken mushroom

While a number of mushrooms are difficult to find, this good edible seems deliberately to hide. This cluster was barely spotted by looking down into grass that had been mowed within the previous week. They are quite variable in color, usually brown shades with yellow, gray, or reddish tones; more often here in Kansas, they are the paler brown, as shown in the picture. The species is of a solid consistency, convex, sometimes with a lobed cap, and with a short, thick stalk. *Lyophyllum decastes* is occasionally found singly but most often grows in large, compact clusters, as depicted here, fruiting mainly in disturbed areas in the summer. One of these clusters might be enough for several good meals.

Description: **Cap**: 3–12 cm broad, convex becoming more planar, smooth, variably pale brown, with tones of yellow, gray, reddish, sometimes bruising brown, caespitose. **Gills**: variably attached, white to whitish. **Stalk**: 3–10 cm long, 1–2.5 cm thick, narrowing downward and often curving to fit in the group. **Spore print**: white. **Spores**: 4–6 µm, round, nonamyloid. **Season**: summer. **Ecology**: saprotrophic.

37. *Asterophora lycoperdoides* Edibility unknown
Syn. = *Nyctalis asterophora*

This bizarre, rare mushroom parasitizes the fruiting bodies of species of *Russula* and *Lactarius*. The specimens illustrated here were found during

37. *Asterophora lycoperdoides*

the summer under hardwoods in eastern Kansas. Their host has become so blackened and rotten that it is scarcely recognizable. *Asterophora lycoperdoides* is white and puffball-like when young; later, hyphal cells on its cap round up, separate, and convert to special spores called **chlamydospores**, which give the mature cap its brown, powdery appearance. The gills, which other mushrooms use to produce spores, are rudimentary and mostly sterile in this species.

Description: **Cap**: 0.5–2 cm broad, nearly round, white and fluffy, becoming brown and powdery. **Gills**: white, thick, widely spaced, rudimentary, attached. **Stalk**: 1–3 cm long, 3–8 mm thick, white or brown, velvety. **Spore print**: white (if obtainable). **Spores**: 5–16 × 3.5–4 μm, oval, smooth, nonamyloid; chlamydospores 12–18 μm, round, spiny, brown. **Season**: summer. **Ecology**: parasitic.

38. *Pleurotus ostreatus* — Edible

Oyster mushroom

The oyster mushroom grows on decaying logs and trees and is particularly prevalent on willow, cottonwood, and elm along the Kansas River floodplain and other river valleys. It fruits in cooler weather all year long but is most abundant during spring and fall. *Pleurotus ostreatus* and closely related species are usually various shades of brown or gray, and may be large, floppy, and fan-shaped in age. The overlapping caps, as in the photograph, can sometimes resemble oysters, and some mycophagists claim that the species also tastes like an oyster. The stalk may be lateral, off center, or entirely absent, depending upon the position of the fruiting body; the gills are decurrent. Shiny black-and-orange beetles often hide between the gills and must be removed before cooking. The mycelium of this mushroom obtains additional nitrogen by paralyzing and digesting wormlike nematodes living in the wood, but this in no way affects the superb edibility of the fruiting bodies. The oyster mushroom is also easily cultivated. The paler *P. pulmonarius* was once considered synonymous, though *P. pulmonarius* usually has a pale purple spore print and occurs in warm weather, while *P. ostreatus* always has a white spore print and occurs in cool weather. The elm oyster, *Hypsizygus ulmarius* (syn. = *Pleurotus ulmarius*), fruits singly or in pairs from wounds on box elder and elm. It has a white to tan cap that often cracks with age and a prominent stalk that is off center to nearly central; its gills are attached but not decurrent. Though edible, the elm oyster usually fruits high above the reach of mushroomers. *Lentinus levis* (syn. = *Panus strigosus* [Ed. 1]), which has decurrent gills, as does *Pleurotus*, usually fruits singly, as does *Hypsizygus*, and is also whitish and fruits on trees. However, *L. levis* has an enormous cap (up to 16 inches broad) and a lateral to off-center stalk that is covered with stiff hairs.

38. *Pleurotus ostreatus*

Description: **Cap**: 5–30 cm broad, fan- or funnel-shaped, white to gray-brown, smooth, often clustered and overlapping. **Gills**: white to yellowish, thick, decurrent. **Stalk**: absent or 0.5–2 cm long, 0.5–2 cm thick, white, velvety, lateral or off center. **Spore print**: white. **Spores**: 8–12 × 3.5–4.5 µm, elliptical, smooth, nonamyloid. **Season**: year-round. **Ecology**: saprotrophic.

39. *Schizophyllum commune* — Not edible

Split gill

The split gill is a ubiquitous mushroom that occurs on fallen hardwood branches in Kansas. The fruiting bodies are capable of drying and reviving according to the whims of the weather; hence, they can be found all year long. Because of its tough, pliant, thin flesh, the split gill is considered more of a polypore than a gilled mushroom. The photograph illustrates its most unique feature, namely, the split nature of its gill-like ridges. During dry weather, the split edges curl over the lateral surfaces of the ridges, presumably to protect the spore-bearing regions from desiccation or marauding insects. The upper surface of the cap (not shown) is white and hairy. The fruiting bodies illustrated here are cup-shaped because they are attached to the wood at their centers, but they are often laterally attached and fan-shaped. The brown, deeply lobed specimens farthest back are probably old and weathered. The

39. *Schizophyllum commune*

ubiquitous *Schizophyllum commune* exploits many habitats and has even been found growing in human (immunocompromised) nostrils. It lends itself to research because it is easily cultured and has become a genetic model in the laboratory.

Description: **Cap**: 0.5–4 cm broad, fan- or cup-shaped with margin often lobed and inrolled, white to gray, hairy, leathery. **Gills**: fuzzy, white to gray, sometimes pale pink; edges split lengthwise and curling when dry. **Stalk**: absent. **Spore print**: white. **Spores**: 3–4 × 1–1.5 µm, cylindrical, smooth, nonamyloid. Season: year-round. **Ecology**: saprotrophic.

Families Bolbitiaceae, Entolomataceae, and Pluteaceae

These three families have spores with a reddish or pinkish cast—from pink and pinkish tan through rust or reddish brown. Other families also have rusty spores—notably the family Cortinariaceae (but also the deadly *Galerina marginata* [no. 58] in the family Hymenogastraceae)—and others can have pale pinkish spores (not the darker pink in *Pluteus*, as shown in Fig. 6), such as some members of the Tricholomataceae and former Tricholomataceae.

Bolbitiaceae are variable in their choice of substrates. Found on dung, wood, and lawns, they are small and fragile and sometimes slimy. The genus *Conocybe*, with rusty (sometimes pale rusty) spores, frequents lawns and is mostly harmless. *Conocybe filaris* is deadly if eaten but fortunately has not yet been found in Kansas. We mention it here because it is widespread and common in adjoining states.

Entolomataceae grow in the woods and usually have attached gills and pink spores. Their spores are microscopically interesting in that they are angular, unlike the spores of most mushrooms. The mushrooms in the genus *Entoloma* are usually midsized to large, and a number are poisonous. Many growing in Kansas are hard to distinguish from one another; they tend to have tan, smooth, wavy caps, though the one presented here is small and dark.

Pluteaceae typically grow on dead wood, which sometimes may be buried, so they might appear to be terrestrial. Free gills and pink spores are characteristic; additionally, the stalks easily and cleanly separate from the softer cap. The genera *Pluteus*, *Volvariella*, and *Volvopluteus* contain great edibles, though some of the smaller species are suspect. *Volvariella* and *Volvopluteus* are distinguished from other species treated here by the possession of a membrane called a **volva**—the remains of a universal veil—enclosing the bottom of the stalk.

Key to species

1a) Spore print (and mature gills) rusty brown — go to **2**

1b) Spore print (and mature gills) some shade of pink — go to **4**

2a) Cap convex, slimy (viscid), yellow fading to tan — *Bolbitius titubans* (no. 40)

2b) Cap conical, dry, pale tan, or brownish — go to **3**

3a) Cap brownish; stalk brown, ring present — *Conocybe filaris* (see no. 41)

3b) Cap pale tan; stalk pale, ring absent *Conocybe apala* (no. 41)

4a) Volva present go to **5**

4b) Volva absent go to **7**

5a) Cap silky/hairy; volva tan; growing on wood
Volvariella bombycina (no. 46)

5b) Cap smooth; volva white; growing in soil go to **6**

6a) Cap medium to large (over an inch to about 6 inches), sticky (viscid)
Volvopluteus gloiocephalus (no. 47)

6b) Cap small (less than an inch to a little over an inch), dry
Volvariella pusilla (see no. 47)

7a) Cap and stalk bright yellow *Pluteus admirabilis* (no. 44)

7b) Cap or stalk violet or some shade of gray or brown go to **8**

8a) Cap dark violet (if only lower part of stalk becoming blue, see lead 9a); stalk scaly, violet; in soil *Entoloma nigroviolaceum* (no. 42)

8b) Cap some shade of gray or brown; stalk smooth or hairy but not scaly, pale or becoming dark blue in lower part only; on wood (sometimes buried)
go to **9**

9a) Lower part of stalk becoming dark blue *Pluteus cyanopus* (see no. 43)

9b) Lower part of stalk remaining pale go to **10**

10a) Cap grayish, striate (appearing pleated); base of stalk with white mycelial fuzz *Pluteus longistriatus* (no. 43)

10b) Cap pale to brownish, with darker center; base of stalk smooth
go to **11**

11a) Cap pale to brownish, with darker streaks in center; fruiting singly
Pluteus cervinus (no. 45)

11b) Cap white with some brown in the center; fruiting in clusters (caespitose)
Pluteus petasatus (see no. 45)

40. *Bolbitius titubans* Edible with caution

Syn. = *Bolbitius vitellinus*

Sunny side up

This gooey little species is not uncommon on wood chips or lawns in the summer. The convex, sticky (viscid), bright yellow cap shown here is typical, though it becomes more open, bell-shaped, and paler with age. All parts are fragile. Smudges of rusty spores can be seen on the stalk of the specimen in the foreground. The pale yellow gills are of variable attachment and become rusty with mature spores. The stalk is an even column of yellow, paler than the cap.

Description: **Cap**: 1–5 cm broad, smooth, even shiny, yellow with a very viscid, gooey surface, convex, then more open and paler. **Gills**: soft pale yellow at first, then rusty, variably attached. **Stalk**: 3–7 cm long, 3–7 mm thick, even, pale yellow; annulus absent. **Spore print**: pale/medium rusty. **Spores**: 10–16 × 6–9 µm, elliptical, smooth. **Season**: summer. **Ecology**: saprotrophic.

40. *Bolbitius titubans*

41. *Conocybe apala* Edibility unknown

Syn. = *Conocybe lactea*
Common cone head
Dunce cap

This little mushroom is common in lawns, looking like tiny tepees scattered about. Typical is the conical tan to whitish cap, the fibrous but fragile stalk, and the fine gills that drop a pale rusty-brown spore print. This species feeds on dead turf. No small lawn mushroom should be eaten (large ones should be individually evaluated). Some are very poisonous, as is a relative of *C. apala*, *C. filaris*, which is deadly. The primary difference is that *C. filaris* has a ring around the stalk and a darker cap. Rings can disappear for various reasons. *Conocybe filaris* has not yet been found in Kansas but is present in adjoining states. *Conocybe apala* usually peaks in summer across Kansas.

Description: **Cap**: 1–2.5 cm broad, conical with flaring edges, sometimes wrinkled, thin flesh, pale tan. **Gills**: fine, pale, then warm light rusty. **Stalk**: 3–11 cm long, 1–2 mm thick, an even column, fragile, without annulus. **Spore print**: pale/medium rusty brown. **Spores**: 11–16 × 6–10 µm, elliptical, smooth. **Season**: summer. **Ecology**: saprotrophic.

41. *Conocybe apala*

42. *Entoloma nigroviolaceum*

42. *Entoloma nigroviolaceum* Edibility unknown
Syn. = *Leptonia nigroviolacea*

Entoloma nigroviolaceum is one of a number of small violet-black or blue-black entolomas that are hard to distinguish from one another, so the pictured specimen may belong to a close relative. However, members of this group are distinct, with a dry, fibrous-scaly deep violet convex cap, pink mature gills, and scaly purple stalk. They are summer mushrooms, found in oak woods, often on moss. This specimen was discovered in southeast Kansas.

Description: **Cap:** 1–3 cm broad, rounded, sometimes with a small dimple in center, fibrous-scaly, intense dark violet or purple. **Stalk:** 5–10 cm long, 0.5–1 cm thick. **Gills:** whitish at first, then pink. **Spore print:** pink. **Spores:** 9.5–11.5 × 7–8.5 μm, angular. **Season:** summer. **Ecology:** saprotrophic.

43. *Pluteus longistriatus* Edibility unknown

There are a number of small *Pluteus* in the woods. This is one of the most common. The clear indicators of a *Pluteus* mushroom are its free gills, pink spores, and growth on wood (sometimes buried). The spores will color the gills pink at maturity, but young *Pluteus* have white gills. This particular species is characterized by its pleated cap and mycelial fuzz at the base of the stalk. In the picture, two tiny primordial fruiting bodies can be seen at the base of the stalk. There are several small *Pluteus* species that become blue on the lower part of the stalk; found in Kansas is *Pluteus cyanopus*. *Pluteus longistriatus* does not become blue on the stalk and grows from spring through fall in different kinds of woodlands.

43. *Pluteus longistriatus*

Description: **Cap**: 1–4 cm broad, bell-shaped, fragile, striate far up the cap, brown to gray-brown. **Gills**: close, whitish at first, then pink, free at maturity. **Stalk**: 2–7 cm long, 1.5–3 mm thick, with white mycelial fuzz at base. **Spore print**: pink. **Spores** 6–7.5 × 5–5.5 µm, nearly spherical, smooth. **Season**: spring–fall. **Ecology**: saprotrophic.

44. *Pluteus admirabilis* — Edibility unknown

This small, delicate *Pluteus* fruits on rotten logs during the summer in Kansas. Its characteristic features, which are shown in the photograph, include free pinkish gills and a yellow cap and stalk. Two of the overturned fruiting bodies are immature, so their gills have not yet turned fully pink. These specimens were collected from a log that supported a troop of about thirty fruiting bodies.

Description: **Cap**: 1–3 cm broad, bell-shaped, then flat with broad central knob, bright yellow becoming duller, smooth, slightly striate along margin, often wrinkled at center. **Gills**: white to pale yellow becoming pinkish, free.

44. *Pluteus admirabilis*

Stalk: 3–6 cm long, 1–3 mm thick, yellow, smooth. **Spore print**: salmon pink. **Spores**: 5.5–7 × 4.5–6 µm, broadly elliptical, smooth. **Season**: summer. **Ecology**: saprotrophic.

45. *Pluteus cervinus* — Edible

Deer mushroom

The deer mushroom, *Pluteus cervinus*, fruits on rotting logs, stumps, and sawdust from spring through fall. Though collected in Kansas woods every year, it is often sporadic in its appearance and strangely absent when most expected. The specimens in the photograph, which were found during a summer foray, illustrate the brown cap and the free gills that are beginning to turn pink. Sometimes the cap is paler or darker. If the stalk is gently twisted, it will readily detach from the cap, revealing the characteristic ball-and-socket attachment of the two parts. The raw flesh has a radish-like flavor that disappears with cooking. Some mycophagists sing this mushroom's praises; others find it mealy and insipid. The larger, meatier *P. petasatus* is better eating and is occasionally found in Kansas, especially on wood chips and sawdust. It has a white cap that is brown in the center and tends to fruit in large clusters. *Pluteus longistriatus* (no. 43) has a cap that is small, gray to grayish brown, and prominently striate. The pink-spored *Entoloma* species, many of which

45. *Pluteus cervinus*

are poisonous, can be distinguished from *Pluteus* by their gills, which are attached, and by their terrestrial growth habit.

Description: **Cap**: 1–15 cm broad, bell-shaped becoming flat when very young, then pale to dark brown or gray-brown, often radially streaked with flattened hairs. **Gills**: white becoming pink or dull red, free. **Stalk**: 5–12 cm long, 0.5–1.5 cm thick, white to brown or gray, smooth. **Spore print**: salmon to brownish pink. **Spores**: 5.5–7 × 4–5 μm, elliptical, smooth. **Season**: spring–fall. **Ecology**: saprotrophic.

46. *Volvariella bombycina* Edible

The beautiful *Volvariella bombycina* fruits during the summer in Kansas from tree wounds, rotting stumps, and logs. Young fruiting bodies are enveloped by a brownish universal veil and appear egg-like. This universal veil is left behind as a sac-like volva (seen in the photograph) after emergence of the large silky-hairy white cap. Note the white gills on the overturned immature fruiting body; these will eventually turn pink, as in the mature cap above it. The rarity of *V. bombycina* is matched only by its excellence as an edible. Other species of *Volvariella* in Kansas grow on the ground rather than on wood.

46. *Volvariella bombycina*

Description: **Cap**: 5–20 cm broad, oval or bell-shaped becoming convex to flat, white to pale yellow, hairy or scaly, silky, fringed at margin. **Gills**: white becoming pink, crowded, free. **Stalk**: 6–20 cm long, 1–2 cm thick, white, smooth, widening toward base; volva white to brown, sac-like, membranous. **Spore print**: pink to salmon. **Spores**: 6.5–10.5 × 4.5–6.5 µm, elliptical, smooth. **Season**: summer. **Ecology**: saprotrophic.

47. *Volvopluteus gloiocephalus* — Edible with caution

Syn. = *Volvariella speciosa* (Ed. 1)

The statuesque *Volvopluteus gloiocephalus* fruits in the hardwood forests of Kansas during late spring or early summer. Its white cap is extremely slimy, especially during wet weather, and often picks up soil and forest debris. Buttons are enclosed by a membranous universal veil and resemble an *Amanita* egg. The remains of the universal veil form a sac-like volva, which is scarcely visible on the large, overturned specimen in the photograph and is missing from the young fruiting body next to it. Part of the ruptured universal veil can also be seen on the upright cap; such volval patches are often not present. The free gill attachment and the change in gill color from white to pinkish are also illustrated; the split cap of the pink-gilled specimen is not typical. Though edible, *V. gloiocephalus* is less than savory. The greatest danger is confusing young, white-gilled specimens with deadly white amanitas (such as *A. bisporigera* [no. 3]), which also have a sac-like volva and free gills. Deadly amanitas differ from species of *Volvariella* in having an annulus, but this is sometimes lost during development, so it is prudent to collect only mature specimens of *V. gloiocephalus* to be sure the spore print is pinkish and not white, as in amanitas. Several similar terrestrial species fruit in Kansas. Among these, *Volvariella pusilla* has a small, dry white cap (0.5–3.5 cm broad). *Volvariella volvacea*, the paddy straw mushroom, has a dry dark gray-brown cap; it doesn't grow in Kansas but is widely cultivated in Asia.

Description: **Cap**: 5–15 cm broad, bell-shaped becoming convex to flat, white to light gray, smooth, slimy, occasionally with volval patches. **Gills**: white becoming pink or reddish pink, free. **Stalk**: 9–20 cm long, 1–2 cm thick, white to cream, smooth; annulus absent; volva white, sac-like, membranous. **Spore print**: salmon to brownish pink. **Spores**: 11.5–21 × 7–12.5 µm, broadly elliptical, smooth. **Season**: spring–summer. **Ecology**: saprotrophic.

47. *Volvopluteus gloiocephalus*

Families Cortinariaceae, Crepidotaceae, and Inocybaceae

The Cortinariaceae is the largest family of gilled mushrooms. Of primary interest is the genus *Cortinarius*, with over two thousand species in North America, including at least two dozen species reported from Kansas. "Corts" are identified by their cobweb-like partial veil, called a cortina, and rusty-brown spore print. The cortina is often visible only on buttons, whereas in mature specimens, it leaves at most a faint hairy zone on the stalk. The fruiting bodies range in color from brilliant blues and yellows to purples and reds, with even some green features and all possible shades of brown. Corts may be dry or slimy, and many have impressively bulbous bases. Some may be abruptly bulbous, that is, marginate, with a ledge above the base. Most species are terrestrial and mycorrhizal and so are often found in association with trees. Several species fruit during the spring in Kansas, but most reach their full glory in late summer and fall.

Species of *Cortinarius* usually *look* distinctive enough to be easily identified to genus level, but most are nearly impossible to identify to species level visually. This is a product of both poor mapping of species characteristics and the vast diversity of species represented. Some contain the toxin orellanine, which has a latent period of three days to two weeks before symptoms occur. It causes kidney and liver damage and can be fatal. Although this toxicity may not extend to its broad diversity, the entire genus is considered unsafe for eating.

The family Inocybaceae consists of small to medium-sized mushrooms that are called fiber heads because the cuticle (a thin membrane on the cap surface) is usually fibrous, splitting into strands and fibers. Many times the cap is peaked or has a knob (umbo) at its center. Like the corts, they always grow on the ground. They often have a strong smell (of very diverse types—floral, fruity, cedarwood-like, and more), and their spore print is usually a muddy brown. They are probably the most prevalent brown-spored LBMs/LWJs. Their spore shape is also interesting in that some species have knobbly spores, and other species have smooth spores. Many members of the family Inocybaceae are poisonous. Recently, gene sequencing has indicated that the family should be split into two new genera plus the original genus *Inocybe*. Although members of the genus *Hebeloma* (family Hymenogastraceae) share many characteristics with these fiber heads, they can often be distinguished by their slimy/sticky caps, radish-like odor, and more robust stature. The small, flabby members of family Crepidotaceae have the same spore color as members of the Inocybaceae but are easily distinguished because they grow on wood and are stalkless (sessile).

Key to species

1a. Very young specimens with a cobweb-like veil (cortina) covering the gills go to **2**

1b. Cortina absent at all stages of development go to **8**

2a. Exterior of cap some shade of purple go to **3**

2b. Exterior of cap some shade of tan, brown, reddish brown, or reddish orange go to **6**

3a. Bulb present at base of stalk go to **4**

3b. Bulb absent at base of stalk go to **5**

4a. Cap with white felty patches *Cortinarius calyptrodermus* (no. 48)

4b. Cap without felty patches *Cortinarius sphaerospermus* (no. 49)

5a. Cap bright violet; both cap and stalk covered in slime *Cortinarius iodeoides* (no. 52)

5b. Cap silky pale lilac; cap and stalk dry *Cortinarius alboviolaceus* (no. 50)

6a. Cap brown, sometimes ringed in darker zones where moist (hygrophanous); gills widely spaced *Cortinarius distans* (no. 53)

6b. Cap yellow to reddish tan or reddish orange, not hygrophanous; gills not widely spaced go to **7**

7a. Fruiting body robust, with cap 2–3 inches broad; cap yellow to reddish tan; flesh quickly (or transiently) turning purple where broken *Cortinarius atkinsonianus* (no. 54)

7b. Fruiting body small, with cap 1–2 inches broad; cap reddish orange; flesh not purple where broken *Cortinarius hesleri* (no. 51)

8a. Growing on wood; stalk absent (sessile) go to **9**

8b. Growing in soil; stalk present go to **10**

9a. Gills yellow to orange until brown with spores *Crepidotus crocophyllus* (no. 55)

9b. Gills pale until brown with spores *Crepidotus mollis* (see no. 55)

10a. Fruiting body brown, bruising wine-colored in all parts *Inosperma adaequatum* (see no. 56)

10b. Fruiting body not bruising go to **11**

11a. Cap yellow tan to ocher, distinctly fibrous *Pseudosperma rimosum* (no. 56)

11b. Cap white, silky *Inocybe geophylla* (see no. 56)

48. *Cortinarius calyptrodermus* Edibility suspect

This beautiful, rare *Cortinarius* was found at Woodridge Primitive Camping Area at Clinton Lake in Douglas County. The species is substantial, purple-violet, with showy, felty, pale white, ragged, often angular patches of universal veil adhering to the sticky (viscid) cap surface, as seen in the foremost specimen illustrated. The young button stage is entirely enclosed by the pale universal veil. The gills are colored as the cap, though mature spores show up as rusty areas in the pictured gills. The stalk is also purple and short, with a thick, rounded, and marginate bulb, which is evident in the upper specimen. The cortina is initially purple but becomes rusty from spores, as seen in the rusty fibers on the middle stalk. The bulb is whitish, covered in the remains of the universal veil and possibly the mycelium that makes a mat through leaf mold where they grow. This mushroom is found in late summer through fall, usually in groups under oak.

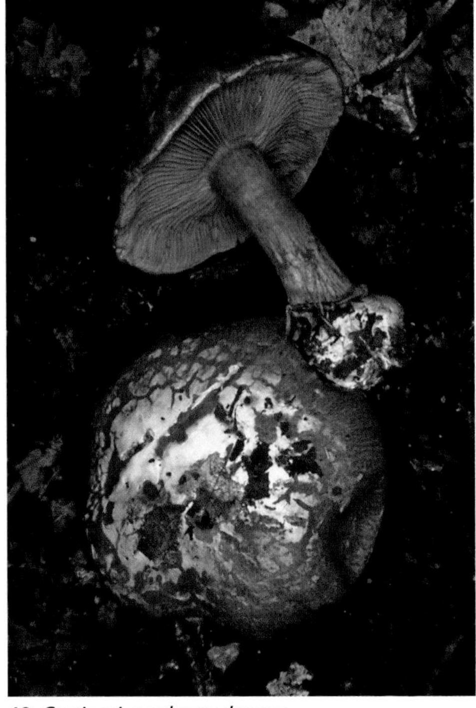

48. *Cortinarius calyptrodermus*

Description: **Cap**: 5–10 cm broad, convex, then opening, whitish when young, with a universal veil that breaks into pale, irregular felty patches on the viscid purple cap surface at maturity. **Gills**: purple until tinged with rusty spores. **Stalk**: 5–9 cm tall, 1–2.5 cm thick, purple, with marginate bulb 3–4 cm thick; cortina purple until covered in rusty spores. **Spore print**: tawny-rust. **Spores**: 10–12 × 6–7 µm, fat almond-shaped, coarsely warted. **Season**: summer–fall. **Ecology**: mycorrhizal.

49. *Cortinarius sphaerospermus* Edibility suspect

Many corts are purple or have purple parts or tones. This one, as pictured, is all purple. Actually, the color here is paler than when it was found in the field, and these specimens are rather young and smaller than typical. The appearance of this mushroom is large and stout, and it is colored an intense purple. The fine fibers of the cortina, which are also purple, are copious and leave a conspicuous hairy ring, laden with dark rusty spores, on the stalk when the fruiting body is fully mature (best seen on the young specimen to the right as a cobwebby material covering the gills). The cap is initially sticky (viscid), though in Kansas weather, it often shows up with a dry, shiny, smooth surface. The stalk is thick and solid and when young has a whitish, marginate bulb (abruptly contracted at the upper edge, forming a little ledge; see left specimen). At maturity the stalk becomes more club-like and more purple with age. It is found in oak woods in Kansas in the fall. Like all corts, it should not be eaten. These specimens were found at Toronto Lake in Woodson County.

49. *Cortinarius sphaerospermus*

Two other purple corts found in Kansas are the smaller white (to pale violet) stalked *Cortinarius iodeoides* (no. 52), common elsewhere, and *C. calyptrodermus* (no. 48). The former species has a slimy cap of light, bright violet whose surface is sometimes spotted with teardrop-shaped splotches. The uncommon *C. calyptrodermus* has a deep purple cap decorated with raised, angular white patches.

Description: **Cap**: 6–12 cm broad, broadly rounded, purple, very viscid, though in dry weather smooth and shining. **Gills**: purple becoming dark rusty with spores. **Stalk**: 6–9 cm tall, 1.5–2 cm thick, stout, purple, whitish when young, dry, hung with dense, rusty fibers, with marginate bulb; cortina deep purple. **Spore print**: deep rusty brown. **Spores**: 7–8 × 6–7.5 µm, globose, roughened. **Season**: fall. **Ecology**: mycorrhizal.

50. *Cortinarius alboviolaceus* — Edibility suspect

This striking cort, with its silky, silvery lilac cap and stalk, fruits during late summer and early fall in hardwood forests of Kansas. Its gills are pale violet at first but later become the cinnamon-brown seen on the sectioned cap in the photograph. Note the cobweb-like cortina covering the gills of the button. As the cap expands, the cortina ruptures and leaves a faint hairy zone on the stalk; this zone is apparent on the medium-sized specimen because the hairs have been covered by a rusty-brown spore deposit. Though often listed as edible, *C. alboviolaceus* and other corts should be avoided since they are difficult to identify and potentially poisonous. The edible blewit, *Lepista nuda* (see no. 30) is also pale purple overall when young but lacks a cortina and produces a pale pink spore print.

50. *Cortinarius alboviolaceus*

Description: **Cap**: 3–6 cm broad, bell-shaped, then flat with broad umbo, silvery lilac, silky. **Gills**: grayish violet becoming cinnamon-brown, attached. **Stalk**: 4–8 cm long, 0.5–2 cm thick, club-shaped, colored as cap, silky; cortina white, leaving faint hairy zone. **Spore print**: rusty brown. **Spores**: 8–12 × 5–6.5 µm, elliptical, minutely roughened. **Season**: summer–fall. **Ecology**: mycorrhizal.

51. *Cortinarius hesleri* — Edibility suspect

Cortinarius cinnabarinus (Ed. 1, misapplied)

Cortinarius hesleri fruits in large troops under deciduous trees during the summer in Kansas. Its entire fruiting body is rich red-orange, including the young gills, which eventually turn rusty brown. The cobweb-like cortina is barely visible on the overturned button in the photograph; this veil ruptures early in development, leaving little if any trace of itself on the stalk. Like all corts, it should not be eaten. In the first edition, this species was identified as *C. cinnabarinus*, a similar species that occurs in Europe.

Description: **Cap**: 3–6 cm broad, convex to flat with broad umbo, cinnabar-red, shiny, silky. **Gills**: cinnabar-red becoming rusty brown, attached. **Stalk**: 3–7 cm long, 0.3–1 cm thick, cinnabar-red, streaked; cortina cinnabar-red, soon disappearing. **Spore print**: rusty brown. **Spores**: 7–9 × 4.5–5.5 µm, elliptical, roughened. **Season**: summer. **Ecology**: mycorrhizal.

51. *Cortinarius hesleri*

52. *Cortinarius iodeoides*

52. *Cortinarius iodeoides* Poisonous

This beautiful, intensely violet little mushroom is often even more spectacular with pale teardrop-shaped splotches scattered across the cap. The top is usually sticky (viscid), especially in wet weather. The cap has a low central raised portion (umbo). The gills are violet, sometimes white, then rusty with mature spores. These rusty spores may be seen on the stalk in the picture, caught on the remains of the cortina. The young stalk is covered in a pale lavender slime that disappears, leaving the white stalk pictured here. The hidden part of the stalk is enlarged below, making a small club shape. The middle part of the stalk often curves. This specimen was found in southeast Kansas among oaks in the summer.

Description: **Cap**: 2–5 cm broad, convex with a low umbo, intense violet, sometimes spotted with pale teardrop-shaped splotches. **Gills**: violet to white, later rusty. **Stalk**: 1.5–2.8 cm long, 0.25–0.5 cm thick, covered in pale violet slime when young, white in age, often curved and enlarging toward the base; cortina violet, slimy. **Spore print**: rusty brown. **Spores**: 7–8 × 4–5 μm, elliptical, slightly roughened. **Season**: summer. **Ecology**: mycorrhizal.

53. *Cortinarius distans*

Edibility suspect

Cortinarius distans fruits gregariously under hardwoods in Kansas from late spring through early fall. Its most distinctive feature—widely spaced gills—is well illustrated in the photograph. In addition, note the broad central knob (umbo) and the cinnamon-brown cap that is hygrophanous and fades to tan with moisture loss. This often shows up as darker rings around the cap. These specimens were among several hundred that fruited on a hillside in September. Though all stages were collected, only pea-sized buttons showed an intact cobweb-like cortina.

Description: **Cap**: 3–10 cm broad, bell-shaped to convex with broad umbo, cinnamon-brown fading to tan, finely scaly; margin often splitting. **Gills**: tan becoming dark cinnamon-brown, widely spaced, attached. **Stalk**: 4–8 cm long, 0.5–1 cm thick, colored as cap, cylindrical to club-shaped; cortina white, leaving whitish zone. **Spore print**: rusty brown. **Spores**: 7–9 × 5–6 µm, elliptical, warty. **Season**: spring–fall. **Ecology**: mycorrhizal.

53. *Cortinarius distans*

54. *Cortinarius atkinsonianus*

Edibility suspect

This cort of many colors begins with an olive-shaded yellow cap that becomes tan to reddish tan. In wet weather especially, the surface of the cap can be sticky (viscid); evidence for this as pictured is the adhering leaf. The flesh, when cut or exposed, becomes a deep purple-violet that fades. The specimen shows this faded aspect. The photo was not taken in the field, as it should have been, and as often happens, the specimen did not react by showing the intense purple color, as it did when freshly picked. Some of the purple tones can be seen in the nick in the cap on right side of the picture. The gills are purple, becoming rusty with spores. The purple stalk is thick, ending with a marginate bulb (with a small ledge above the bulb, which is obscured by the cortina in the photo). Below the bulb, sometimes into the soil, the stalk tapers. The cortina is greenish yellow, although this color is hard to see in the picture. This species is found singly or in groups under oak in late summer and into the fall.

Description: **Cap**: 6–9 cm broad, convex, then opening, yellow, with olive tones at first and then tan to reddish tan, in wet weather somewhat slimy, flesh becoming intense purple when exposed, then fading. **Gills**: purple becoming rusty. **Stalk**: 6–8 cm tall, 1.2–2 cm thick, purple, with a marginate bulb that then tapers; cortina greenish yellow. **Spore print**: rusty. **Spores**: 13–15 × 7–8.5 µm, rounded, pointed at one end, roughened. **Season**: summer–fall. **Ecology**: mycorrhizal.

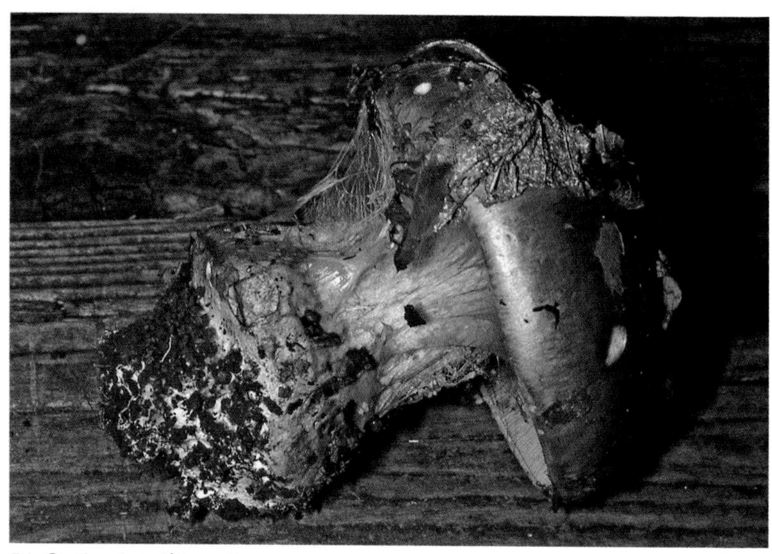

54. *Cortinarius atkinsonianus*

55. *Crepidotus crocophyllus*

55. *Crepidotus crocophyllus* — Edibility suspect

This flabby, shelving genus fruits in the summer and is sometimes mistaken for the edible oyster mushroom (*Pleurotus ostreatus* [no. 38]), but *Crepidotus* species are much smaller and have brown rather than white spores. *Crepidotus crocophyllus* is uncommon and differs from the common *C. mollis* in having yellow to orange rather than whitish gills when immature. (In both species, the gills become brown with mature spores.) The cap is pale with some rusty-brown fibers. *Crepidotus* was formerly included in the family Inocybaceae. However, unlike other members of that family, species of *Crepidotus* have little to no stalk and grow in shelving clusters on dead wood. They are now included in their own family.

Description: **Cap**: 1–5 cm broad, shell-shaped, usually grouped, flabby, white with some small rusty-brown fibers. **Gills**: yellow to orange becoming brown. **Stalk**: absent or tiny. **Spore print**: brown to yellowish brown. **Spores**: 7–11 × 4.5–7 µm, elliptical, smooth. **Season**: summer–fall. **Ecology**: saprotrophic.

56. *Pseudosperma rimosum* — Poisonous

Syn. = *Inocybe fastigiata*

This fiber head is very typical of the family Inocybaceae in Kansas, with its small size, fibrous cuticle (cap surface) that often splits, a central knob (umbo) on the cap, and dull brown spores. Like most fiber heads, *P. rimosum* is mycorrhizal and poisonous and has a strong odor. Other members of the family may smell of green corn, cedarwood, or even sweet peas; *P. rimosum* has a strong spermatic smell. *Pseudosperma rimosum* probably belongs to a group of similar species, differing slightly in size of fruiting body and spores. The stalk in this species is an even, pale column. In the picture, the cap edge of the largest is split through the flesh, as sometimes happens in the genus. I have seen *P. rimosum* as far west as Hays, in Ellis County, growing in a wooded waterway at a rest area.

The family Inocybaceae was once treated as constituting a single genus, *Inocybe*. Evidence from recent genetic data, however, indicate that the family might be split into seven genera. Around thirty different species of Inocybaceae have been found in Kansas, including representatives of three genera; probably just as many species have not been identified. Many of them resemble *P. rimosum*; but others range in appearance from the tiny, silky white *Inocybe geophylla*, which sometimes looks like a multitude of stars on the forest floor, to the much larger, wine-staining *Inosperma adaequatum*.

Description: **Cap**: 3–6 cm broad, yellow tan to ocher, bell-shaped, then flattened, with a distinct umbo and a fibrous, splitting cuticle. **Gills**: off white, then dull pale brown. **Stalk**: 4.5–8 cm tall, 0.7 cm thick. **Spore print**: dull brown. **Spores**: 8–10 × 5–7 μm smooth, bean-shaped. **Season**: summer–fall. **Ecology**: mycorrhizal.

56. *Pseudosperma rimosum*

Families Hymenogastraceae, Psathyrellaceae, and Strophariaceae

These families all have brown spores, many dark brown, and almost all have attached gills. All the species treated here are considered saprotrophic, growing on wood, other dead plant matter, or soil. The Strophariaceae are generally more robust and durable. Members of the genera *Agrocybe* and *Pholiota* of the family Strophariaceae and *Galerina marginata*, the single representative of the Hymenogastraceae, all have medium-brown spores, while species of *Stropharia* have dark, smoky-colored spores. Species of Psathyrellaceae are more fragile, usually smaller, and have very dark spores, with rare exceptions. Based on new DNA work, almost all species formerly included in the genus *Coprinus* of the obsoloete family Coprinaceae have been transferred to the Psathyrellaceae (with the prominent exception of *Coprinus comatus* [no. 70], which can be found in this book in the family Agaricaceae). These "inky caps" grow on dead wood, often in clusters, and dissolve into an inky mass. This "ink" was sometimes used as ink in the Middle Ages. Although *Panaeolina foenisecii* is included with Strophariaceae, its placement in the fungal kingdom is currently uncertain; it has been assigned to several different families in the past.

Key to species

1a) Gills (and sometimes entire cap) dissolving into inky substance (deliquescing); spore print black — go to **2**

1b) Gills not deliquescing; spore print various shades of brown to purplish brown — go to **6**

2a) Growing in clusters (caespitose) on wood (sometimes buried), stumps, and rotting logs — go to **3**

2b) Growing singly or in loose groups in wood, compost, or rarely indoors — go to **5**

3a) Caps tan to light reddish brown, striate, when young with particles that glisten in the sun — *Coprinellus micaceus* (no. 67)

3b) Caps gray to gray-brown, smooth with scaly patches or longitudinal wrinkles but not striate, without glistening particles — go to **4**

4a) Caps gray to grayish brown, with longitudinal wrinkles, often finely scaly at top — *Coprinopsis atramentaria* (no. 66)

4b) Caps pale grayish brown, without wrinkles, broadly covered with brown scaly patches *Coprinopsis variegata* (no. 65)

5a) Fruiting bodies arising from a fuzzy orange mycelial mat; cap rusty tan, scaly (without hairs) *Coprinellus radians* (no. 68)

5b) Fruiting bodies not arising from a mycelial mat; cap gray to grayish brown, with white hairs when young *Coprinopsis lagopus* (no. 69)

6a) Caps slimy or sticky (viscid) when moist and usually scaly go to **7**

6b) Caps not slimy or viscid, smooth, furrowed, or hairy, but not scaly go to **10**

7a) Growing in clusters (caespitose); caps 1.5–6 inches broad go to **8**

7b) Growing singly or in loose groups; caps 0.5–2 inches broad go to **9**

8a) Caps orange, with large patches of reddish-orange scales *Pholiota aurivella* (no. 60)

8b) Caps tan, with pale cottony patches on the cap when young *Pholiota populnea* (see no. 60)

9a) Caps brown to yellowish brown, without scales, ringed with darker bands when moist (hygrophanous) *Galerina marginata* (no. 58)

9b) Caps variably colored red, orange, yellow, purple, or green, with pale scales, not hygrophanous *Pholiota polychroa* (no. 61)

10a) Cap rusty brown, covered with flattened hairs *Lacrymaria lacrymabunda* (no. 64)

10b) Cap variably colored but smooth or furrowed (not hairy) go to **11**

11a) Growing near wood, on wood chips, or in woody debris go to **12**

11b) Growing in grass or on manure go to **13**

12a) Cap tan, sometimes cracked in dry weather; stalk to 0.75 inches thick *Agrocybe praecox* (no. 59)

12b) Cap tan, fragile with shallow grooves; stalk to 0.25 inches thick *Psathyrella candolleana* (no. 63)

13a) Growing on manure; cap yellow fading to near white at maturity; stalk to 4.5 inches long *Protostropharia semiglobata* (see no. 57)

13b) Growing in grass; cap white, yellowish brown, or dark brown go to **14**

14a) Cap dark brown, often with darker hygrophanous rings; ring (annulus) absent *Panaeolina foenisecii* (no. 62)

14b) Cap white or yellowish brown, not hygrophanous; annulus present (though fragile and usually striate) go to **15**

15a) Cap white; stalk to 3 inches long *Stropharia melanosperma* (no. 57)

15b) Cap yellowish brown fading to cream; stalk to 1.5 inches long *Psilocybe coronilla* (see no. 57)

57. *Stropharia melanosperma* Edible with caution

Stropharia melanosperma fruits in lawns, pastures, and prairies during the summer in Kansas. The photograph shows its important features: a smooth white cap, a long stalk, and attached gills that change from white to gray to the purplish black of the mature specimens illustrated. In addition, note the delicate ring that is easily lost during development; not shown are the prominent striations on its upper surface. It is fortunate that *S. melanosperma* is edible since it has undoubtedly been mistaken for the widely collected meadow mushroom *Agaricus campestris* (no. 71), which in contrast has a short stalk and free gills that change from pink to chocolate-brown. Even more easily confused with the meadow mushroom is the poisonous *Psilocybe coronilla* (syn. = *Stropharia coronilla*). Its gills are similar in color to those of *S. melanosperma*,

57. *Stropharia melanosperma*

and it also has a striate ring, but *P. coronilla* has a yellowish-brown cap, fading to cream, and a short stalk (2–4 cm long). Meadow mushroom hunters should be sure to check gill color and attachment! *Protostropharia semiglobata* (syn. = *Stropharia semiglobata*) grows on dung and has a hemispheric yellow cap that fades to near white, supported by a tall, slender stalk (3–12 cm long); its ring is easily lost. *Protostropharia semiglobata* is probably not edible.

Description: **Cap**: 3–6 cm broad, convex to flat, white, smooth; margin often with torn partial veil remnants. **Gills**: white becoming gray, then purple-black, attached. **Stalk**: 3–8 cm long, 4–8 mm thick, white; annulus fragile, striate on upper surface. **Spore print**: dark purplish brown. **Spores**: 10–13 × 6.5–8 μm, elliptical, smooth, with apical germ pore. **Season**: summer. **Ecology**: saprotrophic.

58. *Galerina marginata*

Deadly poisonous

Syn. = *Galerina autumnalis* (Ed. 1)
Deadly galerina

The deadly galerina, *Galerina marginata*, contains amatoxins, which makes it one of the few truly dangerous mushrooms in Kansas. It fruits in clusters or singly on decaying logs during cool weather—that is, in spring, fall, and occasionally winter. This mushroom has a brown to yellow-brown cap that fades with moisture loss (hygrophanous), sometimes making concentric zones of light and dark. The gills are brownish and give a rusty-brown spore print. A well-defined membranous ring is evident on the young specimens in the photograph but often disappears with age. In more mature fruiting bodies, the caps are flatter and the gills and stalks are browner. *Galerina marginata* resembles countless other LBMs and is one of the reasons why LBMs should not be

58. *Galerina marginata*

eaten. Edible mushrooms fruiting on wood that might also be confused with the deadly galerina include the honey mushroom (*Armillaria mellea* group [no. 24]) and the velvet foot (*Flammulina velutipes* [no. 26]), both of which have pale gills and a white spore print.

Description: **Cap**: 2.5–6 cm broad, convex becoming flat, brown to yellowish brown, hygrophanous, smooth, viscid when moist; margin striate when moist. **Gills**: pale brown becoming rusty brown, attached. **Stalk**: 2–7 cm long, 3–8 mm thick, pale brown or darker, streaked, hollow; annulus white, membranous, hairy, often disappearing. **Spore print**: rusty brown. **Spores**: 8–11 × 5–6.5 µm, elliptical, minutely roughened. **Season**: spring, fall, occasionally winter. **Ecology**: saprotrophic.

59. *Agrocybe praecox* — Edible with caution

Spring agrocybe

Often found in the spring, this medium-sized mushroom has a broadly convex, creamy to tan cap that sometimes cracks, as illustrated. The pale gills may be slightly attached at first. At maturity they become dark brown, though those pictured are slightly darker than usual, perhaps shadowed. The edges of the cap here are hung with partial veil remnants. Sometimes the veil clings to

59. *Agrocybe praecox*

the stalk, becoming a ring (annulus). The stalk is fairly even in width along its length and pale, though with age it becomes discolored-brown, as shown. *Agrocybe praecox* grows in and out of town, preferring disturbed areas, including wood chips and gardens. By reports, none of this group is very tasty, but worse, they could be confused with poisonous members of the genus *Hebeloma*, including *H. crustuliniforme* (poison pie), which also produces a brown spore print. Hebelomas are notoriously difficult to identify, differing from *Agrocybe* by such characteristics as the absence of a cellular cap cuticle. However, because hebelomas are mostly mycorrhizal, they typically grow in different habitats.

Description: **Cap**: 5–10 cm broad, rounded, flattening somewhat in age, cream-colored to tan, smooth, sometimes cracked. **Gills**: pale at first, then dark brown, attached in some fashion. **Stalk**: 5–10 cm long, 1.5 cm thick, of the same color as the cap, columnar. **Spore print**: brown. **Spores**: 8–11 × 5–7 μm elliptical, smooth. **Season**: spring. **Ecology**: saprotrophic.

60. *Pholiota aurivella* — Edible with caution

Pholiota aurivella appears infrequently on hardwood trunks and logs during the fall in Kansas. It fruits in clusters (caespitose) and has sticky (viscid) to slimy (when moist) orange caps that are spotted with large reddish-orange

60. *Pholiota aurivella*

scales. The caps illustrated here are beginning to dry out and crack. The scales that are normally present on the lower stalk are not readily apparent on the overturned specimen; note the torn partial veil that leaves little trace of a ring. Mushroom books often list *P. aurivella* as edible, but gastrointestinal poisonings have been reported for the species. *Pholiota polychroa* (no. 61) has a smaller cap that is exceedingly variable in color: olive, green, or purple when young and orange to yellow at maturity. Its slimy cap is covered with small superficial scales that wash off easily. Large fruitings of *P. populnea* (syn. = *P. destruens*) can be found in the fall, mostly on cottonwoods in the lowlands around rivers. When young, it has cottony spots on the cap and a ring that later disappears, leaving large tan-capped clusters.

Description: **Cap**: 4–16 cm broad, bell-shaped to flat, orange fading to yellow or brownish yellow, viscid to slimy when moist, covered with large patches of flat, reddish-orange scales, caespitose. **Gills**: pale yellow becoming rusty brown, attached. **Stalk**: 5–8 cm long, 0.5–1.5 cm thick, colored as cap, hairy at apex, scaly toward base, central or off center; annulus absent or consisting of faint hairy zone. **Spore print**: brown. **Spores**: 7–9.5 × 4.5–6 μm, elliptical, smooth, with apical germ pore. **Season**: fall. **Ecology**: saprotrophic.

61. *Pholiota polychroa* — Edibility unknown

This lovely little mushroom can display most of the colors of the rainbow. At the other end of this log, but out of the photo, were red, yellow, orange, and green specimens, all identical in stature and features. Like many fungi in Kansas, these tend to be smaller than those found in other parts of the country, probably because of the harsh climate. The cap is convex and decorated with white bits of veil, more prevalent toward the edge, which can be washed off. The partial veil (as shown on the central specimen, covering the gills), is textured with soft bumps. The gills (not visible in the image) are attached, sometimes only slightly. They are initially pale but darken with spore maturity. The pale stalk is a column of even width along its length and rough with the pale veil remnants. *Pholiota polychroa* occurs on dead wood mostly in the summer. These specimens were found at Hillsdale Lake in Miami County.

Description: **Cap**: 2–5 cm, convex, variably colored with different pigments, including red, orange, yellow, purple, and green, viscid when moist, sparsely covered with white flakes of veil, more densely toward the margin; veil clinging to the margin and hanging down, fragmenting along the stalk, or becoming

61. *Pholiota polychroa*

an annulus. **Gills**: pale at first, maturing dark brown, attached, notched. **Stalk**: 2–3 cm long, 1 cm thick, pale, rough with pale veil remnants or with an annulus. **Spore print**: brown to dark brown. **Spores**: 5.5–7.5 × 3.5–4.5 µm smooth, elliptical. **Season**: summer. **Ecology**: saprotrophic.

62. *Panaeolina foenisecii* — Poisonous

Syn. = *Panaeolus foenisecii* (Ed. 1)
Syn. = *Psathyrella foenisecii*
Haymaker's mushroom

The haymaker's mushroom, *Panaeolina foenisecii*, is an LBM that frequents Kansas lawns during late spring and early summer. This mushroom has a brown, bell-shaped cap and dark purple-brown gills. An important feature of the cap is the way concentric zones are formed as it fades from moisture loss (hygrophanous). The upright cap in the photograph has dried over most of its surface except near the margin, where there is a darker zone. In contrast, the small cap at its base has dried very little and shows only a faint light zone around its center. The haymaker's mushroom is potentially dangerous to young children, since it may contain low levels of the hallucinogens psilocybin and psilocin and possibly other toxins.

Description: **Cap**: 1–3 cm broad, conical, dark brown, hygrophanous, fading in concentric zones with moisture loss, smooth. **Gills**: dark purple-brown, paler at edges, attached. **Stalk**: 4–8 cm long, 1–3 mm thick, brown, smooth; annulus absent. **Spore print**: purple-brown. **Spores**: 12–15 × 6.5–9 μm, elliptical, minutely roughened, with apical germ pore. **Season**: late spring–early summer. **Ecology**: saprotrophic.

62. *Panaeolina foenisecii*

63. *Psathyrella candolleana* — Edible

Psathyrella candolleana is common and usually abundant where encountered, though not necessarily clustered. When young, the cap is honey-tan, but the color soon fades to almost white with a tan center. The surface can be shallowly grooved (sulcate). At maturity the cap edges are wavy and often have partial veil fragments hanging in small white patches, as seen in the farthest-left cap. The gills are pale at first, then dark with spores; they are attached initially and then recede from an even, smooth, and fragile stalk. Sometimes the veil remains attached to the stalk in a ring. There are many *Psathyrella* that look rather similar; almost all are very fragile and thin-fleshed. This particular species is said to be edible but has so little substance and is so friable that it offers little for the table. Remember that its spores are very dark; the pictured gill section is only beginning to mature. Small, pale mushrooms with fragile veils might be small *Leucoagaricus*, *Lepiota*, or *Leucocoprinus* of the family Agaricaceae, many of which are deadly; these undesirables have white spore prints. *Psathyrella candolleana* grows in Kansas in open woods on woody debris in late spring through early fall.

Description: **Cap**: 3–10 cm broad, conical when young, then expanding, smooth but sulcate, with an uneven surface and margins, sometimes hung

63. *Psathyrella candolleana*

with remnants of a partial veil, initially tan, turning whitish with a tan center at maturity. **Gills**: attached, then receding from stalk; pale at first, then dark. **Stalk**: 4–10 cm long, 5–7 mm thick; annulus sometimes present. **Spore print**: purple-brown. **Spores**: 7–10 × 4–5 µm, elliptical, smooth. **Season**: late spring–early fall. **Ecology**: saprotrophic.

64. *Lacrymaria lacrymabunda* Edible

Syn. = *Psathyrella velutina* (Ed. 1)

Lacrymaria lacrymabunda fruits singly or clustered in lawns, along paths and roads, and near compost heaps from late spring through early fall in Kansas. Its rusty-brown cap is densely covered with flattened hairs, which are not readily apparent in the photograph, though at first glance they often are not clearly seen. The group pictured here is typical of the species in Kansas. The hairy zone on the stalks of the overturned specimens amounts to a ring; the stalk is distinctly white above this zone. Although most authorities list this mushroom as edible, no one rates it better than mediocre. *Psathyrella candolleana* (no. 63), which is also edible, fruits from buried wood, particularly in grassy areas around stumps. It has a smooth light-brown cap that may fade to white; remnants of the torn partial veil often line the margin of young caps.

64. *Lacrymaria lacrymabunda*

Description: **Cap**: 3–12 cm broad, convex becoming flat, rusty brown, densely covered with flattened hairs or scales, margin often with shaggy partial veil remnants. **Gills**: yellow-brown turning dark rusty brown, mottled, with drops of moisture on edges when young, attached. **Stalk**: 5–15 cm long, 0.4–1.2 cm thick, reddish brown, hairy, white and smooth on upper portion, hollow; annulus consisting of hairy zone or ring. **Spore print**: blackish brown. **Spores**: 9–12 × 6–7 µm, elliptical, warty, with apical germ pore on projecting snout. **Season**: spring–early fall. **Ecology**: saprotrophic.

65. *Coprinopsis variegata* — Edible with caution

Syn. = *Coprinus variegatus* (Ed. 1)

Coprinopsis variegata commonly fruits in massive clusters near buried stumps in cities and is probably noticed by more Kansans than any other mushroom. It also occurs on rotting logs in hardwood forests. The fruiting bodies predictably appear following rains from late spring through early fall. This mushroom is identified by its medium-sized cap that is covered with prominent scaly brown patches. The cap deliquesces (turns to "ink") on maturity, as is shown by the blackened fruiting body in the photograph. Although *C. variegata* is widely eaten, it may contain coprine, and poisoning may occur if alcohol is consumed within several days following a meal. Bruce Horn experienced coprine-like symptoms (flushing, rapid heartbeat, nausea)

65. *Coprinopsis variegata*

while drinking a margarita twenty-four hours after a fine feast of *C. variegata* on toast. His dining partner (Richard Kay) also indulged in the meal but did not drink alcohol and suffered no such symptoms. Bitter fruiting bodies occasionally arise from the same stump that produced a savory crop the week before. The species is commonly confused with *Coprinus comatus* (no. 70), the shaggy mane, which is much larger, and with *Coprinopsis atramentaria* (no. 66), which has a smooth to finely scaly gray cap.

Description: **Cap**: 1–3 cm broad and 2–4 cm tall unexpanded, oval becoming bell-shaped, then flat, with margin deliquescing, gray-brown with white to light brown patches, caespitose. **Gills**: white becoming purple, then black, deliquescing, crowded, free. **Stalk**: 4–12 cm long, 0.5–1 cm thick, white, with scaly rings on lower portion, hollow; base with rootlike cords. **Spore print**: black. **Spores**: 7.5–10 × 4–5 μm, elliptical, smooth, with apical germ pore. **Season**: late spring–early fall. **Ecology**: saprotrophic.

66. *Coprinopsis atramentaria*

Edible with caution

Syn. = *Coprinus atramentarius* (Ed. 1)
Inky cap

Coprinopsis atramentaria is a common urban mushroom throughout Kansas. Clusters of fruiting bodies arise from buried wood, often in lawns, next to stumps, or (as shown in the photograph) beside old buildings. It is also found in lowland forests. The fruiting bodies appear primarily during the spring and fall. The gray caps with longitudinal wrinkles and few scales help distinguish this *Coprinopsis* from other species. When mature, the cap and gills deliquesce into a black fluid from the margin inward—hence the common name inky cap. The fruiting bodies in the photograph have not yet begun to deliquesce, and it is at this stage that they are edible. Like *Coprinopsis variegata* (no. 65), *C. atramentaria* contains coprine. The smaller *Coprinellus micaceus* (no. 67), the mica cap, has a tan cap with shiny, minute granules.

Description: **Cap**: 2–6 cm broad and tall unexpanded, bell-shaped, then flat with deliquescing margin, gray to gray-brown, longitudinally wrinkled, often finely scaly at apex, caespitose. **Gills**: white turning gray, then black, deliquescing, crowded, free. **Stalk**: 3–15 cm long, 0.5–1.2 cm thick, white, hollow, with ring at base. **Spore print**: black. **Spores**: 7–9 × 5–6 μm, elliptical, smooth, with apical germ pore. **Season**: spring and fall. **Ecology**: saprotrophic.

66. *Coprinopsis atramentaria*

67. *Coprinellus micaceus* Edible

Syn. = *Coprinus micaceus* (Ed. 1)

Mica cap

The mica cap is a familiar sight in Kansas, where large clusters fruit next to trees and stumps during the spring and fall. It is frequently found while hunting morels. The common name refers to the small, glistening, micalike particles on the cap. These particles are difficult to see unless the sunlight catches them at the proper angle, and they are often washed off by rain early in development. The caps in the photograph do not display any such particles. The mica cap can be otherwise identified by its tan striate cap that deliquesces on maturity. It is a good edible, particularly when fried in butter and served on toast. In fact, the fruiting bodies illustrated were harvested by a marauding mushroomer shortly after the photograph was taken. The orange mat inky, *Coprinellus radians* (no. 68), closely resembles the mica cap but has a woolly mat of orange mycelium at its base; it fruits singly, sometimes in wet basements. The inky cap, *Coprinopsis atramentaria* (no. 66), is larger and grayer and lacks glistening particles on its cap.

67. *Coprinellus micaceus*

Description: **Cap**: 1.5–5 cm broad and 2–4 cm tall unexpanded, cone-shaped, then flat with deliquescing margin, tan to light reddish brown, striate, covered with glistening particles when young, caespitose. **Gills**: white turning gray, then black, deliquescing, crowded, variably attached. **Stalk**: 4–8 cm long, 3–5 mm thick, white, slightly roughened, hollow. **Spore print**: black. **Spores**: 7–12 × 4–5 µm, elliptical, smooth, with apical germ pore. **Season**: spring and fall. **Ecology**: saprotrophic.

68. *Coprinellus radians*

Edibility unknown

Orange mat inky

The most distinguishing characteristic of this species is the fuzzy orange mat from which it grows, illustrated in the left part of the picture. Usually this mat (ozonium) is seen without the scaly, rusty-tan fruiting bodies. This inky's elongated oval and striate cap edge (little close furrows usually following the gills, not necessarily all the way to the stalk, and not clearly illustrated here) are typical of many inkys. *Coprinellus radians* usually grows on dead wood outdoors but is occasionally discovered indoors, extending its summer season in damp, heated structures.

68. *Coprinellus radians*

Description: **Cap**: 5–7 cm broad, oval, rusty tan with small pale scales, striate. **Gills**: white turning gray, then black, deliquescing, crowded, variably attached. **Stalk**: 4–10 cm long, 2–3 mm thick, pale, smooth, even, arising from a prominent orange ozonium. **Spore print**: messy black. **Spores**: 8–10.5 × 4–6 µm, elliptical. **Season**: summer. **Ecology**: saprotrophic.

69. *Coprinopsis lagopus*

Edibility unknown

Syn. = *Coprinus lagopus* (Ed. 1)

Several delicate small to medium-sized species of inky occur in Kansas during late spring and summer. One of these, *Coprinopsis lagopus*, often appears overnight on compost, woody debris, and rich humus, only to deliquesce (dissolve into ink) and collapse several hours later. The young caps are covered with loose white hairs that later disappear. The photograph shows mature specimens with their long stalks and gray striate caps. During dry weather, the margin of the cap curls and splits in the manner illustrated instead of deliquescing.

Description: **Cap**: 1–3 cm broad and 1.5–5 cm tall unexpanded, oval becoming conical, then flat, with margin deliquescing or curling, gray to gray-brown, striate, covered with loose white hairs when young. **Gills**: gray, then black, often deliquescing, crowded, free. **Stalk**: 6–10 cm tall, 2–4 mm thick, white, hairy when young, hollow. **Spore print**: black. **Spores**: 10–12 × 6–7 μm, elliptical, smooth, with apical germ pore. **Season**: late spring–summer. **Ecology**: saprotrophic.

69. *Coprinopsis lagopus*

Family Agaricaceae

The Agaricaceae is a distinctive family of mushrooms made famous by the popularity of the cultivated grocery-store mushroom *Agaricus bisporus*. Once encompassing all gilled mushrooms, the family has most often been represented by the genus *Agaricus*, though several other genera have now been added. These mushrooms are characterized by the presence of a partial veil that manifests as an annulus (a ring around the stalk, the remnants of the veil) and sometimes is fragile or might be present instead as pieces hanging from the edge of the cap, by free gills, and by a chocolate-brown or pale spore print. In the genus *Agaricus*, the gills change from pink (occasionally white) to the chocolate-brown of mature spores. Depending upon the species, the cap may be smooth and white or covered with colored or pale scales. Other useful characteristics in *Agaricus* include the staining reaction of the fruiting body when injured (often bruising yellow or red) as well as the odor of the crushed flesh (smelling of fruit, anise, almonds, or creosote). Staining or bruising does not always occur in all parts of some specimens; the places most likely to stain are the edge (margin) of the cap—when rubbed—and the exterior or interior of the base of the stalk, elicited by breaking or rubbing.

DNA sequencing indicates that most or all of the species formerly included in the family Lepiotaceae now belong to the Agaricaceae, as does a single inky, *Coprinus comatus*, a delectable edible. Most of the former Lepiotaceae have white spores, and some of their new names begin with "leuco-," meaning white. Most of the larger, white-spored former lepiotas are now prefaced with "macro-"; an exception is *Chlorophyllum rachodes*. Seen commonly in lawns but also often in fields, *Chlorophyllum molybdites* is also now a member of the Agaricaceae and has dusty green spores. Species included here in the genera *Lepiota, Chlorophyllum*, *Echinoderma*, *Leucoagaricus*, *Leucocoprinus*, and *Macrolepiota* are often referred to as lepiotoid mushrooms. Collectively, they share a ring that is sometimes friable, free gills, pale spores, and a similar stature, as can be seen in the accompanying images. Some lepiotoid species are deadly, and it's best to avoid consuming any mushroom with this suite of characteristics.

Likewise, not all species of the genus *Agaricus* are safe to eat, so the person who indiscriminately collects the wild relative of the grocery-store mushroom may end up poisoned. The main offenders fruit under trees, but habitat is not always a safe guideline, especially in grassy areas with scattered trees. An *Agaricus* may be confused with some species of *Stropharia*, but the latter have attached gills that change from white to purple-black. Over two dozen species of *Agaricus* have been reported from Kansas; seven are described here. Twelve former Lepiotaceae are also presented, including three species of *Lepiota* as well as *Coprinus comatus*.

Key to species

1a) Spore print brown to black	go to **2**
1b) Spores print white or dull green	go to **9**
2a) Cap elongate or cylindrical, about 1 inch across, up to 6 inches tall; gills dissolving into an inky substance (deliquescing)	*Coprinus comatus* (no. 70)
2b) Cap round, not elongate; gills not deliquescing	go to **3**
3a) Growing in wooded areas; fruiting body bruising distinctly yellow or reddish	go to **4**
3b) Growing in open areas; fruiting body not bruising distinctly yellow or reddish (though bruising pale yellow in *Agaricus arvensis*)	go to **7**
4a) Cap smooth or with very few scales; fruiting body (at least edge of cap and the base of stalk) bruising yellow when rubbed	go to **5**
4b) Cap distinctly scaly; fruiting body bruising reddish, sometimes after bruising yellow	go to **6**
5a) Stalk abruptly expanded to bulbous base	*Agaricus abruptibulbus* (no. 73)
5b) Base of stalk at most only slightly bulbous	*Agaricus sylvicola* (no. 72)
6a) Cap with fine gray scales; fruiting body bruising yellow, then turning reddish	*Agaricus placomyces* (no. 74)
6b) Cap with brown scales; fruiting body immediately bruising reddish	*Agaricus sylvaticus* (see no. 74)
7a) Cap 3–8 inches broad; fruiting body bruising pale yellow	*Agaricus arvensis* (see no. 72)
7b) Cap 1–4 inches broad; fruiting body not bruising	go to **8**
8a) Ring (annulus) single edged; growing in grassy areas	*Agaricus campestris* (no. 71)
8b) Annulus double edged; growing in hard-packed soil	*Agaricus bitorquis* (see no. 71)

9a) Stalk with double-edged movable ring (annulus); stalk up to 12 inches long go to **10**

9b) Stalk without movable annulus; stalk up to 5 inches long go to **12**

10a) Cap white with brown or tan scales; spore print dull green *Chlorophyllum molybdites* (no. 79)

10b) Cap white to pale brown with reddish-brown scales; spore print white go to **11**

11a) Cap with central knob (umbo) and regular reddish-brown scales; fruiting body not bruising reddish (sometimes bruising brown on stalk) *Macrolepiota procera* (no. 78)

11b) Cap without umbo and with coarse, shaggy brown scales; fruiting body bruising reddish *Chlorophyllum rachodes* (see no. 78)

12a) Fruiting bodies clustered (caespitose) go to **13**

12b) Fruiting bodies not caespitose go to **15**

13a) Fruiting body bruising reddish; cap with reddish scales; stalk widest near the middle (spindle-shaped) *Leucoagaricus americanus* (see no. 78)

13b) Fruiting body not bruising; cap with pale or yellow scales; stalk widest at base go to **14**

14a) Cap white to tan, with pale scales; growing on compost *Leucocoprinus cepistipes* (see no. 77)

14b) Cap bright yellow, with yellow scales; growing in flower pots, greenhouses, and similar environments *Leucocoprinus birnbaumii* (no. 77)

15a) Cap a bright shade of pinkish red, radially streaked with fine scales *Leucoagaricus rubrotinctus* (no. 76)

15b) Cap another color, pale to tan, with fine to coarse scales go to **16**

16a) Cap with brown, pyramid-shaped scales; fragile, fibrous partial veil present *Echinoderma asperum* (see no. 78)

16b) Cap smooth, or if scales present, then not pyramidal; fibrous partial veil absent go to **17**

17a) Cap 2–3.5 inches broad, white, tan, or gray, with fine concolorous scales *Leucoagaricus leucothites* (see no. 79)

17b) Cap less than 2 inches broad, pale with contrasting brown scales go to **18**

18a) Stalk shaggy	*Lepiota clypeolaria* (see no. 76)
18b) Stalk not shaggy	go to **19**
19a) Stalk white	*Lepiota cristata* (no. 75)
19b) Stalk pinkish to lilac	*Lepiota lilacea* (see no. 75)

70. *Coprinus comatus* Edible

Shaggy mane

The shaggy mane is the largest inky in Kansas. It fruits singly or in large troops in lawns, pastures, prairies, roadsides, and occasionally woods from late spring through (especially) fall. This mushroom can be identified by its shaggy cylindrical cap and its movable but fragile ring (not visible in the photograph) that often slips to the base of the stalk. Note how the cap margin is initially pressed against the stalk. With maturity, the cap flattens, and its margin and gills deliquesce. This is well depicted by the center specimen, where spore-blackened droplets from the deliquescing cap are running down the adjacent fruiting body. The shaggy mane is praised for its edible qualities. A deliquescing fruiting body is too old for eating. However, if the lower margins are black but the specimen is firm, the mushroom is still good to eat. The younger stages are preferable. *Coprinopsis variegata*

70. *Coprinus comatus*

(no. 65) is often mistaken for the shaggy mane but is considerably smaller.

Description: **Cap**: 3–5 cm broad and 4–15 cm tall unexpanded, cylindrical, then flat with margin deliquescing, white with white to light brown scales, shaggy, often smooth at apex. **Gills**: white turning pink, then black, deliquescing, crowded, free. **Stalk**: 6–20 cm long, 1–2 cm thick, white, slightly hairy, hollow, with movable ring. **Spore print**: black. **Spores**: 11–15 × 6–8 μm, elliptical, smooth, with apical germ pore. **Season**: spring–fall. **Ecology**: saprotrophic.

71. *Agaricus campestris* — Edible

The meadow mushroom
Pink bottom
Champignon

The meadow mushroom, or champignon, is the wild equivalent of the cultivated species *Agaricus bisporus* (or *A. brunnescens* according to some mycologists). It fruits scattered or in fairy rings in lawns, golf courses, pastures, prairies, and sometimes cultivated fields from spring through fall in Kansas. Newly planted lawns are often sites of massive fruitings. The photograph illustrates the dramatic change of the immature pink gills to mature dark ones. The short stalk and fragile single-edged annulus resulting when the partial

71. *Agaricus campestris*

veil (shown in the lower left specimen) pulls away from the cap margin are also evident. The cap in the lower right is slightly scaly, but *A. campestris* often has a smooth cap. Recent reevaluations of this species indicate that it is not as widespread as formerly thought and that most specimens called *A. campestris* in North America actually belong to other species. However, something like the true *A. campestris* shows up in Colorado (Kerrigan 2016), so, pending careful study of specimens from Kansas, we choose to use this name. The wild meadow mushroom tastes the same as, if not better than, its domesticated relative. Collecting your own not only guarantees freshness but also enables you to secure older specimens with darkened gills, which are frowned upon in grocery stores but have a more robust flavor than the relatively flavorless buttons. Avoid specimens near busy streets since *A. campestris* (and other mushrooms) can accumulate toxic heavy metals. The similar but meatier *A. bitorquis* (syn. = *A. rodmanii* [Ed. 1]), with a sheathlike, double-edged annulus, is an equally good edible that fruits primarily during the spring on hard-packed soil near roads and sidewalks. It often remains partially buried, barely cracking the soil surface.

Description: **Cap**: 2.5–10 cm broad, convex becoming flat, white or light brown with age, smooth to slightly scaly; margin sometimes with partial veil remnants. **Gills**: bright pink becoming chocolate-brown, free. **Stalk**: 2–6 cm long, 0.5–2 cm thick, white, discoloring reddish brown, smooth or slightly hairy, tapering toward base; annulus white, delicate, single edged. **Spore print**: chocolate-brown. **Spores**: 6–7.5 × 4.5–5 µm, elliptical, smooth. **Season**: spring–fall. **Ecology**: saprotrophic.

72. *Agaricus sylvicola* — Edible with caution

Woodland agaric

The woodland agaric, *Agaricus sylvicola* (in some guides spelled *A. silvicola*), is perhaps the most common forest-dwelling *Agaricus* in Kansas. It fruits scattered or in partial fairy rings during summer and fall. This mushroom can be recognized by its smooth white cap, skirtlike ring, nonbulbous base, and yellow-staining reaction when bruised. It often smells of anise, particularly when young. Two of the overturned fruiting bodies in the photograph still have their partial veils intact. Once ruptured, the partial veil forms the prominent ring seen on the standing fruiting body. The gills of the other two specimens are beginning to change from pink to chocolate-brown. People eat the woodland agaric, but reports of gastrointestinal poisonings are too numerous to recommend it as an edible. *Agaricus abruptibulbus* (no. 73),

72. *Agaricus sylvicola*

as its name declares, has an abruptly bulbous base but is otherwise nearly identical to *A. sylvicola*. The horse mushroom, *A. arvensis*, also has a large white cap and bruises pale yellow. It is best distinguished from *A. sylvicola* by its preference for pastures and by its larger spores (7–9 × 5–6 μm). The horse mushroom is a fine edible but unfortunately is not common in Kansas.

Description: **Cap**: 4–15 cm broad, round becoming convex, then flat, white, occasionally pale yellow in center, smooth; often bruising yellow, with faint odor of anise. **Gills**: white turning pink, then chocolate-brown, free. **Stalk**: 8–15 cm long, 1–2.5 cm thick, white to pale yellow, smooth or slightly scaly, bruising yellow; base nonbulbous to slightly bulbous; annulus white, skirtlike, membranous, with cottony patches on undersurface. **Spore print**: chocolate-brown. **Spores**: 5–6.5 × 4–4.5 μm, elliptical, smooth. **Season**: summer–fall. **Ecology**: saprotrophic.

73. *Agaricus abruptibulbus* Edible with caution

Agaricus abruptibulbus, with its white cap, skirtlike ring, and yellow-staining reaction, closely resembles *A. sylvicola* (no. 72) and has sometimes been considered only a form of this species. Only careful digging up of the stalk will reveal its identity by the abruptly bulbous base (seen in the photograph). It fruits in the hardwood forests of Kansas during summer and fall. The pinkish-gray gills of the specimen illustrated are beginning to turn chocolate-brown. Though often listed as edible, *A. abruptibulbus* is easily confused with other, potentially poisonous forest-dwelling species of *Agaricus*. Still worse, the young fruiting bodies resemble deadly white amanitas such as *Amanita bisporigera* (no. 3). In addition to producing a bulb and white spores, rather than dark spores, *A. bisporigera* differs in having a sac-like volva. However, inexperienced mushroomers should probably avoid consuming *A. abruptibulbus*, just to be on the safe side.

73. *Agaricus abruptibulbus*

Description: **Cap**: 7–15 cm broad, round becoming convex, then flat, white, smooth, bruising yellow, with odor of anise. **Gills**: white changing to pink, then chocolate-brown, free. **Stalk**: 7–15 cm long, 1–1.5 cm thick, white, smooth, bruising yellow; base abruptly bulbous; annulus white, skirt-like, membranous, with cottony patches on undersurface. **Spore print**: chocolate-brown. **Spores**: 6–8 × 4–5 μm, elliptical, smooth. **Season**: summer–fall. **Ecology**: saprotrophic.

74. *Agaricus placomyces* Poisonous

Agaricus placomyces fruits in the hardwood forests of Kansas during spring and early summer. It can be distinguished from other forest-inhabiting species of *Agaricus* by the fine gray scales on its cap. In addition, the fruiting bodies first bruise yellow and then reddish brown, and the small bulb at the base of the stalk immediately stains yellow when sliced in half. The photograph shows the partial veil still covering the gills on one of the overturned specimens. The pink gills on the other specimen will eventually turn chocolate-brown. *Agaricus placomyces*, like other forest-dwelling species of

74. *Agaricus placomyces*

Agaricus, has caused gastrointestinal upsets. A similar species, *A. sylvaticus*, has brown scales and bruises reddish brown.

Description: **Cap**: 4–10 cm broad, round becoming convex, then flat, covered with radially arranged gray to grayish-brown scales, bruising yellow, then reddish brown, smelling faintly of creosote. **Gills**: pink becoming chocolate-brown, free. **Stalk**: 7–15 cm long, 1–1.5 cm thick, white to pale brown, bruising as cap; base slightly bulbous, staining yellow when sliced; annulus white to pinkish gray, skirtlike, membranous, with cottony patches and yellow droplets on undersurface. **Spore print**: chocolate-brown. **Spores**: 5–6 × 3.5–5 µm, elliptical, smooth. **Season**: spring–early summer. **Ecology**: saprotrophic.

75. *Lepiota cristata* — Edibility suspect

Lepiota cristata is the first of several lepiotoid mushrooms included here. Its cap is convex at first but soon flattens and often bears a very low raised central portion (an umbo). The umbo is colored a warm brown, and around it are paler but similarly colored flat scales that continue to the cap's edge. The gills are not attached to the stalk (free). The stalk is an even width from top to bottom and mostly whitish. A fragile ring, remains of the partial veil, circles the stalk, though sometimes this material sticks to the edge of the cap instead (as seen in one of the specimens). Sometimes there is a small mass of mycelial fuzz at the base. Some people report a strong smell from this species. It is particularly dangerous because it is usually found in the summer in disturbed urban settings around shrubs and in lawns and may be tempting to children. A relative, *L. lilacea*, with a pinkish to pale lavender stalk, is certainly deadly.

75. *Lepiota cristata*

Description: **Cap**: 1–5 cm rounded, soon flattened, whitish with a warm brown umbo, with flat reddish-brown scales up to the edge, which is sometimes decorated with fragments of the partial veil. **Gills**: white, free. **Stalk**: 6 cm long, 2 mm thick, forming an even column, whitish, sometimes with a brownish lower portion and a fuzz of mycelium at the base; annulus white, fragile. **Spore print**: white. **Spores**: 5.5–8 × 4–4.5, narrow, rounded, triangular, dextrinoid. **Season**: summer. **Ecology**: saprotrophic.

76. *Leucoagaricus rubrotinctus* — Edibility unknown

Syn. = *Lepiota rubrotincta* (Ed. 1)

Leucoagaricus rubrotinctus is an infrequent inhabitant of Kansas forests during the summer. Its brilliant pinkish-red cap is unmistakable. As the cap expands, the margin becomes radially streaked with fine scales. The partial veil has barely ruptured on the overturned young specimen in the photograph; it will later form the ring seen on the other fruiting bodies. In addition, note the free white gills on the specimen with the cut-off stalk. None of the small to medium-sized species of *Leucoagaricus*, *Leucocoprinus*, and *Lepiota*, including *L. rubrotinctus*, can be recommended for eating because some species contain deadly amatoxins. Two reportedly poisonous lepiotas frequently found in Kansas forests are *Lepiota cristata* (no. 75), with reddish-brown scales that are arranged concentrically, and *Lepiota clypeolaria*, with

76. *Leucoagaricus rubrotinctus*

yellowish-brown to orangish-brown scales, a shaggy stalk, and an indistinct ring.

Description: **Cap**: 2–8 cm broad, oval becoming flat with broad umbo, pinkish red to dark red, paler toward margin, radially streaked with fine scales. **Gills**: white, free. **Stalk**: 5–10 cm long, 0.3–1 cm thick, white, smooth, slightly club-shaped; annulus white, membranous. **Spore print**: white. **Spores**: 7–10 × 4.5–5 µm, elliptical, smooth, dextrinoid. **Season**: summer. **Ecology**: saprotrophic.

77. *Leucocoprinus birnbaumii* Poisonous

Syn. = *Lepiota lutea* (Ed. 1)

This delicate yellow mushroom often intrigues people because of its unexpected appearance in flowerpots and greenhouses. The fruiting bodies illustrated here were growing under a houseplant, much to the delight of its owner. The powdery yellow cap with prominent striations and the yellow stalk are the distinguishing features. A ring is also visible on the large specimen, but it is rather ephemeral and easily missed. *Leucocoprinus birnbaumii* has caused gastrointestinal poisonings. The related larger *Leucocoprinus cepistipes* has a

77. *Leucocoprinus birnbaumii*

powdery-white to tan cap, often has a green-onion-shaped stalk, and grows in clusters; it prefers compost and is of questionable edibility.

Description: **Cap**: 3–6 cm broad, oval becoming bell-shaped to flat with umbo, yellow, powdery to minutely scaly, deeply striate. **Gills**: pale yellow, hairy at edges, free. **Stalk**: 2.5–8 cm long, 2–5 mm thick, yellow, powdery, enlarged at base; annulus yellow, soon disappearing. **Spore print**: white. **Spores**: 8–13 × 5.5–8 μm, elliptical, smooth, dextrinoid. **Season**: indoors (year-round). **Ecology**: saprotrophic.

78. *Macrolepiota procera* — Edible

Syn. = *Lepiota procera* (Ed. 1)
Parasol mushroom

The stately parasol mushroom fruits in open woodlands during summer and fall. This edible species is not nearly as common in Kansas as it is in Missouri and farther east. The specimen illustrated here shows how the expanding cap breaks into an orderly pattern of reddish-brown scales while leaving the central knob unaltered. The tall, finely scaled stalk is equally characteristic. A movable ring is also present, but only a portion of it is visible below the cap. The fruiting bodies are rarely riddled with insect larvae. Some people who eat this mushroom relish its nutty flavor, while others find it disappointing. It is worth noting that, as with several other mushrooms included in this book, there is some uncertainty regarding the name that should be applied to this species. Strictly speaking, *Macrolepiota procera* appears to be found only in Europe, and the Kansas species is probably an unnamed cousin. This may be a nice reminder that taxonomy is an evolving discipline, but in the meantime, we have no other name for this elegant mushroom.

Care should be taken not to confuse the white-gilled parasol mushroom with poisonous *Chlorophyllum molybdites* (no. 79), which has a smooth stalk and grayish-green gills that are white when young. Several other medium-sized to large *Lepiota*-like (lepiotoid) mushrooms with brown scales occur in Kansas. *Leucoagaricus americanus* (syn. = *Lepiota americana* [Ed. 1]) has a stalk that is widest near the middle (spindle-shaped), bruises yellowish orange, and fruits in clusters near wood; its fruiting body ages and dries reddish brown. *Chlorophyllum rachodes* (syns. = *Lepiota rachodes* [Ed. 1], *Macrolepiota rachodes*) has very coarse scales and a bulbous stalk; bruises orange, then reddish brown; and fruits scattered or in fairy rings. Both *L. americanus* and *C. rachodes* have caused gastrointestinal upsets, so should not be eaten. *Echinoderma asperum* (syn. = *Lepiota acutesquamosa* [Ed. 1]) has brown pyramid-shaped scales on its cap, does not bruise, and has a fragile, cobwebby partial veil that looks almost like a cortina. *Echinodermum asperum* is variable in size and the color of scales; its name is uncertain, and it possibly belongs to a group. Its edibility is unknown.

78. *Macrolepiota procera*

Description: **Cap**: 7–20 cm broad, oval becoming flat, often with umbo, white to pale brown with reddish-brown scales. **Gills**: white to light brown, free. **Stalk**: 15–40 cm long, 0.8–1 cm thick, white with fine tan scales, slightly bulbous; annulus white to brown, double edged, movable. **Spore print**: white. **Spores**: 7–12 × 4–5 µm, elliptical, smooth, dextrinoid. **Season**: summer. **Ecology**: saprotrophic.

79. Chlorophyllum molybdites Poisonous

Chlorophyllum molybdites (syn. = *Lepiota morgana* in the older literature) has probably caused more poisonings in Kansas than any other mushroom. Its fruiting bodies are large and meaty, and they conveniently grow in lawns, pastures, and prairies during summer and early fall, often in large fairy rings (Fig. 5). *Chlorophyllum molybdites* is sometimes found with *Saproamanita thiersii* (no. 8), as they share a similar habitat. The important, and unique, feature for identifying this mushroom is its grayish-green gills, which can be seen in the photograph. Its spore print is also greenish. However, the immature gills are white and do not turn green until well after the cap has expanded. For this reason, *C. molybdites* is often mistaken for the edible parasol mushroom, *Macrolepiota procera* (no. 78), which has white gills. It should not be confused with the meadow mushroom, *Agaricus campestris* (no. 71), which has gills that are pink to chocolate-brown. Young caps of *C. molybdites* are round to oval and smooth; their gills are covered by a membranous partial veil. As the cap expands, its surface breaks into tan scales; the partial veil ruptures to form the prominent ring, which becomes detached and may be moved up and down the stalk, as seen on the overturned specimen. The

79. *Chlorophyllum molybdites*

scales on the upright specimen are rather sparse. Eating *C. molybdites* is a memorable experience. Vomiting begins one to two hours after ingestion, followed by severe diarrhea. Poisonings may require brief hospitalization. Some people have eaten this mushroom without ill effect, possibly owing to individual tolerances or the manner in which the mushroom was cooked. The smaller *Leucoagaricus leucothites* (syn. = *Lepiota naucina* [Ed. 1]) shares the same habitat but has grayish-pink gills. Its cap is white to tan or light gray and bears minute, concolorous scales when young, becoming smooth in age. Though eaten, *L. leucothites* may also cause gastrointestinal upsets.

Description: **Cap**: 10–30 cm broad, round to oval becoming convex or flat, white with tan center and tan scales, smooth when young, slowly bruising yellow or orange, then reddish brown. **Gills**: white becoming grayish green, free. **Stalk**: 10–25 cm long, 0.8–2.5 cm thick, white, smooth, slightly bulbous, bruising as cap; annulus white to pale brown, membranous, double edged. **Spore print**: greenish. **Spores**: 10–12 × 6.5–9 μm, elliptical, smooth, dextrinoid. **Season**: summer–fall. **Ecology**: saprotrophic.

Conventional Order Russulales: Family Russulaceae

This amazing order includes many forms that exploit many ecological niches: mycorrhizal, parasitic, and saprotrophic. In this section, we will deal with the family Russulaceae, the only family in this order with cap, gills, and stalk, which are all very brittle (except in a few species not dealt with here). Later we will treat members of this order that have such diverse shapes as flat parchment, massy spines, and pronged coral.

The Russulaceae is a well-defined family of mushrooms that commonly cover the forest floor with many-colored caps, often red but also purple, green, yellow, and more, even mixtures on one cap. Their fruiting bodies are exceedingly brittle so that the stalks are often described as snapping apart "like a piece of chalk," a feature important in their recognition. These mushrooms are further characterized by attached gills and a white to yellow or orange spore print. The family comprises three genera of the cap, gills, and stalk type: *Lactarius*, *Lactifluus*, and *Russula*. The first two genera named here, commonly called milk caps or lactarii, exude a latex where cut or injured. The latex may be watery, white, or variously colored; it may also stain the injured flesh or change color with exposure to air. Old or dried-up fruiting bodies often deceptively fail to exude latex. In contrast, members of the genus *Russula* lack latex and have a characteristic squatty appearance.

Many species of *Lactarius, Lactifluus,* and *Russula* are fine edibles; others are extremely acrid and may burn your mouth or cause gastrointestinal poisoning. In addition, lactarii are rather grainy and thus are often objectionable to chanterelle purists. All three genera are thought to be strictly mycorrhizal with trees. In Kansas, their members fruit predominantly during hot summer weather. Dozens of species of the family Russulaceae have been reported in the state, including latex-producing species, and more undoubtedly await discovery for those patient enough to tackle their identification.

Key to species

1a) Fruiting body exuding a milky latex (sometimes slowly changing color) when injured — go to **2**

1b) Fruiting body not exuding liquid when injured — go to **10**

2a) Fruiting body with peppery taste — go to **3**

2b) Fruiting body without a peppery taste — go to **8**

3a) Cap zoned orange and tan, becoming vase-shaped at maturity; stalk sometimes shallowly pitted — *Lactarius psammicola* (no. 83)

3b) Cap white, sometimes with a dimple in the center but not vase-shaped; stalk smooth go to **4**

4a) Gills very crowded; cap smooth, white or becoming yellowish or brownish at maturity go to **5**

4b) Gills not crowded; cap smooth, felty, or scaly go to **6**

5a) Latex turning pale blue-green *Lactifluus glaucescens* (no. 82)

5b) Latex not changing color *Lactifluus piperatus* (see no. 82)

6a) Cap initially white, smooth, becoming scaly with brown hints at maturity; latex white, not changing color (although sometimes staining fruiting body brown) *Lactifluus deceptivus* (see no. 82)

6b) Cap white, yellowish, or pale gray, smooth or velvety but not becoming scaly; latex white turning yellow or salmon go to **7**

7a) Cap white; latex turning pale yellow *Lactifluus subvellereus* var. *subdistans* (see no. 82)

7b) Cap white to yellowish or pale gray at maturity; latex turning salmon *Lactarius subplinthogalus* (see no. 80)

8a) Cap zoned blue and silver (at least when young); fruiting body blue, turning green when injured; latex scant, blue, turning green *Lactarius indigo* (no. 81)

8b) Cap orange-brown, often finely felty; latex copious, white, not changing colors go to **9**

9a) Gills crowded; latex staining fruiting body brown; fruiting body with a distinctly fishy smell *Lactifluus volemus* (see no. 80)

9b) Gills widely spaced; latex not staining fruiting body; fruiting body with a mild smell *Lactifluus hygrophoroides* (no. 80)

10a) Cap velvety, often cracking in crust-like patches go to **11**

10b) Cap smooth or with striations go to **12**

11a) Cap a distinct green *Russula virescens* group (no. 88)

11b) Cap yellow to brownish or grayish, sometimes with hints of green *Russula crustosa* (see no. 88)

12a) Cap yellowish brown with striations on the edge, following the gills underneath go to **13**

12b) Cap without striations go to **14**

13a) Cap 2.5–8 inches broad; fruiting body with a fetid odor, though sometimes also with a sweet or almond smell *Russula fragrantissima* (no. 87)

13b) Cap 1–3 inches broad; fruiting body with a fruity odor *Russula pectinatoides* (see no. 87)

14a) Cap initially purple, lavender, yellow, or green (sometimes paler purple with age), not bruising go to **15**

14b) Cap initially white (to reddish brown), turning black or brown when bruised or broken (or as they age) go to **16**

15a) Cap an even, dull green *Russula aeruginea* (no. 84)

15b) Cap mottled, purple, lavender, or yellow (sometimes with hints of green) *Russula cyanoxantha* (no. 86)

16a) Fruiting body turning red-brown when bruised or broken but *not* blackening *Russula compacta* (see no. 87)

16b) Fruiting body turning black when bruised or broken go to **17**

17a) Fruiting body immediately turning black when bruised or broken *Russula albonigra* (no. 85)

17b) Fruiting body turning a shade of brown when broken, then blackening go to **18**

18a) Fruiting body turning brown when bruised or broken, then blackening *Russula adusta* (see no. 85)

18b) Fruiting body turning red-brown when bruised or broken, then blackening *Russula densifolia* (see no. 85)

---

80. *Lactifluus hygrophoroides* Edible

Syn. = *Lactarius hygrophoroides* (Ed. 1)

Mushroom hunters who search Kansas forests during the summer are often rewarded with basketfuls of delectable *Lactifluus hygrophoroides*. The orange-brown cap and widely spaced gills, which are well depicted in the photograph, make this species easy to identify. In addition, the fruiting bodies

80. *Lactifluus hygrophoroides*

prolifically exude sticky white latex with the slightest injury when picked (note the milky droplets on the gills of the overturned specimen). The specimens illustrated were among several dozen collected during a mid-August foray; all were used in a noodle casserole. Another similarly colored species, *Lactifluus volemus* (syn. = *Lactarius volemus* [Ed. 1]), is equally edible; it has crowded gills, white latex that stains the injured flesh brown, and a distinctly fishy odor. *Lactarius subplinthogalus* has a white to yellow or pale gray cap, extremely distant gills, and acrid white latex that stains salmon; it is of unknown edibility.

Description: **Cap**: 3–10 cm broad, convex with inrolled margin, becoming flat or slightly depressed, yellowish brown to orange-brown, slightly velvety, brittle; latex abundant, sticky, mild, white, not staining flesh. **Gills**: white to yellow, widely spaced, attached to slightly decurrent. **Stalk**: 2–5 cm long, 0.5–1.5 cm thick, colored as cap or paler, smooth, brittle. **Spore print**: white. **Spores**: 7–10 × 6–7 µm, broadly elliptical, with amyloid warts and ridges. **Season**: summer. **Ecology**: mycorrhizal.

81. *Lactarius indigo* Edible

Lactarius indigo is a truly spectacular mushroom that is unfortunately rather rare in Kansas. It fruits in hardwood forests during the summer. All parts of the fruiting body are silvery blue when young but gradually turn gray-green

81. *Lactarius indigo*

with age. In the photograph, its brilliant blue latex, though sparse, is readily visible on the cut surface of the cap, a portion of which has been placed in the foreground; the latex eventually turns green. *Lactarius indigo* is a well-known edible but tends to be grainy.

Description: **Cap**: 5–15 cm broad, depressed in center, with inrolled margin when young, silvery blue fading to gray or gray-green, often zoned, sticky, brittle; latex scant, bright blue turning green. **Gills**: bluish, attached to decurrent. **Stalk**: 2–8 cm long, 1–2.5 cm thick, bluish, occasionally spotted with shallow pits, smooth, hollow, central or off center, brittle. **Spore print**: cream. **Spores**: 7–9 × 5.5–7.5 µm, broadly elliptical, with amyloid warts and ridges. **Season**: summer. **Ecology**: mycorrhizal.

82. *Lactifluus glaucescens* Poisonous

Syn. = *Lactarius piperatus* var. *glaucescens* (Ed. 1)

Following drenching summer rains, *Lactifluus glaucescens* often fills the hardwood forests of eastern Kansas with its large white fruiting bodies. If injured, this mushroom exudes an abundant white latex that is acrid enough to melt teeth. In addition, the cap is smooth, and its gills are extremely crowded, as can be seen on the overturned fruiting body in the photograph. When the gills of this specimen were sliced with a knife, the latex they exuded gradu-

82. *Lactifluus glaucescens*

ally dried pale green after half an hour. *Lactifluus piperatus* (syn. = *Lacterius piperatus* [Ed. 1]) is identical, but its milk does not change. Though its hotness diminishes with cooking, this mushroom has nonetheless caused gastrointestinal poisonings. Another large whitish species in Kansas, *Lactifluus subvellereus* var. *subdistans* (syn. = *Lactarius subvellereus* var. *subdistans* [Ed. 1]), has a velvety cap and widely spaced gills; it exudes acrid white latex that dries pale yellow. It also is reportedly poisonous, as is *Lactifluus deceptivus*. The cap begins white and felty and becomes scaly with brown hints; its white latex is unchanging but stains the tissue brown.

Description: **Cap**: 4–15 cm broad, flat or shallowly depressed, with inrolled margin when young, white to pale yellowish brown, smooth, brittle; latex copious, acrid, white, drying pale green. **Gills**: white to cream, extremely crowded, often forked, decurrent. **Stalk**: 3–10 cm long, 1–2.5 cm thick, white, smooth, brittle. **Spore print**: yellow. **Spores**: 5.5–7.5 × 5–6 µm, broadly elliptical, with amyloid warts. **Season**: summer. **Ecology**: mycorrhizal.

83. *Lactarius psammicola* Edible with caution

This striking *Lactarius* commonly fruits during summer and early fall in the deciduous forests of eastern Kansas. The young fruiting bodies in the photograph illustrate the orange-zoned cap with its hairy inrolled margin.

83. *Lactarius psammicola*

The darkened shallow pits on the stalk of the overturned specimen are also characteristic but are sometimes absent. The fruiting bodies eventually become vase-shaped with smooth margins. When waterlogged by heavy rain, the caps are often pale and faintly zoned. Because of its acrid taste, this mushroom is not recommended for eating. Other zoned lactarii occur in Kansas and are distinguishable from *L. psammicola* only with difficulty; all are of suspect edibility.

Description: **Cap**: 4–15 cm broad, centrally depressed with hairy inrolled margin, becoming vase-shaped and smooth margined, zoned orange and brownish yellow, fading with age, covered with sticky, matted hairs, brittle, latex acrid, white, sometimes turning pink. **Gills**: white to yellow, crowded, decurrent. **Stalk**: 1–3 cm long, 1–2 cm thick, white, often spotted with shallow pits, brittle. **Spore print**: yellow. **Spores**: 7.5–9 × 6–7.5 µm, broadly elliptical, with amyloid warts and ridges. **Season**: summer. **Ecology**: mycorrhizal.

84. *Russula aeruginea* Edible

Since green is an unusual color for mushrooms, *Russula aeruginea* always attracts attention among mushroom foragers. The species fruits sporadically during summer and fall in the hardwood forests of eastern Kansas. Its dull green cap is smooth and often sticky. *Russula aeruginea* is a good edible; the three specimens illustrated here are in their prime and would honor the

84. *Russula aeruginea*

palate of any mycophagist. Other greenish mushrooms, belonging to the *R. virescens* group (no. 88), have a velvety cap that cracks into crust-like patches.

Description: **Cap**: 5–8 cm broad, flat to slightly depressed, dull green, sometimes spotted yellow, smooth, viscid when moist, brittle. **Gills**: white to pale yellow, attached. **Stalk**: 4–8 cm long, 1–2 cm thick, white, often with brown stains, brittle. **Spore print**: yellow. **Spores**: 6–10 × 5–7 μm, broadly elliptical, with amyloid warts. **Season**: summer–fall. **Ecology**: mycorrhizal.

85. *Russula albonigra* — Edibility suspect

This distinctive *Russula* fruits under hardwoods during the summer in Kansas. The fruiting bodies are white when young and immediately blacken when cut or bruised. The specimen illustrated here blackened considerably with handling when moved to a lawn for photographing. As the fruiting bodies age, they turn gray and finally black. The edibility of *R. albonigra* is suspect since a very similar species in Asia is poisonous. Others in this group, *R. adusta* (syn. = *R. nigricans*) and *R. densifolia*, turn brown or reddish brown, respectively, before blackening. None of these should be eaten.

Description: **Cap**: 5–15 cm broad, depressed, white becoming gray, then black with age, bruising black, smooth, brittle. **Gills**: white, bruising and aging black, crowded, attached. **Stalk**: 2.5–10 cm long, 2–2.5 cm thick, white,

85. *Russula albonigra*

bruising and aging black, smooth, brittle. **Spore print**: white. **Spores**: 7.5–10 × 6.5–8 µm, broadly elliptical, with amyloid warts and ridges. **Season**: summer. **Ecology**: mycorrhizal.

86. *Russula cyanoxantha* Edible

Russula cyanoxantha fruits under hardwoods during the summer in eastern Kansas. Its large caps are a striking lavender when fresh but may show regions of yellow or green as well. The specimens illustrated here are young, and their deep purple caps will fade and become more lavender as they expand. *Russula cyanoxantha* is a fine edible that rivals the best of the russulas. The deciduous forests of Kansas are rich with other purple, red, and pink species of *Russula*. Many of these are as hot as cayenne pepper and have at one time or another been called *R. emetica*, which fruits primarily in sphagnum bogs, of which there are none in Kansas. Unfortunately, red russulas are often notoriously difficult to identify and will remain a constant source of frustration for mushroom hunters.

Description: **Cap**: 4–15 cm broad, convex becoming depressed, deep purple when very young, then lavender, often with yellow or green regions, paler

86. *Russula cyanoxantha*

with age, smooth, brittle. **Gills**: white, occasionally forked, attached. **Stalk**: 5–13 cm long, 1.5–5 cm thick, white, smooth, brittle. **Spore print**: white. **Spores**: 6.5–9.5 × 5.5–7 μm, broadly elliptical, with amyloid warts. **Season**: summer. **Ecology**: mycorrhizal.

87. *Russula fragrantissima* — Not edible

Syn. = *Russula foetens*
Fetid russula

The yellowish-brown caps of *Russula fragrantissima* often litter Kansas woodlands during wet summer weather. Drab and squatty in appearance, this mushroom is easily hidden by forest debris. Its odor is hardly fragrant and has been variously described as being almondlike with an underlying fetidness to outright nauseating. The former name for the species, *R. foetens*, was probably more descriptive. There seems to be a group of similar russulas with unpleasant odors; their flavor is equally disagreeable, and there is often an acrid aftertaste. This does not deter slugs from dining on the fruiting bodies, as is evidenced by the chewed margin on the smaller cap in the photograph. Other brown russulas occur in Kansas. *Russula pectinatoides* has a smaller cap (3–8 cm broad) with more prominent striations (grooves along the edge of the cap, following the gills) and a fruity odor. The edible *R. compacta* has a

87. *Russula fragrantissima*

white to reddish-brown cap that lacks striations and bruises reddish brown; its cap and stalk are extremely firm.

Description: **Cap**: 7–20 cm broad, flat to slightly depressed with striate margin, yellowish brown, smooth, viscid when moist, fetid, brittle. **Gills**: white becoming yellow, occasionally forked, beaded with clear droplets on edges when young, attached. **Stalk**: 3–6 cm long, 1–2.5 cm thick, white, becoming stained dark yellowish brown at base with age, smooth, brittle. **Spore print**: pale yellow. **Spores**: 6–9 × 5.5–7.5 µm, broadly elliptical, with amyloid warts and ridges. **Season**: summer. **Ecology**: mycorrhizal.

88. *Russula virescens* group — Edible

Mushroom hunters who brave the steamy, tick-infested forests of Kansas during the summer are sometimes rewarded with the *Russula virescens* group, outstanding edibles. These mushrooms, identified by the velvety green cap, actually belong to a group of at least twelve unnamed species that closely resemble one another. As the cap expands, its surface cracks into characteristic crust-like patches, which can be seen on the lower margin of the large cap in the photograph; the neighboring button has not yet formed patches. Because of its moldy appearance, *R. virescens* is often passed by for other edibles, but at great sacrifice; its nutty flavor is surpassed by few other russulas. Unfortunately, insect larvae also delight in its flesh, so it is not unusual to optimistically haul back seemingly prime specimens only to discover that others had previously dined. The ratty, chewed-upon fruiting body illustrated here is typical—even the small button proved to be riddled with larvae. A similar species, *R. crustosa*, has a velvety cracked cap that is yellowish brown to gray or only faintly greenish. *Russula aeruginea* (no. 84), although green, is smooth and sticky. Both species are good edibles.

Description: **Cap**: 5–15 cm broad, round becoming flat or depressed, green to grayish green, often with tan regions, velvety, cracking into crust-like patches, brittle. **Gills**: white, attached. **Stalk**: 3–7 cm long, 1–2 cm thick, white, smooth, brittle. **Spore print**: white. **Spores**: 6–9 × 5.5–7 µm, broadly elliptical, with amyloid warts and ridges. **Season**: summer. **Ecology**: mycorrhizal.

88. *Russula virescens group*

Conventional Order Boletales

The families Boletaceae, Boletinellaceae, Gyroporaceae, and Suillaceae, all belonging to the order Boletales, are treated in this section. DNA research indicates that the Boletales are not yet well defined, so name changes are likely in the future. The members of these families are commonly called boletes and have the traditional cap-and-stalk shape, though the fertile underside (the hymenium) takes the form of tubes, resembling a sponge on the surface, rather than gills. Spores develop on the inner surfaces of the tubes and sift through their openings, or pores, to be borne away on air currents. (Other members of the Boletales do not exhibit these characteristics and will be dealt with later.) The fruiting bodies of boletes are typically soft, and the layer bearing tubes is easily removed from the cap. Polypores, many of which belong to the order Polyporales, may also have a cap, stalk, and pores, but the fruiting bodies tend to be leathery, and their tube layers are not easily removed from their caps. Many boletes have caps and tubes of sharply contrasting colors as well as flesh that stains blue or other colors when bruised or broken.

Boletes are popular edibles and are relatively safe for beginners so long as they avoid two groups that are responsible for gastrointestinal poisonings: the red-pored species and the blue-staining species with red caps and yellow pores. In fact, the king bolete, *Boletus edulis*, regrettably not occurring in Kansas, and the chestnut bolete, *Gyroporus castaneus*, which does occur here, rank with the chanterelles and morels as choice edibles. Unfortunately, insect larvae also have a special fondness for their flesh and commonly monopolize the bolete crop as soon as it cracks the soil surface.

Among the species treated here, the family Boletaceae includes the largest number of genera and species. Most of these have a spore print in some shade of brown, often olive or yellowish. However, species of the genus *Strobilomyces* have black spores, and those of *Tylopilus* have pink to reddish spores. Observing the nature of the shape, color, and surface of the stalk aids in identifying to genus and sometimes to species level. Some stalks have raised networks, tiny groups of hairs (scabers), or sticky "dots"; various other features, including rings, may be present.

In the family Suillaceae, including the genus *Suillus*, the spores are various shades of brown, as are those of the Boletaceae. They are almost always associated with conifers but not the only Kansas native, the eastern redcedar, so the *Suillus* seen here have been brought in with pines from other states for Christmas-tree farms, decorative plantings, and shelter belts. The caps of this group are often sticky (viscid), and the stalks can have sticky matter on them, too. The family Boletinellaceae is represented here by the ash tree bolete, *Boletinellus merulioides*, which grows with ash, low to the ground, with a short, off-center stalk. Species of *Gyroporus*, the only genus of the family Gyroporaceae, are usually small, unfortunately, as they are usually delicious. General characteristics of the species are yellow spores and hollow stalks.

Most bolete species are mycorrhizal and rather specific in their tree associations. The major bolete flush in Kansas occurs during the summer, with a minor flush of *Suillus* in the fall. The caps of boletes in Kansas will often crack in the dry weather, though some are more susceptible than others to becoming areolate (cracking in a pattern through the top layer of the cap). Because boletes are notoriously difficult to distinguish from one another, many found in Kansas have yet to be identified; only the common and distinctive species are described here. The first species dealt with here is the most unusual for a bolete: it is the gilled bolete, *Phylloporus rhodoxanthus*, which does belong to the Boletaceae.

Key to species

1a) Underside of cap with bright yellow "gills," often forked
Phylloporus rhodoxanthus group (no. 89)

1b) Underside of cap with spongelike tubes opening by rounded, elliptical, or elongate pores — go to **2**

2a) Stalk short, off center or lateral; pores radially elongate; always growing under ash — *Boletinellus merulioides* (no. 101)

2b) Stalk not off center or lateral; pores rounded, elliptical or elongate; not (always) growing under ash — go to **3**

3a) Stalk and pores (and in most species also the cap) bruising conspicuously — go to **4**

3b) Cap and stalk not bruising (pores sometimes bruising) — go to **10**

4a) Tubes yellow with yellow, orange, or red pores; cap, stalk, and pores bruising dark blue — go to **5**

4b) Tubes initially white, maturing gray, pink, pinkish brown, or reddish brown with pores of the same color; stalk and pores (and in most species also the cap) bruising grayish brown, bluish green, then rusty, brown, or black but not dark blue — go to **7**

5a) Cap bright red fading to pinkish red; tubes and pores both yellow
Hortiboletus campestris (no. 91)

5b) Cap dark red or yellowish brown to reddish brown; tubes yellow but pores orange to red go to **6**

6a) Cap dark red; stalk with a dark red network of ridges (reticulations) *Boletus rubroflammeus* (see no. 92)

6b) Cap yellowish brown to reddish brown with yellow edges; stalk with fine red granules *Boletus subvelutipes* group (no. 92)

7a) Cap and stalk covered in soft grayish-black scales; pores maturing gray; stalk and cap bruising red, then black *Strobilomyces strobilaceus* (no. 97)

7b) Cap initially wrinkled or smooth, often cracking with age (areolate) but without scales; stalk (and sometimes cap) bruising grayish brown, brown, bluish green, or brown but not black go to **8**

8a) Cap initially wrinkled, areolate at maturity, brown; cap and stalk sometimes bruising pinkish, then always grayish brown *Leccinellum griseum* (no. 96)

8b) Cap not initially wrinkled, areolate or not, reddish brown or purple; stalk bruising bluish green or brown (cap bruising or not) go to **9**

9a) Cap dark reddish brown, velvety, areolate, 1.5–2.75 inches broad; cap and stalk bruising bluish green; pores maturing reddish brown *Porphyrellus sordidus* (no. 99)

9b) Cap dark purple initially, maturing brownish, smooth, not areolate, 3–12 inches broad; cap not bruising; stalk bruising brown; pores maturing pink *Tylopilus rubrobrunneus* (no. 98)

10a) Stalk at least partially covered with a network of ridges (reticulations) go to **11**

10b) Stalk smooth or with minute brown dots go to **13**

11a) Stalk with coarse reticulations on upper two-thirds only; pores nearly extending down stalk (decurrent), yellow with faint rusty discoloration *Xerocomus tenax* (no. 95)

11b) Stalk covered or nearly covered with coarse or fine reticulations; pores not decurrent, yellowish, without rusty discoloration go to **12**

12a) Cap velvety; stalk with very deep reticulations (giving it a shaggy appearance) *Aureoboletus russellii* (no. 90)

12b) Cap smooth; stalk with fine, shallow reticulations *Boletus variipes* (no. 93)

13a) Cap dry go to **14**

13b) Cap sticky (viscid) when moist go to **16**

14a) Fruiting bodies often growing in clusters; pores intensely yellow; spore print olive-brown *Aureoboletus innixus* (no. 94)

14b) Fruiting bodies growing singly; pores initially white becoming pale yellow; spore print yellow go to **15**

15a) Cap and stalk dark burgundy *Gyroporus purpurinus* (no. 102)

15b) Cap and stalk brown *Gyroporus castaneus* (see no. 102)

16a) Stalk with minute brown dots *Suillus granulatus* (see no. 100)

16b) Stalk without dots go to **17**

17a) Tubes often with milky droplets when young; stalk dark at the base *Suillus weaverae* (no. 100)

17b) Tubes without milky droplets; stalk not dark at the base *Suillus brevipes* (see no. 100)

89. *Phylloporus rhodoxanthus* group Edible

The gilled bolete

We begin with an exception to the rule of tubes on the underside of the fruiting body of the *Phylloporus rhodoxanthus* group, which fruits infrequently in the hardwood forests of Kansas during the summer. These curious mushrooms share many characteristics with boletes, including the narrowly elliptical spores and the blue-staining reaction of the gills, and the species are now commonly placed in the family Boletaceae. The specimens in the photograph illustrate several features that help to identify this species, namely, the velvety, reddish-brown cap and the thick, bright yellow decurrent gills. The gills of these fruiting bodies did not stain blue, which suggests that this characteristic is variable.

Description: **Cap**: 2–8 cm broad, convex becoming flat, red to dark reddish brown, velvety, occasionally cracked. **Gills**: bright yellow, thick, widely spaced, often forked, sometimes bruising blue, decurrent. **Stalk**: 4–10 cm

89. *Phylloporus rhodoxanthus* group

long, 0.5–1.5 cm thick, yellow to reddish brown, smooth. **Spore print**: olive-brown. **Spores**: 9–12 × 3.5–5 µm, elliptical, smooth. **Season**: summer. **Ecology**: mycorrhizal.

90. *Aureoboletus russellii* Edible

Syn. = *Boletellus russellii* (Ed. 1)

Aureoboletus russellii is an uncommon bolete in Kansas but one not easily forgotten. It has been reported from the eastern part of the state under oak during the summer. Most distinctive is its tall, shaggy, reddish-brown stalk that is deeply cut into a netlike pattern of ridges. The cap of the specimen illustrated here has not yet fully expanded, and its velvety surface is just beginning to crack into the fine patches characteristic of mature fruiting bodies. Though it is edible, there are few reports on its quality.

Description: **Cap**: 3–13 cm broad, convex becoming flat, yellowish brown, olive gray, or reddish brown, velvety becoming areolate. **Tubes**: yellowish olive, attached, becoming depressed around stalk; pores colored as tubes, greater than 1 mm wide, angular. **Stalk**: 10–18 cm long, 1–2 cm thick, reddish brown, covered with prominent network of ridges, shaggy; base often slimy. **Spore print**: olive-brown. **Spores**: 15–20 µm, elliptical, longitudinally ridged. **Season**: summer. **Ecology**: mycorrhizal.

90. *Aureoboletus russellii*

91. ***Hortiboletus campestris*** Edible with caution

Syn. = *Boletus campestris* (Ed. 1)

Following late-spring and summer rains, the hardwood forests of eastern Kansas often support abundant fruitings of red-topped, yellow-pored boletes. *Hortiboletus campestris* displays all of these characteristics and also stains blue; some of the other red and yellow species do not. This species and other red and yellow species also occur in lawns under trees. The young specimens in the photograph illustrate the important features of this bolete: a velvety, bright-red cap, a red stalk, and yellow tubes. In some red and yellow boletes, fruiting bodies quickly bruise dark blue, as do these, seen on the tubes of the overturned specimen. The caps can eventually become pinkish and crack with age. Though eaten by some Kansans, the group is not recommended since several species have caused gastrointestinal upsets.

Description: **Cap**: 3–4 cm broad, convex, bright red fading to pinkish red, bruising dark blue, velvety, cracking with age. **Tubes**: yellow to greenish

91. *Hortiboletus campestris*

yellow, bruising dark blue, depressed around stalk, pores colored as tubes, 1–2 per mm, round to angular. **Stalk**: 4–5 cm long, 0.5–1 cm thick, red, yellow near apex, bruising dark blue; surface finely granular; base coated with yellow mycelium. **Spore print**: olive-brown. **Spores**: 11–14 × 4.5–6 µm, elliptical, smooth. **Season**: late spring–summer. **Ecology**: mycorrhizal.

92. *Boletus subvelutipes* group Poisonous

Boletus subvelutipes belongs to the red-pored boletes and fruits in the deciduous forests of Kansas during wet summer weather. It may be moved to another genus, perhaps the recently described *Rubroboletus*. It often ushers in the bolete season. The specimens in the photograph show some of the characteristic features: orange-red pores, red granules on the stalk, and dark blue bruising on all parts of the fruiting body. Splitting the tube layer shows that the tubes are actually yellow (before staining), and only the pores (the mouths of the tubes) are orange-red. Red-pored boletes have caused gastrointestinal poisonings and should not be eaten. Another probable relative, *B. rubroflammeus*, has a dark red cap and also bruises dark blue, but its stalk is covered with a dark red network of ridges.

Description: **Cap**: 6–15 cm broad, convex to flat, yellowish brown to reddish

92. *Boletus subvelutipes* group

brown with yellow margin, bruising dark blue, velvety, cracking with age. **Tubes**: yellow, bruising dark blue, attached or slightly depressed around stalk; pores orange to red, about 2 per mm, round. **Stalk**: 3–8 cm long, 1–1.5 cm thick, cylindrical to club-shaped, yellow at apex, redder toward base, bruising dark blue, coated with fine red granules; base with dark red hairs. **Spore print**: olive-brown. **Spores**: 11–16.5 × 4.5–5.5 µm, elliptical, smooth, with minute apical germ pore. **Season**: summer. **Ecology**: mycorrhizal.

93. *Boletus variipes* Edible

Kansas's version of the world-renowned king bolete, *Boletus edulis*, is *B. variipes*. The two species are nearly identical except that *B. variipes* has a dry cap and prefers hardwoods rather than conifers. Though *B. variipes* is a good edible, its flavor is apparently somewhat disappointing compared with its savory relative. The pictured mature specimen shows the typical features: tan cap, tubes receding from the stalk and darkened by ripe spores, and the club-shaped stalk, covered with a fine, raised network. The young fruiting bodies will have a pale pore surface. Species of *Tylopilus* are frequently mistaken for *B. variipes* but at maturity have pink tubes and pink spore prints; many are exceedingly bitter.

93. *Boletus variipes*

94. *Aureoboletus innixus*

Description: **Cap**: 6–25 cm broad, convex to flat, yellowish brown, smooth, dry, often cracking with age. **Tubes**: white becoming yellow, depressed around stalk; pores colored as tubes, 1–2 per mm, round, stuffed with hyphae when young. **Stalk**: 8–15 cm long, 1–3.5 cm thick, club-shaped, white to pale brown, covered with network of ridges that extend nearly to base. **Spore print**: olive-brown. **Spores**: 12–17 × 3.5–5.5 µm, elliptical, smooth. **Season**: summer. **Ecology**: mycorrhizal.

94. *Aureoboletus innixus* Edible

Syn. = *Boletus innixus*

The intense yellow of the pores and the penchant to grow in clusters are the distinguishing features of this species, although *Aureoboletus innixus* does grow singly as well. The dry cap is a pale rusty color, convex when young and flattening in age. The yellow pores are round and fine. The stalk is thick, sometimes bulbous, narrowing below, and is yellow with some reddish-brown tones. Like most or all Kansas boletes, *A. innixus* grows in oak woods in the summer.

Description: **Cap**: 3–8 cm wide, convex, flattening in age, dry, pale rust-colored. **Tubes**: bright yellow, sometime duller in age; pores colored as tubes, 1–2 per mm, angular. **Stalk**: 3–6 cm long, 1–2 cm thick, often club-shaped but narrowing below the club-like swelling, yellow, sometimes with warm brown tones. **Spore print**: olive-brown. **Spores**: 8–11 × 3–5 µm, elliptical, smooth. **Season**: summer. **Ecology**: mycorrhizal.

95. *Xerocomus tenax* Edibility unknown

Syn. = *Boletus tenax*

The distinguishing characteristic of this bolete is the coarse, raised, rust-colored network, more obvious over the top two-thirds of the stalk, well illustrated in the picture. The cap is a dull rusty brown, velvety in texture. The pores are dull yellow, almost extending down the stalk (decurrent), and discoloring slightly rusty, as seen here. The stalk, as stated earlier, is coarsely reticulate and narrows toward the base, which often has dense mycelium around and under it. *Xerocomus tenax* is found in oak woods in the summer.

Description: **Cap:** 4–8 cm wide convex when young, then expanded to plane in age, dull rusty brown, scurfy. **Tubes:** dull yellow staining slightly rusty, nearly decurrent; pores colored as tubes, 1 per mm. **Stalk:** 3–7 cm long, 1–2 cm thick, pale yellow, tapered downward, upper two-thirds with rusty coarse

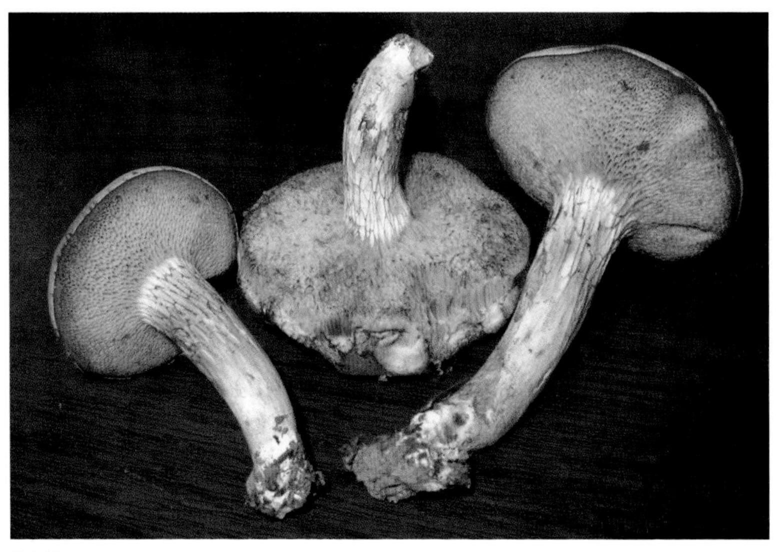

95. *Xerocomus tenax*

reticulation, lower part with dense mycelium. **Spore print:** olive-brown. **Spores:** 9–12 × 4–6 µm elongate, ovoid. Season: summer. **Ecology:** mycorrhizal.

96. *Leccinellum griseum* — Edible

Syn. = *Leccinum carpini*
Syn. = *Leccinum griseum*

There are few members of the genus *Leccinellum* in the broad sense found in Kansas, perhaps because their usual mycorrhizal partners are aspen and birch, trees not often found here. *Leccinellum griseum*, however, will partner with oak and hop hornbeam, which belongs to the same family as birches. The cap pictured on the left (both are elderly) shows the uneven, mature cap with the skin cracked into small areas (areolate); younger individuals have no such cracks but do usually have a wrinkled brown cap surface. The interior flesh slowly darkens to grayish brown with age and handling, sometimes with an initial pinkish stage. The tube mouths are whitish at first but also darken with age and bruising. The fertile surface (here the tubes) is recessed around the stalk, as seen here. What is not apparent are the tufts of tiny dark hairs (scabers) evenly scattered over the stalk; the stalks are also paler in youth and will bruise with handling. The right-most specimen's stalk is dark from larval infestation. This species appears in late summer to fall.

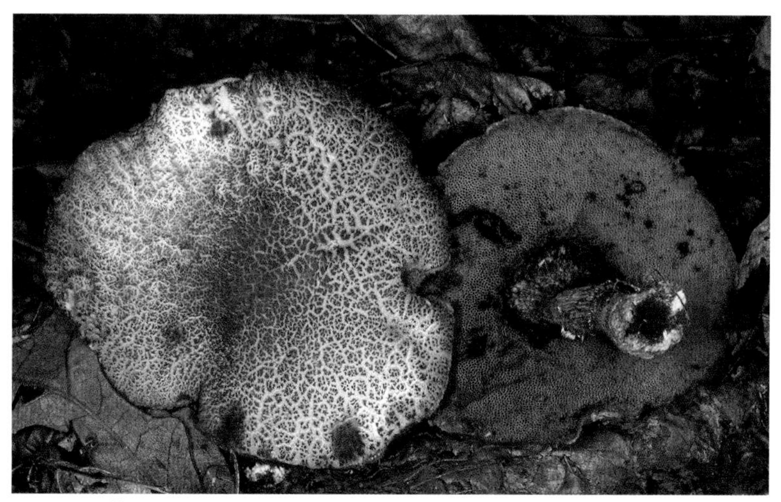

96. *Leccinellum griseum*

Description: **Cap**: 3–10 cm broad, convex, then flattening, dry, wrinkled, brown, areolate in age, flesh bruising pinkish then grayish brown, discoloring grayish brown with age. **Tubes**: whitish at first, bruising and darkening with age, depressed around the stalk; pores colored as tubes, 1–2 per mm, round. **Stalk**: 4–12 cm long, 0.7–2 cm thick, pale, even, having dark scabers, which further darken with time. **Spore print**: rusty brown. **Spores**: 12–18 × 5–6 µm, cylindrical but swollen in the middle. **Season**: late summer–fall. **Ecology**: mycorrhizal.

97. *Strobilomyces strobilaceus* — Edible

Syn. = *Strobilomyces floccopus* (Ed. 1)
Old man of the woods

The old man of the woods is a distinctive bolete that fruits abundantly during the summer in the hardwood forests of Kansas, particularly under oak. The fine pair of fruiting bodies shown here displays the coarse grayish-black scales that cover the cap and stalk. The tubes are gray and give a black spore print. All parts of the fruiting body first bruise reddish, then black. Mushroomers who dine on this bolete usually remove the tubes before cooking. Most rate this mushroom as passably edible, good only when the season is lean.

Description: **Cap**: 4–15 cm broad, convex becoming flat, white to gray with coarse soft grayish-black scales, bruising reddish, then black; margin often with ragged remnants of partial veil. **Tubes**: white becoming gray or darker, bruising as cap, attached or slightly depressed around stalk; pores colored as tubes, 1–3 per mm, angular. **Stalk**: 4–12 cm long, 1–3 cm thick, colored and bruising as cap, scaly; annulus ragged, forming several zones. **Spore print**: black. **Spores**: 9.5–15 × 8.5–12 μm, broadly elliptical, reticulate, with apical germ pore. **Season**: summer. **Ecology**: mycorrhizal.

97. *Strobilomyces strobilaceus*

98. *Tylopilus rubrobrunneus*

98. *Tylopilus rubrobrunneus* Not edible

Among the boletes of Kansas, *Tylopilus rubrobrunneus* is perhaps the most magnificent, with caps that are sometimes larger than dinner plates. It fruits during summer and early fall in hardwood forests. Young caps are deep purple-brown and have white tubes. With maturity, the caps fade to pinkish cinnamon and their tubes turn pink, as in the specimens illustrated here. Occasionally, the stalk is covered with a netlike pattern of ridges next to where it joins the cap. The three specimens in the photograph were part of a troop of about a dozen fruiting bodies, only one of which showed a network of ridges on its stalk. *Tylopilus rubrobrunneus* is meaty and attractive, but its intensely bitter taste will discourage the most courageous of mushroom eaters. Other species of *Tylopilus*, some bitter and others mild, occur in Kansas; most have yet to be identified.

Description: **Cap**: 8–30 cm broad, convex with inrolled margin becoming flat, dark purple-brown fading to pinkish cinnamon, smooth, cracking with age, bitter. **Tubes**: white when young, then pink, attached, becoming depressed around stalk; pores colored as tubes, bruising brown, 1–2 per mm, round. **Stalk**: 8–20 cm long, 1–5 cm thick, club-shaped becoming cylindrical, light purple-brown, whitish near cap, staining olive with age, sometimes covered with network of ridges at extreme apex. **Spore print**: pinkish red. **Spores**: 10–14 × 3–4.5 μm, elliptical, smooth. **Season**: summer–early fall. **Ecology**: mycorrhizal.

99. *Porphyrellus sordidus* Edibility unknown

Syn. = *Tylopilus sordidus*

This unusual little bolete's cap bruises bluish green in the flesh. The pores also stain this color at first and later become the reddish brown of the spores. The cap soon becomes cracked into small flattened scales (areolate), as illustrated in the picture. The pores begin pallid gray but turn reddish with spore maturity; they bruise bluish green and finally dark reddish brown. The stalk is an even ruddy-brown color, sometimes curved at the base. *Porphyrellus sordidus* fruits in the summer to early fall under oaks.

Description: **Cap**: 4–7 cm wide, convex, velvety, reddish brown, soon becoming areolate, bruising bluish green. **Tubes**: pale initially to pinkish brown, then reddish brown, bruising bluish green, then dark reddish brown; pores colored and bruising as tubes, 1–2 per mm, round. **Stalk**: 4–8 cm long, 1–1.5 cm thick, reddish brown. **Spore print**: reddish brown. **Spores**: 10–14 × 4–6 μm, elliptical, smooth. **Season**: summer–early fall. **Ecology**: mycorrhizal.

99. *Porphyrellus sordidus*

100. *Suillus weaverae* Edible

Syn. = *Suillus lactifluus* (Ed. 1)

Syn. = *Fuscoboletinus weaverae*

Though species of the family Suillaceae in the broad sense are mostly mycorrhizal with conifers, they are not associated with Kansas's only native conifer, the eastern redcedar. Hence, in Kansas these boletes should be sought under non-native pines that have been introduced by landscapers and Christmas-tree growers. The survival of these pines outside their natural range may depend to a large degree on their beneficial association with these mushrooms. *Suillus weaverae* fruits under white pine in Kansas during late summer and fall. The pores of the young caps are typically beaded with droplets of milky latex, which dry as the fruiting bodies mature. The specimens in the photograph illustrate the cinnamon-brown cap and the yellow stalk stained dark cinnamon-brown at its base. Like most members of the family Suillaceae, *S. weaverae* is a good edible. *Suillus brevipes* lacks the milky droplets, and the stalk doesn't have a dark base like that of *S. weaverae* but is otherwise similar. *Suillus granulatus*, which is also similar, seems to be a European and/or a Eurasian species and has minute brown dots on the stalk.

Description: **Cap**: 4–10 cm broad, convex becoming flat, pale to dark reddish cinnamon, smooth, viscid when wet; margin membranous, slightly overhanging. **Tubes**: pale yellow becoming brownish yellow, attached; pores

100. *Suillus weaverae*

colored as tubes, beaded with droplets of milky latex when young, bruising brown, 1–3 per mm, round. **Stalk**: 2–5 cm long, 1–2 cm thick, yellow at apex; base staining dark cinnamon-brown. **Spore print**: cinnamon-brown. **Spores**: 7–9 × 3 µm, elliptical, smooth. **Season**: late summer–fall. **Ecology**: mycorrhizal.

101. *Boletinellus merulioides* — Edible

Syn. = *Gyrodon merulioides*
Ash tree bolete

Enormous troops of *Boletinellus merulioides* appear under ash trees from late spring through early fall in Kansas. The association of this species with ash makes it easy to locate. Plantings of ash along city streets are prime collecting habitats; the cluster in the photograph was found in a lawn under an ash tree. The association with ash is complicated and involves an insect; the mushroom is not mycorrhizal. The color of the cap is variable, ranging from yellowish brown to olive-brown. More characteristic are the radially elongate yellow pores; unlike that of most boletes, the tube layer does not readily separate from the cap. The equally diagnostic off-center or lateral stalks are not visible on these specimens. *Boletinellus merulioides* is frequently eaten; its tube layer tends to be slimy and is usually removed. The flesh often bruises blue or red, especially in the stalk.

101. *Boletinellus merulioides*

Description: **Cap**: 5–15 cm broad, convex with inrolled margin, becoming depressed with margin uplifted and wavy, yellowish brown to olive-brown, smooth, sometimes turning bluish green or red when cut. **Pores**: yellow to olive, bruising reddish brown, decurrent; pores radially elongate, often with veinlike ridges. **Stalk**: 2–5 cm long, 0.5–2.5 cm thick, yellow to brown with blackish base, bruising reddish brown or blue, off center or lateral. **Spore print**: olive-brown. **Spores**: 7–10 × 6–7.5 μm, broadly elliptical, smooth. **Season**: late spring–early fall. **Ecology**: mutualistic with ash-tree parasites.

102. *Gyroporus purpurinus* — Edible

Gyroporus purpurinus fruits under hardwoods during summer and early fall in Kansas. It is easily recognized by its velvety, burgundy cap. One of the specimens illustrated here has a slightly sunken cap and a cracked margin, which are characteristic of older fruiting bodies. In addition, note the hollow stalk (which is also brittle) of the overturned specimen, a feature common to all members of the genus *Gyroporus*. The tube layer is initially white but turns light yellow as the spores mature. *Gyroporus purpurinus* is a good edible, and its abundance in Kansas makes it worth gathering. The savory *G. castaneus*, the chestnut bolete, unfortunately is less common; it has a brown cap and stalk.

102. *Gyroporus purpurinus*

Description: **Cap**: 1–5 cm broad, convex becoming flat or slightly depressed, dark burgundy, fading with age, velvety. **Tubes**: white becoming pale yellow, attached, then depressed around stalk; pores colored as tubes, 1–3 per mm, round. **Stalk**: 3–6 cm long, 3–8 mm thick, colored as cap or browner, slightly roughened, hollow at maturity, especially near base. **Spore print**: yellow. **Spores**: 8–11 × 5–6.5 µm, elliptical, smooth. **Season**: summer–early fall. **Ecology**: mycorrhizal.

Orders Hymenochaetales, Polyporales, and some anomalous members of Agaricales and Russulales, mostly with pored hymenia but some with diverse hymenial forms

Polypores, with their pored hymenia (the surface where the spores are produced), are often snubbed by mushroomers who are intent instead on gilled mushrooms and boletes. However, during cold weather and drought—conditions not uncommon in Kansas—these fungi reign supreme in numbers and variety. The fruiting bodies can be crust-like, shelflike, or stalked like boletes, and most produce their spores from a layer of tubes. The tube openings, or pores, may be round, angular, radially elongate, or mazelike (Fig. 4); the pore walls can even resemble gills or break into spines. Polypores differ from boletes, which also bear pores (the openings to their tubes), in their mostly leathery to woody consistency or growth on wood. Terrestrial stalked polypores can be further distinguished from boletes by their tube layers that do not readily separate from the caps. Woody perennial fruiting bodies, or conks, often form stratified tube layers similar to the growth rings on trees. Since these fruiting bodies can be durable, lasting even over several seasons, they have often issued all their spores before being collected, so they will not often produce a spore print.

Many of these fungi are indispensable in helping to recycle woody matter back into the soil. Others are parasitic on trees and may eventually kill their host. Wood is composed primarily of cellulose that is bound together by lignin. Brown-rot polypores attack only cellulose, making wood dark and brittle, whereas white rotters attack both cellulose and lignin, leaving wood white and spongy.

Polyporales are typically tough enough to ruin your dental work, but a few of the flashier species, such as the sulphur shelf, or chicken of the woods (*Laetiporus sulphureus*), and hen of the woods (*Grifola frondosa*) rate among the best edibles. One atypical member of the Polyporales that appears to have soft gills, *Panus conchatus*, begins this section. Kansas is particularly rich in polypores. Members of the order Hymenochaetales treated here, including the genera *Coltricia*, *Cotylidia*, *Hydnoporia*, *Phellinus*, *Pseudoinonotus*, and *Trichaptum*, are of no culinary interest, but some are exotically beautiful.

Some of the families with smooth and other configurations of hymenia belong to our old friends the Agaricales—*Chondrostereum*, *Fistulina*, and *Hohenbuehelia*—and the Russulales—*Bondarzewia*, *Lentinellus*, and *Stereum*—in their anomalous forms. Many of these are commonly called parchment fungi if they are thin, tough, and leathery or are without enough substance to eat. Most are saprotrophic.

Key to species

1a) Fertile undersurface (hymenium), smooth or sometimes creased or wrinkled but not pored (use a hand lens to verify that the surface is not minutely pored) go to **2**

1b) Hymenium gill-like, mazelike, or of pores, which may erode to become teeth go to **7**

2a) Growing on ground; fruiting body pale, vase-shaped; stalk present *Cotylidia diaphana* (no. 132)

2b) Growing on wood or bark of dead trees; fruiting body variously colored but not vase-shaped; stalk absent go to **3**

3a) Fruiting body lying flat on substrate (resupinate), purple, or rarely forming shelflike brown caps *Chondostereum purpureum* (no. 133)

3b) Fruiting body cap-like to shelflike, sometimes shelving but not purple go to **4**

4a) Fruiting body bright coral-pink above, undersurface white (or sometimes white above, coral-pink below) *Byssomerulius incarnatus* (no. 124)

4b) Fruiting body zoned in grays and browns; undersurface yellow, orange, brown go to **5**

5a) Caps with stiff matted hairs; undersurface brown *Stereum hirsutum* (no. 130)

5b) Caps minutely fuzzy or velvety; undersurface orange to brown go to **6**

6a) Caps zoned with gray, tan, and reddish brown *Stereum ostrea* (no. 131)

6b) Caps zoned with yellow and cinnamon-brown *Stereum complicatum* (see no. 131)

7a) Hymenium gill-like or mazelike (composed of large pores that elongate in one direction, usually with some short cross-walls between), at least in part go to **8**

7b) Hymenium of pores, which may erode to become teeth go to **16**

8a) Growing in soil, not growing on wood; cap velvety reddish brown; hymenium of rigid, concentric plates (looking like gills encircling the stalk), sometimes with cross-walls *Coltricia montagnei* (no. 128)

8b) Growing on wood (sometimes buried); hymenium gill-like or mazelike but not of concentric plates go to **9**

9a) Cap funnel-shaped, initially violet, maturing tan; stalk present; gills running down stalk (decurrent) *Panus conchatus* (no. 103)

9b) Cap shell-shaped or fan-shaped; stalk absent (sessile) go to **10**

10a) Cap fuzzy, hairy, or with gelatinous spines; hymenium gill-like go to **11**

10b) Cap smooth; hymenium mazelike, at least in part go to **14**

11a) Cap dark-colored, rather rubbery, finely fuzzy or with gelatinous spines, 1–2 or rarely 3 inches broad go to **12**

11b) Cap pale, tough or soft but not rubbery, finely fuzzy to hairy, up to 4 inches broad go to **13**

12a) Cap dark brown to black, finely fuzzy, especially near attachment to substrate *Hohenbuehelia atrocoerulea* var. *grisea* (see no. 109)

12b) Cap grayish to whitish, with thick, gelatinous spines *Hohenbuehelia mastrucata* (see no. 109)

13a) Cap pale to cinnamon-brown, not zoned; gills soft, with ragged edges *Lentinellus ursinus* (see no. 109)

13b) Caps zoned white, gray, and brown; "gills" tough *Lenzites betulinus* (see no. 104)

14a) Fruiting body partially resupinate, with multiple, attached caps; hymenium elongate and mazelike, cascading down trunk; on eastern redcedar *Brunneoporus juniperinus* (see no. 104)

14b) Fruiting body not resupinate, with separate caps; on wood of dead hardwoods go to **15**

15a) Cap brown, zoned; hymenium variably mazelike or gill-like *Daedaleopsis confragosa* (no. 104)

15b) Cap white; hymenium of fine pores that become mazelike toward edge of cap (margin) *Trametes elegans* (see no. 104)

16a) Growing in soil, not growing on wood; cap concentrically zoned with tiny golden-brown fibers *Coltricia cinnamomea* (no. 129)

16b) Growing on wood (sometimes buried); cap zoned or not, but without golden-brown fibers go to **17**

17a) Hymenium toothed, at least in age; fruiting body shelving to lying flat on substrate (resupinate) go to **18**

17b) Hymenium with pores; fruiting body shelving, without a stalk (sessile) or stalked, but not resupinate (or, if initially resupinate, then appearing as pinkish spots surrounded by white edge and later developing overlapping white caps) go to **22**

18a) Fruiting body shelving, not resupinate; cap zoned pale gray and brown, with edge of cap and adjacent teeth purple *Trichaptum biforme* (no. 105)

18b) Fruiting body partially to entirely resupinate; cap if present not zoned, without purple edge go to **19**

19a) Fruiting body bright golden-orange, entirely resupinate; hymenium central, of tiny, soft teeth *Hydnophlebia chrysorhiza* (no. 107)

19b) Fruiting body white to dull olive-brown, partially or entirely resupinate, with or without shelving caps; hymenium with flexible or rigid teeth go to **20**

20a) Fruiting body dull olive-brown *Hydnoporia olivacea* (see no. 106)

20b) Fruiting body white go to **21**

21a) Fruiting body mostly shelving, with caps cascading down dead wood; hymenium initially with flexible teeth *Irpiciporus pachyodon* (no. 106)

21b) Fruiting body mostly resupinate, sometimes with small shelves protruding; hymenium with rigid teeth *Irpex lacteus* (see no. 106)

22a) Fruiting bodies initiating as shallow cups, eventually developing into fan-shaped caps, white or zoned with brown *Poronidulus conchifer* (no. 126)

22b) Fruiting body without shallow cups go to **23**

23a) Fruiting bodies composed of individual stalked caps go to **24**

23b) Fruiting bodies without stalks or large and compound, with several to many caps sometimes joined to a common stalk go to **30**

24a) Fruiting body apparently growing in soil; stalk central, with a black, rootlike base attached to buried wood *Polyporus radicatus* (no. 121)

24b) Fruiting body obviously growing on wood; stalk lateral or off center, or rarely central, but without black, rootlike base go to **25**

25a) Cap glossy (appearing varnished), dark red to orange-brown, with pale (often yellow) edge when young; stalk colored as cap, lateral or off center *Ganoderma curtisii* (no. 112)

25b) Cap not glossy, tan, yellowish brown, orange, reddish brown, brown, or gray; stalk central or lateral go to **26**

26a) Cap gray to brown; pores white, turning brown dramatically when bruised *Ganoderma applanatum* (no. 111)

26b) Cap tan, yellowish brown, orange, or reddish brown; pores white to pale yellow or brown but not bruising go to **27**

27a) Stalk white, light yellow, or brown; pores 1/32–1/16 inch (0.5–2 mm) wide, angular, or hexagonal go to **28**

27b) Stalk blackened, at least in part; pores less than 1/64 inch (0.3 mm) wide, roughly round go to **29**

28a) Cap orange to orangish brown, smooth to slightly scaly at edge; stalk lateral or off center, to 0.5 inches long *Neofavolus alveolaris* (no. 118)

28b) Cap dark brown to yellowish brown, scaly at edge; stalk central, 0.75–2.5 inches long *Lentinus arcularius* (no. 119)

29a) Cap tan, 0.5–2.75 inches broad; stalk black only at base *Cerioporus leptocephalus* (no. 120)

29b) Cap reddish brown, 1.5–8 inches broad; stalk entirely black or black over lower half *Picipes badius* (see no. 120)

30a) Fruiting body soft and easily broken at maturity (in age more rigid), sometimes with many caps joined to a common stalk (compound) and in some species very large go to **31**

30b) Fruiting body tough and leathery or woody at maturity (if spongy, then exuding clear to brown liquid droplets when young); caps single or arising in groups from the substrate but not joined to a common stalk, often shelving go to **37**

31a) Fruiting body tan, of upright caps; pores white, bruising brown, often covering entire surface of cap; usually on buried wood *Abortiporus biennis* (no. 117)

31b) Fruiting body of one or more mostly horizontal caps; pores not covering surface of cap, if pale and bruising, then bruising dark reddish, gray, or black go to **32**

32a) Fruiting body pink, orange, red, or liver-colored, exuding red liquid when cut; pores a lighter shade than cap or orange or red, bruising dark reddish *Fistulina hepatica* (no. 123)

32b) Fruiting body whitish, yellow, orange, or grayish brown, not exuding liquid when cut; pores white or yellow go to **33**

33a) Fruiting body pale (whitish or tan), faintly zoned; pores white; fruiting body not bruising *Bondarzewia berkeleyi* (no. 115)

33b) Fruiting body yellow, orange, or grayish brown, not zoned; pores white to pale yellow; fruiting body bruising or not go to **34**

34a) Fruiting body pale yellow to grayish brown, bruising gray or black *Meripilus sumstinei* (no. 114)

34b) Fruiting body yellow, orange, or grayish brown but not bruising go to **35**

35a) Fruiting body grayish brown; pores white to pale yellow; usually growing in a rosette *Grifola frondosa* (no. 113)

35b) Fruiting body yellow, orange, or pinkish; pores white to bright yellow; shelving or growing in a rosette go to **36**

36a) Fruiting body bright orange above; pores bright yellow, usually shelving *Laetiporus sulphureus* (no. 116)

36b) Fruiting body pinkish orange; pores white, usually growing in a rosette *Laetiporus cincinnatus* (see no. 116)

37a) Cap bright cinnabar-red, sometimes with subtle, concolorous zoning; not resupinate go to **38**

37b) Cap white, gray, rusty, tan, or brown; if zoned, yellow, red, brown, and blue; shelving, resupinate, or globular go to **39**

38a) Cap dull, rough, to 0.75 inches thick, not zoned *Pycnoporus cinnabarinus* (no. 122)

38b) Cap glossy, smooth, to 0.2 inches thick, subtly zoned *Pycnoporus sanguineus* (see no. 122)

39a) Fruiting body exuding clear or brown droplets when young go to **40**

39b) Fruiting body not exuding droplets go to **41**

40a) Fruiting body shelving, spongy to leathery; cap dark brown, to 1.5 inches thick; on dead wood *Ishnoderma resinosum* (no. 110)

40b) Fruiting body globular; cap pale to tan, to 5 inches thick; on living oak *Pseudoinonotus dryadeus* (see no. 110)

41a) Cap pale brown, densely covered with long, pale tawny or grayish hairs *Coriolopsis gallica* (no. 109)

41b) Cap pale to dark brown or zoned, smooth, velvety or fuzzy but not densely hairy go to **42**

42a) Cap thin (to 0.2 inches thick), pliable, and distinctly zoned with contrasting bands of yellow, red, brown, and blue *Trametes versicolor* (no. 127)

42b) Cap not distinctly zoned (if zoned in brown and yellow, then woody and much thicker), white, brown, or grayish brown go to **43**

43a) Fruiting body initially resupinate, appearing as pinkish spots surrounded by white edge on woody substrate; maturing as small, overlapping white caps; pores dull pink *Vitreoporus dichrous* (no. 125)

43b) Fruiting body shelving, occurring singly or a few together, often woody; pores white, yellow, brown, or nearly black go to **44**

44a) Pores white or pale yellow, bruising dark brown go to **45**

44b) Pores white, yellow, brown, or nearly black but not bruising go to **46**

45a) Cap glossy (appearing varnished), dark red to orange-brown, with pale (often yellow) edge; pores white to pale yellow *Ganoderma resinaceum* (see no. 112)

45b) Cap dull, gray to brown; pores white, turning brown dramatically when bruised *Ganoderma applanatum* (no. 111)

46a) Pores yellowish brown to reddish brown; fruiting body primarily on black locust trees *Phellinus robiniae* (see no. 111)

46b) Pores white, light brown, grayish brown, dark reddish brown, or nearly black; on other tree species go to **47**

47a) Cap pale; pores white or light brown; usually on ash trees *Perenniporia fraxinea* (see no. 111)

47b) Cap dark rusty brown, usually subtly zoned; pores reddish brown at first, then nearly black; fruiting on oak *Phellinus gilvus* (no. 108)

---

103. *Panus conchatus* Not edible

Violet oyster

This lovely little group of *Panus conchatus* is typical of young specimens; with age they change to a dull tan. The concave to somewhat funnel-shaped caps are covered in a short fuzz. The gills run down the off-center stalk; the basal white fuzz (mycelium) pictured is typical. This species grows on wood, as does the true oyster mushroom (*Pleurotus ostreatus* [no. 38]), so they can be confused, but the flesh of *P. conchatus* is thinner and tough. *Panus conchatus* actually does belong to the order Polyporales, though its spore-bearing surface indisputably looks like gills; genetics tell us its family, Panaceae, is a member of the polypores. It is found from summer to early fall in oak woods.

Description: **Cap**: 3–8 cm wide, fuzz-covered, concave to funnel-shaped, violet when young, tan in age. **Hymenium**: decurrent and gill-like, often forking, initially white, yellow, purple, maturing pale brown. **Stalk**: 2–8 cm long, 1–3 cm thick, off center. **Spore print**: white. **Spores**: 4–6 × 2.5–4 µm, nonamyloid. **Season**: summer–early fall. **Ecology**: saprotrophic.

103. *Panus conchatus*

104. ***Daedaleopsis confragosa*** Not edible

Syn. = *Daedalea confragosa*

Daedaleopsis confragosa fruits on dead deciduous wood during late summer and fall in Kansas, but old fruiting bodies may be found year-round. Its caps are smooth, sometimes radially wrinkled, and clearly zoned with various shades of brown, as shown in the photograph. The underlying tube layer is exceedingly variable in pore shape. Pores may be angular, radially elongate, or mazelike. To confuse matters further, the pore walls can even resemble gills. Numerous other polypores with gills or mazelike pores fruit in Kansas. *Trametes elegans* (syn. = *Daedalea ambigua*) has minute, mostly mazelike pores (2–3 per mm), particularly toward the cap edge, and is common. From a distance, its large white caps are often mistaken for the oyster mushroom (*Pleurotus ostreatus* [no. 38]). *Brunneoporus juniperinus* (syn. = *Antrodia juniperina*), which was first described from Kansas, fruits on eastern redcedar (*Juniperus virginiana*) and has large, mazelike pores (greater than 1 mm wide) with thick, blunt walls, often looking like a waterfall down a cedar. *Lenzites betulinus* has a velvety to hairy cap that is zoned brown and gray; its undersurface is whitish and strictly gill-like.

Description: **Cap**: 3–15 cm broad, 0.2–2 cm thick, fan-shaped, concentrically zoned with brown, smooth, often radially wrinkled, leathery. **Hymenium**:

104. *Daedaleopsis confragosa*

mazelike pores or with gill-like walls, white to brown, sometimes bruising pink, 0.5–1.5 mm wide, angular, radially elongate. **Stalk**: absent. **Spore print**: white. **Spores**: 7–9 × 2–2.5 µm, cylindrical, smooth, nonamyloid. **Season**: late summer–fall. **Ecology**: saprotrophic.

105. *Trichaptum biforme*

Not edible

Violet tooth

These purple-edged shelves are beautiful when young but will become whitish with age. The undersurface, where the spores are made (the hymenium), begins as angular pores, but the walls between these pores erode so that the surface becomes toothed. This area, especially the edges, is purple like the upper fuzzy portion. *Trichaptum biforme* grows on dead wood. It is thin but tough so may be found year-round, though bleached.

Description: **Cap**: 2–6 cm broad, 3 mm thick, pale zoned, overlapping shell-shaped. **Hymenium**: pores initially, then teeth. **Stalk**: absent. **Spore print**: white. **Spores**: 5–8 × 2–2.5 µm. **Season**: year-round. **Ecology**: saprotrophic.

105. *Trichaptum biforme*

106. *Irpiciporus pachyodon* Not edible
Syn. = *Spongipellis pachyodon*

Irpiciporus pachyodon is one of a number of "polypores" (actually a member of the family Meruliaceae) whose pores erode into teeth. This species is softer and more flexible than the thin, white, resupinate (lying flat against the wood it's growing on) *Irpex lacteus* or the initially purple-edged, darker *Trichaptum biforme* (no. 105). Another thin, tough, toothed resupinate species, but colored a dull olive-brown, is *Hydnoporia olivacea* (syn. = *Hydnochaete olivacea*). Like *Irpex lacteus, Irpiciporus pachyodon* can be resupinate, but while both have white, furry, shelving caps, *I. pachyodon* has larger, flexible caps and teeth, Still, this species is much tougher than the edible, toothed members of the genus *Hericium*. Very old specimens become rigid. The fruiting bodies are found on dead wood in late spring through fall.

Description: **Fruiting body**: 5–20 cm broad, shelving to resupinate, white. **Hymenium**: flexible teeth, white. **Stalk**: absent. **Spore print**: probably white. **Spores**: 5.5–7.5 × 5–6 µm, ovoid, smooth. **Season**: late spring–fall. **Ecology**: saprotrophic, possibly parasitic.

106. *Irpiciporus pachyodon*

107. *Hydnophlebia chrysorhiza* Not edible

Syn. = *Phanerochaete chrysorhiza*

Golden root

This golden to orange, sprawling, soft, toothed species is found on well-rotted hard wood, usually on the underside or protected areas of that wood. The fruiting body lies flat against its substrate (resupinate). A distinguishing attribute, besides color and tiny teeth, is the presence of thick, bright, ropy strands extending from the edges. *Hydnophlebia chrysorhizon* is usually seen in the summer.

107. *Hydnophlebia chrysorhiza*

Description: **Fruiting body**: approximately 5–12 × 6–11 cm, resupinate, bright golden to orange, sometimes with edge strands that are paler but comparatively thick and cord-like, leading away from the main body. **Hymenium**: teeth, tiny, centrally located. **Stalk**: absent. **Spore print**: not obtained. **Spores**: 3.5–4.5 × 2–2.5 μm. **Season**: summer. **Ecology**: saprotrophic.

108. *Phellinus gilvus* Not edible

Syn. = *Fuscoporia gilva*

Oak conk

This ubiquitous shelf does not necessarily resemble the picture here, as the fruiting body can last through seasons, and so, as expected, its appearance will change. The typically zoned specimen presented is fairly young but not young enough to have the yellow growing edge. The old fruiting bodies turn almost black, though the center part long remains rusty-colored, as can be seen if you break one open. Initially the species is corky, but ultimately it is hard and rigid. It grows in multiples on dead oak.

108. *Phellinus gilvus*

Description: **Fruiting body**: 2.5–15 cm broad, 1–3 cm thick, shell-shaped, when young usually subtly zoned in rust or brown with yellow growing edge, corky, with a velvety surface, in age hard, almost black, uniform, with a rusty interior. **Hymenium**: pores, grayish brown to dark reddish brown, then nearly black, tiny. **Stalk**: absent. **Spore print**: reported whitish (very hard to get prints from some conks). **Spores**: 4–5 × 2.5 µm, elliptical, smooth. **Season**: year-round. **Ecology**: saprotrophic.

109. *Coriolopsis gallica* — Not edible

This furry little polypore fruits in overlapping clusters (and occasionally occurs singly) on dead wood; often this substrate is cottonwood or willow. *Coriolopsis gallica* has pale brown angular pores (which sometimes erode) and, as seen in the picture, a pale tan to grayish, thickly hairy upper surface. Its durable consistency allows it to be found year-round. The species is considered unusual but may just be overlooked because it is unobtrusive. Other hairy-topped shelves are *Lentinellus ursinus* (a member of the Russulales), which is distinguished by its gills with ragged edges, and *Hohenbuehelia*. Like *Lentinellus*, *Hohenbuehelia* species (which are members of the Agaricales, related to oyster mushrooms) also bear gills and differ from *Coriolopsis* in having a gelatinized layer, making them rather rubbery. The cap of *Hohenbuehelia atrocoerulea* var. *grisea* is finely fuzzy, especially near the point of

109. *Coriolopsis gallica*

attachment; however, the cap of *H. mastrucata* is covered with thick, gelatinous spines.

Description: **Cap**: 3–10 cm broad, fan-shaped with pale tawny to grayish dense, long hairs, usually clustered. **Hymenium**: pores, angular, obvious, gray-brown. **Stalk**: absent. **Spore print**: unobtainable. **Spores**: variable in size, 10–16 × 3–5 μm, smooth, cylindrical. **Season**: year-round. **Ecology**: saprotrophic.

110. *Ischnoderma resinosum* Not edible

Ischnoderma resinosum fruits singly or clustered on hardwood logs and stumps during the fall in Kansas. Old fruiting bodies may persist into winter. In contrast to those of woody conks, the caps have a spongy consistency. When young and fresh, they copiously exude brownish droplets, which are well illustrated in the photograph. In addition, note the dark brown upper surface and the white tube layer that often extends downward at the base. Other fleshy annual polypores also exude droplets when young—for example, the rounder, paler *Pseudoinonotus dryadeus* (syn. = *Inonotus dryadeus* [Ed. 1]), which has a thick cap (2.5–12 cm) with a granular core and brown

110. *Ischnoderma resinosum*

tubes and prefers the trunks of living oaks. In age it becomes woody and tough.

Description: **Cap**: 7–25 cm broad, 0.8–4 cm thick, shelflike with rounded margin, dark brown, velvety becoming smooth, concentrically furrowed, radially wrinkled, exuding clear to brown droplets when young, spongy to leathery. **Hymenium**: pores, white to tan; pores 4–6 per mm, round to angular, bruising brown. **Stalk**: absent. **Spore print**: white. **Spores**: 4–7 × 1.5–2 µm, cylindrical to sausage-shaped, smooth, nonamyloid. **Season**: fall. **Ecology**: saprotrophic.

111. *Ganoderma applanatum* — Not edible

Artist's conk

Ganoderma applanatum is the archetypical conk: large, shelflike, and woody. It rarely has a short stalk, which is sometimes varnished-looking. Though widespread and abundant throughout most of North America, it appears to be rather uncommon in Kansas. The fruiting bodies, which are perennial on logs and on dead or dying trees, often attain massive proportions—a well-placed fruiting body can serve as a picnic tray. The gray to brown caps are sometimes powdered with rusty-brown spores that have been carried up by air currents. Underneath are minute white pores that bruise brown so readily that inspired mushroomers often draw or write on the undersurface, which is why this polypore is called the artist's conk. If the mushroom is too dry to write on, soak it overnight, and it will become writable again. By breaking the fruiting body in half, one can see the successive tube layers that resemble the growth rings on trees. Two other common woody tree parasites in Kansas are *Phellinus robiniae* (syns. = *Fomes rimosus*, *P. rimosus*), which has yellowish-brown to reddish-brown pores and a preference for black locust in Kansas, and *Perenniporia fraxinea* (syns. = *Fomes fraxinophilus*, *Fomitopsis fraxinophilus*), which has white to light brown pores and a fondness for ash (occasionally post oak). Both species have hoof- to shelf-shaped fruiting bodies, but their pores, unlike those of *G. applanatum*, do not bruise brown.

Description: **Cap**: 5–60 cm broad, 1.5–10 cm thick, shelf- or hoof-shaped, woody, gray to brown, unpolished, concentrically grooved, often cracked; flesh rusty brown. **Hymenium**: white pores becoming brown with age, stratified with successive layers; pores 4–6 per mm, round, bruising dark brown. **Stalk**: rarely present. **Spore print**: reddish brown. **Spores**: 6–9 × 4.5–6 µm, broadly elliptical, appearing spiny. **Season:** summer through fall. **Ecology**: saprotrophic, sometimes parasitic.

111. *Ganoderma applanatum*

112. *Ganoderma curtisii* Not edible

Ganoderma lucidum (Ed. 1, misapplied)
Lingzhi
Reishi

This polypore commonly fruits in Kansas at the bases of hardwood trees and stumps. Its more famous cousin, *Ganoderma lucidum*, is native to Eurasia, although recent introductions from cultivation appear to have resulted in established populations in some places in the western United States. The fruiting bodies are annual and first appear as white knot-like structures during the summer and fall. A reddish-brown cap later forms and eventually becomes highly varnished. This varnish imparts an artificially lacquered appearance to the fruiting body, making it a favorite for decoration; old fruiting bodies found out of season are dull and unvarnished. If the stalk is absent, then you may have found *G. resinaceum* (syn. = *G. sessile*), which has larger spores and whose internal flesh isn't darkly banded, as it is in *G. curtisii*. The specimen illustrated here was removed from the base of a tree; its underlying white tubes are not visible. In Chinese culture, the varnished ganodermas represent lingzhi, a phrase meaning "divine mushroom of immortality" or "herb of spiritual potency." Traditionally in China, the fruiting bodies are pulverized and used for various medicinal purposes. Currently reishi has an unsubstantiated reputation as a medicament in the Americas.

112. *Ganoderma curtisii*

Description: **Cap**: 2–20 cm broad, fan- or kidney-shaped, dark red to orange-brown, often yellow near margin, lightly zoned or furrowed, varnished, leathery when fresh. **Hymenium**: pores, white to pale yellow, bruising brown, 4–6 per mm, round or angular. **Stalk**: 3–15 cm long, 0.5–4 cm thick, colored as cap, varnished, knobbed, lateral or off center. **Spore print**: brown. **Spores**: 10–12 × –9 µm, elliptical, and appearing warty. **Season**: summer–fall. **Ecology**: saprotrophic, sometimes parasitic.

113. *Grifola frondosa* Edible

Syn. = *Polyporus frondosus*
Hen of the woods

Grifola frondosa, formerly called *Polyporus frondosus* and better known as the hen of the woods, is among the most massive mushrooms found in Kansas. Fruiting bodies of nearly 100 pounds have been reported elsewhere. The specimen illustrated here falls within the more typical 5- to 10-pound range. This mushroom is recognized by its numerous small grayish-brown caps that are laterally joined to a central stalk. The hen of the woods fruits from late summer through fall at the bases of hardwoods, especially oak, and often appears under the same tree for many years. Because of its chewy texture and superb flavor, the location of such a tree is often a closely guarded secret. The

113. *Grifola frondosa*

fruiting bodies tend to be tough unless cooked slowly. *Meripilus sumstinei* (no. 114) has larger caps that bruise black.

Description: **Cap**: 2–8 cm broad, fan-shaped with wavy margin, grayish brown, radially streaked, smooth to faintly hairy, fleshy to leathery, joined together into compound fruiting body up to 60 cm broad. **Hymenium**: pores, white to pale yellow, decurrent, 1–3 per mm, angular. **Stalk**: short, white, smooth, lateral; attached to central common stalk. **Spore print**: white. **Spores**: 5–7 × 3.5–5 µm, broadly elliptical, smooth, nonamyloid. **Season**: late summer–fall. **Ecology**: weakly parasitic and saprotrophic.

114. *Meripilus sumstinei* — Edible with caution

Meripilus giganteus (Ed. 1, misapplied)

This species can be truly gigantic, occasionally reaching 30 pounds or more. It fruits at the bases of hardwood trees and stumps during the late spring and summer in Kansas. When very young, it is pale yellow-cream but soon becomes gray to brown. The caps are joined directly to a stubby central stalk, as is clear from the photograph. The whole fruiting body bruises black, and the pictured specimen soon lost its yellow margins. *Meripilus sumstinei* is best eaten at an immature stage, though caution is advised, since it has caused gastrointestinal upsets, and many complain that it is bitter or sour. Hen of the

114. *Meripilus sumstinei*

woods, *Grifola frondosa* (no. 113), is a much better edible; it has smaller caps that do not bruise black and occurs in the fall.

Description: **Cap**: 6–15 cm broad, fan-shaped, early pale yellow, soon gray-brown, bruising black, radially streaked, slightly hairy, fleshy to leathery, joined together into a compound fruiting body 15 to 60 cm broad. **Hymenium**: pores, white, bruising black, decurrent, 4–7 per mm, angular. **Stalk**: absent on individual caps; central common stalk short, thick, pale yellow becoming brown. **Spore print**: white. **Spores**: 6–7 × 4.5–6 µm, broadly elliptical, smooth. **Season**: late spring–summer. **Ecology**: weakly parasitic and saprotrophic.

115. *Bondarzewia berkeleyi* — Edible

This species is as large as or larger than *Meripilus sumstinei* (no. 114) but does not blacken. The creamy, faintly zoned, thick, fan-shaped fronds are all connected to a short, thick, darker stalk. The dry young caps are smooth (occasionally felty) but become rough and eroded. Rarely seen in Kansas, it was discovered one summer devouring an oak tree in North Lawrence in Douglas County and was written up in the *Transactions of the Kansas Academy of Science* ("Reappearance of the Large Polypore Mushroom, *Bondarzewia berkeleyi*, in Northeastern Kansas"). Amazingly, *B. berkeleyi* is a member of

115. *Bondarzewia berkeleyi*

the order Russulales. It usually grows on living oaks and decaying stumps. When young, the fruiting body is edible, but it later develops an unpleasant taste and a tough consistency. *Bondarzewia berkeleyi* grows in the summer on oaks, probably exclusively.

Description: **Fruiting body**: up to or exceeding 40 cm, large, pale rosette of, initially, somewhat convex, fan-shaped fronds, then flattening and becoming sunken in the center, faintly zoned, surface smooth to felty at first, then eroded and rough. **Hymenium**: pores, white, angular. **Stalk**: 5–10 cm long, 3–5 cm thick, short, distorted. **Spores**: 6–8 μm, spherical, warted, becoming dark blue in iodine or amyloid in Melzer's solution. **Season**: late spring–summer. **Ecology**: parasitic and saprotrophic.

116. *Laetiporus sulphureus* — Edible with caution

Chicken of the woods
Sulphur shelf

Laetiporus sulphureus, also called the sulphur shelf or the chicken of the woods, is a spectacular find in Kansas woodlands. It fruits on logs and stumps and occasionally from tree wounds during summer and fall. Like many polypores, it was formerly placed in the genus *Polyporus*. The photograph illustrates the bright orange cap and the underlying yellow tubes (seen on the

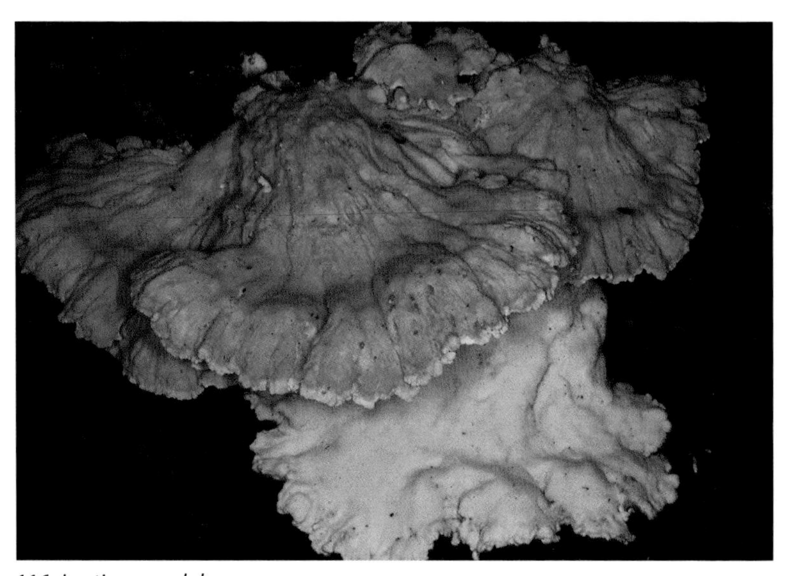

116. *Laetiporus sulphureus*

lower, overturned specimen). Often logs are found littered with the crumbled and bleached remains of large fruitings of this mushroom. These particular fruiting bodies, magnificent as they appear, proved to be thoroughly riddled with insect larvae—an unfortunate circumstance since the sulphur shelf is a choice edible. Tender young caps are best for eating, but the outer growing margin can also be salvaged from older specimens. Gastrointestinal poisonings have been reported, mainly from the western United States, so sample cautiously at first. *Laetiporus cincinnatus*, which is actually the more common species in Kansas, is pinkish orange on top and white beneath. It usually forms rosettes over buried wood, but this is not diagnostic since the more typical sulphur shelf also occasionally grows in this manner.

Description: **Cap**: 5–30 cm broad, fan-shaped with margin lobed and wavy, bright orange to yellow becoming brownish with age, wrinkled, creased, often overlapping, fleshy to leathery. **Hymenium**: pores, yellow, 2–6 per mm, angular. **Stalk**: absent. **Spore print**: white. **Spores**: 5–7 × 3.5–4.5 µm, broadly elliptical, smooth, nonamyloid. **Season**: summer–fall. **Ecology**: parasitic and saprotrophic.

117. *Abortiporus biennis* — Edibility unknown

This distorted, soft tan cap, or perhaps caps, is surrounded and overtaken by coarse white pores that bruise brown in age. Pictured here is a young specimen that will open and show more of the cap(s). Usually found on buried wood even in town, it must be saprotrophic. There are no reports of edibility. It appears in the summer.

117. *Abortiporus biennis*

Description: **Fruiting body**: up to 25 cm broad and tall, with dark tan soft upper cap(s) eventually covered with coarse white pores, bruising brown with age. **Stalk**: absent. **Spore print**: white.

Spores: 5–8 × 3–5 µm, broadly elliptical. **Season**: summer. **Ecology**: saprotrophic.

118. *Neofavolus alveolaris* Not edible

Syn. = *Favolus alveolaris*
Syn. = *Polyporus alveolaris* (Ed. 1)
Syn. = *Polyporus mori*

Neofavolus alveolaris is one of the earliest polypores to fruit in Kansas. Its small orange caps first appear on fallen hardwood branches, especially hickory, during the spring and may persist, weathered and bleached, through the summer. The overturned specimen in the photograph illustrates the large hexagonal pores and the stubby, nearly lateral stalk. The fruiting bodies are reportedly nonpoisonous but tough. Another spring polypore, *Lentinus arcularius* (no. 119), has a scaly brown cap and a well-developed central stalk. Both initially occur in the early spring and may be found through much of the year owing to tough consistency.

Description: **Cap**: 1–8 cm broad, fan- or kidney-shaped, orange to orange-brown, weathering whitish, smooth to slightly scaly, leathery. **Hymenium**: pores, white to light yellow, decurrent, 0.5–2 mm wide, radially elongate, hexagonal. **Stalk**: 0.5–1 cm long, 2–7 mm thick, white to light yellow, lateral or off center. **Spore print**: white. **Spores**: 9–11 × 3–3.5 µm, cylindrical, smooth, nonamyloid. **Season**: spring–summer. **Ecology**: saprotrophic.

118. *Neofavolus alveolaris*

119. *Lentinus arcularius*

119. *Lentinus arcularius* Not edible

Syn. = *Polyporus arcularius* (Ed. 1)

Polypores are scarce in Kansas during the spring except for those that have overwintered. During morel season, *Lentinus arcularius* is the first to appear on decaying hardwood logs and branches. The fruiting bodies may linger into the summer. This stalked polypore is recognized by its scaly brown cap that is centrally attached and by its large angular pores. Several to many fruiting bodies often occur on a single log, as shown in the photograph. *Neofavolus alveolaris* (no. 118) also has large pores but differs in its orange cap and stubby lateral or off-center stalk.

Description: **Cap**: 1–8 cm broad, convex to vase-shaped, dark brown to yellowish brown, scaly, hairy at margin, leathery. **Hymenium**: pores, white to pale yellow, decurrent, 1–2 per mm, angular. **Stalk**: 2–6 cm long, 2–4 mm thick, brown, scaly, central. **Spore print**: white. **Spores**: 7–11 × 2–3 µm, cylindrical, smooth, nonamyloid. **Season**: spring–summer. **Ecology**: saprotrophic.

120. ***Cerioporus leptocephalus*** Not edible

Syn. = *Polyporus elegans* (Ed. 1)

Cerioporus leptocephalus fruits on fallen branches and logs during the fall in Kansas. This stalked polypore can be identified by its tan cap and black foot, both of which are shown in the photograph. The pores on the undersurface of the cap are minute and not visible on the upturned specimen. A similar, more conspicuous species also growing on wood in Kansas, *Picipes badius* (syns. = *Polyporus badius* [Ed. 1], *Royoporus badius*), has a larger reddish-brown cap (4–20 cm broad). Its stalk is entirely black or blackened over the lower half. *Lentinus arcularius* (no. 119) and *Neofavolus alveolaris* (no. 118) lack black stalks.

Description: **Cap**: 1.5–7 cm broad, round to kidney-shaped convex becoming depressed, tan, smooth, leathery. **Hymenium**: pores, white becoming gray or light brown, decurrent, 4–5 per mm, angular. **Stalk**: 0.5–8 cm long, 2–6 mm thick, tan with black foot, smooth, lateral to central. **Spore print**: white. **Spores**: 6–10 × 2.5–3.5 µm, cylindrical, smooth, nonamyloid. **Season**: fall. **Ecology**: saprotrophic.

120. *Cerioporus leptocephalus*

121. ***Polyporus radicatus***

Edible when young

Rooting polypore

The rooting polypore fruits in deciduous forests during late summer and early fall in Kansas. Because of its stalked cap with underlying tubes and its seemingly terrestrial habit, this polypore is commonly mistaken for a bolete. However, the fruiting bodies are leathery, and their tube layers, unlike those of boletes, do not readily separate from the caps. The common name refers to the black rootlike base that penetrates deeply into soil down to buried wood. The specimen illustrated here was carefully excavated to avoid snapping off its root, which is unusually short. Its minute pores are not visible. *Cerioporus leptocephalus* (no. 120) fruits directly on wood and lacks a rooting base.

121. *Polyporus radicatus*

Description: **Cap**: 4–25 cm broad, convex or slightly depressed, yellowish brown, scaly, leathery. **Hymenium**: pores, white to light yellow, decurrent, 2–3 per mm, angular. **Stalk**: 6–13 cm long, 0.5–2.5 cm thick, yellowish brown, scaly, central; base black, deeply rooting. **Spore print**: white. **Spores**: 12–15 × 6–8 µm, elliptical, smooth, nonamyloid. **Season**: late summer–early fall. **Ecology**: saprotrophic.

122. ***Pycnoporus cinnabarinus***

Not edible

The brilliant cinnabar-red cap of *Pycnoporus cinnabarinus* is easily spotted in the forested areas of Kansas, where it fruits on logs and fallen branches during summer and fall. Old, bleached fruiting bodies are often found in other seasons. The caps are roughened, and their underlying tubes (not visible in the photograph) are also colored cinnabar-red. When growing on

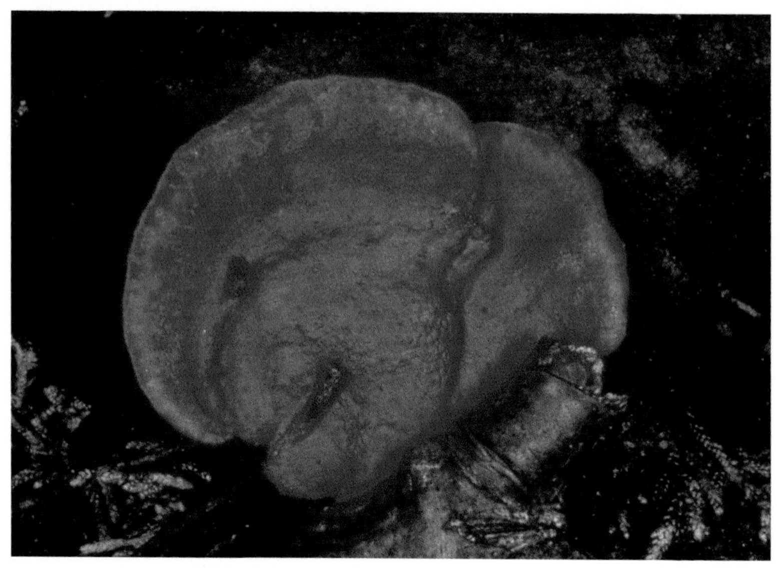

122. *Pycnoporus cinnabarinus*

top of logs, the fruiting bodies rarely form stubby central stalks. *Pycnoporus sanguineus* is similarly colored and subtly zoned and has a smooth, shiny cap that is much thinner (2–5 mm) than that of *P. cinnabarinus*. It is considered more southerly in distribution than *P. cinnabarinus*, but their ranges overlap in Kansas, as do those of many other plants and fungi with northern and southern species.

Description: **Cap**: 2–12 cm broad, 0.5–2 cm thick, fan- to kidney-shaped, cinnabar-red, dull, roughened, often wrinkled, leathery. **Hymenium**: pores, cinnabar-red, 2–4 per mm, round to angular or slightly mazelike. **Stalk**: absent or rarely short and central. **Spore print**: white. **Spores**: 4.5–6 × 2–3 μm, elliptical, smooth, nonamyloid. **Season**: summer–fall. **Ecology**: saprotrophic.

123. *Fistulina hepatica* — Edible

Beefsteak
Ox tongue

This bizarre species is rare in Kansas. The illustration shows a deep, finely mottled pink color, but colors of the beefsteak fungus reportedly range from pink through orange and red to liver-colored, probably darkening with age. The thick, often lobed fruiting body has a soft, felty feel. Internally it has

123. *Fistulina hepatica*

pale streaks and a juicy consistency, even "bleeding" a red liquid. The tubes on the underside are not connected with each other and are a lighter color than the felty, smooth upper surface. Despite its polypore-like appearance, the genus *Fistulina* belongs to the family Fistinulinaceae, a member of the order Agaricales. The taste is sour, not resembling meat except in texture. This specimen was growing from a small oak, about shoulder high, but according to the literature, they usually grow at the base of oaks. The species is found in the summer. Many people call *Discina caroliniana* (no. 178) "beefsteak"; the Latin name helps to distinguish this false morel from *Fistulina hepatica*, at least in conversation.

Description: **Fruiting body**: 7–25 cm broad, 2–6 cm thick, fan-shaped to lobed; pink, orange, red, or liver-colored, felty, soft; interior exuding red juice, having lighter streaks. **Hymenium**: pores, lighter than cap, bruising dark reddish, round, discrete. **Stalk**: absent. **Spore print**: pale reddish brown. **Spores**: 4–6 × 3–4 µm, elliptical, smooth. **Season**: summer. **Ecology**: saprotrophic, weakly parasitic.

124. ***Byssomerulius incarnatus*** Not edible

Syn. = *Merulius incarnatus*
Syn. = *Phlebia incarnata*

This beautiful shelving coral-pink polypore is sometimes found with coloration the reverse of what is pictured here; that is, rather than having a bright pink top and white fertile surface (hymenium), it has a white top and pink underside. The hymenium is not truly pored but instead is wrinkled, which is not clear in the picture. With either color pattern, the cap is minutely fuzzy. The flesh is soft and flabby, becoming hard. The fruiting bodies are found in Kansas, summer through fall, growing on wood.

Description: **Cap**: 2–7 cm broad, several together as overlapping shelves, covered in low fuzz, white or coral-pink wavy scalloped margin. **Hymenium**: wrinkled, white or coral-pink radiating. **Stalk**: absent. **Spore print**: white. **Spores**: 4–5 × 2–2.5 μm, smooth, elliptical. **Season**: summer–fall. **Ecology**: saprotrophic.

124. *Byssomerulius incarnatus*

125. *Vitreoporus dichrous* Not edible

Syn. = *Gloeoporus dichrous*

The pictured *Vitreoporus dichrous* are fully mature; the darker one with a pinkish-brown surface shows the pore-like fertile area. The other specimens illustrate the pale, slightly zoned, scurfy tops of this shelving species. The fruiting body is flexible at first but in old age is hard. In youth, *V. dichrous* may appear as pinkish spots, resupinate—lying flat on its substrate wood—ringed with white. This species will occur fresh in late spring through fall, but tattered remains may be seen all year.

Description: **Fruiting body**: caps 2–5 cm broad, individual, though always found in groups arranged along its substrate, often overlapping when shelving, white, fuzzy, faintly zoned, sometimes in youth completely resupinate as pinkish spots surrounded by white; flexible when young, rigid in age. **Hymenium**: pores, pinkish brown and fine, irregular, stiff but gelatinous. **Stalk**: absent. **Spore print**: unavailable. **Spores**: 3.5–5.5 × 0.7–1.5 µm, slightly curved, sausage-shaped to oval. **Season**: late spring–fall. **Ecology**: saprotrophic.

125. *Vitreoporus dichrous*

126. *Poronidulus conchifer* Not edible

Of the many polypores reported from Kansas, *Poronidulus conchifer* is perhaps the oddest. It fruits gregariously on dead hardwood branches, especially elm, during late summer and fall. Old fruiting bodies are often seen during other seasons. The specimens pictured here were among several dozen that lined the branch of a standing dead elm. The fruiting bodies start as shallow cups, which are present in the photograph. These cups contain asexual spores

126. *Poronidulus conchifer*

that are splashed to distant sites by large raindrops in a manner similar to the dispersal of eggs from the "splash cups" of bird's nest fungi. As seen in the foreground specimens, fan-shaped caps eventually arise from the cups, which remain at the base of the cap. The cap undersurface (not shown here) bears white tubes that produce sexual spores.

Description: **Cap**: 1–5 cm broad, 0.5–1 mm thick, fan-shaped, white or zoned with brown, smooth, leathery, arising from cup at base; cup 0.5–2 cm broad, white or zoned with brown, smooth or bearing tubes on undersurface. **Hymenium**: pores, white to pale yellow, 2–3 per mm, angular. **Stalk**: absent or short and lateral. **Spore print**: white. **Spores**: 5–7 × 1.5–2.5 µm, cylindrical, smooth, nonamyloid. **Season**: late summer–fall. **Ecology**: saprotrophic.

127. *Trametes versicolor* — Not edible

Syn. = *Coriolus versicolor*
Syn. = *Polyporus versicolor*
Turkey tail

Trametes versicolor is possibly the most widespread polypore in Kansas. It fruits in overlapping clusters on hardwood stumps and logs during summer and fall, but faded fruiting bodies often persist through winter and spring. The common name, turkey tail, refers to the zoned, multicolored fan-shaped cap that often resembles a turkey tail in full display. Like snowflakes, no two caps are alike in pattern. The caps illustrated here were clustered on a log, but they also form rosettes when arising from buried wood. Their white

127. *Trametes versicolor*

undersurface, not shown, has minute pores. Other similarly zoned wood rotters fruit in Kansas and can often be distinguished by their undersurface. *Trichaptum biforme* (no. 105) has a purple cap margin and purple-tinged pores, the walls of which become spiny with age. *Stereum hirsutum* (no. 130) and *S. ostrea* (no. 131) are smooth underneath.

Description: **Cap**: 2–7 cm broad, 1–3 mm thick, fan-shaped, overlapping, leathery, concentrically zoned with contrasting shades of yellow, red, brown, and blue; zones alternately velvety and smooth. **Hymenium**: pores, white to pale yellow, 3–5 per mm, angular. **Stalk**: absent. **Spore print**: white. **Spores**: 4–6 × 1.5–2 μm, cylindrical to sausage-shaped, smooth, nonamyloid. **Season**: summer–fall. **Ecology**: saprotrophic.

128. *Coltricia montagnei* — Not edible

This species is quite rare, unusually formed, and beautiful in its own way. Most notable is the fertile surface, which looks like gills that encircle the stalk, spreading in concentric rings out to the underside edge of the cap. These "gills" are rigid and sometimes have connecting walls making them rather like elongated pores, though *Coltricia montagnei* belongs to the order Hymenochaetales rather than Polyporales. The cap is a velvety reddish brown, though reported elsewhere as varying in shades of brown, with a sunken center. The surface is uneven, and so is the edge (margin), as is apparent in

128. *Coltricia montagnei*

the photograph. The "gills" are paler than the cap. The misshapen stalk is also a velvety red-brown and narrows toward the bottom. This fruiting body was found in July under oaks.

Description: **Cap**: 3–14 cm broad, velvety reddish brown or other shades of brown, sometimes faintly zoned, flat to sunken in the center. **Hymenium**: rigid concentric plates, sometimes broken by walls, paler than cap. **Stalk**: 3–12 cm long, 0.5 to 1.5 cm thick, misshapen, narrowing at base, velvety, concolorous with cap. **Spore print**: pale brown. **Spores**: 9–15 × 5–7.5 µm, smooth, elliptical. **Season**: summer. **Ecology**: saprotrophic, though possibly biotrophic.

129. *Coltricia cinnamomea* Inedible

Coltricia cinnamomea is uncommon in Kansas, though it may be regularly overlooked since it is so small. The fruiting bodies are lovely with zoned shades of rusty brown. The sheen of tiny fibers radiating out from the darker center is not well illustrated in the picture. The underside producing the spores is an interesting shallow, pored surface of reddish brown. The small stalk is also rusty brown with a suede-like finish. With its much rarer cousin *C. montagnei* (no. 128), it is found on the ground in Kansas woods.

Description: **Cap**: 1–4 cm, thin, concentrically ringed in rusty-brown colors, textured with tiny shiny fibers. **Hymenium**: pores, even rusty brown, shallow,

129. *Coltricia cinnamomea*

somewhat angular. **Stalk**: 1–4 cm long, 0.1–0.4 thick reddish-brown velvety surface. **Spore print**: yellowish brown. **Spores**: 6–10 × 4.5–7 µm, elliptical, smooth. **Season**: summer. **Ecology**: mycorrhizal and saprotrophic.

130. *Stereum hirsutum* Inedible

Massive overlapping clusters of *Stereum hirsutum* are a common sight on hardwood logs in Kansas. This parchment fungus grows during summer and fall, but old fruiting bodies may be found in other seasons. Concentric zones of stiff, matted hairs, which range from gray to various shades of brown, coat the upper surface. These zones are separated by narrow hairless zones that reveal the underlying reddish-brown surface of the cap. The two overturned caps in the center of the photograph show the smooth brown undersurface where spores are produced. Remarkably, the *Stereum* species belong to the order Russulales. The false turkey tail, *S. ostrea* (no. 131), is only minutely hairy; zoned polypores that are superficially similar, such as *Trametes versicolor* (no. 127), have underlying tubes.

Description: **Cap**: 1–5 cm broad, fan-shaped, clustered with margins often fused, concentrically zoned gray, yellow, and brown, covered with stiff,

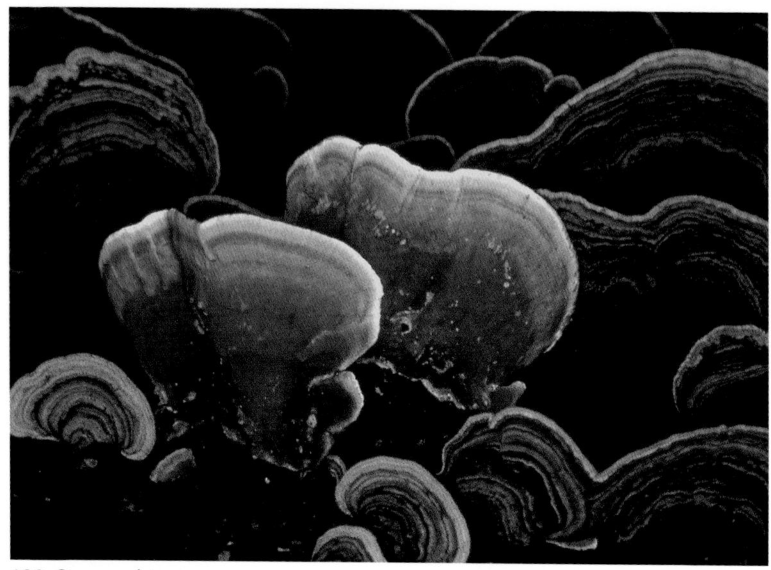

130. *Stereum hirsutum*

densely matted hairs, smooth and reddish brown between zones, leathery. **Hymenium**: smooth to wrinkled, brown, staining yellow when fresh. **Stalk**: absent. **Spore print**: white. **Spores**: 5–8 × 2–3.5 µm, cylindrical, smooth, amyloid. **Season**: summer–fall. **Ecology**: saprotrophic.

131. *Stereum ostrea* Inedible

Syn. = *Stereum fasciatum*

False turkey tail

The false turkey tail fruits clustered on dead wood during summer and fall in Kansas. Old fruiting bodies often persist through the winter and the following spring. The caps are minutely hairy, multicolored, and conspicuously zoned. The spore-bearing undersurface (not shown in the photograph) is smooth and yellow-orange to brown. Similar species include *Stereum hirsutum* (no. 130), which is also multicolored and zoned but can be distinguished from the false turkey tail by its coating of stiff, matted hairs, and *S. complicatum* (syn. = *S. rameale*), which forms dense clusters of smaller, radially furrowed caps that are zoned with yellows and cinnamon-browns. The pores of the true turkey tail, *Trametes versicolor* (no. 127), may be inconspicuous when young; examine your specimen closely with a hand lens.

131. *Stereum ostrea*

Description: **Cap**: 1–6 cm broad, fan-shaped, concentrically zoned gray, tan, and reddish brown, minutely hairy with alternating smooth zones, leathery. **Hymenium**: smooth, yellow-orange to brown. **Stalk**: absent. **Spore print**: white. **Spores**: 5.5–7.5 × 2–3 μm, cylindrical, smooth, amyloid. **Season**: summer–fall. **Ecology**: saprotrophic.

132. *Cotylidia diaphana*

Not edible

Syn. = *Stereum diaphanum*

This odd stalked parchment fungus has been collected during late spring in the hardwood forests of eastern Kansas. With its trumpet-shaped cap and terrestrial growth habit, it superficially resembles an albino horn of plenty (*Craterellus fallax* [no. 136]). However, this mushroom is tougher and belongs in the order Hymenochaetales. The upper surface is often faintly zoned, as seen on the upright fruiting body in the photograph. The overturned fused pair of fruiting bodies illustrates the smooth spore-bearing undersurface.

Description: **Cap**: 1–5 cm broad, 0.5–3 cm tall, funnel-shaped with lobed margin, white to light brown, often zoned, faintly hairy, leathery. **Hymenium**: smooth, often creased, white. **Stalk**: 0.5–4 cm long, 1–5 mm thick, white, smooth, central. **Spore print**: white. **Spores**: 4–6 × 2.5–4 μm, elliptical, smooth, nonamyloid. **Season**: late spring. **Ecology**: possibly biotrophic.

132. *Cotylidia diaphana*

133. *Chondrostereum purpureum* Not edible

Syn. = *Stereum purpureum*

Silver leaf fungus

Of the many crust-like wood rotters reported from Kansas, *Chondostereum purpureum* is one of the few that can be recognized without a microscope. It fruits on hardwood branches and logs during summer and early fall. The

133. *Chondrostereum purpureum*

photograph shows the purple crust-like fruiting bodies that produce spores on their smooth exposed surfaces. The margins on these crusts may also form brown shelflike caps with purple undersurfaces. The common name, silver leaf fungus, refers to the disease caused by the fungus as it attacks hardwood trees, especially apple and plum, and kills their branches or even the entire tree. This disease produces a silvery sheen on the leaves of the host. The fruiting bodies pictured here were found on a recently fallen tree limb.

Description: **Fruiting body**: crust-like, purple, smooth to wrinkled; margin sometimes forming irregular shelflike brown caps 0.5–2 cm broad. **Hymenium**: smooth, purple. **Stalk**: absent. **Spore print**: white. **Spores**: 5–6.5 × 2–3 μm, cylindrical, smooth, nonamyloid. **Season**: summer–early fall. **Ecology**: parasitic and saprotrophic.

Orders Cantharellales, Gomphales, and Thelephorales and some atypical members of other orders: Chanterelles, corals, and tooth mushrooms

To the mushroom hunter with culinary instincts, these orders are worth knowing, as they contain world-class edibles: the vase-shaped chanterelles and dark horn of plenty. In the order Cantharellales, members of the family Cantharellaceae (the chanterelles) are all ground dwelling and probably mycorrhizal. *Hydnum repandum* is also a great edible from the Cantherellales. The corals probably have various lifestyles, from saprotrophic to biotrophic. *Clavulinopsis* belongs to the order Agaricales, while the corals *Clavariadelphus* and *Ramaria* belong to the order Gomphales. Some species of corals are good edibles, but others are of suspect edibility. Two other coral-like genera, *Artomyces* and *Thelephora*, belong to the order Russulales and the order Thelephorales, respectively. Finally, the toothed, wood-inhabiting genus *Hericium* is a member of the Russulales. The capped, tough, toothed species (as well as Sarcodon) belong to the Thelephorales, and the ground-dwelling species *Sebacina schweinitzii* is in the order Sebacinales. There are other surprises in this group, and undoubtedly more will turn up.

Key to species

1a) Fruiting body with cap-like top, the cap sometimes flared or funnel-shaped or reduced to a flat top with a distinct edge (margin) and a thick stalk — go to **2**

1b) Fruiting body without cap, globular-toothed, club-shaped, or highly branched and resembling a coral — go to **12**

2a) Undersurface of cap (hymenium) with teeth — go to **3**

2b) Undersurface of cap (hymenium) undulating, wrinkled, or with blunt, gill-like ridges — go to **6**

3a) Flesh soft, pale to brown; fruiting bodies growing singly — go to **4**

3b) Flesh tough, dark brown, or black; fruiting bodies often fused together — go to **5**

4a) Cap smooth, orangish tan; teeth white to pale tan; flavor mild — *Hydnum repandum* (no. 139)

4b) Cap dark with coarse brown to black scales; teeth pale brown; flavor bitter — *Sarcodon imbricatus* (see no. 139)

5a) Cap gray to black; flesh black; spore print white *Phellodon niger* (no. 140)

5b) Cap brown, zoned with lighter bands; flesh brown; spore print brown *Hydnellum spongiosipes* (see no. 140)

6a) Fruiting body pale purple, cap sometimes reduced to a flat top with a narrow margin overhanging a thick stalk *Pseudocraterellus pseudoclavatus* (no. 143)

6b) Fruiting body yellow or gray to black, cap flared or funnel-shaped go to **7**

7a) Undersurface of cap with blunt, gill-like ridges go to **8**

7b) Undersurface of cap undulating or wrinkled but without gill-like ridges go to **9**

8a) Cap and stalk deep yellow to nearly white *Cantharellus "cibarius"* group (no. 134)

8b) Cap and much of stalk bright red-orange *Cantharellus cinnabarinus* (no. 135)

9a) Cap and stalk yellow *Cantharellus lateritius* (see no. 134)

9b) Cap and stalk gray to black go to **10**

10a) Fruiting bodies often occurring as a clump of distorted caps and stalks, gray or sometimes with a purple cast and a strong, sweet smell *Craterellus foetidus* (no. 138)

10b) Fruiting bodies not clustered, lacking a strong smell go to **11**

11a) Cap 0.75–2.5 inches broad, funnel-shaped with a deep central depression and edges curled back; stalk short, inconspicuous *Craterellus fallax* (no. 136)

11b) Cap to 0.75 inches broad, broadly flaring, with a shallow central depression and a wavy edge; stalk distinct *Pseudocraterellus calyculus* (no. 137)

12a) Growing on wood go to **13**

12b) Growing on ground go to **16**

13a) Fruiting body globular or coral-like but with pendulous spines go to **14**

13b) Fruiting body coral-like, with upright branches go to **15**

14a) Fruiting body a globular mass of white spines, short or long
Hericium erinaceus (no. 142)

14b) Fruiting body consisting of white spines arrayed on short branches
Hericium americanum (no. 141)

15a) Mature fruiting body with branches tipped with minute, crown-like tips; flesh peppery when raw *Artomyces pyxidatus* (no. 148)

15b) Mature fruiting body with pointed tips; flesh bitter
Ramaria stricta (see no. 148)

16a) Fruiting body unbranched, club-shaped or wormlike with even sides, tan or bright yellow go to **17**

16b) Fruiting body branching and coral-like go to **19**

17a) Fruiting body club-shaped, 2.5–8 inches tall; tan bruising brown
Clavariadelphus americanus (no. 144)

17b) Fruiting body wormlike with even sides, 0.5–2.5 inches tall; bright yellow go to **18**

18a) Fruiting bodies growing singly, round in cross-section
Clavulinopsis laeticolor (no. 147)

18b) Fruiting bodies growing in clusters, flattened in cross-section
Clavulinopsis fusiformis (see no. 147)

19a) Fruiting body brilliant pink to red, in age fading to pale orange or yellow *Ramaria araiospora* (no. 145)

19b) Fruiting body not brightly colored, whitish, gray, gray-brown, or pale pastel go to **20**

20a) Fruiting body soft at maturity go to **21**

20b) Fruiting body stiff and cartilaginous at maturity go to **22**

21a) Fruiting body white to various pastel shades at maturity; tips of branches of clustered points *Clavulina coralloides* (no. 146)

21b) Fruiting body gray at maturity; tips of branches blunt
Clavulina cinerea (see no. 146)

22a) Fruiting body white *Sebacina schweinitzii* (see no. 146)

22b) Fruiting body gray-brown go to **23**

23a) Fruiting body with strong, disagreeable odor

Thelephora palmata (see no. 145)

23b) Fruiting body odorless — *Thelephora americana* (see no. 145)

134. *Cantharellus "cibarius"* group — Edible

Yellow chanterelle

Our yellow chanterelle is almost certainly not the *C. cibarius* of European fame, but Kansas does have many yellow to cream-colored delicious chanterelles, apparently associated with hardwoods, particularly oak and hickory, especially in grassy or bushy areas. Teasing out the genetics of these chanterelles is still very much a work in progress. The general shape and characteristics (including the lovely, if faint, fruity odor) of our Kansas species are clearly the same, as they have a stalk and cap, often becoming vase-like. The most important feature, illustrated in the photograph, is the blunt, gill-like ridges that run down the stalk (decurrent) rather than being blade-like, as are true gills. The sunken cap and wavy margin on the upright specimen are characteristic of mature fruiting bodies. It has been claimed that if properly prepared, the yellow chanterelle would "arrest the pangs of death" because of its savoriness. Here is the secret to cooking chanterelles: sauté them slowly, and do not overpower their subtle flavor with harsh spices or thick, greasy sauces. Do not confuse the yellow chanterelle with the poisonous jack-o'-lantern, *Omphalotus illudens* (no. 13), which grows clustered on wood, sometimes buried, and has sharp-edged gills. Another yellow species of chanterelle, *Cantharellus lateritius*, has a smooth to slightly wrinkled undersurface; it is also delectable.

134. *Cantharellus "cibarius"* group

Description: **Cap**: 2–10 cm broad, convex with incurved

margin, becoming flat or depressed with margin wavy, yellow to yellowish orange, smooth; odor often fruity. **Hymenium**: with gill-like ridges, colored as cap or paler, blunt, widely spaced, often forked and cross-veined, decurrent. **Stalk**: 3–8 cm long, 0.5–1.5 cm thick, colored as cap or paler, slowly bruising orange-brown, smooth. **Spore print**: pale yellow. **Spores**: 8–10 × 4.5–5.5 µm, elliptical, smooth, nonamyloid. **Season**: summer–early fall. **Ecology**: mycorrhizal.

135. *Cantharellus cinnabarinus* — Edible

Red chanterelle

The red chanterelle inhabits the hardwood forests of Kansas from late spring through early fall. It differs from the yellow chanterelle, *Cantharellus "cibarius"* group (no. 134), in its cinnabar-red color and smaller size. Note the blunt, decurrent, gill-like ridges running down the stalk of the upturned specimens in the photograph. The fruiting bodies are often redder than those shown here. The red chanterelle commonly fruits in large troops, making it worth collecting for the table. Its flavor rivals that of *C. "cibarius"* group (no. 134).

Description: **Cap**: 1–4 cm broad, convex with incurved margin, becoming flat or depressed with margin wavy, cinnabar-red to pinkish orange, smooth.

135. *Cantharellus cinnabarinus*

Hymenium: with gill-like ridges, colored as cap or paler, gill-like, blunt, usually forked and cross-veined, decurrent. **Stalk**: 2–6 cm long, 0.3–1 cm thick, colored as cap, often with white base, smooth. **Spore print**: pale pink. **Spores**: 7–9 × 4.5–5.5 µm, elliptical, smooth, nonamyloid. **Season**: late spring–early fall. **Ecology**: mycorrhizal.

136. *Craterellus fallax* — Edible

Horn of plenty
Trumpet of death

The unmistakable horn of plenty fruits in deciduous forests during late summer and fall in Kansas. The dark trumpet-shaped fruiting bodies in the photograph are typical. Their somber appearance is no doubt responsible for another common name for this mushroom: the trumpet of death. Note the small scales within the trumpet and the bloom of spores on its smooth outer surface. When sliced and fried, the horn of plenty resembles a shredded tire: never has a fungus looked so unappetizing yet tasted so wonderful. Its chewy texture, fruity aroma, and cheesy flavor make it well worth finding, which in Kansas is all too infrequent. The European *C. cornucopioides* has white spores, while *C. fallax* has salmon-colored spores.

136. *Craterellus fallax*

Description: **Cap**: 2–6 cm broad, 4–8 cm tall, funnel-shaped with curled margin, dark brown, grayish brown, or nearly black, scaly, thin-fleshed; odor fruity. **Hymenium**: smooth to slightly wrinkled, colored as cap, often with light orange bloom. **Stalk**: short, inconspicuous, hollow. **Spore print**: pale salmon. **Spores**: 12–16.5 × 7–10 µm, elliptical, smooth, nonamyloid. **Season**: late summer–fall. **Ecology**: mycorrhizal.

137. *Pseudocraterellus calyculus* — Edibility unknown

Syn. = *Craterellus calyculus*

This minuscule mushroom is probably more prevalent than found. It has a distinct gray stalk about the same color as the dainty, sometimes ruffled, dimpled cap. The undersurface of the cap, where the spores are produced (the hymenium), is lighter and slightly uneven. Oaks are *Pseudocraterellus calyculus*'s preferred mycorrhizal partner. The fruiting body may be edible, but is too tiny to be of any real interest to the mycophagist. Usually this species appears in the summer.

137. *Pseudocraterellus calyculus*

Description: **Cap**: 0.5–2 cm broad, tiny, gray, depressed at center, with wavy margin, thin-fleshed. **Hymenium**: smooth, uneven, pale gray. **Stalk**: 1.5–3.5 cm long, 0.1–0.3 cm thick, columnar, gray, sometimes bowed. **Spore print**: white. **Spores**: 9–12 × 5–7 µm. **Season**: summer. **Ecology**: mycorrhizal.

138. *Craterellus foetidus* — Edible

Like all *Craterellus*, this species is uncommon in Kansas, but it is more conspicuous than the others, as it tends to grow in clumps and has a strong, sweet scent, not altogether pleasant. The undersurface is wrinkled and veined, and the caps are contorted, features that are well illustrated in the picture. Often

138. *Craterellus foetidus*

the cap color has hints of purple and is grayer than shown, although there are reports that this species is lighter-colored in dry weather. *Craterellus foetidus* occurs in oak woods from midsummer into the fall. This particular specimen was found at Perry Lake in Jefferson County.

Description: **Cap**: individually 3.5–10 cm broad, clustered, pale grayish tan, sometimes with purple tones, with a strong, cloying, sweet smell. **Hymenium**: shallowly wrinkled and veined, paler than cap. **Stalk**: 1–3 cm long, distorted by joining other stalks, narrower at base, colored as undersurface of caps. **Spore print**: pale orangish. **Spores**: 8.5–12 × 5–7 µm, elliptical, smooth. **Season**: midsummer–fall. **Ecology**: mycorrhizal.

139. *Hydnum repandum* — Edible

Syn. = *Dentinum repandum*
Hedgehog mushroom
Sweet tooth

Hydnum repandum fruits sporadically under hardwoods during summer and early fall in Kansas. With its commonplace cap and stalk, this mushroom is easily missed within the tedious multitude of gilled mushrooms and boletes—unless overturned to reveal its underlying spines (Fig. 4), which are shown in the photograph. The caps are orange but may fade to tan with age.

139. *Hydnum repandum*

Though specimens in the photograph are not from the central United States, they appear identical in all respects to those from Kansas. *Hydnum repandum* is a first-rate edible with a slight pepperiness reminiscent of watercress. More common in Kansas is *Sarcodon imbricatus*, which has a large cap with coarse, raised brown to black scales and pale brown spines. Though eaten widely in Europe, it tends to be bitter.

Description: **Cap**: 2–15 cm broad, convex with inrolled margin, becoming flat to depressed with margin wavy, orange to tan, bruising dark orange, smooth. **Hymenium**: of spines 0.3–1 cm long, white to pale tan, pendant, pointed, decurrent. **Stalk**: 3–10 cm long, 1–2 cm thick, white to pale orange or tan, smooth, central or off center. **Spore print**: white. **Spores**: 6–8 × 5.5–7 µm, broadly elliptical to round, smooth, nonamyloid. **Season**: summer–early fall. **Ecology**: mycorrhizal.

140. *Phellodon niger* Not edible

Phellodon niger is a European species, so the name of ours will likely be changed, possibly to *P. alboniger*. Our species grows low to the ground, often in moss and under oak. It can be found singly, as shown, but also occurs in clusters with irregular margins grown together. The lumpy cap, often with a depressed center, is gray—sometimes pale, sometimes almost black. The pictured specimen looks almost white, but the margins are often paler than the rest of the cap. The surface is soft and suede-like but hard and black underneath. The soft teeth are whitish at first, then increasingly gray and extend down the stalk. The stalk is brown, thick, irregular, and less suede-like. There are a number of tough, inedible toothed species in Kansas; the variety increases in the southeast. The genus *Hydnellum* is similar. Some *Hydnellum* species found here are brightly colored—orange, yellow, and even blue—though the cap of *H. spongiosipes* is brown with lighter bands. The big difference between the genera *Phellodon* and *Hydnellum* is spore color: *Phellodon* has white spores, and *Hydnellum* has brown, but it is hard to get them to drop their spores. All seem to be mycorrhizal (mutualistic or symbiotic in some manner) with trees, probably oak, where they are most often found in the summer into the fall.

Description: **Cap**: individually 3–5 cm broad, often clustered with fused margins but also found singly, lumpy, with a depressed center, pale to dark gray but margins often lighter and flesh black, with a soft, suede-like exterior and hard interior. **Hymenium**: of teeth, paler than cap, decurrent. **Stalk**: 4–6 cm tall, 1–4 cm thick, brown, irregular, not as suede-like as cap. **Spore color**: white. **Spores**: 3.5–5 × 3–4.5 globose, spiny. **Season**: summer–fall. **Ecology**: mycorrhizal.

140. *Phellodon niger*

141. *Hericium americanum* — Edible

Bear's head

The bear's head fruits on hardwood logs and stumps during late summer and fall in Kansas, where it is most often collected along the floodplains of major rivers. This spectacular mushroom is easily recognized by its coral-like fruiting body, which has clusters of spines hanging from the ends of short

141. *Hericium americanum*

branches. Strangely enough, the genus *Hericium* belongs to the order Russulales. The specimen illustrated here was the smallest of three fruiting bodies that appeared for several consecutive falls on the same log. Though a choice edible that goes well with most mushroom recipes, the bear's head is often left unpicked, its beauty being its best protection. *Hericium coralloides*, mentioned as a synonym of *H. americanum* in the first edition of this book, is a different species.

Description: **Fruiting body**: 10–30 cm broad, 20–40 cm tall, coral-like with clusters of spines on branch ends, white aging to yellow or brown. **Hymenium**: of spines 0.5–1.5 cm long, pendant, pointed. **Stalk**: absent. **Spore print**: white. **Spores**: 5–6.5 × 4.5–5.5 µm, broadly elliptical to round, smooth or finely roughened, amyloid. **Season**: late summer–fall. **Ecology**: saprotrophic, possibly parasitic

142. *Hericium erinaceus* — Edible

Lion's mane

This beautiful *Hericium* fruits from wounds on hardwood trees during the fall in Kansas. It also occasionally occurs on logs and stumps. The white globular fruiting body with its long, hanging spines is unmistakable. *Hericium erinaceus* is a fine edible but tends to be tough unless cooked slowly. Some *H. erinaceus* have short spines (less than 0.5 cm long) and are called subspecies *erinaceo-abietis*, and others have long ones. One Kansas short-spined specimen that was found in Lawrence, in Douglas County, tipped the scales at 25 pounds.

Description: **Fruiting body**: 10–25 cm broad, globular, unbranched, white to yellow-brown. **Hymenium**: of spines 1–6 cm long, pendant, pointed. **Stalk**: short or absent. **Spore print**: white. **Spores**: 5–6.5 × 4.5–5.5 µm, broadly elliptical to round, smooth or finely roughened, amyloid. **Season**: fall. **Ecology**: saprotrophic, possibly parasitic.

142. *Hericium erinaceus*

143. ***Pseudocraterellus pseudoclavatus*** Edibility unknown

Syn. = *Gomphus pseudoclavatus*

In Kansas, found only under oaks, these small, pure lavender fruiting bodies are probably edible but have not been tried, having been discovered just a few times. *Gomphus clavatus* probably does not occur in Kansas and grows exclusively with pines. It is commonly called pig's ears (a good edible) and has an appearance very similar to our *P. pseudoclavatus*, though pig's ears often become yellowish tan and *P. pseudoclavatus* seems to keep its pale purple coloring. On the largest specimen, you can see the bumpy riblike surface of the stalk/hymenium as well as the yellowish color of the spores, if you look carefully at the area between the large one and the small group. *Pseudocraterellus pseudoclavatus* is smaller overall, including the spores, which also differ from *G. clavatus* in being smooth rather than decorated. This specimen was found in the summer under oaks north of Atchison, in Atchison County.

Description: **Cap**: 3–7 cm broad, pale purple, flat on top, with a paler, wavy margin. **Hymenium**: colored as cap, bumpy, riblike. **Stalk**: 2–6 cm long, 2–5 cm thick. **Spore print**: dull yellow. **Spores**: 9–11 × 2–5 μm smooth, long, elliptical, nonamyloid. **Season**: summer. **Ecology**: mycorrhizal.

143. *Pseudocraterellus pseudoclavatus*

144. *Clavariadelphus americanus*

144. *Clavariadelphus americanus* Edible

Clavariadelphus pistillaris (Ed. 1, misapplied)

Club coral

The distinctive club coral, *Clavariadelphus americanus*, fruits during late summer and fall in Kansas under hardwoods. The specimens pictured here were among a troop of several dozen collected in late summer. The fruiting bodies are club-shaped and have a spongy flesh that bruises brown with handling. The club coral is bitter when raw and only marginally edible when cooked.

Description: **Fruiting body**: 1–5 cm broad, 6–20 cm tall, club-shaped with rounded to flattened apex, rarely forked, yellowish brown to reddish brown, bruising brown, wrinkled, spongy. **Stalk**: indistinct, base white, finely hairy. **Spore print**: white. **Spores**: 11–16 × 6–10 µm, elliptical, smooth, nonamyloid. **Season**: late summer–fall. **Ecology**: mycorrhizal.

145. *Ramaria araiospora* Edible with caution

This brilliant pink to red coral fruits under hardwoods in eastern Kansas during late summer. For years it defied identification, but it appears to be *Ramaria araiospora*. This species had previously been reported only from

145. *Ramaria araiospora*

146. *Clavulina coralloides*

the West Coast under conifers. The specimen illustrated here is young. Older fruiting bodies fade to orange or yellow and lose all trace of their original splendor. Numerous other *Ramaria* species in Kansas remain to be identified and may prove equally intriguing. Unrelated branched species that appear similar but are leathery belong to the genus *Thelephora*. Fairly common in Kansas is the drab, stinking *Thelephora palmata* and its odorless look-alike, *T. americana*. Although the western *R. araiospora* is often listed as edible, specimens collected in Kansas should be sampled with caution, since edibility may vary from region to region.

Description: **Fruiting body**: 2–8 cm broad, 5–12 cm tall, highly branched, bright pink to red, often yellow at branch tips, fading to orange, yellow, or pinkish tan. **Stalk**: 2–3 cm long, 1–3 cm thick, sometimes absent, colored as branches or paler; base white. **Spore print**: pale yellow. **Spores**: 8–13 × 3–4.5 μm, cylindrical, finely roughened, nonamyloid. **Season**: late summer. **Ecology**: mycorrhizal.

146. *Clavulina coralloides* — Edible

Syn. = *Clavulina cristata*
Crested coral

This common little coral is white to various pastel shades. The branches have uneven clustered points, sometimes with flattened tips. The specimen pictured here is typical. *Clavulina coralloides* is found on the ground in wooded areas. This somewhat fragile species is said to be edible, though some corals are not. It grows from summer into the fall. Another coral, larger, pale at first but becoming gray and having blunt tips, is the more common *C. cinerea*. Similar in appearance to *C. coralloides* is the whitish *Sebacina schweinitzii* (syn. = *Tremellodendron pallidum*). This species is usually larger but is most different in context, being stiff and cartilaginous.

Description: **Fruiting body**: 2–7 cm high, 2–5 cm broad, pale all over, irregularly branched with pointed, multiple, sometimes flattened tips. **Stalk**: 0.5–2 cm high, comparatively thick. **Spore print**: white. **Spores**: 7–11 × 6.5–10 μm, spherical, smooth, nonamyloid. **Season**: summer–fall. **Ecology**: mycorrhizal.

147. *Clavulinopsis laeticolor* — Edibility unknown

These lovely, tiny corals are a beautiful yellow that will fade with age. Cylindrical, occasionally a little flattened, and always unbranched, they can occur in clusters, as pictured, or singly. Probably saprotrophic, they are found

147. *Clavulinopsis laeticolor*

148. *Artomyces pyxidatus*

under hardwoods in the summer. The larger *Clavulinopsis fusiformis*, also yellow and unbranched, is more often flattened and grows in dense clusters; it is reportedly edible.

Description: **Fruiting body**: 1.5–6.5 cm high, 1–5 mm thick, bright yellow, fading. **Stalk**: indistinct. **Spore print**: white. **Spores**: 4.5–7 × 3.5–5.5 µm, generally irregularly globose, nonamyloid. **Season**: summer. **Ecology**: saprotrophic.

148. *Artomyces pyxidatus* Edible

Syn. = *Clavicorona pyxidata* (Ed. 1)

Crown-tipped coral

Most Kansas corals are terrestrial, but the crown-tipped coral, which grows on fallen wood, is an exception. It fruits in summer, often during dry weather. The crown-like tips of its branches (shown in the photograph) are its hallmark. However, young fruiting bodies may deceptively lack these crowns. If your specimen is mature, perhaps two or four inches high, but still has pointed tips and is growing on wood, it is likely to be *Ramaria stricta* instead; this has a bitter taste and is usually darker in color. The teeth on the crowns of *Artomyces pyxidatus* often continue to develop into new branches, giving this fungus its orderly branching pattern. It is peppery when raw but delicious when fried in butter.

Description: **Fruiting body**: 2–8 cm broad, 5–13 cm tall, highly branched, crown-like at branch tips, pale yellow to pinkish or tan. **Stalk**: short, brown; base with brown hairs. **Spore print**: white. **Spores**: 4–5 × 2–3 µm, elliptical, smooth, amyloid. **Season**: summer. **Ecology**: saprotrophic.

Order Tremellales and other jellies

Jelly mushrooms, commonly called "jellies," constitute a diverse group particularly suited for mushroomers who yearn for the esoteric. The fruiting bodies are typically slippery and gelatinous and consist almost entirely of water. During dry weather, they shrivel into hard, scarcely recognizable forms, only to revive quickly with the next rain. Most species fruit on rotten wood, though several are terrestrial.

Fruiting bodies may be crust-like or may resemble brains, leaves, ears, or horns; others mimic coral and spine fungi. Their colors range from white, brown, and black to brilliant yellows and oranges. No poisonous species are known, and several are popular edibles in Asia; what they lack in taste they make up for with texture.

Because Kansas has a rather dry climate, the state is generally not thought of as prime jelly fungus territory. However, a number of species can be found here after prolonged rains, especially in the eastern half of the state. Jelly fungi are separated into orders according to the morphology (the way they look) and the shape of their spore-bearing cells (basidia); consequently, a microscope is often needed just to determine which order a specimen belongs to. Of the species described here, *Calocera cornea* and *Dacryopinax elegans* are members of the order Dacrymycetales, while *Auricularia americana* and *Ductifera pululahuana* belong to the Auriculariales; all other species belong to the main order of jelly fungi, the Tremellales. All or most of the Tremellales are parasites on other fungi, often species that are small or overtaken by the jelly, so that identifying the host is not much of an aid to identification of the *Tremella*.

Key to species

1a) Fruiting body on ground, often around living plant stems, white to translucent *Helvellosebacina concrescens* (see no. 153)

1b) Fruiting body on or beside wood go to **2**

2a) Fruiting body less than an inch tall, pointed, columnar or with a narrowed, stalk-like base go to **3**

2b) Fruiting body 0.5–10 inches broad, brain-like or lobed and without a stalk-like base go to **5**

3a) Fruiting body brown when moist, hollowed like rabbit ears, with granular stalk *Dacryopinax elegans* (no. 151)

3b) Fruiting body yellow when moist, of a different shape go to **4**

4a) Fruiting body petal-shaped, broad at the tip, narrowed to a stalk-like base *Dacryopinax spathularia* (see no. 150)

4b) Fruiting body horn-shaped, columnar or usually narrowed at the tip *Calocera cornea* (no. 150)

5a) Fruiting body white, yellow, or orange when moist go to **6**

5b) Fruiting body some shade of brown when moist go to **8**

6a) Fruiting body yellow to orange *Tremella mesenterica* (no. 154)

6b) Fruiting body white go to **7**

7a) Fruiting body translucent, lobed or of broad branches *Tremella fuciformis* (no. 153)

7b) Fruiting body opaque and waxy, brain-like *Ductifera pululahuana* (see no. 153)

8a) Fruiting body ear- or cup-shaped, usually several together in overlapping clusters *Auricularia americana* (no. 149)

8b) Fruiting body lobed or brain-like go to **9**

9a) Fruiting body a mass of thin, leaf-like lobes, looking like loose heads of (brown) lettuce *Phaeotremella frondosa* (no. 152)

9b) Fruiting body brain-like or lobed but not thin and leaf-like go to **10**

10a) Fruiting body pale brown to reddish brown with embedded white granules *Myxarium nucleatum* (see no. 154)

10b) Fruiting body blackish brown, without granules *Exidia glandulosa* (see no. 154)

149. *Auricularia americana*

149. *Auricularia americana* Edible

Auricularia auricula (Ed. 1, misapplied)
Tree ear

The tree (or cloud) ear, *Auricularia americana*, is a ubiquitous jelly fungus in Kansas. It fruits on dead wood from spring through fall. The fruiting bodies are brown, rubbery, and ear- or cup-shaped; they frequently grow in overlapping clusters. The spore-bearing undersurface (not shown in the photograph) is often ribbed or veined, giving the appearance of a human ear. The fruiting bodies become hard when dried but rapidly revive in water. The related *A. polytricha* is imported into the United States from Asia, where it is widely cultivated; this is the species you will find in the grocery store. Both species have little flavor but add interesting texture to dishes. *Phaeotremella frondosa* (no. 152) is similar, but its leaf-like lobes are joined into loose heads. Brown cup fungi (members of the genus *Peziza*, belonging to the phylum Ascomycota) are more cup-shaped and brittle and often grow on the ground.

Description: **Fruiting body**: 2–10 cm broad, ear- or cup-shaped, yellow-brown to reddish brown, rubbery, drying hard; upper surface velvety; undersurface smooth, often ribbed and veined. **Spore print**: white. **Spores**: 12–14 × 4–6 µm, sausage-shaped, smooth. **Season**: spring–fall. **Ecology**: saprotrophic.

150. *Calocera cornea*

150. *Calocera cornea* Edibility unknown

Jelly fungi assume many unusual forms. For example, the fruiting bodies of *Calocera cornea* are shaped like tiny elongate horns or columns. This fungus grows in clusters on rain-soaked logs during late summer and fall in Kansas. The fruiting bodies are rubbery but become hard upon drying; they revive with wet weather. The specimens illustrated here are turning reddish brown at their tips, indicating that they are beginning to dry out. A related species, *Dacryopinax spathularia*, has yellow to orange petal-shaped fruiting bodies. Coral fungi are generally larger and brittle.

Description: **Fruiting body**: 0.2–1.5 cm tall, horn-shaped, simple or forked, rarely branched, pointed, bulbous at base, yellow to orange, rubbery, drying reddish brown and hard. **Spore print**: yellow. **Spores**: 7–10 × 3–4 µm, cylindrical, slightly curved, smooth, becoming 2-celled. **Season**: late summer. **Ecology**: saprotrophic.

151. *Dacryopinax elegans* Edibility unknown

This tiny, unobtrusive jelly might be mistaken for very young tree ear (*Auricularia americana* [no. 149]) and does look like little, elongate animal ears. The cap is a rubbery medium brown. The stalk is a lighter color (sometimes darker) and granular in texture, as can be seen in one of those pictured. *Dacryopinax elegans* grows on dead wood, mostly in the summer.

Description: **Cap**: 0.2–1.5 cm tall, rounded elongate, upright cups, rubbery composition. **Stalk**: 0.1–0.3 cm, columnar, paler or darker than the cap, grainy. **Spore print**: unobtainable. **Spores**: 11–17 × 4–6 μm, cigar-shaped, with a small curve/hook at one end. **Season**: summer. **Ecology**: saprotrophic.

151. *Dacryopinax elegans*

152. *Phaeotremella frondosa*

152. ***Phaeotremella frondosa*** Edible

Syn. = *Phaeotremella foliacea* (Ed. 1, misapplied as *Tremella foliacea*)
Syn. = *Tremella frondosa*

Phaeotremella frondosa is the largest species of jelly fungus found in Kansas. It fruits at the bases of stumps and logs during summer and early fall. Characteristic are its rubbery, leaf-shaped lobes, which form loose clusters resembling heads of lettuce. The specimen illustrated here is rather young—as it ages, its lobes will become thinner and darken to reddish brown. A local mycophagist regularly uses this fungus in Chinese cooking and prefers it to the tree ear, *Auricularia americana* (no. 149), which fruits in overlapping clusters and is more tedious to collect.

Description: **Fruiting body**: 5–25 cm broad, consisting of leaf-shaped lobes loosely joined into a lettuce-like head, tan becoming reddish brown, gelatinous to rubbery. **Spore print**: white to pale yellow. **Spores**: 8–9 × 7–9 µm, round to broadly elliptical, smooth. **Season**: summer–early fall. **Ecology**: parasitic on *Stereum*.

153. ***Tremella fuciformis*** Edible

White jelly mushroom

The delicate, translucent *Tremella fuciformis* fruits on fallen tree limbs in Kansas following summer rains. The fruiting bodies consist of upright gelatinous

153. *Tremella fuciformis*

branches and lobes that often sag when fully hydrated, as in the specimens illustrated here. It is cultivated in Asia and imported to the United States canned in light syrup. Other white jelly fungi in Kansas are more opaque. The mycorrhizal *Helvellosebacina concrescens* (syn. = *Sebacina concrescens* [Ed. 1]) usually wraps around the bases of living herbaceous stems and has a special fondness for poison ivy. The saprotrophic *Ductifera pululahuana* (syn. = *Exidia alba* [Ed. 1]), also white and more opaque, is lobed to brain-like and waxy; like *T. fuciformis*, it fruits on dead wood.

Description: **Fruiting body**: 1–8 cm long, 1–4 cm tall, consisting of rounded, upright branches and lobes, white, extremely translucent, gelatinous, hollow, drying hard. **Spore print**: white. **Spores**: 6–11 × 5–8.5 µm, broadly elliptical, smooth. **Season**: summer. **Ecology**: parasitic.

154. *Tremella mesenterica* — Edible

Witch's butter

The witch's butter is a fitting name for this convoluted yellow to orange jelly fungus that appears to exude from wood like half-melted butter. During the summer in Kansas, it often fruits aboveground on dead deciduous trees, as shown in the photograph. The fruiting bodies dry into hard, shriveled masses but quickly revive with moisture. *Exidia glandulosa* is similar in form to *Tremella mesenterica* but is blackish brown; it is frequently found in the spring during morel hunting season. Another brain-like jelly fungus, *Myxarium nucleatum* (syn. = *E. nucleata*),

154. *Tremella mesenterica*

ranges from pale brown to reddish brown and has white granules embedded in its jelly. Both *E. glandulosa* and *M. nucleatum* are saprotrophs.

Description: **Fruiting body**: 1–10 cm broad, 3–4 cm tall, brain-like to somewhat lobed, yellow to orange, gelatinous, drying hard. **Spore print**: pale yellow. **Spores**: 7–15 × 6–10 µm, elliptical, smooth. **Season**: summer. **Ecology**: parasitic.

Order Phallales: Stinkhorns

Mushroom hunters are always captivated by the beautiful and often suggestive Phallales, better known as stinkhorns. Phallales are considered gasteroid fungi, as they begin with spores enclosed in a membrane and do not eject their mature spores. The fruiting bodies rank among the most elaborate in the fungal kingdom and are commonly adorned with colorful branches, arches, lattices, and nets. Simpler forms that are shamelessly phallic have evoked much folklore and not a little mycological humor. The fruiting bodies arise from a mostly subterranean egg that has an inner gelatinous layer; remnants of the egg form a sac-like volva at the base of the stalk. "Hatching" and full expansion of the fruiting body are extremely rapid, often occurring in less than two hours. The eggs can be easily transplanted for leisurely observation of the hatching process.

Stinkhorns are more often scented than sighted. Unlike puffballs, which produce spores in a powdery mass, stinkhorns suspend their spores in a thick, putrid slime (gleba) that coats the fertile surface of the fruiting body. Their odor strongly mimics that of rotten meat and can drift considerable distances on a light breeze. This rank smell serves to attract insects (chiefly flies but also moths in the evening), which wallow in the slime and eat it, then inadvertently disperse the spores to distant sites.

The eggs and stalks of stinkhorns are considered delicacies in Asia, but most Westerners are reluctant to stray from more conventional edible mushrooms. Stinkhorns thrive in areas disturbed by humans, even in gardens, and several species have been introduced into the United States from the tropics, where these fungi attain their greatest diversity. Kansas, with its sweltering subtropical summers, supports a surprising number of species.

Key to species

1a) Fruiting body without head, slime covering the top portion of the stalk — go to **2**

1b) Fruiting body with slime-covered head, separate from the stalk — go to **3**

2a) Stalk gradually tapering toward slime-covered top — *Mutinus elegans* (no. 157)

2b) Stalk more abruptly tapering to slime-covered top — *Mutinus caninus* (see no. 157)

3a) Fruiting body up to about 10 inches tall; stalk white — go to **4**

3b) Fruiting body up to about 7 inches tall; stalk orange or red (sometimes pale) go to **7**

4a) Fruiting body with white net resembling a skirt hanging from bottom of the head *Phallus indusiatus* (see no. 155)

4b) Fruiting body without netlike skirt go to **5**

5a) Fruiting body head more or less smooth under slime *Phallus ravenelii* (no. 156)

5b) Fruiting body with ridges under slime go to **6**

6a) Fruiting body arising from a pink egg *Phallus hadriani* (no. 155)

6b) Fruiting body arising from a white egg *Phallus impudicus* (see no. 155)

7a) Fruiting body with a small slime-covered, peaked, helmetlike structure *Phallus rubicundus* (see no. 155)

7b) Fruiting body with round head or with armlike structures, either joined at the tip or not go to **8**

8a) Fruiting body head round, divided into portions with orange-red lattice *Lysurus periphragmoides* (no. 158)

8b) Fruiting body tapering toward the top of the head, divided into several armlike structures go to **9**

9a) Fruiting body with round stalk; arms separating widely at maturity *Lysurus borealis* (see no. 158)

9b) Fruiting body with angular stalk; arms narrowly separate *Lysurus mokusin* (see no. 158)

155. *Phallus hadriani* Edible (egg)

The powerfully putrid *Phallus hadriani* is the commonest stinkhorn in Kansas, where it flourishes in cities and forests from late spring through fall. It is recognized by its conical, slime-covered head, which has a netlike pattern of ridges beneath the slime, and by its pink to purple egg and volva. The fruiting bodies hatch from a partially buried egg, the remnants of which form the volva seen in the photograph. Ripe specimens are particularly attractive to insects, which swarm after the foul-smelling spore slime in great numbers, often licking the head clean. One front lawn that sported hundreds of these

155. *Phallus hadriani*

stinkhorns filled the neighborhood with the smell of rotten meat and the noise of buzzing flies. After the slime (gleba) is removed, the cap shows up as a pure white, apparently pitted head that has been mistaken for a morel (morels are not white). In Kansas, *P. hadriani* has been traditionally called *P. impudicus*, which differs in having a white egg and volva. It is unclear whether *P. impudicus* actually occurs in Kansas. *Phallus indusiatus* (syn. = *Dictyophora duplicata* [Ed. 1], *P. duplicatus*), perhaps the most beautiful of Kansas's stinkhorns, is adorned with a delicate netlike skirt that hangs below its head, which also has a network of ridges beneath the slime. The smaller *P. rubicundus* grows to about 7 inches tall and has a smooth head and orange to red stalk; it prefers prairies with sandy soil but adapts well to wood chips, where it is often seen in town. The species used to be rare in Kansas but is now more frequently seen.

Description: **Head**: 1.5–3 cm broad, 3–4 cm tall, conical, flat topped with an apical hole, hanging freely around stalk, covered with spore slime, white and covered with network of ridges underneath; fruiting body hatching from pink to purple egg with inner gelatinous layer. **Stalk**: 7–20 cm long, 2–3 cm thick, white, spongy, hollow; volva pink to purple, sac-like, membranous. **Spore mass**: olive-green or olive-brown, slimy, putrid. **Spores**: 3–4 × 1.5–2 µm, elliptical, smooth. **Season**: summer. **Ecology**: saprotrophic.

156. *Phallus ravenelii* Edible (egg)

This stinkhorn resembles, in stature, the more common *Phallus hadriani* (no. 155), but under the stinky olive gleba, the cap is fairly smooth rather than having a raised network. The egg from which this species grows is white to pale pink. *Phallus ravenelii* also grows in woodlands and lawns and on wood chips, usually in summer to early fall. Illustrated here is the stinkhorn's method of spore dispersal: large and small flying insects, especially flies.

156. *Phallus ravenelii*

Description: **Head**: 1.5–3 cm broad, 3–4 cm tall, conical, peaked top with pale, thick opening, initially covered in greenish sticky gleba, under which the surface is smooth to granular. **Stalk**: 7–20 cm long, white. **Spores**: 3–4.5 × 1–2 µm, elliptical, smooth. **Season**: summer. **Ecology**: saprotrophic.

157. *Mutinus elegans* Edible (egg)
Devil's dipstick

Mutinus elegans fruits in the rich hardwood forests of eastern Kansas during summer and early fall. This stinkhorn has a pink to orange fruiting body that is stalk-like and gradually tapers to a point. The upper portion of the fruiting body is covered by a fetid brown spore slime. The fruiting bodies hatch from a white egg that remains behind as a sac-like volva (not clearly visible in the photograph). This specimen was diligently smelled out during a foray in the early-summer woods; flies had not yet removed its spore slime. The odor, though putrid, is not quite as offensive as that of other species. *Mutinus elegans* is probably edible in its egg stage, though it may be more of a challenge

157. *Mutinus elegans*

than a delicacy. The similar *M. caninus*, the dog stinkhorn, is also stalk-like but tapers abruptly near the apex; it is rare in Kansas.

Description: **Fruiting body**: 1.5–2.5 cm broad, 6–18 cm tall, cylindrical, stalk-like, gradually tapering from midportion upward, often with an apical hole, pink to pale orange with base white, covered by spore slime on upper third (2–5 cm), spongy, hollow, hatching from white egg with inner gelatinous membrane. **Spore mass**: greenish brown, slimy, fetid. **Spores**: 4–7 × 2–3 µm, cylindrical, smooth. **Season**: summer. **Ecology**: saprotrophic.

158. *Lysurus periphragmoides*

Edibility unknown

Syn. = *Simblum sphaerocephalum* (Ed. 1)

The delicate beauty of this small stinkhorn easily distracts from its putrid odor. It has been collected from lawns, cultivated fields, prairies, and thin woods in Kansas during spring and fall. The specimen illustrated here was found on a neighbor's front lawn. The distinctive round head is divided into portions with an orange to red lattice; the fetid spore slime, which flies find so irresistible, rests in the depressions formed by the lattice. The fruiting bodies hatch from a white egg that remains as a membranous volva (seen in the photograph). The arms of the lizard's claw, *Lysurus borealis*, separate clearly at maturity. It is much rarer in Kansas, where it fruits on a round stalk in cultivated soil. The lantern stinkhorn, *L. mokusin*, has become common on wood chips. Its head splits vertically into pink, pointed arms that separate slightly to expose their inner spore slime, and its stalk is angular. In both, the head appears to taper toward the top.

Description: **Head**: 1.5–2.5 cm broad, round to slightly flattened, divided into an orange to red lattice; depressions formed by lattice filled with spore slime; fruiting body hatching from white egg with inner gelatinous layer. **Stalk**: 6–8 cm long, 0.5–1.5 cm thick, orange to red, spongy, hollow; volva white, sac-like, membranous. **Spore mass**: olive-brown, slimy, fetid. **Spores**: 3.5–4.5 × 1.5–2 μm, elliptical, smooth. **Season**: summer. **Ecology**: saprotrophic.

158. *Lysurus periphragmoides*

Conventional Class Gasteromycetes: Gasteroid fungi

The gasteroid fungi include such diverse fungi as puffballs, earthstars, stalked puffballs, earthballs, and bird's nest fungi. Unlike those of other members of the Basidiomycota, the spores of the gasteroid fungi are born enclosed within the fruiting body and are not forcibly discharged from their basidia. "Gasteroid" comes from the Greek word for stomach; gasteroid fungi appear as little stomachs full of spores. To disperse their spores, these fungi often rely instead upon ingenious mechanisms involving rain or animals. Once considered to belong to their own fungal class, called the Gasteromycetes, the gasteroid fungi are now known to belong to several distinct lineages of fungi, including the Agaricales and Boletales.

Gasteroid fungi are commonly slighted by mushroom books, a tradition not shared by this guide because although puffballs, large and small, fruit in diverse habitats, they are particularly prevalent in dry, treeless areas where relatively few gilled mushrooms occur. Since a large portion of Kansas is prairie, they deserve special emphasis here. Though much maligned and often kicked, puffballs have their own special beauty. Many are decorated with scales, granules, warts, or spines, and what they lack in complexity they make up for in resourcefulness. It has been estimated that the giant puffball (*Calvatia gigantea*) contains seven trillion spores, which suggests that these fungi know their odds of producing viable offspring. Often the lower part of the fruiting body is not involved in spore production. This "sterile base" may appear stalk-like and commonly persists long after the upper spore-bearing portion has disappeared.

Two genera of puffballs—*Calvatia* and *Lycoperdon*—predominate in Kansas. *Calvatia* species simply shed their outer skin to expose the inner powdery spore mass to the wind and elements. In contrast, species of *Lycoperdon* puff their spores through an apical pore (at the top of the fruiting body) when jolted by animals or large raindrops. Aptly enough, *Lycoperdon* means "wolf flatulence"; Linnaeus, who named it, obviously had a sense of humor. Earthstars (genus *Geastrum*) also release their spores through pores. Their star-shaped fruiting bodies arise when the outer skin layers split and peel back as rays, leaving behind an inner spore case.

Most puffballs are edible if entirely white inside; the texture should be soft, sort of like a marshmallow. Properly prepared, they are choice edibles. Always slice the fruiting bodies in half, from top to bottom, before cooking to be certain they are not poisonous *Amanita* eggs (Fig. 7). Species can be difficult to identify; it is often necessary to examine several developmental stages, particularly mature fruiting bodies with powdery spore masses.

A big surprise of gene sequencing is that all of our common puffballs, stalked puffballs, and bird's nest fungi, with their tiny packets of spores, belong to the order Agaricales. The gasteroid fungi with a firm interior, species of the genera *Scleroderma* (some of which are poisonous) and *Pisolithus*, the dye-maker's false puffball, are surprisingly members of the order Boletales, as is the earthstar genus *Astreus*, but the other lovely earthstars belong to the order Geastrales. The strangest gasteroid fruiting body, a member of the order Ustilaginales, is corn smut (*Ustilago maydis*), which parasitizes corn. A whopping dozen or so species each of *Geastrum* and *Lycoperdon*, as well as seven species of *Calvatia*, a couple of stalked puffballs (genus *Tulostoma*), several species of *Scleroderma*, one *Pisolithus*, and *U. maydis* are reported from Kansas.

Key to species

1a) Fruiting body infecting corn (*Zea mays*), lobed, amorphous-spherical, with thin silvery-gray skin — *Ustilago maydis* (no. 175)

1b) Fruiting body growing on wood, wood chips, or soil, without silvery-gray skin — go to **2**

2a) Fruiting body cup-shaped, top initially covered by thin membrane that ruptures at maturity; each cup bearing several egg-like spore packets — go to **3**

2b) Fruiting body beginning as a rough sphere, sometimes stalked or with rays that separate to reveal a round spore case — go to **5**

3a) Membrane velvety, tan; egg-like spore packets white — *Crucibulum laeve* (no. 168)

3b) Membrane smooth, whitish; egg-like spore packets dark gray to black — go to **4**

4a) Interior of cup smooth — *Cyathus stercoreus* (no. 169)

4b) Interior of cup with prominent striations — *Cyathus striatus* (see no. 169)

5a) Fruiting body at maturity with triangular or roughly triangular rays extending from a spherical spore case (or sometimes just a powdery mass), giving it a flower- or starlike appearance — go to **6**

5b) Fruiting body at maturity without rays — go to **11**

6a) Spore case firm, with interior soon becoming dark purple before maturity; spores shed as outer layer of spore case breaks down go to **7**

6b) Spore case soft with a white interior before maturity; spores shed through an apical pore in spore case go to **8**

7a) Fruiting body 0.75–1.5 inches broad at maturity, skin less than 0.04 inches (1 mm) thick *Scleroderma flavidum* (no. 173)

7b) Fruiting body 2.75–6 inches broad at maturity, skin 0.04–0.2 inches (1–5 mm) thick *Scleroderma polyrhizum* (see no. 173)

8a) Fruiting body 1–4 inches broad at maturity, initially bulblike and sometimes partially buried, opening as rays part, often cracking at their base so that the spore case appears to rest on a saucerlike platform *Geastrum triplex* (no. 170)

8b) Fruiting body 0.75–2 inches broad at maturity, rays not cracking basally go to **9**

9a) Spore case with a distinct circular groove around the apical pore *Geastrum saccatum* (no. 171)

9b) Spore case lacking a circular groove around the apical pore (although typically with a striate ring around apical pore) go to **10**

10a) Rays folding over spore case when dry, unfolding when moist (hygroscopic) *Geastrum campestre* (see no. 171)

10b) Rays not hygroscopic, arching back so that the spore case is raised off the ground *Geastrum coronatum* (see no. 171)

11a) Fruiting body consisting of a round spore case up to 0.75 inches broad, borne on a tough, slender stalk up to 1.5 inches long go to **12**

11b) Fruiting body mostly more than 0.75 inches broad, stalkless, although sometimes with a stout sterile base go to **13**

12a) Spore case reddish brown; apical pore with smooth edge *Tulostoma simulans* (no. 167)

12b) Spore case gray or tan; apical pore lobed or ragged *Tulostoma fimbriatum* (see no. 167)

13a) Spores shed through an apical pore in spore case; spore case with fine scales, warts, or cone-shaped or shaggy spines go to **14**

13b) Spores shed as outer layer of spore case breaks down; spore case smooth or with scales or warts but not spiny go to **18**

14a) Fruiting body growing on wood; spore case ornamented with fine scales or warts *Apioperdon pyriforme* (no. 166)

14b) Fruiting body not growing on wood; spore case ornamented (at least initially) with cone-shaped or shaggy spines go to **15**

15a) Fruiting body covered with cone-shaped spines of two sizes, which remain through maturity *Lycoperdon perlatum* (no. 165)

15b) Fruiting body initially covered with shaggy spines, which are shed as fruiting body matures go to **16**

16a) Spines sloughing off in sheets to reveal brown, velvety inner layer *Lycoperdon marginatum* (no. 164)

16b) Spines shed individually, not in sheets go to **17**

17a) Skin of mature fruiting body with a netlike pattern of scars from sloughed-off spines *Bovistella utriformis* (no. 163)

17b) Skin of mature fruiting body smooth and shiny *Lycoperdon pulcherrimum* (see no. 163)

18a) Immature spore case pale, with or without brown scales; interior firm, soon becoming dark; growing under trees go to **19**

18b) Immature spore case white; interior soft and white; growing in open areas go to **21**

19a) Fruiting body round to club-shaped, up to 6 inches broad and 10 inches tall; interior with pea-sized nodules embedded in black gelatin *Pisolithus arhizus* (no. 172)

19b) Fruiting body round, up to 2 inches broad; interior uniformly dark purple go to **20**

20a) Fruiting body with fine, dark brown scales; skin thin, becoming papery *Scleroderma areolatum* (no. 174)

20b) Fruiting body without scales; skin thick, often developing a fine network of cracks at maturity *Scleroderma cepa* (see no. 174)

21a) Fruiting body bruising bright yellow, becoming orangish brown at maturity *Calvatia rubroflava* (no. 161)

21b) Fruiting body not bruising, becoming brownish at maturity go to **22**

22a) Fruiting body lacking stalk-like sterile base; fruiting body often very large (up to 55 inches broad) *Calvatia gigantea* (see no. 162)

22b) Fruiting body with thick, short, persistent, stalk-like sterile base; fruiting body up to 10 inches broad but usually smaller go to **23**

23a) Fruiting body light brown, smooth; spore mass purplish brown at maturity go to **24**

23b) Fruiting body white to tan or yellowish brown, smooth or with flattened warts; spore mass olive or yellowish brown at maturity go to **25**

24a) Fruiting body 2–6.5 inches broad; sterile stalk well developed *Calvatia cyathiformis* (no. 160)

24b) Fruiting body 1–3 inches broad; sterile stalk poorly developed *Calvatia fragilis* (see no. 160)

25a) Fruiting body covered with flattened warts; spore mass olive-brown at maturity *Calvatia bovista* (no. 159)

25b) Fruiting body surface smooth to undulate but without warts; spore mass yellowish brown at maturity *Calvatia craniiformis* (no. 162)

159. *Calvatia bovista*

159. *Calvatia bovista* Edible

This large puffball has only rarely been reported from Kansas. The specimens in the photograph were collected on the open prairies of central Kansas in late spring, though it has also been found in pastures of eastern Kansas during April. The fruiting bodies are typically skull-shaped and adorned with flattened warts; the small specimen shown here has split on top, perhaps due to drying. Mature fruiting bodies have an olive-brown spore mass that eventually blows away, leaving a cup-like sterile base behind. *Calvatia craniiformis* (no. 162) prefers woodlands and has a smooth to wrinkled surface.

Description: **Fruiting body**: 5–25 cm broad, 10–20 cm tall, skull-shaped, white to pale yellowish brown, covered with flattened warts; skin cracking and flaking with age. **Sterile base**: stalk-like, persistent. **Spore mass**: olive to olive-brown, powdery. **Spores**: 4–6.5 µm, round, minutely roughened. **Season**: spring. **Ecology**: saprotrophic.

160. *Calvatia cyathiformis* Edible

This medium to large puffball fruits in lawns, pastures, and prairies throughout Kansas during summer and fall. It often forms fairy rings. Brown patches on the surface of the specimen shown here are beginning to crack, and its skin

160. *Calvatia cyathiformis*

will eventually flake away to expose the purple-brown spore mass. The prominent sterile base, not visible, often persists through the winter, long after the spores have been dispersed. Young fruiting bodies are particularly solid and make an excellent edible. *Calvatia fragilis* (syn. = *Calvatia cyathiformis* forma *fragilis* [Ed. 1]) is smaller and has a poorly developed sterile base; it has been reported mainly from central and western Kansas. *Calvatia bovista* (no. 159) and *C. craniiformis* (no. 162) have yellowish-brown or olive spore masses.

Description: **Fruiting body**: 5–16 cm broad, 5–11 cm tall, round or slightly flattened, light brown with faint pale patches, areolate, smooth; skin cracking and flaking with age. **Sterile base**: prominent, persistent. **Spore mass**: purple-brown, powdery. **Spores**: 3.5–7.5 µm, round, spiny. **Season**: summer and fall. **Ecology**: saprotrophic.

161. *Calvatia rubroflava* — Edibility unknown

Syn. = *Calvatia candida* var. *rubroflava*

Calvatia rubroflava was described to science under the name *Lycoperdon rubroflavum* from specimens found in Shawnee County in 1885 and later transferred to *C. rubroflava*. It is common in Kansas and has been frequently reported from forests, gardens, and lawns throughout central and eastern parts of the state. The flesh of this puffball stains bright yellow when injured,

161. *Calvatia rubroflava*

a feature not exhibited by any other puffball in the state. Young fruiting bodies are white but gradually acquire the orange-brown color of the specimen illustrated here. Fully mature fruiting bodies are extremely light and cottony. It fruits during summer and early fall. Some authors consider this species to be a synonym of the older name *C. rugosa*. However, application of that name appears uncertain in North America, so we retain *C. rubroflava* for the species found in Kansas.

Description: **Fruiting body**: 2–10 cm broad, 1.5–5 cm tall, round or flattened, white becoming orangish brown, bruising bright yellow, smooth; skin cracking and flaking with age. **Sterile base**: pointed, narrowly attached to ground. **Spore mass**: greenish orange, powdery. **Spores**: 3–5 μm, round, minutely roughened. **Season**: summer–early fall. **Ecology**: saprotrophic.

162. *Calvatia craniiformis* Edible

Calvatia craniiformis is perhaps the most frequently collected large puffball in Kansas. It is particularly prevalent in dry, scrubby woods and along forest edges during late summer and fall (occasionally spring). Fruiting bodies are skull-shaped owing to their stalk-like sterile base and have a smooth to undulate surface. When mature, the skin sloughs away, exposing the powdery yellowish-brown spore mass. Eventually the spores will blow away entirely,

162. *Calvatia craniiformis*

leaving a cup-like sterile base that often overwinters. The young white specimens of known edible calvatias should be cut in two, most importantly to be sure they are not *Amanita* eggs but also because if there are yellow tones, they will be bitter. A similar species, *C. bovista* (no. 159), is covered with flattened warts. *Calvatia cyathiformis* (no. 160) differs in its purple-brown spore mass and preference for open grassy areas. The giant puffball, *C. gigantea* (syn. = *Langermannia gigantea*), is smooth and round and lacks a sterile base. This prized edible fruits in prairies, in thin woods, and along streams, where it often attains gigantic proportions (10–140 cm broad). *Calvatia gigantea* is more common in the western two-thirds of the state. It seems to fruit in cycles across years, so some years it is plentiful and others not.

Description: **Fruiting body**: 8–20 cm broad, 6–20 cm tall, skull-shaped, white to tan, smooth becoming wrinkled; skin cracking and flaking with age. **Sterile base**: stalk-like, persistent. **Spore mass**: yellowish brown, powdery. **Spores**: 2.5–3.5 μm, round, smooth to slightly roughened. **Season**: late summer–fall. **Ecology**: saprotrophic.

163. *Bovistella utriformis* — Edible

Syn. = *Lycoperdon americanum*
Syn. = *Lycoperdon echinatum* (Ed. 1)

The beautiful *Bovistella utriformis* has been collected in eastern Kansas during late summer and fall under hardwoods. The fruiting bodies are covered with long, shaggy spines and can easily be mistaken for the acorn caps of bur oak. The spines are white at first but later turn brown. They eventually fall off and leave a netlike pattern of scars on the underlying skin, as can be seen in the photograph. The white spot represents the location of the future pore. Another spiny puffball, *Lycoperdon pulcherrimum*, is probably more abundant in Kansas. When young, it is identical to *Bovistella utriformis*, but its spines remain white and leave a smooth, shiny surface when shed. These two species appear to intergrade in Kansas, and specimens whose spines turn brown but do not leave a network of scars are common.

Description: **Fruiting body**: 2–4 cm broad, 2–3.5 cm tall, round to flattened, white to yellow becoming brown, covered with long, shaggy spines, opening by an apical pore; inner surface brown, with network of scars from shed spines. **Sterile base**: small. **Spore mass**: purplish brown, powdery. **Spores**: 4–6 μm, round, warted. **Season**: late summer–fall. **Ecology**: saprotrophic.

163. *Bovistella utriformis*

164. *Lycoperdon marginatum*

164. *Lycoperdon marginatum* Edible

Lycoperdon marginatum fruits in prairies, lawns, and open woods throughout Kansas during late spring and summer. It prefers sandy soil. As the fruiting bodies approach maturity, their short, pointed spines slough away in sheets, exposing the underlying brown, velvety skin. This manner of shedding spines can be seen in the photograph. Strange to say, *L. marginatum* is reportedly used as a hallucinogen in Mexico, though chemists have been unable to discover any hallucinogenic compounds in this species. Other spiny puffballs, such as *Bovistella utriformis* (no. 163), do not shed their spines in sheets.

Description: **Fruiting body**: 1–5 cm broad, round to flattened, white becoming brown, covered with spines that fall off in sheets, opening by an apical pore; inner surface brown, velvety. **Sterile base**: small. **Spore mass**: olive to grayish brown, powdery. **Spores**: 3.5–4.5 µm, round, minutely roughened. **Season**: late spring–summer. **Ecology**: saprotrophic.

165. *Lycoperdon perlatum* — Edible

Syn. = *Lycoperdon gemmatum*
Gemmed puffball

Lycoperdon perlatum is a common puffball in the hardwood forests of Kansas during summer and fall. Its characteristic feature (shown in the photograph) is the patterned arrangement of both fine and coarse cone-shaped spines that are reminiscent of gems—hence its common name, the gemmed puffball. Upon shedding, the coarse spines leave prominent scars on the fruiting body. The specimens illustrated here have nipple-like apices that have not yet formed pores for release. The impressive manner in which the spores are

165. *Lycoperdon perlatum*

puffed out is alluded to in another common name for this species: the devil's snuffbox. Like most puffballs, *L. perlatum* is a good edible if entirely white inside.

Description: **Fruiting body**: 1.5–6 cm broad, 2–8 cm tall, pear- or turban-shaped, white, covered with short cone-shaped spines of two sizes, opening by an apical pore. **Sterile base**: short to stalk-like. **Spore mass**: olive to olive-brown, powdery. **Spores**: 3.5–4.5 µm, round, minutely spiny. **Season**: summer–fall. **Ecology**: saprotrophic.

166. *Apioperdon pyriforme* Edible

Syn. = *Lycoperdon pyriforme* (Ed. 1)
Pear-shaped puffball

Of the many species of puffballs found in Kansas, only *Apioperdon pyriforme* occurs on wood. It fruits on rotten logs and stumps, mostly during cool fall weather. The fruiting bodies are typically pear-shaped, but when growing in massive clusters, such as those illustrated here, they become compressed and distorted. The fruiting bodies arise directly from rootlike mycelial cords, which can be seen by carefully removing the bark and wood around such clusters. Specimens vary from white to brown and are covered with patches of fine scales that feel like sandpaper. The fruiting bodies in the photograph

166. *Apioperdon pyriforme*

have dark slit-like markings where their pores will form. *Apioperdon pyriforme* is one of the better puffballs for eating; be certain, however, that all specimens are white throughout, for otherwise the flavor will be bad.

Description: **Fruiting body**: 2–4 cm broad, 1.5–3 cm tall, pear-shaped, white, yellow-brown, or brown, covered with fine scales or warts, opening by a round to slit-like apical pore. **Sterile base**: small. **Spore mass**: olive to olive-brown, powdery. **Spores**: 2.5–3.5 μm, round, smooth. **Season**: late summer–fall. **Ecology**: saprotrophic.

167. *Tulostoma simulans*

Not edible

Stalked puffball

Tulostoma simulans, like most stalked puffballs, thrives on sandy soil in dry habitats. It has been collected from lawns, fields, and wooded ravines in Kansas from spring through fall. The fine collection illustrated here was gathered from a sandy field near the Kansas River. The fruiting bodies were buried in sand with only their spore cases showing. *Tulostoma simulans* is recognized by its reddish-brown spore case, which has a persistent coating of sand, provided sand comprises its substrate. Also diagnostic is its tubular, smooth-edged pore, which is particularly evident on several specimens in the photograph. The bulb at the base of the stalk consists of mycelium and

167. *Tulostoma simulans*

adherent sand. *Tulostoma fimbriatum* (syn. = *T. campestre* [Ed. 1]) has a pale gray to tan spore case covered with warts of sand that eventually fall off. Its lobed or ragged pore is only slightly raised.

Description: **Fruiting body**: 1–1.5 cm broad, round or acorn-shaped, reddish brown, with persistent coating of sand; apical pore tubular, smooth edged. **Stalk**: 1.5–3 cm long, 3–4 mm thick, rusty brown to gray, scaly; basal bulb consisting of compact sand and mycelium. **Spore mass**: brown, powdery. **Spores**: 4–6 µm, round, warted. **Season**: spring–fall. **Ecology**: saprotrophic.

168. *Crucibulum laeve*

Not edible

Syn. = *Crucibulum vulgare*
Common bird's nest

Crucibulum laeve is probably the most frequently encountered bird's nest fungus in Kansas. It fruits from late spring through fall on fallen tree limbs, corn stubble, corncobs, hickory husks, wood chips, and other assorted woody matter. This bird's nest mushroom is easily identified by its white eggs. Several stages of development can be seen in this photograph: Some nests are still covered with suede-like rusty-brown membranes, while in others, the membrane has ruptured and the eggs are exposed. New fruiting bodies often arise within the empty nests.

168. *Crucibulum laeve*

Description: **Fruiting body**: 0.5–1 cm broad and tall, cylindrical becoming cone- to cup-shaped with slightly flared margin, tan to cinnamon, velvety becoming smooth; top initially covered by a shaggy orange to rusty-brown membrane; inner surface white to pale brown, smooth; eggs 1–2 mm broad, lens-shaped, white, attached to an extensible cord. **Spores**: 7–10 × 4–6 µm, elliptical, smooth, formed inside eggs. **Season**: late spring–fall. **Ecology**: saprotrophic.

169. *Cyathus stercoreus* — Not edible

Bird's nest

This widespread bird's nest fungus fruits on manure and wood or in soil enriched with these substrates during late spring and summer in Kansas. The specimens illustrated here were part of an extensive fruiting on a pile of wood chips around the base of a tree that had been removed. *Cyathus stercoreus* is identified by its shaggy brown exterior, smooth inner surface, and black eggs. The photograph shows the fungus in various stages of development. Many of the fruiting bodies have not yet opened and resemble small fuzzy puffballs; others have opened, but their eggs are still concealed by a delicate white membrane that eventually tears open. The eggs are attached to a coiled, cordlike apparatus, but this often aborts during development. A similar black-egged species, *C. striatus*, has prominent striations on its shiny inner surface.

169. *Cyathus stercoreus*

Description: **Fruiting body**: 4–8 mm broad, 0.5–1.5 cm tall, vase-shaped, brown, shaggy, becoming smooth and nearly black; top initially covered by a white membrane; inner surface gray to bluish black, smooth; eggs 0.5–2 mm wide, lens-shaped, dark gray to black, sometimes attached to a thin, coiled cord. **Spores**: 22–40 × 18–30 µm, elliptical, smooth, formed inside eggs. **Season**: late spring–fall. **Ecology**: saprotrophic.

170. *Geastrum triplex* — Not edible

Geastrum triplex is one of the largest earthstars reported from Kansas. Like all other members of *Geastrum*, it belongs to the family Geastraceae of the order Geastrales. It has been collected during the summer from wet woodlands in eastern sections of the state. Young fruiting bodies are bulblike and mostly buried; they become visible only after their rays have curled back from the inner spore case to form a star. The spore case rests on a saucerlike platform that is formed when the fleshy rays crack around its perimeter. The rays of the three fruiting bodies in the photograph are just beginning to crack. At times the platform fails to develop, but size alone will usually distinguish *G. triplex* from similar species.

Description: **Fruiting body**: 1–4 cm broad unopened, round, pointed at apex, 3–10 cm broad opened, star-shaped with 4–8 curled, reddish-brown,

170. *Geastrum triplex*

fleshy, cracked rays; spore case 2–3 cm broad, pinkish gray to reddish brown, stalkless, resting on a saucerlike platform, opening by an apical pore. **Spore mass**: brown, powdery. **Spores**: 3.5–4.5 µm, round, warted. **Season**: summer. **Ecology**: saprotrophic.

171. *Geastrum saccatum* — Not edible

Common earthstar

Geastrum saccatum is the most prevalent earthstar in eastern Kansas, where it fruits under hardwoods from spring through fall. Young fruiting bodies are buried in the leaf litter and resemble small, pointed puffballs. The slightly opened specimen in the photograph was found by grubbing around mature fruiting bodies. It will eventually form rays that curl back in the lovely starlike manner of the two opened specimens. Characteristic are the sunken inner spore case and the apical pore that is delimited by a circular groove. Other earthstars in Kansas include *G. campestre*, with hygroscopic rays that fold over the spore case as they dry out and reopen when moistened again, and *G. coronatum* (syn. = *G. quadrifidum*), with a stalked spore case and arched rays that lift the fruiting body off the ground. Both typically have a striate ring around the apical pore but lack the circular groove.

Description: **Fruiting body**: 0.5–1.5 cm broad unopened, pointed at apex, white to tan; 2–5 cm broad opened, star-shaped with 4–8 curled pink to brown rays;

171. *Geastrum saccatum*

spore case 0.5–2 cm broad, white becoming brown, stalkless with apical pore delimited by circular groove. **Spore mass**: purplish brown, powdery. **Spores**: 3.5–4.5 µm, round, warted. **Season**: spring–fall. **Ecology**: saprotrophic.

172. *Pisolithus arhizus* Edible with caution

Syn. = *Pisolithus arenarius*
Syn. = *Pisolithus tinctorius* (Ed. 1)
Dead man's hand
Dye-maker's false puffball

Pisolithus arhizus is often maligned for its ugliness, yet few fungi evoke as much fascination among mushroomers. It fruits in Kansas during late summer and early fall under oak and might also be expected under planted pine. These specimens were collected in town under oak. The exterior can be whitish but may be brown, as can be seen in the uncut specimen. They also may be partially buried. The interior of this unusual fungus consists of pea-sized nodules that are embedded in a black gelatin. These nodules are clearly visible on the sectioned specimens in the photograph. Spores eventually form within the nodules. As the fruiting body matures, the nodules disintegrate from the top down, releasing their powdery cinnamon-brown contents. *Pisolithus arhizus* is an important mycorrhizal associate of pine and oak, and it contributes invaluably to their success on nutrient-poor soils. One of its common names, the dye-maker's false puffball, stems from its use as a source of dyes. The entire fruiting body gives a brown to black dye, whereas the gelatin between the nodules provides a bright olive-yellow pigment.

172. *Pisolithus arhizus*

Description: **Fruiting body**: 5–15 cm broad, 4–25 cm tall, round or club-shaped with rootlike base, whitish, olive-yellow, brown, or black, smooth or slightly lumpy; skin thin, flaking with age; interior divided into pea-sized nodules surrounded by black gelatin; nodules white or yellow becoming blackish purple, then cinnamon-brown, finally disintegrating. **Spore mass**: cinnamon-brown, powdery. **Spores**: 7–12 μm, round, spiny. **Season**: summer–early fall. **Ecology**: mycorrhizal.

173. *Scleroderma flavidum* — Edible with caution

Scleroderma flavidum thrives in sandy, windblown habitats that few other fleshy fungi tolerate. It fruits uncommonly in Kansas during the fall. The fruiting bodies are round and remain mostly buried in sand until mature. As shown in the photograph, the skin eventually splits into lobes that curl back in a starlike manner to expose the inner spore mass. The cup-like remains of empty fruiting bodies often persist through the winter. *Scleroderma polyrhizum* (syn. = *S. geaster*) also opens in a starlike manner but is much larger (up to about 6 inches broad) than *S. flavidum* and has an extremely thick skin (1–5 mm), and the interior spore mass doesn't appear to be enclosed in a separate membrane. It fruits in lawns, flowerbeds, and cultivated fields.

Description: **Fruiting body**: 2–4 cm broad, nearly round with rootlike base,

173. *Scleroderma flavidum*

yellowish brown, smooth becoming cracked or scaly; skin 0.5–1 mm thick, splitting, then curling back in a starlike manner; interior whitish when extremely young, soon dark purple. **Spore mass**: brown, powdery. **Spores**: 9–14 µm, round, spiny. **Season**: fall. **Ecology**: possibly saprotrophic and/or mycorrhizal.

174. *Scleroderma areolatum* — Edible with caution

Common earthball

Scleroderma areolatum is the most abundant earthball in central and eastern Kansas. It fruits under hardwoods during summer and fall. The species is an exception to the rule that earthballs have thick skins, since its skin is rather thin, as seen in the photograph, and becomes paperlike when mature. When very young, the interior is puffball pale but hard, unlike the interior of a puffball. However, the dark purple interior of the sectioned immature specimen leaves little doubt that it is an earthball. Later, as the spores ripen, the fruiting bodies become olive-brown and powdery inside. The delicate brown scales on these specimens are also characteristic. Earthballs have a bad reputation as edibles, and *S. areolatum* may be no exception. Another Kansas species, *S. cepa*, has caused gastrointestinal poisonings. It has a smooth, thick skin that often cracks into a fine network with age.

174. *Scleroderma areolatum*

Description: **Fruiting body**: 0.5–5 cm broad, round to flattened with rootlike base, light brown with fine dark brown scales; skin thin, becoming papery, rupturing irregularly; interior whitish when extremely young, soon dark purple. **Spore mass**: olive-brown, powdery. **Spores**: 10–18 µm, round. **Season**: summer–fall. **Ecology**: mycorrhizal.

175. *Ustilago maydis* Edible

Syn. = *Ustilago zeae*
Corn smut
Cuitlacoche
Huitlacoche

This is a very interesting fungus belonging to the order Ustilaginales, whose members may fit between the two phyla of interest in this book: the Basidiomycota and the Ascomycota. The multiple bulbous appendages of this species conform to the gastroid definition in that the spores are enclosed in a skin, in this case a thin and silvery gray one. The picture shows a young clump of large, pale gray lumps parasitizing an ear of corn. Found only on corn or its close relative teosinte (members of the plant species *Zea mays*), *Ustilago maydis* is often considered a pest, but the nutritional content complements that of corn since it has more protein and is also rich in lysine, a building

175. *Ustilago maydis*

block of proteins. Many Mexican recipes use corn smut, and the species has some of the corn flavor. The fruiting bodies should be used before they begin to show the dark, mature spores. *Ustilago maydis* has a complex, not entirely understood life cycle.

Description: **Fruiting body**: bulbous lumps and appendages, initially silvery gray, at maturity a powdery dark mass of spores. **Stalk**: absent. **Spore print**: dark olive to black. **Spores**: round to elliptical, bristly. S**eason**: spring–fall. **Ecology**: parasitic.

Phylum Ascomycota

The Ascomycota greatly exceed the Basidiomycota in number of species, but about one-third of Ascomycota are microscopic and are of little interest to mushroomers. The spores are borne within microscopic sac-like cells called asci (Fig. 8A and B). When mature, asci typically discharge their spores into the air, often with explosive force (though, exceptionally, animals disperse truffle spores). These seven orders of Ascomycota are divided into two groups of four orders and three orders, respectively, which are united by the morphology of their fruiting bodies.

Orders Helotiales, Leotiales, Pezizales, and Phacidiales: Mostly cup fungi

The cup fungi consist of mostly minute cups or cushion-shaped species, some with stalks that thrive on rotting plant litter (though notable exceptions, such as true truffles, form mycorrhizal relationships). The more obvious species attract mushroom hunters because of their brilliant colors or fine edibility. Cup fungi tend to be highly seasonal, particularly those that fruit during the spring—as anyone who has ever hunted morels can attest.

Morels, with their stalked and pitted heads, seem a far cry from simple cup-shaped forms, but they are actually modified stalked cups that have become everted and folded into pits. Mushroomers cherish morels, often so much that they neglect other, equally delectable edibles. However, not all kinds of morels are savory; moreover, some of their relatives—the false morels—contain potentially dangerous toxins. An unfortunate few experience gastrointestinal distress from eating morels. There are also reports that some people become allergic after safely eating morels for years.

The hymenium produces spores on the inner surface of the cups of cup fungi, on the top surface of cushions (as in the order *Leotiales*), or inside the pits of morels. The spores are often discharged in spectacular bursts, sometimes seen as a white cloud when the fruiting bodies are jarred or suddenly removed from a bag. Morels, false morels, and other obvious cups belong to the order Pezizales, as does the genus *Tuber* (the true truffle); *Calycina* and *Hymenoscyphus* are members of the order Helotiales; *Leotia* belongs in the order Leotiales; and *Bulgaria* has recently been placed in the order Phacidiales

Key to species

1a) Fruiting body underground, solid and roundish; stalk absent go to **2**

1b) Fruiting body borne aboveground, variously shaped but not solid and roundish; stalk present or absent go to **3**

2a) Fruiting body cream-colored to brown with lighter furrows *Tuber brennemanii* (no. 176)

2b) Fruiting body pale reddish brown, without contrasting furrows *Tuber lyonii* (see no. 176)

3a) Fruiting body cup- or goblet-shaped, usually with even rim, at least initially (sometimes flattening or becoming ragged with age); often without a distinct stalk go to **4**

3b) Fruiting body with a head-shaped, bell-shaped, saddle-shaped, or lobed cap, sometimes pitted, not cup-shaped with an even rim; with a distinct stalk go to **17**

4a) Fruiting body colored bright yellow, orange, or red go to **5**

4b) Fruiting body gray, tan, brown, or black (if pale yellow, then growing on nuts or growing in soil) go to **10**

5a) Fruiting body orange to red with tiny dark hairs around the edge of the cup *Scutellinia scutellata* (no. 188)

5b) Fruiting body without hairs around the edge of the cup go to **6**

6a) Fruiting body yellow; growing on wood *Calycina citrina* (no. 191)

6b) Fruiting bright orange or red (although exterior of cup sometimes whitish due to the presence of hairs); growing on wood (sometimes buried) or in soil go to **7**

7a) Interior of cup orange; growing in soil *Aleuria aurantia* (see no. 186)

7b) Interior of cup bright red; growing on wood (sometimes buried) go to **8**

8a) Fruiting body exterior covered in shaggy white hairs *Microstoma floccosum* (no. 185)

8b) Fruiting body exterior smooth or cottony but not shaggy go to **9**

9a) Cups to 2.5 inches broad; stalks to 0.75 inches high; fruiting in early spring *Sarcoscypha dudleyi* (no. 186)

9b) Cups to 0.75 inches broad; stalks to 1.5 inches long; fruiting in late spring–fall *Sarcoscypha occidentalis* (no. 187)

10a) Fruiting body minute (cup less than 0.2 inches broad), white to pale yellow; growing on nuts *Hymenoscyphus fructigenus* (see no. 191)

10b) Fruiting body larger, gray, brown, or black go to **11**

11a) Fruiting body initially cup-shaped but becoming flat and irregular at maturity; interior of cup tan, exterior often paler; growing in human environments (including indoors or on concrete) *Peziza domiciliana* (no. 184)

11b) Fruiting body remaining cup- or goblet-shaped at maturity; interior of cup pale or dark; growing in soil or wood go to **12**

12a) Fruiting body pale gray or grayish brown, typically with a paler interior; growing mostly in soil (rarely on wood) go to **13**

12b) Fruiting body brown or black, with a dark brown, reddish-brown, or black interior; growing on wood go to **15**

13a) Fruiting body with a distinct stalk, equaling or exceeding the cup in length *Helvella macropus* (see no. 180)

13b) Fruiting body without a stalk go to **14**

14a) Fruiting body brown to tan, to about 2.5 inches broad, exuding liquid that turns yellow; exterior smooth; growing in soil or among mosses *Paragalactinia succosa* (see no. 184)

14b) Fruiting body gray, to about 1 inch broad, not exuding liquid; exterior densely hairy; growing in soil or rarely on rotting wood *Humaria hemisphaerica* (see no. 177)

15a) Fruiting body shallowly cup-shaped (sometimes becoming convex at maturity), with brown exterior and contrasting black interior; stalk absent *Bulgaria inquinans* (see no. 189)

15b) Fruiting body deeply cup- or goblet-shaped, with brown exterior and brown or reddish-brown interior; stalk present, 0.2–1.5 inches long go to **16**

16a) Fruiting body cup-shaped, with dark brown exterior and contrasting tan to reddish-brown interior *Galiella rufa* (no. 177)

16b) Fruiting body goblet-shaped, completely dark brown *Urnula craterium* (no. 189)

17a) Fruiting body with round to flattened greenish-yellow or olive-green head go to **18**

17b) Fruiting body with variously shaped head, but some shade of brown, gray, or black go to **19**

18a) Fruiting body with greenish-yellow head and stalk *Leotia lubrica* (no. 190)

18b) Fruiting body with olive-green head and yellow to orange stalk *Leotia lubrica* (color variant "*L. viscosa*"; see no. 190)

19a) Head wrinkled or deeply pitted, typically oval to conical in outline, up to 5 inches tall go to **20**

19b) Head smooth to undulate, bell-shaped, saddle-shaped, or lobed, less than 2 inches tall go to **26**

20a) Head wrinkled, sometimes becoming convoluted and brain-like; stalk chambered go to **21**

20b) Head deeply pitted; stalk and head hollow go to **23**

21a) Head yellowish brown to reddish brown, with several distinct wrinkled lobes, with margins forming raised seams *Discina fastigiata* (no. 179)

21b) Head reddish brown, convoluted and brain-like go to **22**

22a) Head with vertical ridges *Discina caroliniana* (no. 178)

22b) Head without distinct vertical ridges, irregularly convoluted *Gyromitra esculenta* (see no. 179)

23a) Ridges between pits pale at maturity go to **24**

23b) Ridges between pits dark at maturity go to **25**

24a) Head with rounded pits and irregularly arranged ridges *Morchella americana* (no. 181)

24b) Head with elongated pits and vertical ridges *Morchella diminutiva* (see no. 181)

25a) Head fully connected to stalk *Morchella angusticeps* (see no. 181)

25b) Head connected to stalk for only about half its length, with lower part of head free *Morchella punctipes* (no. 182)

26a) Head bell-shaped, connected only to top of stalk; stalk white with yellow bands of scales *Verpa conica* (no. 183)

26b) Head saddle-shaped or lobed; undersurface smooth, granular, or hairy; stalk smooth or ribbed and pitted but not scaly go to **27**

27a) Stalk ribbed and pitted *Helvella crispa* (see no. 180)

27b) Stalk smooth go to **28**

28a) Head with grayish-brown upper surface and smooth undersurface *Helvella elastica* (see no. 180)

28b) Head with pale tan to brown upper surface and hairy or granular undersurface *Helvella latispora* (no. 180)

176. *Tuber brennemanii* Edible

This species is a true and edible truffle with many close relatives, some of which may not be so edible. Because it measures an approximate roundish inch and grows just underground, finding it is not easy, and unless you have a friend with a good nose, your find may not be ripe. This truffle's cream to brown surface is smooth but with shallow, paler furrows, giving it a knobby look. The one pictured here has been cut in two, showing the typical marbled interior; the furrows on the exterior are deeper because it has dehydrated.

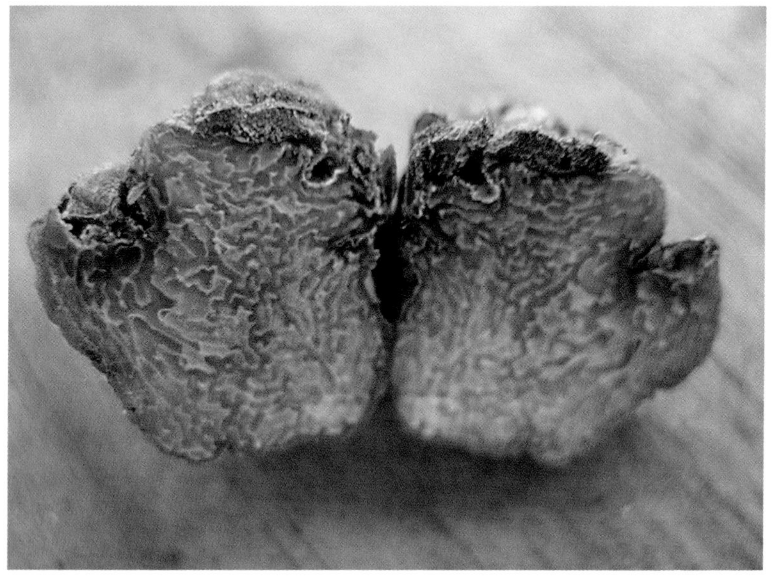

176. *Tuber brennemanii*

This species also presents as small white mats that look rather like simple mycelium but are an alternate form (anamorph) of the truffle. The mycorrhizal partners are often pecan, which is native in Kansas, and oak. The odor is pleasant, and the taste is nutty. Ralph Brown found this Kansas truffle on his property in the town of Hope, in Dickinson County, and it was named by some truffle experts in Matthew Smith's lab at the University of Florida. This specimen was found in the summer. *Tuber lyonii* is also found in Kansas in similar habitats, though it is larger, reaching 4 cm across, and has a pale reddish-brown exterior.

Description: **Fruiting body**: 1–2.6 × 0.8–1.6 cm, roughly round, cream to brown, with lighter-colored furrows, smooth but with a knobby appearance; interior light tan with white marbling. **Stalk**: absent. **Spores**: 24–61 × 12–36 µm, ellipsoid to broadly ellipsoid. **Season**: summer. **Ecology**: mycorrhizal.

177. *Galiella rufa*

Edibility unknown

Peanut butter cup

Galiella rufa fruits in clusters on decaying sticks during the summer in the hardwood forests of Kansas. Its thick, rubbery cups are tan to reddish brown inside and have a dark, hairy exterior. Young, unopened fruiting bodies resemble small puffballs. The much smaller *Humaria hemisphaerica* also has a

177. *Galiella rufa*

hairy exterior, but its inner surface is whitish, and its flesh is thin and brittle; it is typically terrestrial but occasionally fruits on rotten wood.

Description: **Cup**: 1–3 cm broad, cup-shaped with ragged margin, rubbery or gelatinous; inner surface tan to reddish brown; exterior dark brown to black with fine blackish-brown hairs. **Stalk**: 0.5–2 cm long, 4–6 mm thick, dark brown, hairy, occasionally lacking. **Spores**: 19–21 × 9–12 μm, elliptical, minutely roughened. **Season**: summer. **Ecology**: saprotrophic.

178. *Discina caroliniana* Poisonous

Syn. = *Gyromitra caroliniana* (Ed. 1)
Big red
Beefsteak

This rare false morel is sometimes larger than a person's head and can be an impressive, if not frightening, sight in the early-spring woods. It fruits under hardwoods during April before the first morels appear. The reddish-brown head is brain-like and often has vertical ridges that run its length. The massive stalk is highly convoluted and chambered when examined in cross-section. *Discina caroliniana* is referred to locally in Kansas as the beefsteak, an unfortunate name that is used elsewhere for other types of mushrooms. Though eaten by some people, it is suspected of containing toxic monomethylhydrazine (MMH) and is therefore not recommended for the table. Boiling *D. caroliniana* is intended to remove toxins; however, illness and death have been reported from inhaling the steam from the cooking mushrooms.

178. *Discina caroliniana*

Description: **Head**: 5–20 cm broad, 5–11 cm tall, round to oval, reddish brown, convoluted and brain-like, often with prominent vertical ridges; lower margin closely appressed against stalk. **Stalk**: 3–15 cm long, 3–8 cm thick, white, ribbed; interior convoluted. **Spores**: 22–35 × 11–16 µm, elliptical, reticulate, with 1 to several short knobs at each end. **Season**: spring. **Ecology**: saprotrophic.

179. *Discina fastigiata*

Poisonous

Syn. = *Gyromitra brunnea*
Syn. = *Gyromitra fastigiata* (Ed. 1)
Elephant ears

Discina fastigiata is the most abundant of the so-called false morels in Kansas. It fruits in rich woodlands during March and April, shortly before morel season. The head consists of several wrinkled lobes that may resemble elephant ears—hence the common name for it in Kansas. In the photograph, note the raised seam where two adjacent lobes join on the specimen. Equally characteristic is the stout white stalk. Many Kansans relish the elephant ears and have no regrets during poor morel years. However, related false morels, such as *Gyromitra esculenta*, with a dark reddish-brown, brain-like head, often contain toxic levels of monomethylhydrazine (MMH). As long as mycologists are uncertain whether *D. fastigiata* also contains MMH, it is prudent not to eat this species. The massive *D. caroliniana* (no. 178) has a brain-like head with vertical ridges.

179. *Discina fastigiata*

Description: **Head**: 4–8 cm broad, 5–12 cm tall, yellowish brown to reddish brown, wrinkled, consisting of several distinct lobes; margins of adjacent lobes forming raised seams where joined; lower portion of lobes free of stalk. **Stalk**: 2–9 cm long, 2.5–6 cm thick, stout, white, often ribbed; interior sometimes channeled. **Spores**: 24–30 × 13.5–15 µm, elliptical, reticulate, with 1 to several short knobs at each end. **Season**: early spring. **Ecology**: saprotrophic.

180. *Helvella stevensii* — Edibility unknown

This delicate relative of the morel fruits during late spring in the forests of eastern Kansas. It is identified by its smooth, slender stalk and its saddle-shaped or lobed head. Young fruiting bodies, such as the one illustrated here, have heads with prominently curled margins that cover the upper spore-bearing surface. As the fruiting body matures, its head uncurls and often assumes a more lobed appearance. The granular or hairy undersurface of the head is also an important characteristic; this is best observed with a hand lens. Other *Helvella* species reported from Kansas include the darker, grayish-brown *H. elastica*, with a head that is smooth underneath as well as above and not curled when young, and *H. crispa*, with a ribbed and pitted stalk. If you look carefully, *H. macropus* (a small, simple gray cup on a plain stalk) can also be found in Kansas.

180. *Helvella latispora*

Description: **Head**: 0.8–3.5 cm broad, 1–4.5 cm tall, saddle-shaped or lobed, with margin curled over upper surface when young, pale tan to brown; undersurface white, granular or hairy. **Stalk**: 1–6 cm long, 0.2–0.6 cm thick, light tan, smooth to hairy, round in cross-section. **Spores**: 17.5–20 × 11–13.5 µm, elliptical, smooth. **Season**: late spring. **Ecology**: mycorrhizal.

181. *Morchella americana* Edible

Morchella esculenta (Ed. 1, misapplied)
Yellow morel
Common morel
Sponge mushroom

People seek the yellow morel, also known as the common morel or sponge mushroom, more than any other wild mushroom in Kansas. This morel is often the first, if not the only, exposure novices have to the joys of mushroom hunting. It fruits under hardwoods during April or early May, depending upon the weather. "Morels are found where they're at," but mushroomers can increase their odds by searching under dying elms, around old apple orchards, and along rivers. The fruiting bodies have a pitted yellowish-brown head that is fused along the stalk through its lower margin, forming a continuous hollow. The pits are rounded and irregularly arranged, as in the specimen illustrated. Young fruiting bodies are gray and have white ridges surrounding their pits. They are often considered different from the yellow morel but in fact will eventually turn yellowish brown if left undisturbed. To do so would be a foolhardy act, however, since the yellow morel is an esteemed edible, whether fried in butter or baked after being stuffed with meats and vegetables. Two less common morel species in Kansas have vertical ridges and elongated pits: *M. diminutiva*, similar in color to the yellow morel but smaller, and the black morel, *M. angusticeps*, with vertically arranged black ridges surrounding pits. *Morchella diminutiva* is an excellent edible, but *M. angusticeps* is not.

181. *Morchella americana*

Description: **Head**: 2–7 cm broad, 2–10 cm tall, oval or elongate with lower margin fused to stalk, yellow-brown to brown, hollow; pits rounded, irregularly arranged. **Stalk**: 2–8 cm long, 2–5 cm thick, white to light yellow, granular on outer surface, hollow. **Spores**: 21–25 × 12–16 μm, elliptical, smooth. **Season**: spring. **Ecology**: mycorrhizal and saprotrophic.

182. *Morchella punctipes* — Edible

Morchella semilibera (Ed. 1, misapplied)
Half-free morel

The half-free morel is frequently collected in Kansas, where it fruits under deciduous trees in April or early May. It typically appears shortly before the yellow morel. The species is easily identified by slicing its head in two lengthwise: the upper half is fused to the stalk, while the lower half hangs skirtlike. All other species of *Morchella* in Kansas have heads that are fused to the stalk by their lower margins. Young fruiting bodies have short stalks and tan heads; more mature specimens, such as the one illustrated here, display greatly elongated stalks and blackened vertical ridges on the head. The flavor of the half-free morel is disappointing, but this is not apparent when it is smothered by the juices of the yellow morel, which can thus be extended when in short supply.

182. *Morchella punctipes*

Description: **Head**: 1.5–3 cm broad, 1.5–4 cm tall, conical; upper half fused to stalk; lower half free and skirtlike; pits vertically elongate, tan with ridges eventually blackening. **Stalk**: 5–15 cm long, 1–2 cm thick, white to light yellow, granular on outer surface, hollow. **Spores**: 24–34 × 15–21 µm, elliptical, smooth. **Season**: spring. **Ecology**: mycorrhizal and saprotrophic.

183. *Verpa conica* — Edible with caution

Bell morel

The bell morel fruits in the forested areas of Kansas during April and early May. It is recognized by its smooth bell-shaped head, which hangs freely around the stalk and is joined to it only at the apex. Though edible when well cooked, the bell morel is of poor flavor.

Description: **Head**: 1.5–3.5 cm broad, 1.5–3 cm tall, bell-shaped, skirtlike around stalk, tan to dark brown, smooth or creased. **Stalk**: 5–10 cm long, 0.5–1.5 cm thick, white with yellow bands of fine scales, hollow. **Spores**: 21–24 × 12–13.5 µm, elliptical, smooth. **Season**: spring. **Ecology**: mycorrhizal.

183. *Verpa conica*

184. *Peziza domiciliana* Edibility unknown

This nondescript brown cup fungus attracts attention by its intrusions into domestic settings. Favored habitats include rugs, shower stalls, cellars, and greenhouses. The fruiting bodies illustrated here were discovered in a limestone cave near Atchison in Atchison County during midwinter. They were growing on a wooden flat full of composted grain on which the grocery-store mushroom, *Agaricus bisporus*, was being grown commercially. The humid conditions needed for *A. bisporus* were obviously also ideal for this cup fungus, as the lush mycelium at the base of the upper fruiting body indicates. Young cups often exhibit the prominent stalks shown here. Upon maturing, these cups flatten, and their white granular exteriors become smooth and of the same color as their inner surfaces. Several other brown to tan species of pezizas occur outdoors in Kansas; all are difficult to identify. One species, *Paragalactinia succosa* (syn. = *Peziza succosa* [Ed. 1]) fruits in soil and exudes juice that turns yellow.

184. *Peziza domiciliana*

Description: **Cup**: 1–10 cm broad, cup-shaped becoming flat and irregular, tan with exterior often lighter. **Stalk**: present when young, becoming inconspicuous. **Spores**: 13–15 × 8–10 µm, elliptical, smooth or slightly roughened. **Season**: year-round. **Ecology**: saprotrophic.

185. *Microstoma floccosum*

185. ***Microstoma floccosum*** Edibility unknown
Syn. = *Sarcoscypha floccosa*
Fairy goblet

Clusters of the delightful fairy goblet, *Microstoma floccosum*, appear under hardwoods during late spring and summer in Kansas. The red goblet-shaped cups, adorned with shaggy white hairs, are distinctive. The fruiting bodies are attached to buried tree limbs by long stalks. The specimens in the photograph show how the fruiting body begins as a stalked fuzzy ball and then opens at the top to form a cup.

Description: **Cup**: 5–8 mm broad, 0.7–1.2 cm tall, goblet-shaped, red; exterior with shaggy white hairs. **Stalk**: 3–5 cm long, 2–5 mm thick, white, hairy. **Spores**: 20–35 × 15–17 μm, elliptical, smooth. **Season**: late spring–summer. **Ecology**: saprotrophic.

186. ***Sarcoscypha dudleyi*** Edibility unknown
Sarcoscypha coccinea (Ed. 1, misapplied)
Scarlet cup

The scarlet cup fruits under hardwoods in Kansas during March or early April at the same time that the first wildflowers appear. It is a welcome sight

186. *Sarcoscypha dudleyi*

after a long, desperate winter and is the harbinger of a new year of mushrooming. Cups arise from buried sticks; their brilliant red interior contrasts sharply with the white exterior. Rarely, a yellow form will be found. The fruiting bodies in the photograph are young and will continue to expand. *Sarcoscypha occidentalis* (no. 187), which is often confused with the scarlet cup, fruits during late spring and summer; it has smaller cups and a more pronounced stalk. The orange peel, *Aleuria aurantia*, is bright orange and terrestrial, with a minutely fuzzy underside in youth; it also fruits later and is uncommon in Kansas.

Description: **Cup**: 2–6 cm broad, cup- to saucer-shaped with incurved margin; inner surface red; exterior white and cottony. **Stalk**: 0.5–2 cm long, 3–5 mm thick, white, sometimes absent. **Spores**: 26–40 × 10–12 µm, elliptical, smooth, with two fairly large oil droplets (within) at either end. **Season**: early spring. **Ecology**: Saprotrophic.

187. *Sarcoscypha occidentalis* Edibility unknown

This bright red cup fungus is extremely abundant in the deciduous forests of Kansas during late spring and summer and even into the fall. It may fruit singly but often occurs in clusters, as in the photograph. The fruiting bodies are attached to buried twigs by long white stalks. The stalks on the specimens illustrated are longer than usual and were exposed by removing a neighboring piece of wood. Mushroomers frequently confuse *Sarcoscypha occidentalis* with the scarlet cup, *S. dudleyi* (no. 186), which fruits in early spring. However, their fruiting seasons do not overlap, and *S. dudleyi* has a larger cup and shorter stalk.

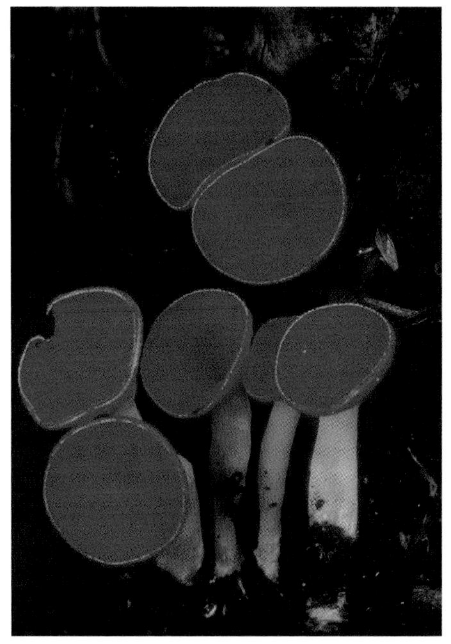

187. *Sarcoscypha occidentalis*

Description: **Cup**: 0.5–1.5 cm broad, cup- to saucer-shaped; inner surface red; exterior white and smooth. **Stalk**: 0.5–3.5 cm long, 2–4 mm thick, white. **Spores**: 18–20 × 10–12 µm, elliptical, smooth, and with two fairly large oil droplets (within) at either end. **Season**: late spring–fall. **Ecology**: saprotrophic.

188. *Scutellinia scutellata*

188. *Scutellinia scutellata* Edibility unknown

Eyelash cup

The eyelash cup can usually be found during the summer in Kansas by carefully searching boggy areas where timber has fallen. Its stalkless orange to red cups occur singly or clustered on rotten logs and exposed tree roots or on nearby soil. The eyelash cup is aptly named for the dark hairs that project from its margin (visible in the photograph). Similar species in Kansas are difficult to identify; they often lack hairs at the margin or are differently colored.

Description: **Cup**: 0.3–1.5 cm broad, saucer-shaped, orange to red; outer surface with stiff brown to black hairs that extend beyond margin. **Stalk**: absent. **Spores**: 18–19 × 10–12 µm, elliptical, slightly roughened. **Season**: summer. **Ecology**: saprotrophic.

189. *Urnula craterium* *Edibility unknown*

Devil's urn

The devil's urn is a distinctive cup fungus that appears in Kansas woods during March and April before the appearance of the first morels. The fungus, which causes cankers on oaks, fruits on the tree limbs it has killed after they have fallen and become buried under leaf litter. The fruiting bodies are

189. *Urnula craterium*

urn-shaped and leathery; they are often filled with rainwater. The inside of the cup appears black in subdued light but is actually dark brown, as revealed here by flash illumination. Another black cup fungus, *Bulgaria inquinans*, is gelatinous, somewhat flattened, and stalkless; it fruits on logs during the summer and fall.

Description: **Cup**: 3–10 cm broad, 4–8 cm tall, urn-shaped with toothed margin, blackish brown, leathery; exterior with brown scales. **Stalk**: 3–4 cm long, 3–5 mm thick, tapered. **Spores**: 22–37 × 10–15 µm, elliptical to sausage-shaped, smooth. **Season**: early spring. **Ecology**: parasitic and saprotrophic.

190. *Leotia lubrica* — Edible

Jelly babies

Leotia lubrica fruits during the summer in the moist woodlands of Kansas. Though mushroom-like in appearance, its fruiting body lacks gills and instead produces spores on the upper surface of the head. The fruiting bodies are greenish yellow, rubbery, and very slippery. The form sometimes called *Leotia viscosa*, which has an olive-green head and yellow to orange stalk, appears merely to be a color variant of typical *L. lubrica*.

Description: **Head**: 0.5–3 cm broad, round to flattened, with wavy, inrolled margin, greenish yellow, smooth or creased, slippery, rubbery. **Stalk**: 1–6 cm long, 0.3–1 cm thick, colored as head, smooth or granular, hollow. **Spores**: 16–23 × 4–6 µm, spindle-shaped or slightly curved, smooth, 5–7-celled. **Season**: summer. **Ecology**: saprotrophic.

190. *Leotia lubrica*

191. ***Calycina citrina*** Edibility unknown

Syn. = *Bisporella citrina* (Ed. 1)

This bright yellow cup fungus fruits abundantly in Kansas on rotten logs during mid- to late fall, after the weather has become decidedly cool. The fruiting bodies are minute and sometimes have a tiny stalk, but their habit of growing in large, dense clusters makes them stand out in the woods. Another species from the order Helotiales, equally minuscule, is *Hymenoscyphus fructigenus*. This species is cup-like, stalked, and pale and grows only on nuts.

Description: **Cup**: 1–3 mm broad, saucer- or disc-shaped; upper surface bright yellow; lower surface paler and smooth. **Stalk**: short or absent. **Spores**: 9–14 × 3–5 µm, elliptical, smooth, 1- or 2-celled. **Season**: mid–late fall. **Ecology**: saprotrophic.

191. *Calycina citrina*

Orders Boliniales, Hypocreales, and Xylariales

These three orders all bear their spores in groupings of asci (plural of ascus: microscopic sac-like structures found embedded in the hymenium of Ascomycetes; Fig. 8A). These groups are each contained in flask-shaped structures called perithecia (Fig. 8B). Although they are mostly embedded, the tops of the perithecia may protrude, making tiny, visible bumps, sort of like pimples.

Claviceps purpurea, commonly called ergot, belongs to the order Hypocreales and causes ergotism, or St. Anthony's fire, which is characterized by gangrene and convulsions. Many epidemics attributable to ergot have been recorded since the Middle Ages. Ergot parasitizes grasses, especially rye, and replaces their grains with fungal tissue rich in LSD-like alkaloids; this then would be made into flour that, when consumed, would cause the terrible illness. *Claviceps purpurea*, along with many other fungi producing perithecia, has been reported from Kansas. Those discussed here that reside in the order Hypocreales are the genera growing on insect larvae or truffle-like fungi, *Nectria* (growing on plants), and *Hypomyces* (growing on cap-and-stalked russulas). The genera *Biscogniauxia*, *Daldinia*, *Entonaema*, *Kretzchmaria*, and *Xylaria* belong to the order Xylariales, and the single member of the order Boliniales represented here is the rare genus *Camarops*.

Key to species

1a) Growing on insect larvae	go to **2**
1b) Growing on fungi or wood	go to **3**
2a) Growing on June bug larvae	*Ophiocordyceps melolonthae* (no. 192)
2b) Growing on butterfly or moth larvae	*Cordyceps militaris* (see no. 192)
3a) Growing on fungi	go to **4**
3b) Growing on wood	go to **8**
4a) Growing on buried, spiny, truffle-like fungi	go to **5**
4b) Growing on cap-and-stalk mushrooms	go to **6**
5a) Fruiting body with a blackish, club-shaped head and yellowish stalk	*Tolypocladium ophioglossoides* (no. 193)
5b) Fruiting body with a yellowish, round head and yellowish stalk	*Tolypocladium capitatum* (see no. 193)

6a) Growing over *Lactarius*, *Lactifluus*, or *Russula*, becoming a distorted, bright orange, pimply mass, becoming firm at maturity
Hypomyces lactifluorum (no. 194)

6b) Growing over *Amanita* or bolete species, at first white, then pink, golden, or brown; remaining soft at maturity go to **7**

7a) Growing over boletes, at first white, then golden, then brown
Hypomyces chrysospermus (no. 195)

7b) Growing over *Amanita* species, at first white, then pink
Hypomyces hyalinus (see no. 195)

8a) Fruiting body surface soft, sticky, or rubbery at maturity go to **9**

8b) Fruiting body hard at maturity go to **10**

9a) Fruiting body yellow, round-amorphous, hollow but filled with liquid, with a rubbery surface *Entonaema liquescens* (no. 199)

9b) Fruiting body black, cushion-shaped, solid with a sticky surface
Camarops petersii (no. 200)

10a) Fruiting body of bright coral or orange becoming brown, bead-like, pimply bumps *Nectria cinnabarina* (see no. 194)

10b) Fruiting body gray or typically black at maturity go to **11**

11a) Fruiting body lying flat on the substrate (resupinate) go to **12**

11b) Fruiting body not resupinate go to **13**

12a) Fruiting body black at all stages
Biscogniauxia mediterranea (see no. 200)

12b) Fruiting body initially gray ringed with white, later black
Kretzschmaria deusta (no. 197)

13a) Fruiting body roundish to amorphous, showing internal concentric rings when cut *Daldinia childiae* (no. 198)

13b) Fruiting body not spherical, longer than broad, club-shaped or branched go to **14**

14a) Fruiting body stout, unbranched, club-shaped, broadened at tip
Xylaria polymorpha (no. 196)

14b) Fruiting body slender, branched, and coral-like, often pointed at tips
Xylaria hypoxylon (see no. 196)

192. *Ophiocordyceps melolonthae* Edibility unknown
Syn. = *Cordyceps melolonthae* (Ed. 1)

This fantastic, if not morbid, fungus parasitizes June bug larvae, or grubs. It fruits in the hardwood forests of eastern Kansas during late spring and summer. The mummified larva in the photograph was carefully dug out from leaf litter to reveal its connections with the fruiting bodies aboveground; note that the head and legs are still visible on the host. Only a single white to orange-yellow fruiting body normally arises from one larva. These unusual twin fruiting bodies are immature and resemble plant sprouts more than fungi. They will eventually form a club-shaped head that consists of patches of minute spore-producing perithecia; the extreme apex of the head usually remains sterile. *Cordyceps militaris* is smaller than *Ophiocordyceps melolonthae*, orange to reddish orange, and fertile at its apex. It parasitizes the larvae and pupae of butterflies and moths.

Description: **Head**: 1–1.5 cm broad, 2–3 cm tall, club-shaped, white to yellow or orange-yellow, covered with irregular patches of perithecia; apex usually sterile. **Stalk**: 5–7 cm long, 0.3–1 cm thick, light yellow-orange to brown, smooth, arising from buried beetle larvae. **Spores**: needle-shaped, breaking into smooth elliptical segments 6–8 × 1.5–2.5 µm. **Season**: late spring–summer. **Ecology**: parasitic.

192. *Ophiocordyceps melolonthae*

193. *Tolypocladium ophioglossoides* Edibility unknown
Syn. = *Cordyceps ophioglossoides* (Ed. 1)
Syn. = *Elaphocordyceps ophioglossoides*

Although most species of this group parasitize insects, *Tolypocladium ophioglossoides* attacks a truffle-like fungus, namely, the deer truffle, *Elaphomyces* (not a true truffle), which grows underground. In Kansas, fruiting bodies arise from parasitized *E. granulatus* during the summer. The specimen illustrated here was carefully dug up and propped on a log to show both the parasite and its attached host. *Tolypocladium ophioglossoides* is characterized by its blackish club-shaped head and yellow stalk. It is attached indirectly to its spiny host by yellow mycelial cords. Like true truffles, deer truffles are excavated and eaten by animals, who then disperse the spores. The deer truffle was once considered an aphrodisiac by herbalists. *Tolypocladium ophioglossoides* might be confused with some species of *Xylaria*, but the latter grow on woody matter. Another species, *T. capitatum* (syns. = *Cordyceps captata* [Ed. 1], *Elaphocordyceps capitata*), which is also found in Kansas, differs in having a round head and being entirely yellowish.

193. *Tolypocladium ophioglossoides*

Description: **Head**: 3–6 cm broad, 1–2 cm tall, club-shaped, yellow becoming reddish brown or black, roughened by perithecia. **Stalk**: 3–8 cm long, 1–3 mm thick, yellow to olive, attached to underground *Elaphomyces granulatus* by yellow mycelial cords. **Spores**: needle-shaped, breaking into smooth elliptical segments 2–4 × 1.5–2 µm. **Season**: summer. **Ecology**: parasitic.

194. *Hypomyces lactifluorum*

194. *Hypomyces lactifluorum* Edible with caution
Lobster mold

The lobster mold parasitizes large white species of *Lactarius*, *Lactifluus*, and *Russula*, turning their fruiting bodies into misshapen, bright-orange masses. Its appearance in Kansas naturally coincides with the emergence of its hosts under hardwoods, generally in summer and early fall. The parasitized mushrooms often are barely able to crack the soil surface. Spores of *Hypomyces lactifluorum* are produced in minute flask-shaped perithecia that coat the undersurface of the host and give it a sandpaperlike texture. Note in the photograph how the gills of the host are nearly obliterated by the parasite. Most mushroom books do not recommend the lobster mold as an edible because its host is impossible to identify. However, mushrooms infected by *H. lactifluorum* are commonly eaten with no ill effects, and those from Kansas are clearly delectable. Chopped up and fried in butter, they impart a rich, saffron-like color to rice dishes. Another often bright coral or orange species that dulls with age manifests as tiny, hard, discrete, pimply, bead-like bumps parasitizing wood. It is *Nectria cinnabarina*, commonly called coral spot.

Description: **Fruiting body**: minute perithecia coating gills of mushroom host; parasitized host bright orange to orange-red, distorted, with gills ridgelike or obliterated. **Spores**: 35–50 × 6–8 µm, spindle-shaped, warted, 2-celled. **Season**: summer–early fall. **Ecology**: parasitic.

195. *Hypomyces chrysospermus* Not edible

This mold is a common parasite of boletes during summer and early fall in Kansas. Its three stages are distinguished by the type of spore produced and the color imparted to the host. Initially, the bolete becomes covered with a white, cottony mycelium. This is the rather brief "*Verticillium*" stage; patches of it can be seen on the hosts illustrated here. The next stage, designated "*Sepedonium chrysospermum*," is bright yellow, powdery, and much more prolonged. It is the dominant stage in the photograph and the one by which the mold is most often identified. In the final stage, *Hypomyces chrysospermus* turns the host reddish brown. Fortunately, this stage is rarely seen since by then the host is very rotten. The first two stages form asexual spores and are called anamorphs, and the last stage is called a teleomorph and is sexual, producing sexual spores within minute flask-shaped perithecia. Since the sexual stage is most important in fungi (at least to the people naming them), *H. chrysospermus* is the proper name when referring to the fungus as a whole. Parasitized boletes should not be eaten, since the host is difficult to identify, and bacteria participate in its decomposition. Another mushroom parasite, *H. hyalinus*, turns *Amanita* species into white to pink club-shaped masses.

195. *Hypomyces chrysospermus*

It has a preference for the edible blusher, *A. "amerirubescens,"* but can also parasitize deadly amanitas. It is definitely not recommended for eating.

Description: **Fruiting body**: perithecia covering bolete host during final red-brown stage; parasitized host initially white (*Verticillium* stage), then bright yellow (*Sepedonium* stage), finally red-brown (*Hypomyces* stage). **Spores**: *Verticillium* stage, 10–30 × 5–12 µm, elliptical, smooth; *Sepedonium* stage, 10–25 µm, round, warted; *Hypomyces* stage, 25–30 × 5–6 µm, spindle-shaped, smooth, 2-celled. **Season**: summer–early fall. **Ecology**: parasitic.

196. *Xylaria polymorpha*

Not edible

Syn. = *Xylosphaera polymorpha*

Dead man's fingers

Xylaria polymorpha commonly fruits on logs and stumps in Kansas. When arising from buried wood, its blackened, fingerlike fruiting bodies resemble hands groping to be free of the grave—hence its common name, dead man's fingers. The fruiting bodies first appear in late spring or early summer. At this time, they are covered with a white bloom of asexual spores. Later, during summer and fall, sexual spores form inside perithecia that are embedded within the fruiting body; the specimens illustrated here are in this sexual state. Old fruiting bodies often persist through the winter. Another common species in Kansas is *X. hypoxylon* (syn. = *Xylosphaera hypoxylon*), the candle-snuff fungus, which also fruits on wood but is slender, branched, and coral-like. When young, the pointed tips of its branches are also whitened by asexual spores.

196. *Xylaria polymorpha*

Description: **Head:** 0.5–12 cm broad, 2–8 cm tall, club- or finger-shaped, black, covered with white bloom when young, wrinkled or cracked. **Stalk**: short, narrower than head. **Spores**: (sexual) 20–30 × 5–10 μm, spindle-shaped, flattened on one side, smooth, dark brown. **Season**: late spring–fall. **Ecology**: saprotrophic.

197. *Kretzschmaria deusta* — Not edible

Bird poop

This funny little Ascomycete shows up as many little patches of bubbly gray to grayish brown, ringed with white, looking more like bird poop than a fungus, as shown here. The mature organism is hard, textured black, and easily overlooked. The growth habit of both forms is resupinate (lying flat on its substrate of dead wood). *Kretzschmaria deusta* is probably found year-round in its aged form.

Description: **Fruiting body**: 2–10 cm, irregularly round or amorphous, resupinate, initially soft, lumpy, gray to grayish brown, surrounded by white, at maturity hard, blackish, with a rough, bumpy texture. **Spore print**: dark brown. **Spores**: 32–34 × 7–10, roughly elliptical, one side shorter. **Season**: year-round. **Ecology**: saprotrophic.

197. *Kretzschmaria deusta*

198. *Daldinia childiae*

198. *Daldinia childiae* Not edible

Daldinia concentrica (Ed. 1, misapplied)

Carbon balls

King Alfred's cakes

Unobtrusive, dark, usually hard, fruiting bodies are prevalent in Kansas forests, many looking like burned lumps. *Daldinia childiae* is one of the largest of these. This species is generally round to round amorphous, as pictured in the larger uncut specimen. The distinguishing features are the concentric rings of the interior, which are apparent when cut. Initially, the finely roughened surface is reddish brown, but older fruiting bodies become black with a dull sheen. *Daldinia childiae* grows on dead hardwood in Kansas. Because of its sturdy nature, this species may be found year-round.

Description: **Fruiting body**: 2–5 cm wide, thick, hard, round to irregular lumps, initially rusty brown, later black, surface finely roughened. **Stalk**: absent. **Spores**: 12–17 × 6–7.5 µm, irregularly elliptical, smooth. **Season**: year-round. **Ecology**: saprotrophic.

199. *Entonaema liquescens*

199. *Entonaema liquescens* — Edibility unknown

This strange tropical fungus has been collected in the United States near the Gulf Coast, in southern Illinois, and, oddly enough, in eastern Kansas, where it is fairly common on fallen logs during the summer. It is recognized by its yellow, round to convoluted fruiting bodies, which are hollow and filled with liquid. One of the specimens in the photograph is split open to show the hollow interior from which fluid has spilled. Spore-bearing perithecia are embedded in the gelatinous wall. Jelly fungi are also gelatinous, but none of these are filled with liquid.

Description: **Fruiting body**: 1–13 cm broad, 1–6 cm tall, round to convoluted, bright yellow to olive-yellow (easily rubbed off) with dark undersurface, gelatinous, hollow, filled with liquid. **Spores**: 9.5–12 × 5–6 µm, elliptical to rectangular, smooth, with longitudinal germ slit, brown. **Season**: summer. **Ecology**: saprotrophic.

200. *Camarops petersii* — Not edible

The rare and exotic *Camarops petersii* has been reported from a handful of states in the eastern half of the United States, including Kansas. The three fruiting bodies shown here were discovered in August during a group foray at Fort Leavenworth in Leavenworth County and caused mixed exclamations of disgust and wonder. The fungus typically fruits singly on rotting oak logs but may also occur clustered, as in the photograph. *Camarops petersii* is identified by its black, cushion-shaped fruiting body, the upper fertile surface of which is encircled by a ragged margin, visible on these specimens. This margin represents the remnants of an overlying membrane that sloughs away early in development. Spore-bearing perithecia are embedded beneath the fertile surface, giving it a pimple-like texture. The shiny, tar-like, sticky coating on these specimens is due to spores that have been exuded through the mouths of the perithecia. *Daldinia childiae* (no. 198), commonly called carbon balls, is more or less spherical and lacks a ragged margin and sticky surface; concentric zones are visible within its fruiting body when it is sliced in half. *Biscogniauxia mediterranea* (syn. = *Hypoxylon mediterraneum* [Ed. 1]) and other black species of *Hypoxylon* are similar in color to *C. petersii* but are hard and crust-like, not cushion-shaped, and lack ragged margins; *B. mediterranea* is a common species that prefers oak.

Description: **Fruiting body**: 2–7 cm broad, cushion- or top-shaped, black, rubbery when fresh; upper surface shiny, tar-like, roughened by perithecia, initially covered by a membrane that sloughs away, leaving a ragged margin. **Spores**: 6–8 × 3.5–4 µm, elliptical, smooth, with minute apical germ pore, dark brown. **Season**: summer. **Ecology**: saprotrophic.

200. *Camarops petersii*

Myxomycetes or Mycetozoa: The Slime Molds

Other organisms that might be mistaken for mushrooms are slime molds, also called Myxomycetes or Mycetozoa. These belong to the kingdom Protista rather than the fungal kingdom. The organisms traditionally included in Mycetozoa encompass several distantly related groups of amoeboid organisms within the Protista that have independently adopted nutritional and reproductive modes that are similar to those of fungi. Many slime molds are very tiny and will go unnoticed by all but the most careful observer. The species pictured are all plasmodial slime molds, which have an active unicellular, multinucleate stage, which in some species may reach very large sizes before the slime mold settles down to produce its delicate fruiting structures. *Fuligo septica* (no. 205), for instance, commonly called dog vomit slime mold or scrambled egg slime, can reach 8 inches in diameter. Some people eat this slime and compare it favorably to scrambled eggs. *Fuligo septica* is often found consuming microorganisms on mulch or grass in lawns and does not look appealing. While young, it is bright yellow, and in age, it is textured tan with a black powdery interior. Other slimes are miniature, exotic beauties, such as the tiny bubblegum-pink or neon-orange blobs of *Lycogala epidendrum* (no. 203), the feathery fronds of *Stemonitis fusca* (no. 202), and the tempting *Tubifera ferruginosa* (aptly named raspberry slime) shown here (no. 204).

201. *Physarum polycephalum*

Before fruiting, many plasmodial slime molds are brightly colored, and some species, such as *Physarum polycephalum* (no. 201, pictured here exploring *Auricularia americana*), are deftly able to find their way to nutritional rewards. This species is world famous for learning how to solve mazes and has occasionally been employed by urban planners in determining the most efficient route from one place to another. The easiest way to distinguish a fruiting slime mold from a mushroom is to touch it; when mature, the slime fruit is very fragile, and the entire fruiting structure will crumble to almost nothing with a little puff of dusty spores, but a mushroom is more durable.

202. *Stemonitis fusca*

203. *Lycogala epidendrum*

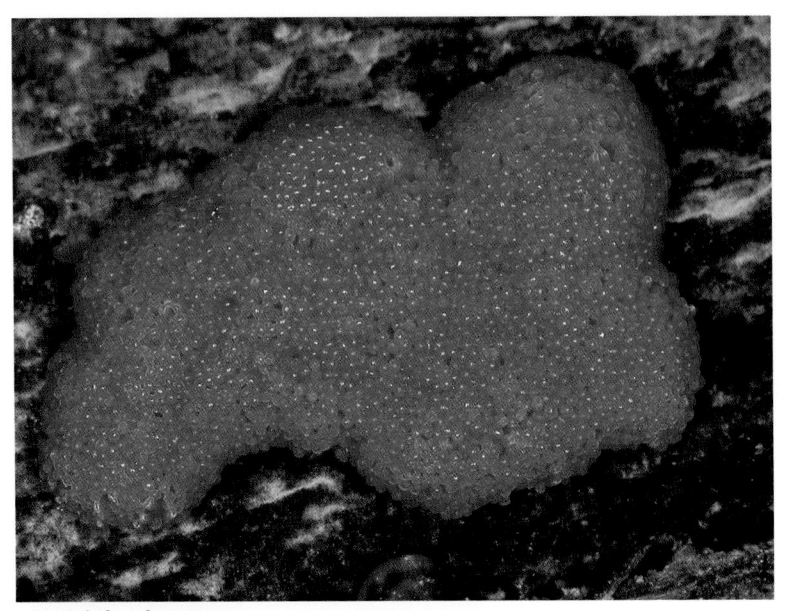

204. *Tubifera ferruginosa*

205. *Fuligo septica*

More on Mushrooms

Sex, Lies, and the Truth about Mushrooms

Dean Abel, Sherry Kay, and Benjamin Sikes

The Naming of Mushrooms

Mushrooms—like T. S. Eliot's cats—can have three names. First, they often have a common name, such as inky cap or yellow morel or bear's head. These are sensible everyday English names that identify the mushroom friends we know well. Common names can vary from region to region: what is "beefsteak" in Kansas is called "big red" in Missouri, though if you ask both Kansas and Missouri mycologists, they will tell you it is *Discina caroliniana* (no. 178) (if they are keeping up with current taxonomy). Likewise, many different species of *Coprinopsis* and *Coprinellus* are called "inky caps." Many less familiar mushrooms have no common name at all.

Second, mycologists give each species its own scientific name, such as *Coprinopsis atramentaria* (no. 66), *Morchella americana* (no. 181), or *Hericium americanum* (no. 141). This name never belongs to more than one kind of mushroom. The scientific naming of organisms is called binomial nomenclature because the name consists of two words. The first word is always capitalized and indicates the genus to which the mushroom is assigned; the second word is the specific epithet, which, when combined with the generic name, forms a binomial that indicates the species of the mushroom. The specific epithet is adjectival and describes the genus name. So, for instance, the common grocery-store mushroom, *Agaricus bisporus*, would be translated as "the two-spored agaric." This specific epithet is not capitalized even when the mushroom is named after a person, such as *Saproamanita thiersii* (no. 8), named for Dr. Harry D. Thiers. The entire binomial is italicized.

Last, like Eliot's cats, mushrooms have their own deep and inscrutable singular names that no mycologist can discover.

The avid reader will notice many name changes in this book, most of which are driven by changes to scientific names over time. These changes have three main sources. First, a single species may have been given more than one scientific name, usually because a species was "discovered" and named independently by different scientists. Taxonomists must determine which name should be adopted, usually based on priority. The *International*

Code of Nomenclature for Algae, Fungi, and Plants tells us that the first name to be published is the one to use. Although rare, this sometimes causes names long in use to be replaced by more obscure ones simply because they were published earlier, causing confusion. In the end, each species has one binomial name accepted by most taxonomists as the correct one and perhaps one or more other scientific names, which are called synonyms. In this book, synonyms are marked "syn. ="; in several cases, the scientific name used in the first edition is now considered a synonym.

More commonly these days, however, scientific names change as we refine our understanding of the evolutionary relationships among species. In these cases, the specific epithet (the second part of a binomial) is sometimes transferred from one genus to another (occasionally with a slight change in the ending to make it the correct Latin gender). The genus name is new, and may be unfamiliar, but the specific epithet remains the same. It can be frustrating and confusing to call the species formerly known as *Boletus campestris* (a common red-and-yellow bolete) by the new name, *Hortiboletus campestris* (no. 91), or to call the elm oyster *Hypsizygus ulmarius* (see no. 38) after learning it as *Pleurotus ulmarius*, but at least the specific epithet is there to guide you.

In other instances, scientists learn that mushrooms in multiple regions that were considered to belong to the same species are actually genetically distinct and deserve recognition as two (or more!) separate species. Again, following the rules laid out in the *Code*, each species gets its own binomial name, and sometimes we must learn to distinguish between the old, more broadly defined species and the new, more narrowly defined ones. Along these lines, readers who are familiar with the first edition of this guide may be surprised to learn that *Morchella esculenta* (see no. 181), once considered to occur in Europe and North America (including Kansas), is now considered to be found in Europe only, and our species of yellow morel is called *Morchella americana*. In this case, the name used in the first edition was merely an incorrect—or "misapplied"—name, due not to an error of the authors but to our understanding of this difficult species group at the time of publication.

For all the confusion these new names may engender, the reader might well wonder why we have chosen to take them up at all. We emphasize scientific names for individual mushrooms and groupings of mushrooms (families, orders, classes, and the like) throughout this book because we believe that these are the names that convey the most accurate (sometimes vital) information about the identity of the species. For instance, many mushrooms may informally be referred to as fairy-ring mushrooms and do form arcs and rings (as does the most common poisoner, *Chlorophyllum molybdites* [no. 79]), but only one, a good edible, *Marasmius oreades* (no. 16), is so called. The book reflects science's current understanding of the fungal kingdom, including some surprises (e.g., the polypore *Bondarzewia berkeleyi* [no. 115] is now known to be in the Russulales). As detailed in "Online Resources for Identifying Mushrooms," the Index Fungorum (http://www.indexfungorum.org) or Mycobank (http://www.mycobank.org) websites provide complete lists of synonyms for each mushroom's scientific name to satisfy the intrepid reader who wants to learn the evolution of a mushroom's names. We also struggle with the many ongoing name changes, particularly following the application of genetic tools. Many of these are new to us, so we have tried, with each entry in the Anthology, to include obsolete scientific names and any common names. The index lists the mushrooms included not only by current genus and species but also by some frequently encountered synonyms (especially those used in the first edition) and common names if available.

Microscopic Features

Not everyone has or wants to use a microscope to help them identify mushrooms. The fact is, though, that observing microscopic features not only aids in identification but is sometimes the only way to distinguish some mushrooms, barring DNA sequencing. This section describes these microscopic features, including the specialized terms (in bold) used to describe them. Don't worry—there won't be a test! As you use the book, if you come to a term you don't remember, they are also listed at the end of the book in the glossary (p. 369).

A **hymenium**, or layer of microscopic spore-bearing cells, covers the surfaces of **gills** of the gilled members of the Basidiomycota. In the non-gilled Basidiomycota, the hymenium lines the inner surface of the **tubes** of boletes and polypores, covers the teeth of spine fungi (Fig. 4, page 4) and the branches of corals, or resides within a tissue sack (as in puffballs). In the Ascomycota, spores develop within a microscopic, elongated, sac-like cell called an **ascus** (Fig. 8A), which typically contains eight **spores**. The orders Helotiales, Leotiales, Pezizales, and Phacidiales of Ascomycota develop an exposed layer of asci (Fig. 8A), as on the inner surface of cup fungi or within the pits of morels. The Boliniales, Hypocreales, and Xylariales produce minute, flask-shaped structures called perithecia (Fig. 8B), within which the asci develop. So the Basidiomycota have spore-producing cells that protrude, while the Ascomycota spore-producing cells are embedded, all microscopically, for the most part.

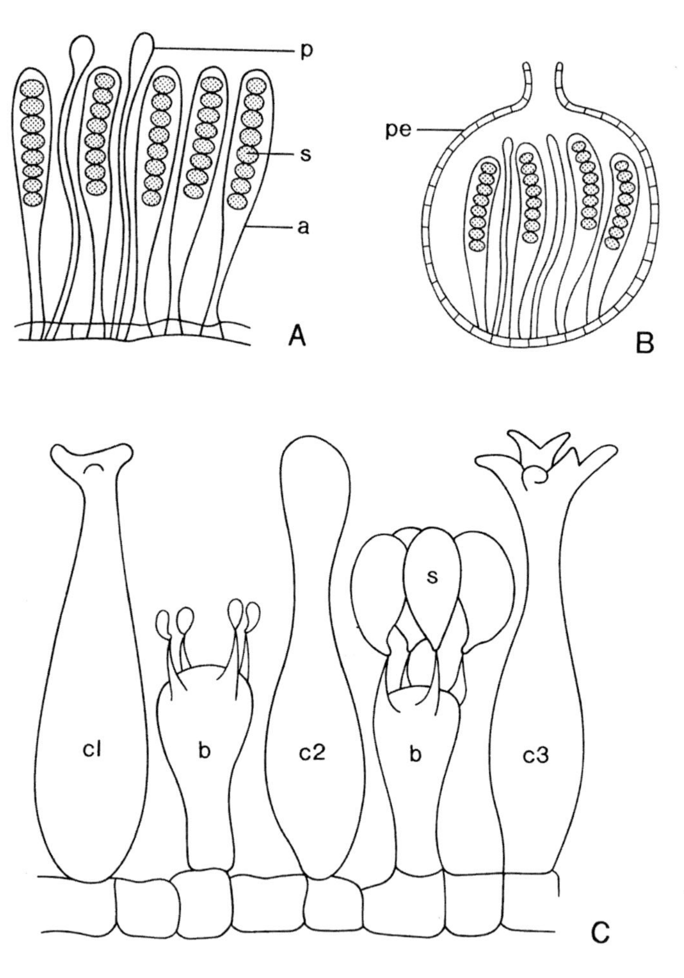

Figure 8. Spore-producing cells. Ascomycota represented in A and B; Basidiomycota represented in C.

A. Portion of the hymenium of a cup fungus, or relatives thereof. Each ascus (a) typically contains eight spores (s). Long, thin paraphyses (p) are interspersed among the asci.

B. Sectioned hymenium of a perithecium (pe) of a flask fungus. Both asci and paraphyses are present.

C. Hymenium of a gilled mushroom. Each basidium (b) typically produces four spores at the tips of pointed sterigmata; both young and nearly mature spore(s) are shown. Interspersed among the basidia are examples of large sterile cells, or cystidia (c), from three species of *Pluteus*: (c1) *P. petasatus*, (c2) *P. admirabilis*, (c3) *P. cervinus*. (Not drawn to scale.)

In the Basidiomycota, usually four spores develop on the tips of thin projections called **sterigmata**, which extend from a club-shaped cell called a **basidium** (Fig. 8C). The gleba is the fertile portion of the Gasteromycetes and the Phallales and may become powdery in the puffballs or slimy in the stinkhorns. The basidia of the jelly fungi are often not club-shaped and sometimes look like a tuning fork.

In the hymenium of the Ascomycota, there may also be threadlike sterile cells called **paraphyses** interspersed with the asci (Fig. 8A and 8B). Similar structures called **cystidia** often occur within the hymenium of members of Basidiomycota (Fig. 8C). Many types of cystidia exist, and the determination of their shape and size can be important to verify the correct identification of a mushroom.

The most important feature for identification, used in most guides, is the spores themselves. Their color, shape, size, ornamentation, septation (walls within the spore), and reaction to chemical tests often can be the crux of an identification (Fig. 9). Spores of Basidiomycota often have a protrusion at one end, called an **apiculus**, which is the point of attachment to the basidium. The opposite end of the spore may also be flattened due to an opening, termed the apical **germ pore** (Fig. 9A, H, J), from which the **hypha** emerges when the spore germinates.

Sex and Mushrooms

In plants and animals, fertilization results from the union of a sperm and an egg, which forms a zygote that divides and grows into an embryo. Mushrooms, on the other hand, produce cells called spores from which a filament, or hypha, emerges upon germination (Fig. 10). There is initially no baby mushroom or embryo.

The hypha grows, branches, and forms a mass of hyphae called a **mycelium** (Fig. 1, p. 2). Only when hyphae from one spore comes into contact with hyphae from another spore that is of a compatible "mating type" do the hyphae fuse into a single organism that is able to fruit. Since mushrooms may have a great number of mating types, it may be said that they have many sexes.

The genetic control and determination of mating can be quite complex. For example, a feature peculiar to mushrooms is that upon the fusion of two compatible hyphae, the nuclei from each mating type do not fuse, as they do in fertilization between sperm and egg. The nuclei, one from each parent, are maintained as separate entities within each cell, a condition called **dikaryotic** that is unique to mushrooms. Upon the formation of a dikaryotic

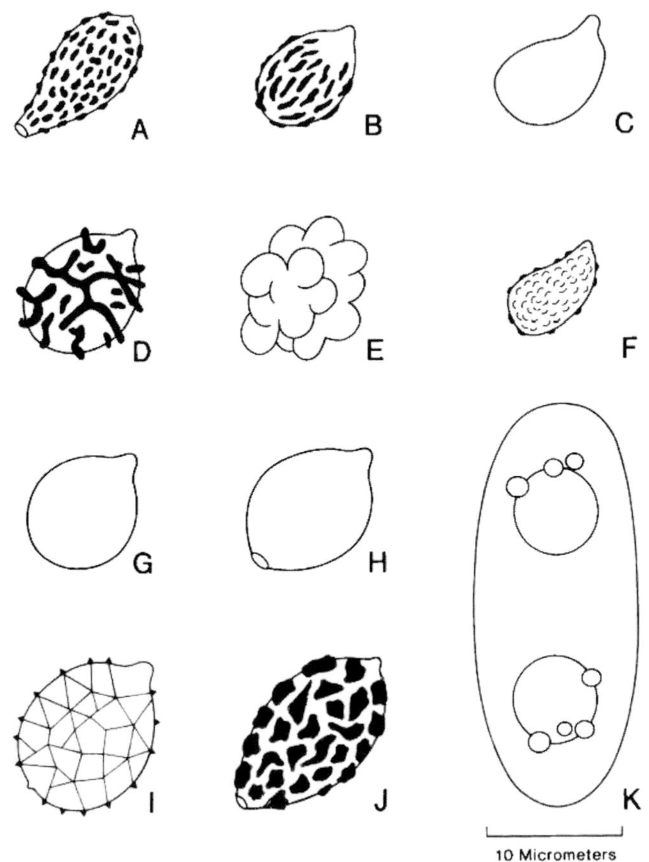

Figure 9. Mushroom sexual spores.
A. *Lacrymaria lacrymabunda*.
B. *Galerina marginata* (the deadly galerina).
C. *Gyroporus purpurinus*.
D. *Lactarius psammicola*.
E. *Inocybe* species.
F. *Ramaria stricta*.
G. *Amanita bisporigera* (the destroying angel).
H. *Chlorophyllum molybdites*.
I. *Strobilomyces strobilaceus* (the old man of the woods).
J. *Panaeolina foenisecii* (the haymaker's mushroom).
K. *Sarcoscypha dudleyi* (the scarlet cup), with oil droplets visible inside spore.
Spores A, H, and J have an apical germ pore at their lower end. A nipple-like apiculus where the spore was attached to the basidium is present at the upper end of all spores except E (not visible) and K (not present).

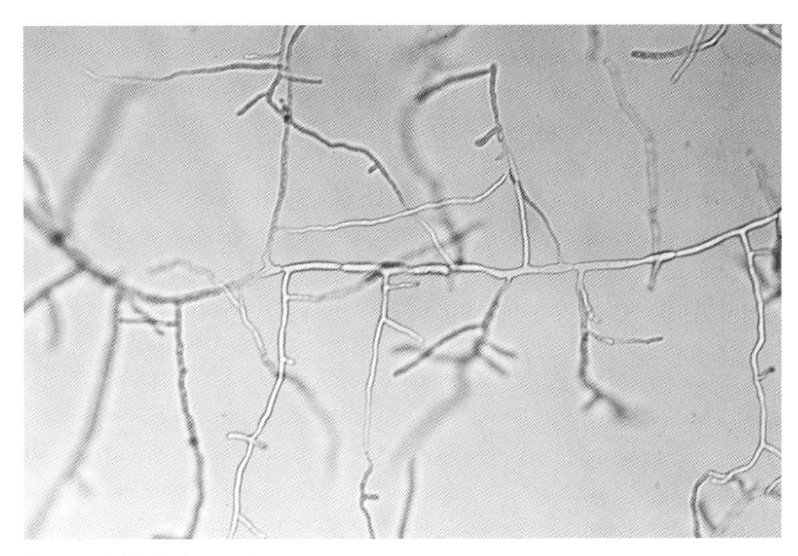

Figure 10. Hyphal strand.

mycelium, when the conditions are appropriate, the hidden mass of mycelium growing inside a dead log, in animal dung, or on leaf litter will form tiny nodules that develop into the spore-bearing fungal fruiting bodies we call mushrooms.

The above discussion pertains to nearly all the known mushrooms in the phylum Basidiomycota. Sex and fruiting body formation in the other large subdivision of mushrooms, the phylum Ascomycota, are more diverse and often more complex. Nevertheless, many of these mushrooms also have mating types and ultimately form spores from dikaryotic hyphae.

Mushrooms within these groups produce spores within asci or on the tips of basidia (Fig. 8), which gives the phyla their respective names. It is only within each ascus or basidium that the two parental nuclei finally fuse to become a zygote. Immediately following fertilization, the zygote nucleus divides twice to produce four spores. In the Ascomycota, an additional nuclear division is usual and results in eight spores. The details of these biological events vary greatly among mushrooms, and this discussion is only a peek though the fungal bedroom window.

Some mushrooms can also produce **asexual** spores that are not the result of fertilization and zygote formation. For example, *Asterophora lycoperdoides* (no. 37) develops a powdery layer of asexual spores on the surface of the cap, while immature specimens of *Xylaria polymorpha* (no. 196), or dead man's fingers, are often frosted with a white layer of asexual spores before the development of asci within perithecia. Like sexual spores, asexual spores typically germinate into young hyphae.

The spores of many mushrooms are forcibly discharged. They are shot off the tips of basidia or blown out of the asci by a buildup of hydrostatic pressure. Puffballs, however, do not discharge their spores but simply rely upon the wind and rain to disperse them. Stinkhorns attract insects to their smelly slime, or gleba, in order to spread the spores it contains. Bird's nest fungi form splash cups that exploit the energy of falling raindrops to drive their packets of spores, or "eggs," out of the nest and into the world. The diverse mechanisms of spore dispersal emphasize how mushrooms have evolved to use animals, wind, and rain to ensure their survival.

The Molecular Revolution in Mushroom Taxonomy

Like nearly all life on Earth, mushrooms have instructions for their growth, function, and reproduction encoded in DNA. This DNA is made up of nucleic acids (represented by A, C, G, and T), and differences in the letters within a common region provide critical information about how two mushrooms are related and hence how we should name them. Since the latter part of the twentieth century, scientists have increasingly relied on this genetic information to give fungi scientific names that better convey information about their evolutionary relatedness. However, using DNA in this way relies on choosing a gene region that can be equally compared among all (or most) fungi and that evolves at a rate consistent with the speed at which new species are formed.

The main gene region that scientists use to identify fungal species is called the internal transcribed spacer (ITS). This ITS region fits the criteria above and is commonly used for both taxonomy and, to a lesser extent, establishing ancestral relationships among mushrooms (known as their phylogeny). The effect of evolutionary forces such as natural selection on this region is relatively weak, and as a consequence, the ITS is highly variable among closely related species. The degree to which two similar mushrooms differ in this gene region can then be used to tell how closely they are related. Information from other gene regions has been combined to provide a more accurate picture of the higher phylogenetic relationships of fungi (e.g., family, order, class, phylum), but the ITS region has now been established as a convenient and useful region for identifying individual species.

Genetic information, including ITS sequences, is now commonly used to augment traditional trait-based taxonomy and has revolutionized our understanding of the fungal kingdom in two ways. First, it has shown that our understanding of the morphological characteristics that suggest that one kind of organism is different from another is basically correct. Mushrooms that look like yellow morels all belong to the genus *Morchella*. In many cases, genetic data have confirmed that mushrooms we have always considered distinct species by their appearances are genetically distinct as well.

One the other hand, gene sequencing has shown us that our ability to discern the relationships *among* species—in particular, which are the important morphological characteristics to use in assigning different species to one genus or another—have often been wrong. For example, the production of a latex-like substance has long been considered a key feature of mushrooms included in the genus *Lactarius*, the name applied to all latex-producing mushrooms in the first edition of this guide. It took gene sequencing to show us that the production of latex in the Russulales evolved at least twice, and latex-producing species now included in the genus *Lactifluus* (nos. 80, 82) are actually more closely related to species of *Russula* (nos. 84–88), which lack latex, than to latex-producing species of *Lactarius* (nos. 81, 83).

Similarly, at higher taxonomic levels, the absence of gills in mushrooms once defined a large fungal order called Aphyllophorales—which included such diverse fungi as polypores, chanterelles, and coral fungi—but this group is now understood to represent many different independent lineages. Some of these lineages are much more closely related to gilled mushrooms than to one another. In many cases where we have adopted a new name for a species in this edition, this is the reason: our traditional, morphology-based classification often underestimated the fact that the traits we used to group species had in fact evolved independently multiple times, sometimes in very distantly related groups.

Second, and perhaps more exciting, is that this DNA revolution has shown us that there is still a vast diversity of fungal life to discover, even in species we thought we knew well. The genetic data on yellow morels helped us identify subtle morphological differences that confirmed what should have been obvious: the European *Morchella esculenta* is not, after all, the same species as the one that occurs in Kansas, *M. americana*. Even when we are able to make out morphological differences between these species, the genetic data give us confidence that these differences represent something important. Genetic data of seemingly identical species (morphologically and ecologically) have in some cases been shown to be as distinct genetically as humans are from chimpanzees. This "hidden" diversity has shown that previous estimates of fungal diversity on Earth may be off by a factor of ten or more. Moreover, they show the continued importance of discovering, documenting, and conserving species in these times of ever-growing threats to global biodiversity.

These are exciting times in mycology. Genetic evidence from the ITS and other gene regions will continue to improve our understanding of the evolution of different mushrooms and their common ancestors. However, visible traits, such as those outlined in the first section, are still the most effective tools we have to identify mushrooms in the field without the cost, specialized equipment, and time needed for DNA sequencing.

Bibliography

Alexopoulos, C. J., and C. W. Mims. *Introductory Mycology*. 3rd ed. New York: John Wiley & Sons, 1979.

Brodie, Harold J. *Fungi: Delight of Curiosity*. Toronto, ON: University of Toronto Press, 1978.

Kendrick, Bryce. *The Fifth Kingdom*. 3rd ed. Mycologue Publications, 2000.

Kerrigan, Richard W. *Agaricus of North America*. Bronx, NY: New York Botanical Garden, 2016.

Margulis, Lynn, and Karlene V. Schwartz. *Five Kingdoms: An Illustrated Guide to the Phyla of Life on Earth*. San Francisco: W. H. Freeman, 1982.

Moore-Landecker, Elizabeth. *Fundamentals of the Fungi*. 3rd ed. Englewood Cliffs, NJ: Prentice-Hall, 1990.

Ramsbottom, J. *Mushrooms and Toadstools*. London: Collins, 1960.

Schoch, Conrad L., Keith A. Seifert, Sabine Huhndorf, Vincent Robert, John L. Spouge, C. André Levesque, Wen Chen, and Fungal Barcoding Consortium. "Nuclear Ribosomal Internal Transcribed Spacer (ITS) Region as a Universal DNA Barcode Marker for Fungi." *Proceedings of the National Academy of Sciences*, April 17, 2012: 6241–6246.

Kansas Habitats: Where to Find Mushrooms

Benjamin Sikes and Bruce Horn

Myths about Kansas die slowly. The state's image as a flat desert of endless wheat fields is likely perpetuated by travelers who, with visions of rugged mountains or ocean beaches, drive across its length without ever leaving the freeway. Kansans know differently. There are expansive wind-blown prairies, undulating hills with waist-high grasses, parklike savannas, and richly forested uplands and stream valleys. These diverse habitats also dispel a similar myth circulated among East and West Coast mushroomers—that Kansas is a mycological wasteland. The success of the first edition of this book and the number of species we've added to this new edition demonstrate, in fact, that Kansas is a very good place to hunt mushrooms.

Climate

Understanding the haunts and habitats of mushrooms in Kansas requires familiarity with the state's climate and its effect on the vegetation. Fungi thrive under conditions of high moisture and are thus directly influenced by climate. More profoundly, mushrooms grow on organic matter provided by plants by acting as parasites, as decomposers of litter (for example, wood and leaves), or as mycorrhizal partners with a plant's root systems. By dictating the types of plants available as food sources, climate again affects the distribution of mushrooms within the state.

Most of the state's moisture arrives on southerly breezes from the Gulf of Mexico. Since Gulf moisture tends to be deflected eastward, precipitation is greatest at the eastern boundary, where approximately 40 inches fall yearly, and progressively declines to about 18 inches on the semiarid High Plains of western Kansas. Pacific storms drop their moisture on the Rocky Mountains and are relatively dry once they cross over into Kansas. However, these low-pressure systems are responsible for drawing up moisture from the Gulf. Fortunately for mushrooms, three-fourths of the year's precipitation falls during the growing season (April–September). May and June are the wettest and most volatile months. During these months, warm, moist Gulf winds often collide with cooler, dry northern air masses, setting off violent thunderstorms. Morels may be washed from hillsides during flash floods or shredded by large hail. Temperatures are equally extreme, and subzero weather during winter and consecutive days over 100 degrees Fahrenheit in summer are not uncommon. The latter conditions are often encountered by mushroom hunters, and, when combined with the high humidity of eastern Kansas, help breed determination and character.

Vegetation

The moisture gradient from east to west accounts for the different vegetation zones that divide Kansas (Fig. 11). From the map, it is apparent that most of the state is prairie. Tallgrass prairie covers much of the eastern half of the state and is dominated by big bluestem, little bluestem, switchgrass, and Indian grass—plants that are adapted to higher precipitation. In contrast, the shortgrass prairie of the western High Plains contains plants that thrive under semiarid conditions: blue gramma, buffalo grass, and sand sagebrush (in the windblown sands bordering the Arkansas River). The mixed-grass prairie represents the transitional zone between tall- and shortgrass prairies, with species from both zones. All three prairie zones also support an abundance of wildflowers that often bloom in spectacular displays. Unfortunately, much of the Kansas prairie was plowed under by the early pioneers; the map illus-

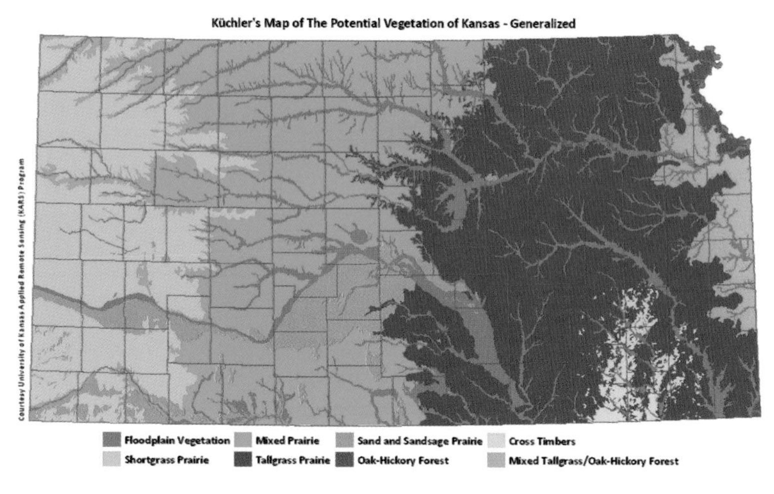

Figure 11. Vegetation zones of Kansas. Original vegetation map by Kuchler (1974). Digitized and updated by Dana Peterson at the Kansas Applied Remote Sensing (KARS) program within the Kansas Biological Survey and Center for Ecological Research. A. W. Kuchler, "A New Vegetation Map of Kansas," *Ecology* 55 (1974): 586–604, https://doi.org/10.2307/1935149.

trates the vegetation as it was before settlement or as it would be if the land were abandoned and natural processes were allowed to take their course. However, large expanses of prairie can still be found in the state, most notably in the Flint Hills at the western edge of the tallgrass prairie.

Newcomers are often surprised by the dense hardwood forests near the eastern edge of the state, which represents the westernmost extension of the eastern deciduous forest that encompasses much of the eastern United States. Here drier uplands are dominated by northern red and chinquapin oak on limestone and black and post oak on sandstone. North-facing slopes have white oak and, on limestone, lindens. Our common upland hickories are shagbark and bitternut. The riparian areas are populated with bur oak, elms, green ash, hackberry, sugarberry, black walnut, sycamore, some pecan, and kingnut and mockernut hickory. Flat woods contain silver maple, black willow, pin oak, and pecan. The understory (besides the herbaceous plants) is dominated by red mulberry, pawpaw, hop hornbeam, western buckeye, hazelnut, wahoo, and bladdernut. Upland oak-hickory forests extend into the tallgrass prairie farther west, forming a mosaic of discrete forest "islands" surrounded by prairie. These forest islands gradually decrease from east to west in size, height, and number of species. Toward their western boundary (indicated on the map), they are confined primarily to the north-facing slopes of stream valleys. In contrast, the Chautauqua Hills of southeastern Kansas are covered by a savanna of scattered oaks with a tallgrass prairie understory. Forests of western Kansas are restricted to the floodplains of major rivers and consist mostly of cottonwood and willow. Successional seminatural woodlands are dominated by yellow and black locusts and Osage orange and eastern redcedars. This is not an exhaustive list of tree species in Kansas but rather a good representative selection.

Mushroom Habitats

Judging from the collection data in Kansas, it might seem that most mushroom species occur in the counties surrounding Lawrence, Pittsburg, Topeka, and Manhattan—all in the eastern third of the state. In fact, all that these records actually reflect is the distribution of universities and the activities of their mycologists. Elam Bartholomew's collections from Rooks County in the mixed-grass prairie of north-central Kansas represent the only extensive record of mushrooms from the state's western two-thirds. Even in the more extensively collected forests of eastern Kansas, at least one new species for the state usually turns up during a day's foray, with no evidence as yet of saturation. During 1951, a year of record rainfall and ravaging floods,

Rogerson and Shaffer substantially increased the number of Kansas species; many of these have not been collected since. This suggests that the mycelia of numerous unreported mushrooms live unobserved in Kansas, patiently awaiting extremely favorable weather conditions for fruiting. Hence, Kansas holds many surprises for mushroom hunters with adventurous spirits. Particularly promising and virtually unexplored regions include the previously mentioned Chautauqua Hills and the Red Hills and sand prairies of south-central Kansas.

Mushrooms in the western half of the state are as sporadic and unpredictable as the rainfall that supports them. Thunderstorms may unload copious rains in one region while leaving areas several miles away parched. The best way to handle such uncertainty is to live in the region for many years or to become very lucky in your mushrooming talents. That mushrooms occur on the prairies is evident from Bartholomew's early reports and hearsay from plant collectors and local residents. Large puffballs (*Calvatia* species, nos. 159–162) often emerge from the open prairies like giant white bubbles and may be joined by smaller *Lycoperdon* species (nos. 164–165), stalked puffballs (*Tulostoma* species, no. 167), and even stinkhorns (especially *Lysurus periphragmoides* [no. 158] and *Phallus rubicundus* [see no. 155]). Gilled mushrooms are also represented on the prairies, particularly by species of *Agaricus*, *Lepiota*, *Leucoagaricus*, *Leucocoprinus*, *Marasmius*, *Stropharia*, *Psilocybe*, *Panaeolus*, *Agrocybe*, and *Conocybe*. Interestingly, many of these same mushrooms now inhabit lawns and fields and often grow on cattle dung, perhaps having adopted these new habitats with the introduction of the plow and the extermination of the buffalo. Other rarities—such as *Saproamanita prairiicola* (syn. = *Amanita prairiicola*), last reported in Kansas from Rooks County in 1927 but in Colorado in 1998—await the patient mushroomer.

Mushrooming in western Kansas is most productive in the forested draws and river valleys. Here morels sometimes fruit prolifically in spring under thickets of cottonwood, willow, and elm, later to be replaced by the savory oyster mushroom (*Pleurotus ostreatus* [no. 38]) and other assorted gilled mushrooms, polypores, and puffballs common to forested regions farther east. Under wet conditions, even isolated trees in the middle of prairies support abundant mushrooms. A search under one such tree in late May revealed a dozen stinkhorn eggs (*Phallus hadriani* [no. 155]) in all stages of hatching, a large cluster of *Coprinopsis variegata* (no. 65), and numerous edible *Chlorophyllum rachodes* (see no. 78).

Eastern Kansas, with its greater precipitation and hardwood forests, is far richer in mushrooms than western Kansas. Plant species from many areas of the United States, with the possible exception of the far West, converge in this region, creating particularly diverse fungi. These overlapping ranges may also account for the state's richness in mushrooms. The species described in this book are mostly widespread in the eastern United States and probably reach their western limit in Kansas, where the eastern deciduous forest converges with the Great Plains. Particularly intriguing is the co-occurrence in Kansas of northern species of *Pycnoporus cinnabarinus* (no. 122) and *Bovistella utriformis* (no. 163) with their more southerly counterparts, *P. sanguineus* (see no. 122) and *Lycoperdon pulcherrimum* (see no. 163). The spectacular red coral, *Ramaria araiospora* (no. 145), from the West Coast is perhaps an anomaly.

Mushrooming in eastern Kansas is often feast or famine. When blessed with periodic thunderstorms, stupendous fruitings occur during July and August under hardwoods. Lesser fruitings take place in the spring with the appearance of morels and related fungi and in the fall with the advent of the cool-weather mushroom crop. However, abundant spring rainfall will bring out summer species prematurely, and late-summer rains following drought often induce them to fruit later than usual. Droughts of several weeks' duration are not uncommon in Kansas and are stoically endured by resident mushroom hunters, who in response turn to mushroom books and silently ponder the insufferably sunny skies.

The joy of mushroom hunting is expecting the unexpected, and unless they are hunting morels, most mushroomers in eastern Kansas simply head for the woods with empty baskets and no specific quarry. Oak-hickory forests support a wealth of mycorrhizal fungi that include species of *Amanita*, *Russula*, *Lactarius*, *Hygrophorus*, and *Cortinarius* as well as boletes. Mycorrhizal associations may be rather specific—for instance, the bolete *Aureoboletus russellii* (no. 90) fruits primarily under oak, while *Leccinellum griseum* (no. 96) is found under hop hornbeam. Often, scrubby second-growth forests are more productive than those heavily shaded by large trees. However, pastures overgrown with Osage orange (hedge apple) generally prove disappointing unless mixed with other trees.

Other mushrooms thrive on leaf litter or dead wood. During dry weather, logs and stumps hold moisture the longest and are the best sources for mushrooms. These include *Pluteus* (nos. 43–45) and inky species, the *Armillaria mellea* group (honey mushroom, no. 24), *Omphalotus illudens* (jack-o'-lantern, no. 13), *Flammulina velutipes* (velvet foot, no. 26), *Pleurotus ostreatus*, *Galerina marginata* (deadly galerina, no. 58), and the ubiquitous polypores and parchment fungi. Alternatively, during droughts, many Kansans practice urban mycology and prowl city streets for fleshy fungi. Here massive clusters of inky caps (particularly *Coprinopsis variegata*, *Coprinopsis atramentaria*, and *Coprinellus micaceus* [nos. 65–67]) and *Desarmillaria tabescens* (ringless honey [no. 25]) arise from buried stumps, and well-watered lawns blossom with *Agaricus campestris* (meadow mushroom [no. 71], a close relative of the typical store mushroom), *Stropharia melanosperma* (no. 57), and fairy rings of *Saproamanita thiersii* (no. 8) and poisonous *Chlorophyllum molybdites* (no. 79). Forest-dwelling mycorrhizal mushrooms also invade the city under planted oaks and non-native pines.

Whether scouring cities, forests, or prairies, mushroom enthusiasts have much to be thankful for in Kansas. With attentive preservation of the natural landscape, the state's unique blend of climate and vegetation will undoubtedly continue to unveil mycological treasures.

Bibliography

Bare, J. E., and R. L. McGregor. "An Introduction to the Phytogeography of Kansas." *University of Kansas Science Bulletin* 48 (1970): 869–949.

Buchanan, Rex C., and James R. McCauley. *Roadside Kansas: A Traveler's Guide to Its Geology and Landmarks*. Lawrence: University Press of Kansas, 1987.

Collins, Joseph T., ed. *Natural Kansas*. Lawrence: University Press of Kansas, 1985.

Haddock, Michael John, and Craig C. Freeman. *Trees, Shrubs, and Woody Vines in Kansas*. Lawrence: University Press of Kansas, 2019.

Reichman, O. J. *Konza Prairie: A Tallgrass Natural History*. Lawrence: University Press of Kansas, 1987.

Self, Huber. *Environment and Man in Kansas: A Geographical Analysis*. Lawrence: Regents Press of Kansas, 1978.

Forays: A Basic Kit and Some Risks

Sherry Kay

Going into the field safely, comfortably, and successfully is the general goal of a mushroom foray. You may be personally interested in only a subset of mushrooms—morels, for instance. Nevertheless, just in case, you ought to have some smaller bags for other species in addition to a container that can be comfortably carried (a rigid basket works well). Waxed sandwich bags are probably best for bagging your finds, followed by paper ones. Unlike plastic bags, these bags do not contain the heat and moisture of your finds so that they begin to spoil. Probably next most important is a cell phone, preferably with GPS, partly to get a fix on where you have found what but also to enable you to contact your companions, to keep in touch and keep from being lost, and to provide you with photo capabilities. Hours before going out, it's a good idea to spray your clothes with permethrin to keep the critters off, especially ticks. An additional precaution to this end is to pull your socks (white are best so you can see what's crawling) over your pant legs and wear a long-sleeved shirt. To avoid an infestation of chiggers, spread flowers of sulfur on your boots, socks, and pant legs just after you arrive. This is a smelly option but can save you much misery. Comfortable, sturdy footwear is also important.

In the first edition, Dean Abel offered a good list of things to take into the field, some of which we include here:

A knife or two (large and small), preferably with a brush, attached or separate, to brush off finds to see them better

A loupe (a small magnifying glass or hand lens), preferably one that can be attached to a cord to hang around your neck or to a belt

Waxed or paper bags

Cell phone

Notepad and pen or pencil, or a list of mushrooms likely to be found

Drinking water

A walking stick

A hat

There is a lot more private property in Kansas than public, so if you plan to go on private property, it's an excellent idea to obtain permission. You could offer to share your finds, but you could also ask about the property; the landowner might have some good pointers that will make for a more pleasant foray.

The dangers in the field are probably not more numerous than in town, but they are not as familiar and are certainly different. Mostly they can be avoided by taking precautions and paying attention, knowing what poison ivy (*Toxicodendron radicans*), stinging nettles (*Urtica dioica*), and wood nettle (*Laportea canadensis*) look like, and being careful where you put your feet to avoid falls.

Ticks come in four species here: the American dog tick (*Dermacenter variabilis*), the lone star tick (*Amblyomma americanum*), the deer tick (*Ixodes scapularis*), and the relapsing fever tick (*Ornithodoros turicata*). Ticks are not just a nuisance; they can cause a number of diseases in humans, both crippling and deadly. In addition to ticks and chiggers, be aware of spiders, who love to make webs across the path. They were there first, so I carry a stick to carefully move them out of the way. We also have venomous snakes, including copperheads and several varieties of rattlesnake. Joe Collins, the late snake expert, recommended tall boots to protect against snakebite. He also advised never reaching into rock crevices or under rock ledges, hollow logs, or stumps and wearing gloves.

In spite of spraying your clothes, you may carry home a few ticks and perhaps other unwanted critters, so it's best to immediately have a good scrub-down in the shower as soon as you get home, before you set up to obtain spore prints (if you haven't started these in the field) or make other arrangements to identify your catch.

Bibliography

Collins, Joseph T., and Suzanne L. Collins. *A Pocket Guide to Kansas Snakes*. 3rd ed. Wichita, KS: Friends of the Great Plains Nature Center, 2010.

Vajnar, Mary Ella. "Observations on Tick-Borne Disease in Kansas." Kansas Department of Health and Environment, *Epi Updates* 9, no. 3 (March 2018): 1–5.

Online Resources for Identifying Mushrooms

Benjamin Sikes

An increasing supply of digital resources in the form of websites and smartphone apps can provide the amateur mushroom enthusiast with new tools to compare with specimens and even catalog them for others to see. Below are descriptions of some of the key online resources at the time this edition of the book was published. As with many digital resources, changes in web addresses, maintenance of information, and usefulness for determining the identity of a mushroom found in Kansas may cause issues over time.

Websites

Michael Kuo's MushroomExpert.com
http://www.mushroomexpert.com

Mushroom Expert is an excellent website that is a must when learning a new species or group. Michael Kuo is an "amateur" mycologist from Illinois, so many of the mushrooms descriptions and details are relevant to the Midwest (including Kansas). His descriptions are easy to read, provide useful identification tips, and often detail interesting facts or name changes. Based on his experiences, he also discusses ecology, habitats, and look-alikes. If you have some idea what you might be looking at (possibly from working from this book), Mushroom Expert can often help you learn more about the group and how to tell individual species apart.

MycoKeys MMI (Morphing Mushroom Identifier)
http://www.mycokey.com/

MycoKeys is an online (and downloadable) key-based mushroom identifier created by Scandinavian researchers based on collections from their region. It is also a journal, so don't be confused! The online MycoKeys MMI tool lets you click through individual steps to "key out" your specimen. MycoKeys MMI provides helpful illustrations to describe the different traits to choose from at each step. Although these traits can be helpful to get you in the region, be warned that many of the species are those of Europe, not necessarily Kansas.

Mycobank
http://www.mycobank.org/

Mycobank is an online database that focuses on fungal nomenclature and associated data (descriptions and illustrations). Anyone can provide content (i.e., a new name for a found mushroom species) to Mycobank, and this information is vetted by nomenclature experts. For a given name, Mycobank also provides links to other online initiatives, such as Index Fungorum (see below) and the Global Biodiversity Information Facility (GBIF), the latter of which has details about distributions. Data on DNA or locations of living cultures may also be linked. Mycobank is spearheaded by the International Mycological Association, the Westerdijk Fungal Biodiversity Institute in the Netherlands, and the German Mycological Society (DGfM).

Index Fungorum
http://www.indexfungorum.org/

Index Fungorum is a website that focuses solely on up-to-date fungal nomenclature and is based at the Royal Botanic Gardens, Kew, in the United Kingdom. Index Fungorum has no pictures, descriptions, or information to help you identify mushrooms. As we've outlined in other sections, however, the taxonomy of fungi is constantly changing. If you are eager to see whether your mushroom's scientific name has changed or find its synonyms, Index Fungorum is a simple place to go. Fungal taxonomists constantly update this website to make sure all the names are current and also add new names.

Smartphone Apps

There are dozens of different mushroom identifier apps available for both Apple and Android devices. We do not review them here, but many of them are relatively similar in what they provide: detailed descriptions and pictures of the most common one hundred to two hundred mushrooms people encounter. They include both free and pay-based apps and often market themselves to foragers trying to determine whether a mushroom is edible (beware!). None have been in existence long, despite their number of downloads, and very few are location based; therefore, proposed identifications may belong to species that do not even occur in Kansas. The iNaturalist app, detailed below, is a citizen-science project that has been around a long time, charges nothing to use, and can be very helpful locally for both amateurs and the broader mushroom community.

iNaturalist/SEEK

iNaturalist is a citizen-science project that helps amateurs identify and collect information about all kinds of organisms, including mushrooms. The website (and now app) was started in 2008 and is a product of the California Academy of Sciences. With it, you can take pictures of a mushroom you observe/collect and add location information, and it can then help you identify it. From your photograph(s) and the location, the app will suggest several identifications. It bases these suggestions on the vast database curated over time by the iNaturalist community (called "crowdsourcing"). Each candidate species has a detailed description, including features, habitat (whether it has been seen "nearby"), and edibility. Other users can also check/verify the identification you provide. If more than two people confirm the identity, it becomes "research grade" and may then be used for future work. If you aren't sure about the identity, you can simply identify the specimen to a higher taxonomic level (for instance, family or order). Other users can then help refine your identification, and you are notified as they do so. This iterative process allows users to both catalog their own mushroom observations and help identify other users' mushrooms. If you get to know one mushroom well, assisting other nearby users to confirm their finds can be very rewarding. In this way, your mushroom observations and assistance with identifications can help populate a broad database that others can use.

Some people are intimidated by this, so the group behind iNaturalist created a new app, called SEEK, that simply uses the database to help you identify unknown things. By pointing your camera at a mushroom or pointing to a photo on your phone, SEEK can help you identify it to the family or sometimes genus level. From there, you can use other tools to get more specific. With either tool, you will quickly see that iNaturalist is much bigger than mushrooms.

Mushrooms in the Kitchen

Sherry Kay

Why, you ask, should we complicate our walk in the woods with gathering mushrooms? I believe it satisfies both a certain primitive need to be hunters and gatherers and a more modern need, born of the work ethic, to do something productive during leisure time. Beyond that, the hedonist anticipates the luxury of feasting on wild mushrooms at the end of the day.

Wild mushrooms do not come in one generic flavor. Some taste pretty much like the common store-bought mushroom (*Agaricus bisporus*), but many more have distinct flavors and textures of their own. The hottest thing I have ever tasted was *Lactifluus piperatus* (see no. 82), which was like eating white-hot iron. A hot one like that is usually telling you not to eat it because it will make you sick as well as burn your mouth. The peppery taste will often disappear with cooking, but the sick-making qualities will not always follow suit. (Not all mushrooms are so straightforward, however; *Amanita bisporigera* [no. 3] is said to be quite delicious but is certainly deadly.)

My personal favorites among the edibles are *Craterellus fallax* (no. 136), which tastes cheesy to me, like a good brie with more substance; *Grifola frondosa* (no. 113), with a crisp, nutty flavor; *Boletus variipes* (no. 93), firm, delicious, perhaps also nutty but really indescribable; *Russula virescens* group (no. 88), flavored like hazelnuts; the chanterelles (nos. 134–135), of course, with their slight apricot odor and smooth, delightful texture; and finally, if you want to take the risk, *Hypomyces lactifluorum* (no. 194), which is firm, crisp, and mushroomy, with a hint of seafood, perhaps suggested by its nickname, the lobster mold. I could go on, but suffice it to say that it is worth trying a number of different edibles. Tastes do differ, however, and you may not enjoy certain species as much as I do. I have had *Lactarius indigo* (no. 81) highly recommended to me but find it coarse and not at all pleasant.

In choosing mushrooms to pick for the pot, BE CERTAIN that they are not poisonous. (Take this book into the field—it's not heavy!) Remember, distinguishing characteristics that are visible in the natural setting can disappear before you get home. Still worse, important clues may be washed away by rain or munched by fauna. If the mushroom you would like to eat is a kind you do not recognize, you may well want to consult a fellow mycophile, as well as other books, once you are at home without the nagging call of more mushrooms to collect over the next hill. There you can determine at leisure what species you really have, perhaps sitting with friends over numerous books, a plate of sautéed, firmly identified mushrooms, and a glass of good wine (but keep in mind that some inkys mix poorly with alcohol).

Proper precautions, however, begin back in the woods. Even when harvesting an old friend, do look closely at each one to avoid adding a look-alike to the edibles bag; with new species, take extra care. Be prepared with an adequate number of brown paper bags (five or six) or, better yet, a package of waxed ones to keep the varieties separate. If you are not certain what species you are gathering, collect specimens at several stages of development. Dig with your knife to get the whole fruiting body, observing closely for volval remnants, checking whether the stalk extends far down to form a rootlike appendage, and noting whether a specimen found on the ground is actually growing in soil or only on buried wood. Now examine all your specimens for ephemeral characteristics. Are there water droplets anywhere on the gills, cap, or stalk? Are there tiny cobweb-like threads (a cortina) connecting the cap edge to the stalk? Are there powdery remains on the stalk? Anything else notable? Take a few written notes (you can even use a permanent marker to write directly on the bag), collect these typical specimens, and save them to make spore prints when you get home. Then harvest the rest of the group, giving them the same thorough examination to be sure they are identical to your specimens because poisonous and nonpoisonous look-alikes can share the same area. In harvesting (*if* you are sure you have an edible), cut off the stipe above the soiled portion and brush away as much debris as possible so that when you arrive home, your choice edibles will not be thoroughly begrimed by batting about in a bag with excess dirt. As with any other food, be sure that your pot mushrooms are in good repair, with no sign of deterioration or spoilage.

Having brought your pristine catch home and identified the uncertain ones, where now? The first stage in kitchen preparation is cleaning. I brush as much as possible and wash as little as necessary. Washing waterlogs most mushrooms, changing their texture unpleasantly; in addition, important flavors are lost. Some of the firmer shelf fungi can be soaked a bit to loosen dirt, but do so gingerly. I am squeamish and do not like extra protein in larval form. This way I eat fewer mushrooms but maintain my appreciation. Next, I cut each one in half and trim off the infested parts. I put the discarded pieces into the water I used for washing. Later they can be thrown on the lawn with the expectation of fruiting in the future. Usually I only provide an immediate banquet for the squirrels, but sometimes we have lovely surprises. One might think twice about infecting prized trees with wood-rotting fungi, however. For example, I never pour water filled with *Grifola frondosa* spores close to our oak trees.

I recommend that all but a few wild mushrooms be cooked before eating. Mushroom cell walls are made of chitin, like insect cell walls, which is hard to digest. *Agaricus campestris* (no. 71), like its close relative from the supermarket, is good raw, as are puffballs. I like to take firm white puffballs and add them raw to tossed salads. What looks like a puffball could of course be the egg stage of a deadly *Amanita*, so they should be checked first by cutting them in half from top to bottom to be sure that the interior is a homogeneous white mass, similar to cream cheese, which is characteristic of puffballs. If instead it has a preformed button inside or appears to be layered like an onion, you probably have the egg of a poisonous *Amanita* (Fig. 7). If trying a new species, always sauté a few of them in nothing but butter to get the true flavor. This will give you a good idea of how best to use the rest of the batch. You will find that different parts of the mushroom differ in desirability and quality. For instance, the stems of *Marasmius oreades* (no. 16) are almost impossibly tough, whereas those of *Pluteus cervinus* (no. 45) are so tasty that I like them better than the caps. You can even experiment with the sauté, as some fungi do best with a quick fire and others with a gentle one. Thus, chanterelles will become tough if cooked quickly, but puffballs will become soggy if cooked slowly. A note of caution: Do not eat great quantities the first time you try any particular mushroom, even a variety known to be safe. Some people experience unexpected, highly individual allergic reactions, notably to species of the *Armillaria mellea* group (no. 24), *Desarmillaria tabescens* (no. 25), and morels (nos. 181–182), although the allergenic fungi are by no means limited to these. Moreover, an individual's sensitivity may develop after repeated exposure. One friend actually had no trouble with morels for years and then experienced increasing stomach difficulties with successive spring crops. (For further discussion of poisons and allergies, see "The Edibility Issue," p. 10.)

There are a number of approaches to a large surplus. First, you might just invite all your nonmycophobic friends and treat them to a feast. A party of us gathered puffballs in tremendous quantities one year when enormous puffballs burgeoned over acres, so the woods looked as though they had been overrun by hundreds of neglectful ostrich hens. Never were we out of sight of dozens. We came home, called more friends, and spent an enchanting evening taking turns in the kitchen experimenting with puffball recipes, eating them, or going out for more supplies. Wine and congeniality flowed with equal bounty. I might add that mushroom dishes are almost always enhanced by a glass of wine, if not in the sauce, then at the table. The exception to this rule is several of the inky caps, some of which contain coprine, a substance that becomes toxic when mixed with alcohol (again, "The Edibility Issue," p. 10). This will cause wretched misery for anyone who drinks alcohol after eating these inkys—even several days later.

Short-term storage varies with the mushroom. Many mushrooms will easily keep for a week in the refrigerator; the more robust and firm fleshed, like *Grifola frondosa*, will stay reasonably fresh for at least two weeks. As a rule, the more fragile the fungus, the more susceptible to early deterioration. Among the quickest to spoil are the inkys (nos. 65–67). Hope Miller (late wife and partner of the late mycologist Orson Miller) suggested a way of keeping fresh inky caps for up to ten days. She submerged them completely in cold water—a bowl of water with a plate placed on top will keep the contents wholly underwater. Then the bowl is refrigerated. Puffballs often keep poorly as well. Many times I have gathered a quantity and saved some for the morning omelet, only to find that they have turned yellow overnight. In this condition, they are bitter and hence unusable. Cooking does end maturation and so is one solution to those rapidly maturing fungi. As with other foods, refrigeration is the best overall aid to maintaining edibility in the short run.

Another way of dealing with a profusion of fungi is to preserve as many as you can. There seem to be three main methods: canning, drying, and freezing. I hesitate to recommend canning for fear of botulism, to which mushrooms as well as green beans are quite susceptible. If you insist, however, follow the directions included with your pressure cooker, and follow them exactly. Drying is the oldest method of keeping the excess; it was the customary way of preserving morels in Kansas a century ago. Boletes positively seem to gain flavor from this treatment, although the texture is lost; some other species also lose something with desiccation. I have dried only *Marasmius oreades* for the table, and they were very good. In fact, Kansas mycophagist Ansel Stubbs, at age 105, recommended them for delicate stomachs. Both *Marasmius* and *Auricularia* (no. 149) are well known for their ability to revive after being dried. To reconstitute any dried mushroom, soak it in warm water until it is as soft as desired. Do not throw the water out, as it contains many good mushroomy flavors.

There are many different ways of drying. Commercial driers work quite as well on mushrooms as on vegetables. I have dried both in an oven with a pilot light and in a frost-free refrigerator. In either case, the mushrooms must be left uncovered. I find that the oven is more satisfactory because in the refrigerator, they will sometimes pick up odors; this way also takes longer. Another popular approach to drying uses a box of some kind. The top is left open and draped with cheesecloth to keep out insect pests, and at least one rack, screen, or perforated shelf is centrally located inside the box. As a heat source, install at least one 100-watt lightbulb in the bottom of the box, or more if needed. Sun drying also works, but you must protect your mushrooms from insects in some way.

Perhaps the most popular and successful method of preserving mushrooms today is freezing. Opinions differ as to whether precooking is necessary. Some recommend lightly brushing whole caps clean, popping them into baggies, and then freezing them. Others make complex sauces or simple purees and freeze them, sometimes in ice-cube trays so that small quantities can be added to a recipe as flavor and thickener. (Put the cubes in baggies after they are frozen because if left in the tray, they will dehydrate and pick up odors.) I prefer simply to slice and sauté, then pack and freeze. Hope Miller also had a trick for dealing with quick-frozen uncooked morels. She cut them in half and removed vermin from the hollow stems, then put the mushrooms in the freezer. She recommended popping them frozen into very hot oil (butter burns before it gets hot enough) and cooking them for no more than thirty seconds. In this way, they retain their body and almost-fresh flavor.

Children, those notoriously picky eaters, can be persuaded to try wild mushrooms and then eat them with gusto, especially if they have had a hand in the gathering. Of course, if the supply is short, you may not want to introduce your offspring to this delight. We have often regretted it when our daughter picked all the chanterelles, which she favored, off the serving dish. Children can learn to identify mushrooms, even with their Latin names, often more easily than adults. I'll never forget driving our four-year-old to nursery school one fine fall day. As we drove down a lovely tree-lined street in an older neighborhood, she suddenly cried out, "*Caput ursi! Caput ursi!*" And sure enough, in the crotch of a tree was an enormous *Hericium erinaceus* subspecies *erinaceo-abietis* (see no. 142), which at that time we were mistakenly calling *Hericium caput-ursi*. We took some to nursery school as a wonder to share, and Sally ate her fill for dinner.

I hesitate to give more than a few basic recipes because there are already so many good mushroom cookbooks, a selection of which I list in the bibliography. There are also many good individual recipes online. However, I will offer a few simple suggestions other than the sauté. Something to keep in mind while cooking is how much liquid is contained in the particular mushroom you are handling. Most mushrooms are made up of a high proportion of water. The worst of these are the inkys. When cooking these, it is best to add little or no liquid unless you do not mind spending the time to reduce the excess. Herbs and onions—and their relatives, shallots and the like—are wonderful in mushroom dishes when used in proper proportions. In *The New*

Savory Wild Mushroom, Angelo M. Pellegrini mentions that Italian chefs call oregano "the mushroom herb" (*erba da funghi*), and he also suggests, in addition to more traditional herbs, the use of pennyroyal and catnip. Mushrooms seem to lend themselves to sauces, and a good white sauce can improve almost any dish, especially dry meats such as chicken, turkey, pork, and veal. Somehow, the mushroom flavor is absorbed and amplified by the sauce. Eggs and mushrooms are an excellent combination, whether in a plain omelet or an exotic quiche. If using the store-bought *Agaricus*, the older ones with open caps have more flavor than the buttons. Yet the young ones have a wonderful firm quality of their own, so I usually mix both kinds if possible. Particularly delicious are sautéed mushrooms mixed with rice in pilafs and risottos. In our carefree days before dieting, we frequently fried our fungi after dipping them lightly in a batter of egg and flour, sometimes seasoned and sometimes not. We especially like *Laetiporus sulphureus* (no. 116) prepared in the modified tempura style, perhaps because it is reminiscent of shrimp. This dish has made many converts to mycophagy. I have not often made soup out of mushrooms but have read many mouthwatering recipes for it, which I keep meaning to try. Usually half the quantity is blended and used as a thickener for the other portion, which is cut into pieces. A good chicken broth is most often the principal liquid ingredient, sometimes with cream added. Now, with these few guidelines, invent your own recipes, experiment, and enjoy!

One final comment. My experience has been that the taste of a species can sometimes vary depending on when and where it was gathered as well as the manner in which it was prepared. So don't give up on a choice edible if it proves disappointing the first time. Conversely, if it is perfect, look for it again in the same spot next year.

Bibliography

Czarnecki, Jack. *Joe's Book of Mushroom Cookery*. New York: Atheneum, 1986.

Freedman, Louise. *Wild about Mushrooms: The Cookbook of the Mycological Society of San Francisco*. Berkeley, CA: Aris, 1987.

Grigson, Jane. *The Mushroom Feast*. New York: Knopf, 1975.

Leibenstein, Margaret. *The Edible Mushroom: A Gourmet Cook's Guide*. New York: Fawcett Columbine, 1986.

McKenny, Margaret, and Daniel E. Stuntz. *The New Savory Wild Mushroom, Revised and Enlarged*. Seattle: University of Washington Press, 1987.

Nelson, Kay Shaw. *Cooking with Mushrooms*. New York: Dover, 1971.

Puget Sound Mycological Society. *Wild Mushroom Recipes*. Seattle, WA: Pacific Search, 1969.

Growing Mushrooms in Kansas

Terry Shistar

Several saprophytic mushrooms are cultivated commercially in Kansas, including shiitake (*Lentinula edodes*), a variety of oyster mushrooms (*Pleurotus ostreatus* [no. 38], *P. djamor*, *P. pulmonarius* [see no. 38], and *P. tuber-regium*), elm oyster (*Hypsizygus ulmarius* [see no. 38]), lion's mane (*Hericium erinaceus* [no. 142]), black poplar (*Agrocybe aegerita*), brown beech (*Hypsizygus tessulatus*), and nameko (*Pholiota nameko*). When produced commercially, they are grown on bags of straw, sawdust, or wood chips under controlled conditions that are not always available to the amateur grower.

However, some mushrooms are easy to grow indoors or outdoors in Kansas. Kits in which the mycelium has grown through the substrate are readily available. Oysters are particularly easy to grow and make a good choice for the beginner. After the substrate is spent, it can be used to inoculate wood chips, sawdust, or coffee grounds. Shiitake mushrooms (*Lentinula edodes*) are easy to grow by inoculating logs with dowels containing mycelium. Unless the logs are given extra care, they will probably take longer to fruit in Kansas than in more friendly environments. The same is true for *Stropharia rugoso-annulata*, the wine-red stropharia, which can be established in beds of straw or wood chips.

The more adventurous mycophile can try growing mushrooms starting with stem butts or spores. In stem butt (bottom part of the stem) culture, a piece of the butt of a mushroom stem is sandwiched in corrugated cardboard that has been moistened and split apart. When the mycelium starts to grow, the cardboard can be transplanted to wood chips or used to produce dowels for inoculating logs. A number of species, including morels, oysters, *Stropharia*, and *Psilocybe* species, have been grown this way. It is a great way to reproduce locally adapted varieties.

Commercial growers start with pure cultures grown from spores. This is a multistep process that requires a high degree of sanitation. Spores collected in a spore print are placed on sterilized culture plates containing nutritionally enhanced agar and then incubated at a suitable temperature. When the mycelium has colonized no more than three-quarters of the plate, the agar can be used to inoculate grain, which is the principal way to increase the amount of "spawn" (a fungal seed of substrate and mycelium). Grain spawn can be used to make more grain spawn or to inoculate dowels or other substrates.

Mycelium Running by Paul Stamets contains ideas for cultivating these and other mushrooms. The Fungi Perfecti website contains updated information, including a table of tree species best suited for cultivating specific mushrooms. The serious grower will find the detailed instructions for propagation in *The Mushroom Cultivator* by Stamets and Jeff Chilton to be helpful.

Resources for growing mushrooms

Sources of Mushroom Spawn

There are many sources of ready-to-fruit kits and mushroom spawn for edible and medicinal mushrooms in the form of sawdust, plugs, and/or grain. A few of them are the following:

Fungi Perfecti, www.fungi.com

Field and Forest Products, www.fieldforest.net

Penn State Department of Plant Pathology and Environmental Microbiology attempts to maintain a comprehensive list at http://plantpath.psu.edu/facilities/mushroom/resources/usa-commercial-suppliers.

Fungi Perfecti also sells pure cultures in test tubes and will provide cultures and spawn made from wild mushrooms provided by the customer.

Sources for *Psilocybe* species also exist online. Spores are sold separately from kits. One company selling kits does so with this disclaimer: "[We do] not advocate growing any illegal substance, such as *Psilocybe cubensis* (magic mushrooms). While these kits are capable of growing *Psilocybe cubensis* mushrooms (magic mushrooms), it is not advised by [us] for anybody to do so unless legally licensed by their local agricultural or research authorities. Check your country's laws and regulations regarding exotic species." Similarly, spores are sold for scientific purposes.

Resources

Stamets, Paul. *Mycelium Running: How Mushrooms Can Help Save the World.* Berkeley, CA: Ten Speed, 2005.

Stamets, Paul, and J. S. Chilton. *The Mushroom Cultivator: A Practical Guide to Growing Mushrooms at Home.* Olympia, WA: Agarikon, 1983.

Mycological Latin

Richard Kay

The Latin scientific names of mushrooms are a formidable stumbling block, not only to beginners but even to the professional mycologists who use them daily. Then why use them? Simply to have a standardized terminology. Without an international standard, it would be difficult to know that the German *Steinpilz*, the French *cèpe*, the Italian *porcino*, and the English king bolete all refer to the same species—*Boletus edulis*. Even in the United States, mushroom names in English can be confusing—for example, what Lincoff (now departed) called the "Common Laccaria," Arora termed the "Lackluster Laccaria" and McKnight's book called the "Deceiver." It is much easier to call it by its precise name, *Laccaria laccata* (no. 34). Therefore, this guide regularly refers to species by their Latin scientific names, although some widely used English common names are also given.

Latin names have two drawbacks. The first is that they change as mycologists change their concepts of classification, and with the gene sequencing revolution, these changes are occurring much more rapidly. This is inconvenient if one consults older guidebooks that use outmoded terminology. Usually only the genus is changed, so the species can still be located by the second half of its old name in an index that lists both names separately (for example, *campestris*, *Agaricus*, as well as *Agaricus campestris*—no. 71). This guide does index both elements of the Latin name, but it gives only a token selection of "synonyms" (as obsolete names are called).

The other drawback is how to pronounce those Latin names. The simplest solution, recommended by David Arora,[1] is to pronounce them any which way, which is pretty much what you will hear professionals and amateurs alike doing at the annual meeting of the North American Mycological Association (NAMA). The first edition and this new edition recommended classical Latin (CL) based on William T. Stearns's standard handbook *Botanical Latin*.[2] Included here are the rules of CL; however, a rough-and-ready and mightily simplified version would be to pronounce every letter and remember that all the **c**'s and **g**'s are hard. The accents are easy: two-syllable words are accented on the first, and longer words are accented on the next to the last. But many deviations have occurred in biological Latin over the years, as was evidenced in the recording of Alexander Smith and Rolf Singer speaking 368 different mycological names and terms. This recording is available online at http://www.scmsfungi.org. Smith gives what was the American/British interpretation and Singer the German/European one. Change has certainly continued since these giants of the twentieth century dominated field mycology, so I suggest that the emphasis should be on communication more than pronunciation: therefore, listen to knowledgeable speakers and feel your way to the best way to communicate about mycological matters. For instance, according to Sterns, "*Clitocybe*" would have two hard **c**'s ; however, I first heard this genus spoken of with an initial hard **c** while the second was soft, and this way seems to be generally acceptable. So be patient, persistent, and unembarrassed by your efforts to communicate in mycology.

The Rules of Classical Latin

Sounds of the Letters

1. A vowel is long or short, depending on whether it is drawn out or not. Dictionaries mark long vowels with a macron (¯) and short ones with a breve (˘). The equivalent English sounds are as follows:

ā as in *father*, **ă** as in *idea*

ē as in *they*, **ĕ** as in *pet*

ī as in *machine*, **ĭ** as in *sin*

ō as in *note*, **ŏ** as in *obey*

ū as in *rude*, **ŭ** as in *put*

ȳ as *u* in French *pur*, **y̆** as *u* in French *du*

Less precisely, the sounds of the Latin **i** can be used instead of those of the French *u*.

2. Double vowels are pronounced separately unless they are **diphthongs**, which have their own sounds, all of which are long:

ae like *ai* in *aisle*

ei as in *eight*

oe like *oi* in *oil*

au like *ow* in *how*

The combination **eu** (as in *Pluteus* and *Pleurotus*) is pronounced as two short, separate vowels. Similarly, **ui** is like *we* (for example, *Suillus*). Just so, but oddly to our ears, the co*mbination* **oi** *is pronounced as two separate* vowels, so the ending *-oides*, "having the form of," would have three syllables: *-o-i-des.*[3]

3. Most **consonants** are pronounced just as in English, namely, **b**, **d**, **f**, **h**, **k**, **l**, **m**, **n**, **p**, **r**, **qu**, **z**. A few, however, are treated differently.

c and **g** are hard, as in *come*, *get*; never soft, as in *city*, *gem*

j when a consonant (for example, *juniperina*) like *y* in *yet*

ng as in *finger*

s as in *sea*, *lips*: never as in *ease*

t is always a plain *t*; never with a *sh* sound, as in *nation*

v like *w*

x always like *ks*; never like English *gz* or *z*

In the heyday of CL, the letters in the pairs **ph**, **th**, and **ch** were pronounced separately, but most modern Latinists drop the *h* in these combinations, saying simply *p*, *t*, and *c*.

Syllables

4. Every vowel or diphthong makes a separate syllable. A single consonant is joined to the following vowel, but doubled consonants are separated. Thus, *ae-ru-gin-ne-a*, *ro-sei-brun-ne-us*, *mi-ca-ce-us*, and *can-tha-rel-lus*.

Accent

5. Words of two syllables are accented on the first syllable: for example, *ful′-va*, *al′-ba*, *ru′-fa*.

6. Words of more than two syllables are accented on the next-to-the-last syllable (penult) if it is a long syllable; if it is short, the stress falls instead on the second-from-the-last (antepenult). A long syllable is one containing a long vowel or a diphthong or a short vowel followed by two consonants or by *x* or *z*. Examples with a long penult: *a-ma-nī-ta* and *tre-mēl-la*; with a short penult: *plu′-tĕ-us*, *po-ly′-pŏ-rus*, *le-pi′-ŏ-ta*, and *pa-nae′-ŏ-lus*.

Recommended Exceptions

The purist who wants to sound like Cicero will observe all these rules. I would, however, recommend a few exceptions. The first concerns proper names that have been Latinized to commemorate modern individuals. Stearn suggests a sensible method of dealing with them: simply pronounce the name as it would be said in its own language and then add the Latin endings. Whether the stress should follow native or Latin rules is a matter of taste. Thus, *petersii* can be accented either *pe′-ters-i-i* or *pe-ter′-si-i*. Of course there are mixed-in Greek syllables that are not addressed here at all.

Since some of the rules given above are, in my opinion, more flexible than others, I will give some suggestions for bending them. I will begin with those I strongly recommend and proceed with ever-diminishing enthusiasm. Since even the Romans eventually came to pronounce **ph** as *f*, some classicists recommend this, as I do. Moreover, since the Romans pronounced **th** with some sort of an *h* sound, it seems no worse to use the familiar English *th* than to omit the *h* altogether, as most classicists recommend. Furthermore, in botanical usage, I would not hesitate to treat **oi** as a diphthong pronounced as *oi* in *oil*. I would, however, hesitate to abandon the pronunciation of **v** as *w* because this is a hallmark of the classical pronunciation of Latin, not just a fine point, and I would not even consider softening **c** or **g**.

Practical Considerations

The principal drawback in applying these rules, whether modified or not, is that a Latin dictionary is needed to determine whether the vowels are short or long.[4] Still worse, botanical names are frequently nonclassical in origin; hence, considerable philological finesse may be required to determine the length of their vowels.

Perhaps the easiest way to acquire the knack of pronouncing CL is by hearing and imitating. The recording by Rolf Singer mentioned above closely approximates CL; however, it deviates from CL in the following respects: **ae** as long *e* in English *they*; **c** soft before *e* and *i*; **oi** as *oi* in English *oil*; **ti** softened to *shi*; and **v** as in English. Otherwise, it provides an excellent model.

Exercises

Hard consonants: cervinus, coprinus, clitocybe, cordyceps, limacella, morchella, mycena, polychroa; bisporigera, fastigiata, fragilis, geastrum, giganteus; rubescens, scleroderma, virescens; lateritius, leotia; pyxidata, xylaria, rhodoxanthus.

Diphthongs: aeruginea, cepaestipes, laeve, sphaerocephalum, foenisecii, aurantia, auricula.

Divide into syllables: craniiformis, flammulina, foenisecii, giganteus, lepiota, merulioides, molybdites, prairiicola, pleurotus, pluteus, polychroa, pycnoporus, roseibrunneus, schizophyllum, variipes.

Which syllable is stressed? (only the length of the penult is indicated): asterophŏra, boletacĕae, inquinăns, molybdĭtes, hygrophŏrus, dryophĭla, velutĭpes, velutīna, oreădes, clitocȳbe, favŏlus, pycnŏporus, tramētes, tylopĭlus, sanguinĕus, volvacĕa.

How is it pronounced? (unmarked vowels are short): a-ga-ri-cā-ce-ae, bom-bȳ-ci-na, ē-rī-nā-ce-us, fo-li-ā-ce-a, gi-gan-tē-us, le-pi-o-ta, mī-ca-ce-us, po-ly-po-rus, quad-ri-fi-dus, sul-phu-re-us.

Proper names: candolleana, everhartii, hadriani, petersii, russellii, stevensii, sullivantii, thiersii.

Notes

1. David Arora, *Mushrooms Demystified*, 2nd ed. (Berkeley, CA: Ten Speed, 1986), 8.

2. William T. Stearn, *Botanical Latin: History, Grammar, Syntax, Terminology, and Vocabulary*, 3rd ed., rev. (North Pomfret, VT: David & Charles, 1983), 53–56. Among its many other benefits is how to understand the meaning of plant names.

3. Although Greek has a diphthong *oi* (pronounced like the *oi* in *oil*), it does not appear in the Greek suffix *-oeides*, from which the CL *-oides* is derived. But in English, *-oid* has become one syllable (although the French follow Latin and say *oïd*). Speaking strictly CL, then, one must say *ly-co-per-do-í-des*. But see my recommended exceptions above.

4. For the full vocabulary of CL, see Charlton T. Lewis and Charles Short, *A New Latin Dictionary* (New York, 1878), reprinted as *A Latin Dictionary* (Oxford: Clarendon, 1980); and P. G. W. Glare, ed., *Oxford Latin Dictionary* (Oxford: Clarendon, 1982).

Mycology in Kansas: A Brief History

Richard Kay

The scientific study of mushrooms is hardly older than America. Although the Greeks and Romans prized mushrooms as a delicacy, they knew them by sight rather than by science and so left recognizable descriptions of barely twenty species. The work of describing and classifying European mushrooms was largely accomplished in the eighteenth century and culminated in the catalogs of C. H. Persoon (1801) and Elias Fries (1821–1829). Europeans then looked farther afield for new species and found enthusiastic allies among American amateur naturalists, who supplied them with specimens. On both sides of the Atlantic, competition was keen for the honor of making a scientific discovery, and consequently many common species of fleshy fungi east of the Mississippi were already known to science when Kansas entered the Union in 1861.[1]

After the Civil War, American science became academic. New universities and colleges sprang up in the West, and government subsidies encouraged them to investigate practical applications to agriculture. The new schools were staffed by professionals with academic degrees; the first teachers had bachelor's degrees obtained in the United States, but many of the new generation went abroad for advanced degrees and returned to produce graduate students of their own. At the University of Kansas, Lawrence, biologists studied birds, insects, and flowering plants but had little time for fungi. In 1873, J. H. Carruth covered the subject in one brief sentence, which is the earliest reference to Kansas mushrooms in the professional literature: "Fungi are not common though I have seen specimens of the puffball family four or five inches in diameter."[2] In 1881, however, he published "a list of some larger fungi in the Blue River Valley" that had been compiled by Mrs. E. C. Jewell, who consequently has the honor of being the first Kansas mycologist.[3] Carruth himself also collected mycological data, which he later contributed to the first biological survey of Kansas.

This project was organized a decade later at Washburn College by F. W. Cragin (B.Sc.), who in 1884 began to publish lists of the flora and fauna of Kansas. Perhaps half of the lists were created by collaborators, but when Cragin could find no one else, he did the work himself—for example, on mammals, reptiles, spiders, fishes, and ferns. His survey of Kansas fungi fell between these extremes, for although Cragin assembled the data, he relied on the expertise of eastern mycologists C. H. Peck and J. B. Ellis. Unlike most later lists of Kansas fleshy fungi, Cragin's are annotated and thus provide glimpses of fieldwork in the 1880s. Washburn students combed the woods around Topeka, the Santa Fe Railroad gave Cragin a free pass to roam the state, and he received specimens from colleagues in Lawrence and Manhattan as well as from numerous correspondents. In all, Cragin reported 292 species, 15 of which he claimed as new, although he was correct in only a few cases, such as *Calvatia rubroflava*.[4]

In 1883, a year before Cragin began publishing his lists, the Kansas State Agricultural College hired its first professional mycologist, W. A. Kellerman (Ph.D., Zurich). His interests were narrowly focused on parasitic fungi, such as rusts and smuts, and Cragin was quick to enlist his help. Within a year, Kellerman listed 183 species that he had personally collected in Kansas. This was only the first of many such lists to be published by him and by a long, distinguished line of successors and associates.[5] Kellerman established a herbarium at Kansas State, which in over a century accumulated thousands of specimens; in 1885 he also founded the *Journal of Mycology*, which was published in Manhattan until Kellerman left to teach at Ohio State University in 1891.[6] In just eight years, he had developed a program for the study of plant pathogenic fungi at Kansas State that continues to flourish more than a century later. Although these studies of rots, rusts, smuts, wilts, blights, and molds undoubtedly have great scientific and economic significance, they fall outside the scope of this work and hence of this historical sketch, which recognizes their achievement only in passing, although the interested reader can follow their progress as it pertains to Kansas in the *Transactions of the Kansas Academy of Science*.[7]

Kellerman's enthusiasm turned several Kansas farmers into serious mycologists, most notably Elam Bartholomew (1852–1934), who became the greatest collector of American fungi in his generation.[8] Twenty-one-year-old Bartholomew emigrated from Illinois to Rooks County, Kansas, where he worked as a farmhand until he could afford to homestead a farm of his own near Rockport, about ten miles north of Stockton. By 1885, he was not only a successful farmer but also an accomplished self-taught botanist who had assembled a collection of the flora of Rooks County. In June 1885, Kellerman visited Bartholomew's farm, where he found Elam cultivating corn; as they talked in the field, Kellerman picked up a bit of pigweed and pointed out a fungus growth on it. By the time the professor left, Bartholomew was determined to learn all about fungi.[9] He taught himself Latin, assembled a mycological library, and combed his county for specimens. By 1898, his thesis on the rusts of Kansas had earned him a master's degree from Kansas State.

In 1901, Elam Bartholomew assumed the editorship of *Fungi Columbiani*, an annual collection of dried specimens, which he continued to produce for subscribers until the end of his life, along with a similar one, *North American Uredinales*, devoted exclusively to rusts, which he began in 1911. To secure specimens, and employed as an agent of the USDA, he systematically visited every state in twenty annual forays (1899, 1906–1925) and gathered 292,380 specimens of fungi, which he divided and distributed in 427,700 labeled packets. Some 118,000 he kept for himself, however, in the largest private herbarium in the country. The core of his collection—some 30,000 specimens—eventually went to Harvard's Farlow Herbarium, while smaller lots were sold to other schools.

Although rusts were Bartholomew's first love, on which he published a scientific monograph, he did not neglect the higher fungi, as other Kansas academic mycologists of his generation did. Instead, in 1919, he produced the first monograph on the edible mushrooms of Kansas,[10] and in 1927, he compiled the first checklist of all Kansas fungi since Cragin's survey.[11] Bartholomew estimated that previous lists had reported about 465 species from Kansas; his own with its supplements raised the total to over 1,900 (many of which were microscopic and/or plant pathogens of no interest to the general mushroom hunter), some 406 of which were new to science when first reported from Kansas.

Bartholomew's checklist was nothing more than a list of scientific names arranged in alphabetical order, without indications (such as Cragin had provided) of when, where, or how abundantly the species appeared. In the 1930s, however, local studies were made of the fleshy fungi around Manhattan, Junction City, and Pittsburg. The first two localities were the subject of the master's thesis of Ethel B. Feese, who cataloged the higher fungi of Riley and Geary Counties but unfortunately never published her work.[12] Shorter but more accessible was a five-page guide to the fleshy fungi of Crawford County that was prepared by two biologists at the state teachers' college in Pittsburg, Gerald Travis and H. H. Hall. Their list groups 120 species by family and, in addition to providing the scientific name of each species, notes its edibility and fruiting season. Travis and Hall also appended a key to the genera that was designed to be helpful to the amateur.[13]

Another approach to the regional mycology of Kansas was taken by C. Rajagopalan, who focused his studies in 1960–1963 on a functional group of fungi: wood-rotting fungi from northeastern Kansas.[14] He reported 75 species, 18 of which were new reports for Kansas.

Before 1950, Kansas had no professional mycologists who cared to focus their talents and training on the fleshy fungi. As a result, many of the discoveries that had been enthusiastically announced during the previous seventy years had never been adequately verified and documented. But in that year, Clark T. Rogerson arrived at Kansas State with a fresh Ph.D. in mycology from Cornell, a talent for scientific bibliography, and an abiding love of fieldwork.[15] Almost immediately, he began to explore the wooded ravines around Manhattan, often in the company of Robert L. Shaffer, then a graduate student studying the state's Basidiomycota but later to become a noted agaricologist at the University of Michigan herbarium.[16] Together, Rogerson and Shaffer collected thousands of specimens for the Kansas State herbarium, many previously unreported from Kansas, among which were a few notable rarities.[17]

More important still was Rogerson's attempt to compile a definitive list of all the fungi that had been reported from Kansas. He systematically surveyed all the mycological literature from 1873 to 1958 and recorded every reported collection. Moreover, he also noted which ones had been preserved in the herbaria of Kansas State University and the New York Botanical Garden. In 1958, he left Kansas to join the staff of the New York Botanical Garden but continued to perfect his compilation until 1960, when he produced a preliminary draft titled "Fungi of Kansas: Annotated Checklist of the Fungi Reported from Kansas."[18] The author warned that his references to the literature should be rechecked and that the herbarium specimens should be reexamined before any record could be accepted as authentic for Kansas, but unfortunately, the press of other duties prevented him from bringing the work to completion. Although for most species, Rogerson simply noted references to the literature and to herbarium specimens, he gave much more elaborate treatment to the Conventional Class Gasteromycetes (for example, puffballs). Each species was described and keyed, and details were given for every reported collection, together with the author's own observations and a critical discussion of the species and its synonyms.

In the past century, the amateur mycologists of Kansas have come into their own. A folk tradition was already well established in 1885, when Cragin wrote of *Morchella americana*,

> This fine edible fungus, known in England as the *Morel*, is known in Kansas both by that name and by the misnomer of "mushroom," and its edible qualities appear to be better known and appreciated by many of our people than those of the true mushroom, *Agaricus campestris*. Our foreign-born citizens speedily discover the "morel-grounds," and many of them not only count upon them for a frequent and delicious treat during

the "morel season," but also gather them to dry and lay away to be used for soups in winter. The humbler portion of our native population, both white and [Black], is rapidly learning the virtues of the Edible Morel, but very few of the "educated" class appear to know even that such a plant exists.[19]

Such an educated person was Ansel Hartley Stubbs, who was born at Emporia in 1884 and grew up in Garden City and Kansas City. He was educated on scholarships, first at the University of Chicago and then at Munich, where he learned to eat mushrooms in 1910. Guided by Charles McIlvaine's *One Thousand American Fungi* (1900), Stubbs collected, studied, and consumed mushrooms during his years as a businessman in Kansas City. In 1951, he published a list of 243 identified specimens in his collection, most of which he had also tested for edibility,[20] and in 1971, he wrote the first field guide to the fungi of Kansas and adjacent states (122 species).[21] In 1991, at 107, the father of Kansas mycophagy was still enjoying mushrooms in a Lenexa retirement home.[22]

Stubbs's field guide was the regional manifestation of a nationwide upsurge in interest in mushroom hunting, the principal landmarks of which are the founding of the North American Mycological Association (NAMA, 1960) and the appearance of a new generation of American field guides, notably those by Alexander H. Smith (1958) and Orson K. Miller (1972).[23] Individual Kansans, such as Frederick Baselt in Wellington and Elizabeth Moses in Manhattan, hunted alone or attended NAMA's national forays, while in Lawrence, the number of amateurs grew steadily in the 1970s and 1980s because solid training was available from Robert Lichtwardt's class in field mycology. In October 1986, after a decade of informal forays, the Lawrence mycophiles, on the initiative of Dean Abel, formed the Kaw Valley Mycological Society (KVMS), which by 1989 had nearly one hundred members throughout the state.

To serve the needs of this amateur group, Richard Kay compiled *A Checklist of Kansas Mushrooms* (Lawrence, 1989), which is based chiefly on the unpublished work of Rogerson but also records more recent collections. Additions to (and subtractions from) the 727 items in Kay's list were regularly reported in *The Kansas Mycolog*, the newsletter of the KVMS, and entered into an electronic database. The first edition of this field guide was the next but not the last stage in the exploration of Kansas fungi that began with Mrs. Jewell in 1880.

Since Richard Kay, professional historian, wrote these words, Kansas mycologists have continued to add to the list of mushrooms found in the state.

The Kansas Mycolog *is no more, but foray lists have been kept and over 1,200 different macrofungi have now been recorded from Kansas. In addition, members of the Kaw Valley Mycological Society and others have begun depositing voucher specimens to serve as permanent records of their discoveries in R. L. McGregor Herbarium at the University of Kansas. A good recent estimate of the number of fleshy/macrofungi in the world is between 30,000 and 35,000. Therefore, I believe that thousands more species could be identified in Kansas, some of which have yet to be named (scientifically); every time I foray, I see mushrooms I cannot identify. I have had the great pleasure of leading most of the forays for the KVMS. This new edition is just a beginning for the reader. New finds await.—Sherry N. Kay*

Notes

1. For a national conspectus, see D. P. Rogers, *A Brief History of Mycology in North America* (Amherst, MA: Newell, 1977; 2nd ed., New York: Mycological Society of America, 1981). Selected topics in John H. Haines and Ira F. Salkin, eds., "A Symposium on the History of North American Mycology," *Mycotaxon* 26 (1986): 1–79; reprinted as *History of North American Mycology* (Albany: New York State Museum, 1986).

2. J. H. Carruth, "Catalogue of Plants Seen in Kansas," *Transactions of the Kansas State Board of Agriculture for 1872* (Topeka, KS: Office of the State Board of Agriculture, 1873), p. 347.

3. Mrs. E. C. Jewell, "A List of Some Larger Fungi in the Blue River Valley," in J. H. Carruth, "Botanical Addenda for 1879 and 1880," *Transactions of the Kansas Academy of Science* 7 (1881): 131.

4. F. W. Cragin, "First Contribution to the Catalogue of the Hymenomycetes and Gasteromycetes of Kansas," *Bulletin of the Washburn College Laboratory of Natural History* 1 (1884): 19–28, 33–42: "Second Contribution to the Catalogue of the Hymenomycetes and Gasteromycetes of Kansas," *Bulletin of the Washburn College Laboratory of Natural History* 1 (1884): 65–67; "A Contribution to the Knowledge of the Lower Fungi of Kansas," *Bulletin of the Washburn College Laboratory of Natural History* 1 (1884): 67–72.

5. W. A. Kellerman, "A Partial List of the Kansas Parasitic Fungi, Together with Their Host-Plants," *Bulletin of the Washburn College Laboratory of Natural History* 1 (1884–1885): 72–81.

6. "Obituary of W. A. Kellerman," *Journal of Mycology* 14 (1908): 49–53. He died of malaria on a field trip to Guatemala.

7. *Transactions of the Kansas Academy of Science* 13 (1893): 103; 15 (1898): 65–73; 16 (1899): 164–167; 30 (1919): 171–179; 38 (1935): 101–103; 39 (1936): 95–101; 55 (1952): 280–284; 56 (1953): 53–60; 57 (1954): 280–282; 59 (1956): 39–48, 233–235, 483–484; 60 (1958): 370–375; 61 (1958): 262–272. Also see *Journal of Mycology* 1–6 (1885–1890): passim; *Erythea* 4–5 (1896–1897): passim; *Bulletin of the Torrey Botanical Club* 11 (1884): 114–116, 121–123.

8. Leonard Erie Muir, *Elam Bartholomew: Pioneer, Farmer, Botanist* (Stockton, KS: privately published, 1981).

9. W. T. Swingle told a similar story of his conversion to mycology, which is quoted in "Obituary of W. A. Kellerman," 52.

10. Elam Bartholomew, "The Edible Mushrooms of Kansas," *Transactions of the Kansas Academy of Science* 30 (1919): 174–179.

11. Elam Bartholomew, *The Fungous Flora of Kansas*, Agricultural Experimental Station, Kansas State College, Contribution No. 268 from the Department of Botany (Topeka, KS: State Printer, 1927). *Addenda in Transactions of the Kansas Academy of Science* 33 (1930): 82–83 and 36 (1933): 71.

12. Ethel B. Feese, "The Fleshy Fungi of Riley and Geary Counties, Kansas" (M.S. thesis, Kansas State College, Manhattan, 1930).

13. Gerald Travis and H. H. Hall, "The Fleshy Fungi of Crawford County, Kansas," *Transactions of the Kansas Academy of Science* 42 (1939): 197–201.

14. C. Rajagopalan, "Some Wood-Rotting Fungi from Northeastern Kansas," *Transactions of the Kansas Academy of Science* 68 (1965): 553–562, which summarizes his Ph.D. dissertation, "Studies on Some Wood-Rotting Fungi from Northeastern Kansas" (University of Kansas, Lawrence, 1963).

15. *Mycological Contributions Celebrating the 70th Birthday of Clark T. Rogerson*, ed. Gary J. Samuels, *Memoirs of the New York Botanical Garden*, vol. 49 (Bronx: New York Botanical Garden, 1989), biography and bibliography, pp. ix–xiv. The "Fungi of Kansas" project is not noted.

16. Robert Lynn Shaffer, "Kansas Basidiomycetes (Exclusive of the Teliosporeae)" (M.S. thesis, Kansas State College, Manhattan, 1952).

17. Clark T. Rogerson and R. L. Shaffer, "Underwoodia in Kansas," *Mycologia* 44 (1952): 582; and C. M. Slagg and Clark T. Rogerson, "A 'Tuckahoe' Found in Kansas," *Transactions of the Kansas Academy of Science* 57 (1954): 66–68.

18. Robert W. Lichtwardt had a carbon copy of the original typescript. In 1960, the following sections had been completed: Myxomycetes, Phycomycetes, Ascomycetes (including Lichens), Basidiomycetes (except Ustilaginales and Uredinales, which were still in preparation), and a 46-page bibliography. The deuteromycetes section was also in preparation, as was a host index. The sections of interest to the amateur mycologist total about 260 pages of typescript. An addendum was issued in 1961. Rogerson also prepared a monograph, "Gasteromycetes of Kansas" (preliminary draft dated May 1960), which documents all previous reports.

19. F. W. Cragin, "A Contribution to the Knowledge of the Lower Fungi of Kansas," *Bulletin of the Washburn College Laboratory of Natural History* 1, no. 2 (January 1885): 69–70.

20. Wendell V. Showalter and Ansel H. Stubbs, "The Stubbs Collection of Fleshy Fungi at the University of Kansas," *Transactions of the Kansas Academy of Science* 54 (1951): 221–225.

21. Ansel Hartley Stubbs, *Wild Mushrooms of the Central Midwest* (Lawrence: University Press of Kansas, 1971). It is still in print under the title *Wild Mushrooms Worth Knowing* (Kansas City, MO: Lowell Press, 1980).

22. Interview by Nancy Smith, *Lawrence Journal-World*, April 9, 1989, 2C.

23. Alexander H. Smith, *The Mushroom Hunter's Field Guide* (Ann Arbor: University of Michigan Press, 1958); Orson K. Miller, Jr., *Mushrooms of North America* (New York: Dutton, 1972). Smith's earlier *Mushrooms in Their Natural Habitat* (Portland, OR: Sawyer's, 1949), illustrated with spectacular stereoscopic color slides, was too expensive to become popular.

A Life List for the Kansas Mycophile

Sherry Kay

Over 1,200 species of fungi have been reported from Kansas, including many lichens and plant pathogenic fungi. Of these, 200 are fully described and illustrated in this guide, and over 320 species can be identified using the taxonomic keys; others can be found in the current field guides to North American fungi or online. The following list gives a conspectus of a great number of approximately 1,080 Kansas species that are likely to be found and identified by amateurs.

Such a list can be useful in several ways. Obviously, a life list encourages the mycophile to keep a personal record of all the species encountered, and to facilitate this, a check-off space has been provided. Furthermore, this list can not only stimulate the curious Kansan to consult more comprehensive guides but also help to bridge the gap between this guidebook and national or continental ones. For example, when David Arora vaguely states in *Mushrooms Demystified* that a species is "eastern"—that is, not found west of the Rockies—the Kansan may well wonder whether it has in fact been found here. This life list will indicate whether it has been reported from Kansas.

The original *A Checklist of Kansas Mushrooms* (compiled by Richard Kay) provided 548 of the entries here. The additional items are from addenda to that list. The *Checklist* provides fuller information on each species—for example, English common names; Latin synonyms; who reported the find; what guidebooks describe the species; and occasional notes on where, when, and under what conditions it has been found as well as an index by specific as well as Latin scientific names. The addenda have a reduced amount of information. These checklists include many doubtful or questionable reports, however, and must therefore be used critically. The names in these earlier lists are woefully out of date since the gene sequencing revolution but have been updated in the following list.

For convenient reference, the life list is in alphabetical order. For a systematic arrangement, see the cladograms (phylogenetic trees) for Basidiomycota and Ascomycota, which describe the evolutionary relationships among at least the species included in the book. The "Systematic List of Kansas Fungi" found in the *Checklist* is now out of date.

Species have been included only if their identification is reasonably certain. Most have been looked up online and are pictured there. A selection of the species in the list are followed by a name; this indicates that the species was first found in Kansas and refers to the professional who gave that name. These include Elam Bartholomew, Francis W. Cragin, Job B. Ellis, Benjamin M. Everhart, Elizabeth Moses, Charles H. Peck, Alexander H. Smith, and Rodham E. Tulloss. For the most part, these species names are included for their historical interest, as a nod to the state's long history of mycological studies, as many of them are now considered to be synonymous with other names. It may be worthwhile to note that leafspots, rusts, smuts, and leaf curls, which are as inconspicuous as they are economically important, have been omitted from this list. Also missing are many of the resupinate, shelving species; conks; and the myriad tiny cups, cushions, and prongs, though a few of each of the more representative are present. All of the above are so numerous and often so hard to distinguish from one another that they are usually not of interest to the amateur, though many have been identified in Kansas. While these fungi are generally beyond the scope of a field guide to mushrooms, several eminent Kansas mycologists, including Bartholomew, William A. Kellerman, Arthur J. Mix, and Clark T. Rogerson, described species new to science in these groups from Kansas specimens.

Species found in this guide are identified by their species account numbers. Those that are pictured and fully described are indicated by the number alone (for example "96"), while others that are mentioned within the description of a numbered species are designated by that number preceded by *see* (for example, "see 96"). If a genus is followed by "sp." then the species is unknown. Scientific names are not italicized here, for ease of reading.

__ Abortiporus biennis (117)
__ Acanthophysium oakesii
__ Acrospermum compressum
__ Agaricus abruptibulbus (73)
__ Agaricus arvensis (see 72)
__ Agaricus bilamellatus
__ Agaricus bisporus
__ Agaricus bitorquis (see 71)
__ Agaricus caesifolius Peck
__ Agaricus campestris (71)
__ Agaricus comptulus
__ Agaricus cretacellus
__ Agaricus micromegethus
__ Agaricus placomyces (74)
__ Agaricus rutilescens
__ Agaricus subrutilescens
__ Agaricus sylvaticus (see 74)
__ Agaricus sylvicola (72)
__ Agaricus xanthodermus
__ Agrocybe acericola
__ Agrocybe dura
__ Agrocybe pediades
__ Agrocybe praecox (59)
__ Agrocybe sororia
__ Agrocybe vermiflua
__ Agrocybe vervacti

__ Alutaceodontia alutacea
__ Albotricha albotestacea
__ Aleuria aurantia (see 186)
__ Aleuria cestrica
__ Amanita abrupta
__ Amanita aestivalis
__ Amanita albocreata
__ Amanita "amerirubescens" (provisional name) (7)
__ Amanita "banningiana" (provisional name)
__ Amanita bisporigera (3)
__ Amanita borealisorora
__ Amanita brunnescens
__ Amanita ceciliae
__ Amanita citrina
__ Amanita cokeri
__ Amanita cothurnata
__ Amanita flavoconia (2)
__ Amanita flavorubescens (see 7)
__ Amanita fulva (4)
__ Amanita gemmata
__ Amanita longipes
__ Amanita microlepis
__ Amanita multisquamosa (6)
__ Amanita muscaria (see 2)
__ Amanita peckiana
__ Amanita populiphila Tulloss & Moses (1)
__ Amanita solaniolens
__ Amanita spreta (5)
__ Amanita vaginata (see 4)
__ Amanita "whetstoneae" (provisional name)
__ Amanita verna
__ Amanita volvata
__ Anthracobia melaloma
__ Antrodia albida
__ Antrodia heteromorpha
__ Antrodiella semisupina
__ Apioperdon pyriforme (166)
__ Apiosporina morbosa
__ Arachnion album
__ Arachnopeziza aurelia
__ Arcryria cinerea (myxomycete)
__ Arcryria denudata (myxomycete)
__ Arcryria nutans (myxomycete)
__ Armillaria mellea group (24)
__ Arrhenia epichysium
__ Artomyces pyxidatus (148)
__ Ascobolus furfuraceus
__ Ascocoryne cylichnium
__ Aspropaxillus giganteus
__ Asterophora lycoperdoides (37)
__ Astraeus hygrometricus
__ Atheniella flavoalba
__ Aureoboletus auriporus
__ Aureoboletus innixus (94)
__ Aureoboletus roxanae
__ Aureoboletus russellii (90)
__ Auricularia americana (149)
__ Auriscalpium vulgare
__ Biscogniauxia atropunctata
__ Biscogniauxia mediterranea (see 200)
__ Bjerkandera adusta
__ Bjerkandera fumosa
__ Bogbodia uda
__ Bolbitius coprophilus
__ Bolbitius sordidus
__ Bolbitius titubans (40)
__ Boletinellus merulioides (101)
__ Boletus aurantiosplendens
__ Boletus bicolor
__ Boletus fairchildianus
__ Boletus glabellus
__ Boletus rubroflammeus (see 92)
__ Boletus subvelutipes (92)
__ Boletus variipes (93)
__ Bondarzewia berkeleyi (115)

__ Bovista cinerea Ellis
__ Bovista pila
__ Bovista pusilla
__ Bovistella utriformis (163)
__ Brevicellicium olivascens
__ Britzelmayria multipedata
__ Brunneoporus juniperinus (see 104) (syn. = Antrodia juniperina Murril)
__ Bryoperdon acuminatum
__ Bulgaria inquinans (see 189)
__ Butyriboletus peckii
__ Byssomerulius corium
__ Byssomerulius incarnatus (124)
__ Callistosporium luteo-olivaceum
__ Caloboletus calopus
__ Caloboletus firmus
__ Caloboletus inedulis
__ Calocera cornea (150)
__ Calocera viscosa
__ Calvatia bovista (159)
__ Calvatia craniiformis (162)
__ Calvatia cretacea
__ Calvatia cyathiformis (160)
__ Calvatia elata
__ Calvatia fragilis (see 160)
__ Calvatia gigantea (see 162)
__ Calvatia lilacina
__ Calvatia rubroflava (161) (syn. = Lycoperdon rubroflavum Cragin)
__ Calvatia sculpta or subsculpta
__ Calycina citrina (191)
__ Camarops petersii (200)
__ Cantharellus "cibarius" group (134)
__ Cantharellus cinnabarinus (135)
__ Cantharellus flavus
__ Cantharellus lateritius (see 134)
__ Cantharellus minor
__ Cantharellus phasmatis
__ Cantharellus spectaculus
__ Cantharellus subalbidus
__ Cerioporus leptocephalus (120)
__ Cerioporus mollis
__ Cerioporus squamosus
__ Cerioporus varius
__ Ceriporia spissa
__ Cerrena unicolor (syn. = Daedalea tortusosa Cragin)
__ Chalciporus pseudorubinellus
__ Chalciporus rubinellus
__ Chlorociboria aeruginascens
__ Chlorophyllum agaricoides
__ Chlorophyllum molybdites (79)
__ Chlorophyllum rachodes (see 78)
__ Chondrostereum purpureum (133)
__ Clavaria cretacea
__ Clavaria fumosa
__ Clavaria fragilis
__ Clavariadelphus americanus (144)
__ Clavariadelphus ligula
__ Claviceps purpurea
__ Clavulina cinerea (see 146)
__ Clavulina coralloides (146)
__ Clavulinopsis corniculata
__ Clavulinopsis fusiformis (see 147)
__ Clavulinopsis laeticolor (147)
__ Climacodon septentrionalis
__ Clitocella mundula
__ Clitocybe americana
__ Clitocybe dealbata
__ Clitocybe eccentrica
__ Clitocybe morbifera
__ Clitocybe multiceps
__ Clitocybe nebularis
__ Clitocybe odora (29)
__ Clitocybe phaeophthalma
__ Clitocybe phyllophila
__ Clitocybe revoluta
__ Clitocybe truncicola
__ Clitocybula familia

__ Clitopilus prunulus
__ Collybia alboflavida
__ Collybia amabilipes
__ Collybia zonata
__ Collybiopsis confluens
__ Collybiopsis luxurians
__ Coltricia cinnamomea (129)
__ Coltricia montagnei (128)
__ Coniophora puteana
__ Conocybe apala (41)
__ Conocybe deliquescens
__ Conocybe fragilis
(syn. = Galera fragilis Peck)
__ Conocybe tenera
__ Coprinellus disseminatus
__ Coprinellus domesticus
__ Coprinellus ephemerus
__ Coprinellus marculentus
__ Coprinellus micaceus (67)
__ Coprinellus radians (68)
__ Coprinellus subimpatiens
__ Coprinopsis atramentaria (66)
__ Coprinopsis cinerea
__ Coprinopsis lagopus (69)
__ Coprinopsis nivea
__ Coprinopsis picacea
__ Coprinopsis radiata
__ Coprinopsis variegata (65)
(syn. = Coprinus ebulbosus Peck)
__ Coprinus calyptratus Peck
__ Coprinus comatus (70)
__ Coprinus laniger Peck
__ Coprinus semilanatus
__ Coprinus sulphureus
__ Cordyceps farinosa
__ Cordyceps militaris (see 192)
__ Coriolopsis gallica (109)
__ Cortinarius albidus
__ Cortinarius alboviolaceus (50)
__ Cortinarius argentatus
__ Cortinarius atkinsonianus (54)
__ Cortinarius basalis
__ Cortinarius bolaris
__ Cortinarius calyptrodermus (48)
__ Cortinarius camphoratus
__ Cortinarius coloratus
__ Cortinarius cotoneus
__ Cortinarius crassus
__ Cortinarius cylindripes
__ Cortinarius distans (53)
__ Cortinarius elegantior
__ Cortinarius hesleri (51)
__ Cortinarius infractus
__ Cortinarius iodeoides (52)
__ Cortinarius multiformis
__ Cortinarius obliquus
__ Cortinarius rimosus
__ Cortinarius rubripes
__ Cortinarius sphaerospermus (49)
__ Cortinarius subpulchrifolius
__ Cortinarius triumphans
__ Cortinarius violaceus
__ Cotylidia diaphana (132)
__ Craterellus fallax (136)
__ Craterellus foetidus (138)
__ Craterellus tubaeformis
__ Creosphaeria sassafras
__ Creosphaeria verruculosa
__ Crepidotus applanatus
__ Crepidotus bresadolae
__ Crepidotus cinnabarinus
__ Crepidotus crocophyllus (55)
__ Crepidotus epibryus
__ Crepidotus mollis (see 55)
__ Crepidotus versutus
__ Crinipellis piceae
__ Crinipellis scabella
__ Crinipellis subtomentosa (syn. = Marasmius subtomentosus Peck)
__ Crucibulum crucibuliforme

__ Crucibulum laeve (168)
__ Crustoderma dryinum
__ Cuphophyllus pratensis
__ Cyanoboletus pulverulentus
__ Cyanosporus caesius
__ Cyathus hirsutus
__ Cyathus olla
__ Cyathus rufipes
__ Cyathus stercoreus (169)
__ Cyathus striatus (see 169)
__ Cystoderma amianthinum
__ Cystolepiota seminuda
__ Cytospora ceratosperma
__ Cytospora leucostoma
__ Cytospora nivea
__ Cytospora populina
__ Dacrymyces capitatus
__ Dacrymyces deliquescens
__ Dacrymyces minor
__ Dacryopinax elegans (151)
__ Dacryopinax spathularia (see 150)
__ Daedalea quercina (syn. = Trametes kansensis Cragin)
__ Daedaleopsis confragosa (104)
__ Daedaleopsis ticolor
__ Daldinia childiae (see 198)
__ Daldinia vernicosa
__ Daleomyces petersii
__ Deconica montana
__ Dendrothele nivosa
__ Desarmillaria tabescens (25)
__ Diatrype stigma
__ Discina ancilis
__ Discina brunnea
__ Discina caroliniana (178)
__ Discina fastigiata (179)
__ Disciotis venosa
__ Disciseda candida
__ Disciseda circumscissa
__ Disciseda subterranea
__ Dissingia leucomeleana
__ Donadinia nigrella
__ Ductifera pululahuana (see 153)
__ Echinoderma asperum (see 78)
__ Efibula tuberculata
__ Elaphomyces granulatus (see 193)
__ Elaphomyces muricatus group
__ Entoloma byssisedum
__ Entoloma clypeatum
__ Entoloma incanum
__ Entoloma nigroviolaceum (42)
__ Entoloma rhodopolium
__ Entoloma sericeum
__ Entoloma sinuatum
__ Entoloma strictius
__ Entoloma vernum
__ Entomophthora culicis
__ Entonaema liquescens (199)
__ Exidia glandulosa (see 154)
__ Exidia recisa
__ Exidia thuretiana
__ Fistulina hepatica (123)
__ Flammulaster erinaceellus
__ Flammulina velutipes (26)
__ Fomes fomentarius
__ Fomes fulvus
__ Fomes igniarius
__ Fomitiporia punctata
__ Fomitopsis betulina
__ Fuligo septica var. septica (myxomycete)
__ Fuligo varians (myxomycete)
__ Fulviformes inermis
__ Fusarium graminearum
__ Fuscoporia contigua
__ Fuscoporia ferruginosa
__ Fusicolla merismoides
__ Galerina marginata (58)
__ Galerina venenata
__ Galiella rufa (177)

__ Ganoderma applanatum (111)
__ Ganoderma curtisii (112)
__ Ganoderma lucidum (see 112)
__ Ganoderma resinaceum (see 112)
__ Geastrum campestre (see 171)
__ Geastrum corollinum
__ Geastrum coronatum (see 171)
__ Geastrum elegans
__ Geastrum fimbriatum
__ Geastrum floriforme
__ Geastrum fornicatum
__ Geastrum javanicum
__ Geastrum kotlabae
__ Geastrum lageniforme
__ Geastrum limbatum
__ Geastrum minimum
__ Geastrum morganii
__ Geastrum nanum
__ Geastrum pectinatum
__ Geastrum pedicellatum
__ Geastrum rufescens
__ Geastrum saccatum (171)
__ Geastrum smardae
__ Geastrum smithii
__ Geastrum striatum
__ Geastrum triplex (170)
__ Geopora arenicola
__ Geopora arenosa
__ Gerronema strombodes
__ Gerronema subclavatum
__ Gliophorus psittacinus (10)
__ Globiformes graveolens
__ Gloeophyllum berkeleyi
__ Gloeophyllum odoratum
__ Gloeophyllum sepiarium
__ Gloeophyllum trabeum
__ Gomphus clavatus (see 143)
__ Granulobasidium vellereum
(syn. = Corticium vellereum
Ellis & Cragin)
__ Grifola frondosa (113)
__ Gymnopilus fulvosquamulosus
__ Gymnopilus liquiritiae
__ Gymnopilus luteofolius
__ Gymnopilus penetrans
__ Gymnopilus picreus
__ Gymnopilus punctifolius
__ Gymnopilus sapineus
__ Gymnopus alcalinolens
__ Gymnopus androsaceus
__ Gymnopus dryophilus (14)
__ Gymnopus foetidus
__ Gymnopus fuliginellus
(syn. = Collybia fuligenella Peck)
__ Gymnopus fuscopurpureus
__ Gymnopus microsporus
(syn. = Collybia microspora Peck)
__ Gymnopus semihirtipes (15)
__ Gymnopus spongiosus (see 15)
__ Gymnopus subnudus
__ Gymnopus subsulphureus (see 14)
(syn. = Collybia subsulphurea)
__ Gyromitra esculenta (see 179)
__ Gyromitra gigas
__ Gyromitra infula
__ Gyroporus castaneus (see 102)
__ Gyroporus purpurinus (102)
__ Gyroporus subalbellus
__ Hapalopilus rutilans
__ Harrya chromipes
__ Hebeloma colvinii
__ Hebeloma crustuliniforme
__ Hebeloma fastibile
__ Hebeloma gregarium
__ Heliocybe sulcata
__ Helotium craginianum (syn. =
Peziza craginiana Ellis & Everhart)
__ Helvella acetabulum
__ Helvella cripsa (see 180)
__ Helvella elastica (see 180)

__ Helvella fibrosa
__ Helvella lacunosa
__ Helvella macropus (see 180)
__ Helvella stevensii (180)
__ Helvellosebacina concrescens (see 153)
__ Hemileccinum hortanii
__ Hemileccinum subglabripes
__ Hemistropharia albocrenulata
__ Hemitricia calyculata (myxomycete)
__ Hericium americanum (see 141)
__ Hericium cirrhatum
__ Hericium coralloides (141)
__ Hericium erinaceus (142)
__ Hericium erinaceus subsp. erinaceo-abietis (see 142)
__ Hohenbuehelia approximans
__ Hohenbuehelia atrocoerulea (see 109)
__ Hohenbuehelia angustata
__ Hohenbuehelia mastrucata (see 109)
__ Hohenbuehelia petaloides
__ Hortiboletus campestris (91)
__ Hortiboletus fraternus
__ Humaria hemisphaerica (see 177) (syn. = Peziza hemisphaerica var. subcalva Ellis)
__ Hydnellum aurantiacum
__ Hydnellum caeruleum
__ Hydnellum concrescens
__ Hydnellum peckii
__ Hydnellum spongiosipes (see 140)
__ Hydnophlebia chrysorhiza (107)
__ Hydnoporia olivacea (see 106)
__ Hydnum repandum (139)
__ Hygrocybe acutoconica
__ Hygrocybe conica (11)
__ Hygrocybe miniata
__ Hygrophoropsis aurantiaca
__ Hygrophorus occidentalis
__ Hygrophorus roseobrunneus (12)
__ Hygrophorus sordidus
__ Hygrophorus subsalmonius (see 12)
__ Hymenochaete rubiginosa
__ Hymenogaster citrinus
__ Hymenopellis radicata group (28)
__ Hymenopellis rubrobrunnescens
__ Hymenoscyphus fructigenus (see 191)
__ Hyphodontia granulosa
__ Hyphodontia pallidula
__ Hypholoma cutifractum Peck
__ Hypholoma fasciculare
__ Hypholoma lateritium
__ Hypocopra kansensis Ellis & Everhart
__ Hypomyces chrysospermus (195)
__ Hypomyces hyalinus (see 195)
__ Hypomyces lactifluorum (194)
__ Hypomyces rosellus
__ Hypoxylon fragiforme
__ Hypoxylon fuscum
__ Hypoxylon howeanum
__ Hypoxylon perforatum
__ Hypoxylon rubiginosum
__ Hypsizygus ulmarius (see 38)
__ Hysterobrevium mori
__ Hysterographium fraxini
__ Hysterographium kansense Ellis & Everhart
__ Imleria pallida
__ Infundibulicybe gibba (see 29)
__ Inocutis dryophila
__ Inocybe albodisca
__ Inocybe asterospora
__ Inocybe caesariata
__ Inocybe calospora

__ Inocybe decipientoides
__ Inocybe flocculosa
__ Inocybe geophylla (see 56)
__ Inocybe hirtella
__ Inocybe intricata
__ Inocybe lorillardiana
__ Inocybe mixtilis
__ Inocybe pusio
__ Inocybe pyriodora
__ Inocybe suaveolens
__ Inocybe subochracea
__ Inonotus cuticularis
__ Inonotus hispidus
__ Inosperma calamistratum
__ Inosperma cookei
__ Inosperma fastigiellum
__ Inosperma maculatum
__ Inosperma adaequatum (see 56)
__ Irpex lacteus (see 106)
__ Irpiciporus pachyodon (106)
__ Isaria sp.
__ Ischnoderma resinosum (110)
__ Jackrogersella multiformis
__ Jafnea semitosta
__ Jattaea cornina
__ Kauffmania larga
__ Kretzschmaria deusta (197)
__ Kretzschmaria zonata
__ Kuehneromyces mutabilis
__ Laccaria amethystina (see 35)
__ Laccaria laccata (34)
__ Laccaria ochropurpurea (35)
__ Lacrymaria echiniceps
__ Lacrymaria lacrymabunda (64)
__ Lactarius alnicola
__ Lactarius argillaceifolius
__ Lactarius atroviridis
__ Lactarius chrysorrheus
__ Lactarius corrugis
__ Lactarius fuliginosus
__ Lactarius helvus
__ Lactarius hibbardiae
__ Lactarius hygropheroides var. lavandulaceus
__ Lactarius indigo (81)
__ Lactarius maculatipes
__ Lactarius pallidus
__ Lactarius psammicola (83)
__ Lactarius rufulus
__ Lactarius subdulcis
__ Lactarius subplinthogalus (see 80)
__ Lactarius subserifluus
__ Lactarius subvernalis
__ Lactarius uvidus
__ Lactarius vietus
__ Lactarius westii
__ Lactarius zonarius
__ Lactiarus theiogalus
__ Lactifluus deceptivus (see 82)
__ Lactifluus glaucescens (82)
__ Lactifluus hygrophoroides (80)
__ Lactifluus luteolus
__ Lactifluus piperatus (see 82)
__ Lactifluus subvellereus
__ Lactifluus subvellerus var. subdistans (see 82)
__ Lactifluus volemus (see 80)
__ Laetiporus cincinnatus (see 116)
__ Laetiporus persicinus
__ Laetiporus sulphureus (116)
__ Langermannia pachyderma
__ Leccinellum crocipodium
__ Leccinellum griseum (96)
__ Leccinellum rugosiceps
__ Leccinum murinaceostipitatum
__ Leccinum scabrum
__ Leccinum snellii
__ Leccinum subtestaceum
__ Lentinellus cochleatus

__ Lentinellus semivestitus (syn. = Tricholoma semivestitum Peck)

__ Lentinellus ursinus (see 109)

__ Lentinellus vulpinus

__ Lentinula reticeps

__ Lentinus arcularius (119)

__ Lentinus brumalis

__ Lentinus levis (see 38)

__ Lentinus squamosus

__ Lentinus substrictus

__ Lenzites betulinus (see 104)

__ Leocarpus fragilis (myxomycete)

__ Leotia atrovirens

__ Leotia lubrica (190)

__ Leotia lubrica (form "L. viscosa" see 190)

__ Lepiota asperula

__ Lepiota atrodisca

__ Lepiota caloceps

__ Lepiota castanea

__ Lepiota clypeolaria (see 76)

__ Lepiota clypeolarioides

__ Lepiota cortinarius

__ Lepiota cristata (75)

__ Lepiota erminea

__ Lepiota juniperina

__ Lepiota mutata Peck

__ Lepiota neophana

__ Lepiota pratensis

__ Lepiota roseotincta

__ Lepiota rugulosa

__ Lepiota sanguiflua

__ Lepiota sublilacea Peck

__ Lepista amara

__ Lepista graveolens

__ Lepista nuda (see 30)

__ Lepista personata

__ Lepista tarda (30)

__ Leucoagaricus americanus (see 78)

__ Leucoagaricus coerulescens

__ Leucoagaricus leucothites (see 79)

__ Leucoagaricus rubrotinctus (76)

__ Leucocoprinus birnbaumii (77)

__ Leucocoprinus cepistipes (see 77)

__ Leucocoprinus fragilissimus

__ Leucocoprinus ianthinus

__ Leucocybe candicans

__ Leucopaxillus albissimus (see 31)

__ Leucopaxillus gentianeus

__ Leucopaxillus laterarius

__ Leucopaxillus tricolor (31)

__ Limacella kaufmannii

__ Lopharia cinerascens

__ Lycogala epidendrum (myxomycete)

__ Lycogala flavofuscum (myxomycete)

__ Lycoperdon atropurpureum

__ Lycoperdon candidum

__ Lycoperdon caudatum

__ Lycoperdon curtisii

__ Lycoperdon delicatumum

__ Lycoperdon elegans

__ Lycoperdon excipuliforme

__ Lycoperdon flavotinctum

__ Lycoperdon floccosum

__ Lycoperdon marginatum (164)

__ Lycoperdon molle (syn. = Lycoperdon molle var. occidentale Cragin)

__ Lycoperdon perlatum (165)

__ Lycoperdon pratense

__ Lycoperdon pulcherrimum (see 163)

__ Lycoperdon radicatum

__ Lycoperdon rima-spinosum Cragin

__ Lycoperdon rimulatum

__ Lycoperdon sigillatum Cragin

__ Lycoperdon spadiceum
__ Lycoperdon subincarnatum
__ Lycoperdon umbrinum
__ Lyomyces crustosus
__ Lyophyllum decastes group (36)
__ Lysurus borealis (see 158)
__ Lysurus cruciatus
__ Lysurus mokusin (see 158)
__ Lysurus periphragmoides (158) (syn. = Simblum rubescens var. kansense Cragin)
__ Macrolepiota excoriata
__ Macrolepiota procera (78)
__ Macrotyphula sp.
__ Maireina ochracea
__ Marasmiellus candidus
__ Marasmius badiceps Peck
__ Marasmius campanulatus
__ Marasmius capillaris
__ Marasmius cohaerens
__ Marasmius delectans
__ Marasmius detonianius
__ Marasmius elongatipes
__ Marasmius epiphyllus
__ Marasmius glabellus
__ Marasmius graminum
__ Marasmius nigrodiscus
__ Marasmius oreades (16)
__ Marasmius rotula (17)
__ Marasmius rubrophyllus
__ Marasmius siccus (18)
__ Marasmius sullivantii (19)
__ Megacollybia rodmanii (32)
__ Melanoleuca acris
__ Melanoleuca melaleuca
__ Melanophyllum haematospermum
__ Melastiza chateri
__ Mensularia radiata
__ Meripilus sumstinei (114)
__ Meruliporia incrassata
__ Microstoma floccosum (185)
__ Mollisia cinerea
__ Morchella americana (181)
__ Morchella angusticeps (see 181)
__ Morchella crassipes
__ Morchella diminutiva (see 181)
__ Morchella punctipes (182)
__ Mutinus caninus (see 157)
__ Mutinus elegans (157)
__ Mutinus ravenelii
__ Mycena alcalina (see 22)
__ Mycena corticola
__ Mycena eburnea
__ Mycena galericulata
__ Mycena haematopus (see 22)
__ Mycena hemisphaerica
__ Mycena inclinata (22)
__ Mycena leaiana
__ Mycena luteopallens (23)
__ Mycena niveipes
__ Mycena pelianthina
__ Mycena pseudoinclinata
__ Mycena pulchrifolia
__ Mycena pura (21)
__ Mycena subcaerulea
__ Mycenastrum corium
__ Mycetinis scorodonius
__ Mycorrhaphium adustum
__ Myriostoma coliforme
__ Myxarium nucleatum (see 154)
__ Nectria cinnabarina (see 194)
__ Nectria vulpina
__ Nemania caries
__ Neoantrodia serialis
__ Neoboletus praestigiator
__ Neofavolus alveolaris (118)
__ Neolentinus lepideus
__ Niptera fuscorubra
__ Niveoporofomes spraguei
__ Omphalina mutila

__ Omphalina pyxidata
__ Omphalotus illudens (13)
__ Onnia tomentosa
__ Ophiocordyceps melolonthae (192)
__ Ophiocordyceps ravenelii
__ Orbilia cruenta
__ Otidea alutacea
__ Oxyporus corticola
__ Oxyporus populinus
__ Pachyella clypeata
__ Pachyphloeus virescens
__ Panaeolina foenisecii (62)
__ Panaeolus papilionaceus
__ Panaeolus semiovatus
__ Panaeolus solidipes
__ Panellus stipticus
__ Panus conchatus (103)
__ Panus neostrigosus
__ Panus rudis
__ Paragalactinia succosa (see 184)
__ Paragymnopus perforans
__ Paragyrodon sphaerosporus
__ Parasola plicatilis
__ Paxina queletii
__ Peniophora cinerea
__ Peniophora incarnata
__ Peniophora versiformis
__ Perenniporia bartholomaei (syn. = Polyporus bartholomaei Peck)
__ Perenniporia fraxinophila (see 111)
__ Perenniporia ohiensis
__ Perenniporia semistipitata (syn. = Polyporus semistipitatus Lloyd)
__ Perenniporia subacida
__ Peziza arvenensis
__ Peziza domiciliana (184)
__ Peziza repanda
__ Peziza vesiculosa
__ Phaeocalicium polyporaeum
__ Phaeohelotium carneum
__ Phaeotremella foliacea
__ Phaeotremella frondosa (152)
__ Phalllus impudicus (see 155)
__ Phallus hadriani (155)
__ Phallus indusiatus (see 155)
__ Phallus ravenellii (156)
__ Phallus rubicundus (see 155)
__ Phanerochaete velutina
__ Phellinus everhartii
__ Phellinus gilvus (108)
__ Phellinus igniarius
__ Phellinus pomaceus
__ Phellinus robiniae (see 111)
__ Phellodon melaleucus
__ Phellodon niger (140)
__ Phlebia radiata
__ Phlebia tremellosa
__ Phlebiopsis flavidoalba
__ Pholiota adiposa
__ Pholiota aurivella (60)
__ Pholiota polychroa (61)
__ Pholiota populnea (see 60)
__ Pholiota squarrosa
__ Pholiota terrestris
__ Phylloporus rhodoxanthus (89)
__ Phyllotopsis nidulans (33)
__ Physarum didermoides (myxomycete)
__ Physarum leucophaeum (myxomycete)
__ Physarum polycephalum (myxomycete)
__ Picipes badius (see 120)
__ Picipes melanopus
__ Picipes rhizophilus (syn. = Polyporus cryptopus Ellis & Bartholomew)

__ Pilobolus sp.
__ Pisolithus arhizus (172)
__ Pithya cupressina
__ Pleurocybella porrigens
__ Pleurotus cornucopiae
__ Pleurotus dryinus
__ Pleurotus ostreatus (38)
__ Pleurotus pulmonarius (see 38)
__ Plicaturopsis crispa
__ Pluteus admirabilis (44)
__ Pluteus cervinus (45)
__ Pluteus cyanopus (see 43)
__ Pluteus leoninus
__ Pluteus longistriatus (43)
__ Pluteus nanus
__ Pluteus petasatus (see 45)
__ Pluteus romellii
__ Polyporus radicatus (121) (syn. = Polyporus kansensis Ellis & Bartholomew)
__ Polyporus umbellatus
__ Polystigma rubrum subsp. rubrum
__ Porodaedalea pini
__ Poronia punctata
__ Poronidulus conchifer (126)
__ Porphyrellus indecisus
__ Porphyrellus sordidus (99)
__ Postia tephroleuca
__ Protodontia fascicularis
__ Protostropharia semiglobata (see 57)
__ Psathyrella bartholomaei Peck
__ Psathyrella brachycystis Smith
__ Psathyrella brooksii Smith
__ Psathyrella candolleana (63)
__ Psathyrella debilis Peck
__ Psathyrella delicatella Smith
__ Psathyrella delineata
__ Psathyrella fuscofolia
__ Psathyrella gracillima Peck
__ Psathyrella hymenocephala
__ Psathyrella incerta
__ Psathyrella kauffmanii
__ Psathyrella leucostigma Peck
__ Psathyrella limicola
__ Psathyrella obscura (syn. = Psilocybe obscura Peck)
__ Psathyrella ovatispora Smith
__ Psathyrella riparia Smith
__ Psathyrella rugocephala
__ Psathyrella sepulcreti Smith
__ Pseudocolus fusiformis
__ Pseudocraterellus calyculus (137)
__ Pseudocraterellus pseudoclavatus (143)
__ Pseudohydnum gelatinosum
__ Pseudoinonotus dryadeus (see 110)
__ Pseudoomphalina compressipes
__ Pseudosperma rimosum (56)
__ Pseudosperma sororium
__ Pseudovalsaria allantospora
__ Psilocybe coronilla (see 57)
__ Psilocybe cubensis
__ Psilocybe sabulosa Peck
__ Pterula plumosa
__ Puccinia podophylli
__ Pulveroboletus curtisii
__ Pulvinula convexella
__ Punctularia strigosozonata
__ Pycnoporus cinnabarinus (122)
__ Pycnoporus sanguineus (see 122)
__ Pyrenochaeta graminis
__ Pyronema omphalodes
__ Ramaria apiculata
__ Ramaria araiospora (145)
__ Ramaria aurea
__ Ramaria caulifloriformis
__ Ramaria fennica

__ Ramaria flava
__ Ramaria formosa
__ Ramaria formosa var. concolor
__ Ramaria rasilispora var. scatesiana
__ Ramaria stricta (see 148)
__ Resinomycena rhododendri
__ Resupinatus applicatus
__ Retiboletus ornatipes
__ Rhizomarasmius pyrrhocephalus
__ Rhodocollybia butyracea
__ Rhodocollybia maculata
__ Rhodofomes cajanderi
__ Rhodotus palmatus (27) (?syn. = Agaricus alveolaris Cragin)
__ Rhytidhysteron hysterinum
__ Rickenella fibula
__ Rosellinia quercina
__ Russula adusta (see 85)
__ Russula aeruginea (84)
__ Russula albida
__ Russula albonigra (85)
__ Russula atropurpurea
__ Russula ballouii
__ Russula betularum
__ Russula brevipes
__ Russula brunneola
__ Russula cessans
__ Russula compacta (see 87)
__ Russula cremeirosea
__ Russula crustosa (see 88)
__ Russula cyanoxantha (86)
__ Russula decolorans
__ Russula densifolia (see 85)
__ Russula dissimulans
__ Russula emetica group
__ Russula faginea
__ Russula flaviceps
__ Russula flavida
__ Russula foetentula
__ Russula fragrantissima (87)
__ Russula graveolens
__ Russula heterophylla
__ Russula incarnaticeps
__ Russula maculata group
__ Russula mariae
__ Russula michiganensis
__ Russula modesta
__ Russula nigrescentipes
__ Russula nobilis
__ Russula paludosa
__ Russula pectinatoides (see 87)
__ Russula polyphylla
__ Russula pulchra
__ Russula pulverulenta
__ Russula rosea
__ Russula rubescens
__ Russula sanguinea
__ Russula sericeonitens
__ Russula sororia group
__ Russula subnigricans
__ Russula subpunctata
__ Russula veternosa
__ Russula vinosa
__ Russula virescens (88)
__ Ruzenia spermoides
__ Saproamanita prairiicola (syn. = Amanita prairiicola Peck)
__ Saproamanita thiersii (8)
__ Sarcodon imbricatus (see 139)
__ Sarcodontia unicolor
__ Sarcomyxa serotina
__ Sarcoscypha dudleyi (186)
__ Sarcoscypha occidentalis (187)
__ Schizophyllum commune (39)
__ Schizopora paradoxa
__ Scleroderma arenicola
__ Scleroderma areolatum (174)
__ Scleroderma cepa (see 174)
__ Scleroderma citrinum
__ Scleroderma flavidum (173)

__ Scleroderma hypogaeum
__ Scleroderma lycoperdoides
__ Scleroderma polyrhizum (see 173)
__ Scleroderma verrucosum
__ Scutellinia scutellata (188)
__ Scutellinia setosa
__ Sebacina candida
__ Sebacina incrustans
__ Sebacina schweinitzii (see 146)
__ Sebacina sparassoidea
__ Serpula lacrymans
__ Singerocybe adirondackensis
__ Sphaerobolus stellatus
__ Steccherinum ochraceum
__ Stemonitis ferruginea (myxomycete)
__ Stemonitis fusca (myxomycete)
__ Stereum complicatum (see 131)
__ Stereum gausapatum
__ Stereum hirsutum (130)
__ Stereum lobatum
__ Stereum ostrea (131)
__ Stereum striatum var. ochraceoflavum
__ Strobilomyces strobilaceus (97)
__ Stropharia aeruginosa
__ Stropharia inuncta
__ Stropharia melanosperma (57)
__ Stropharia rugosoannulata
__ Stropharia umbonatescens
__ Suillellus luridus
__ Suillus brevipes (see 100)
__ Suillus granulatus (see 100)
__ Suillus weaverae (100)
__ Syzygospora mycetophila (see 14)
__ Tarzetta bronca
__ Tetrapyrgos nigripes (see 17)
__ Thelephora americana (see 145)
__ Thelephora pallida
__ Thelephora palmata
__ Thelephora terrestris group
__ Tolypocladium capitatum (see 193)
__ Tolypocladium ophioglossoides (193)
__ Trametes elegans (see 104) (syn. = Daedalea ambigua var. coronata Cragin)
__ Trametes hirsuta
__ Trametes ochracea
__ Trametes pubescens
__ Trametes suaveolens
__ Trametes trogii
__ Trametes versicolor (127)
__ Trametes villosa
__ Trametopsis cervina
__ Tratraea macrospora
__ Tremella fuciformis (153)
__ Tremella mesenterica (154)
__ Tremella obscura
__ Tremellodendropsis tuberosa
__ Trichaptum biforme (105)
__ Trichia varia
__ Tricholoma aurantium
__ Tricholoma caligatum
__ Tricholoma columbetta
__ Tricholoma fulvum
__ Tricholoma inamoenum
__ Tricholoma odorum
__ Tricholoma populinum (see 32)
__ Tricholoma portentosum
__ Tricholoma sejunctum
__ Tricholoma subresplendens
__ Tricholoma sulphurescens
__ Tricholoma ustale
__ Tricholoma ustaloides
__ Tricholomopsis sulfureoides
__ Tubaria decurrens (syn. = Flammula decurrens Peck)

__ Tubaria furfuracea
__ Tuber brennemanii (176)
__ Tuber candidum
__ Tuber gardneri
__ Tuber lyonii (see 176)
__ Tuberifera ferruginosa (myxomycete)
__ Tulostoma americanum
__ Tulostoma brumale
__ Tulostoma campestre (see 167)
__ Tulostoma fimbriatum (see 167)
__ Tulostoma kansense Peck
__ Tulostoma minutum
__ Tulostoma obesum
__ Tulostoma occidentale
__ Tulostoma poculatum
__ Tulostoma punctatum Peck
__ Tulostoma rufum
__ Tulostoma simulans (167)
__ Tylopilus ferrugineus
__ Tylopilus rubrobrunneus (98)
__ Tylopilus violatinctus
__ Typhula juncea
__ Tyromyces chioneus
__ Tyromyces galactinus
__ Tyromyces lacteus
__ Underwoodia columnaris
__ Urnula craterium (189)
__ Ustilago maydis (175)
__ Verpa bohemica
__ Verpa conica (183)
__ Verpa digitaliformis
__ Vitreoporus dichrous (125)
__ Volutella bartholomaei Ellis & Everhart
__ Volvaria striatula Peck
__ Volvariella bombycina (46)
__ Volvariella pusilla (see 47)
__ Volvariella stercoraria (syn. = Pluteus stercorarius Peck)
__ Volvariella taylorii
__ Volvopluteus gloiocephalus (47)
__ Wolfiporia cocos
__ Xanthoconium affine
__ Xanthoconium affine var. maculosus
__ Xanthoconium affine var. reticulatum
__ Xanthoconium purpureum
__ Xanthoconium separans
__ Xanthoporia andersonii
__ Xerocomus illudens
__ Xerocomus subtomentosus
__ Xerocomus tenax (95)
__ Xeromphalina kauffmanii
__ Xeromphalina tenuipes
__ Xylaria cubensis
__ Xylaria digitata
__ Xylaria filiformis
__ Xylaria hypoxylon (see 196)
__ Xylaria multiplex
__ Xylaria polymorpha (196)
__ Xylobolus frustulatus
__ Xylodon papillosus
__ Xylodon sambuci
__ Zhuliangomyces illinitus (9)

Appendix A

Relationships among the Species of Phylum Basidiomycota

Benjamin Sikes

These figures depict our current understanding of the relatedness among species in the phylum Basidiomycota that are presented in this book. Recent genetic work has helped to clarify the evolutionary history of these species, revealing that morphological or ecological traits that are helpful for field identification do not necessarily indicate close relationships. The following pages are an extended cladogram, an evolutionary tree that depicts those relationships. At the tip of each branch of the tree is the scientific name of the fungus as well as the species account number in which it is described. The branches represent evolutionary paths. Two species that share a fork of the tree also have a common ancestor that they do not share with any other species in the tree. In fact, you might imagine each fork in the tree to represent an ancestor species and the branches its descendants. At the tips, these forks display the relationships among close relatives, with fewer forks between species meaning they share a more recent common ancestor. This is true at the "deeper" forks of the tree as well. Species at the tips of a deep fork are still (collectively) more closely related to one another than any of them is to a species at the tip of the other path from that deep fork. It is probably the case that any two closely related species on this tree actually have even more closely related cousins, which are not included in this tree; what is presented in the tree is only the small subset of species we choose for this book.

Basidiomycota represent the lion's share of mushrooms presented here, and therefore, it is not possible to display a cladogram for all the species on a single page (or even ten pages). The first page shows the "deep" relationships among major groups of Basidiomycota, with numbers and shading to represent the grouped subsets of species that appear on the pages to follow. For example, the third cladogram (Agaricales 3) depicts relationships among the species of Agaricaceae and Lycoperdaceae in the book. These two groups are more closely related to one another than they are to species on other pages, with their broader relatedness to other Agaricales and Basidiomycota depicted in the initial figure of major groups. Each of the subsequent pages also has shading and letters to represent taxonomic groups (often families) of note. A key for those is detailed below. The first six pages are species all found

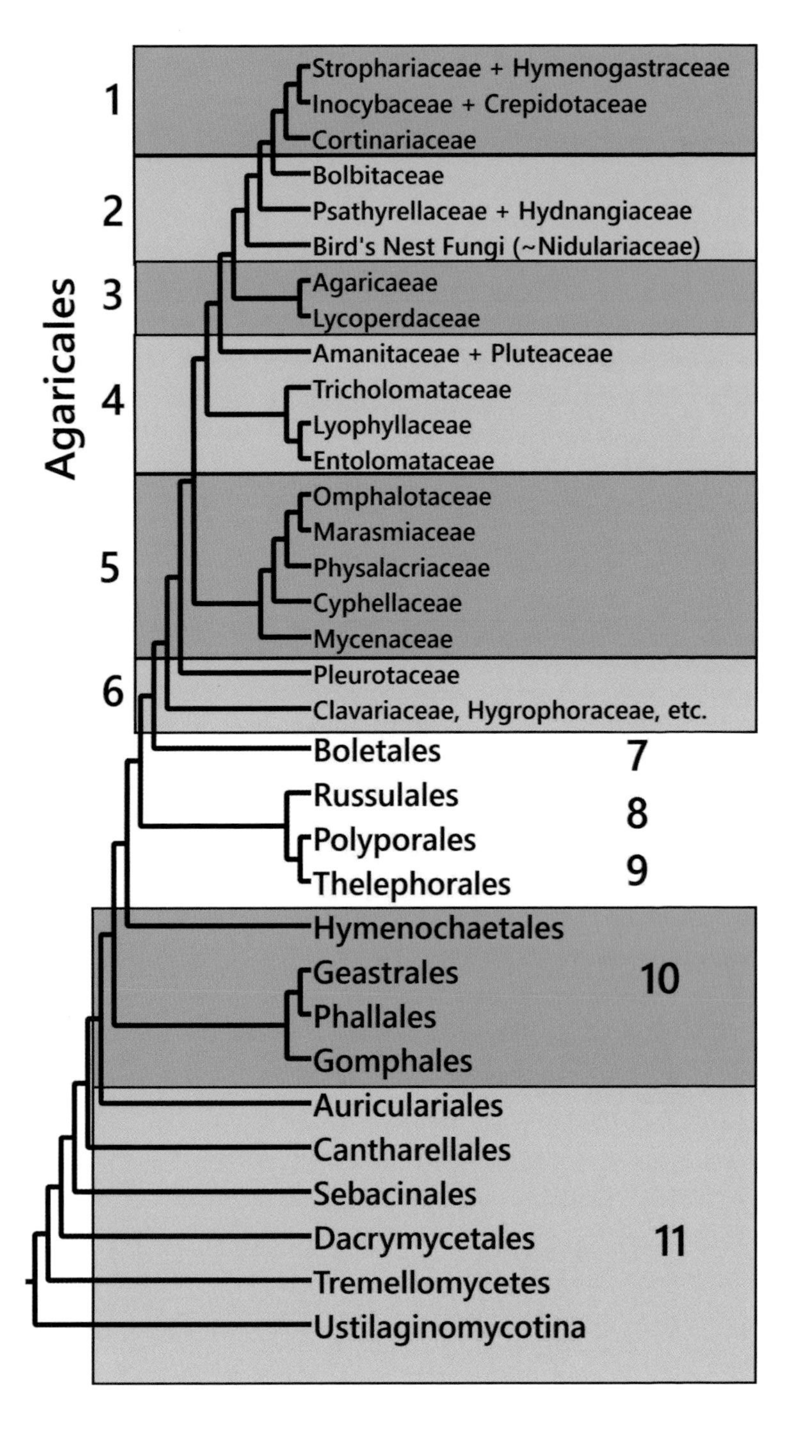
Agaricales
1
2
3
4
5
6
Strophariaceae + Hymenogastraceae
Inocybaceae + Crepidotaceae
Cortinariaceae
Bolbitaceae
Psathyrellaceae + Hydnangiaceae
Bird's Nest Fungi (~Nidulariaceae)
Agaricaeae
Lycoperdaceae
Amanitaceae + Pluteaceae
Tricholomataceae
Lyophyllaceae
Entolomataceae
Omphalotaceae
Marasmiaceae
Physalacriaceae
Cyphellaceae
Mycenaceae
Pleurotaceae
Clavariaceae, Hygrophoraceae, etc.
Boletales
7
Russulales
8
Polyporales
9
Thelephorales
Hymenochaetales
Geastrales
10
Phallales
Gomphales
Auriculariales
Cantharellales
Sebacinales
Dacrymycetales
11
Tremellomycetes
Ustilaginomycotina

in the order Agaricales, the lineage of most mushrooms. The final page (Basal Basidiomycota) represents the basal clades of Basidiomycota, including *Ustilago maydis*, the sole representative outside the subphylum Agaricomycotina. The Tremellomycetes and Dacrymycetes (order Dacrymycetales) are the only two Basidiomycota groups that are not part of the class Agaricomycetes.

Within each page, you will find relationships among closely related species; when their circumscriptions are clear, higher taxonomic groups are boxed and labeled with letters. For the first 9 pages, these shaded areas represent clusters of species at the family level (ending in "–aceae"). As one moves towards the groups at the base of this phylogenetic tree (the "basal" groups), genetic differences often grow bigger and the labels represent orders (ending in "-ales"). A key to the letters indicating family or order assignment is in the table on p. 348; these higher groups are presented in the cladogram on p. 346. Species represented in these pages include both those with photos and species accounts and related fungi discussed in the species account. Both species treated in full and those keyed and mentioned in passing are numbered with the relevant species account. Finally, it is important to remember that many more species, genera, and even entire families of Basidiomycota, are not represented in the cladogram because they are not in the book. That does not, however, mean that they are not present in Kansas! Truly the diversity of fungi, both known and unknown, leaves much to discover.

Agaricales 1 S = Strophariaceae C = Cortinariaceae	**Agaricales 2** B = Bolbitaceae P = Psathyrellaceae Nest = bird's nest fungi
Agaricales 3 Ag = Agaricaceae Ly = Lycoperdaceae	**Agaricales 4** Am = Amanitaceae Pl = Pluteaceae
Agaricales 5 Om = Omphalotaceae Ma = Marasmiaceae Ph = Physalacriaceae My = Mycenaceae	**Agaricales 6** Pl = Pleurotaceae Hy = Hygrophoraceae
Boletales Bo = Boletaceae Sc = Sclerodermataceae	**Russulales** Ru = Russulaceae
Polyporales + Thelephorales Po = Polyporaceae Th = Thelephoraceae	**Hymenochaetales + Geastrales + Phallales** Hy = Hymenochaetales Ge = Geastrales Ph = Phallales
Basal Basidiomycota Au = Auriculariales Ca = Cantharellales	

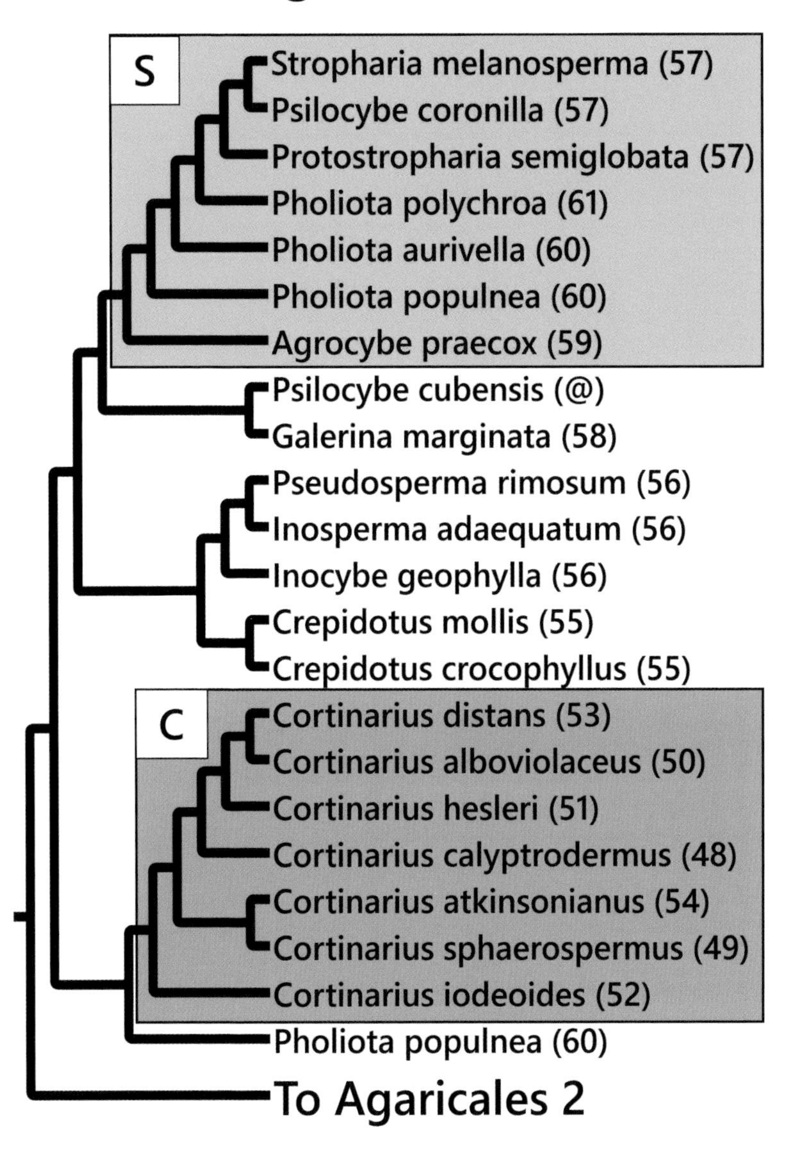
Agaricales 1
S
Stropharia melanosperma (57)
Psilocybe coronilla (57)
Protostropharia semiglobata (57)
Pholiota polychroa (61)
Pholiota aurivella (60)
Pholiota populnea (60)
Agrocybe praecox (59)
Psilocybe cubensis (@)
Galerina marginata (58)
Pseudosperma rimosum (56)
Inosperma adaequatum (56)
Inocybe geophylla (56)
Crepidotus mollis (55)
Crepidotus crocophyllus (55)
C
Cortinarius distans (53)
Cortinarius alboviolaceus (50)
Cortinarius hesleri (51)
Cortinarius calyptrodermus (48)
Cortinarius atkinsonianus (54)
Cortinarius sphaerospermus (49)
Cortinarius iodeoides (52)
Pholiota populnea (60)
To Agaricales 2

Agaricales 2

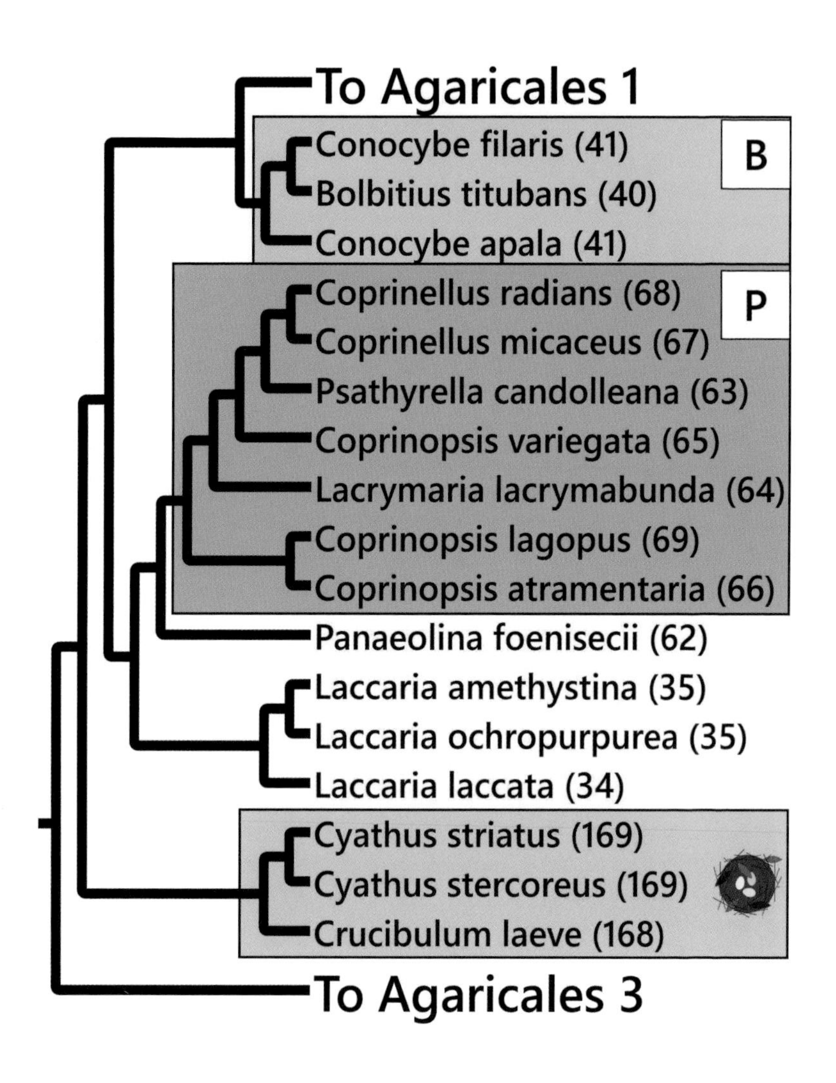

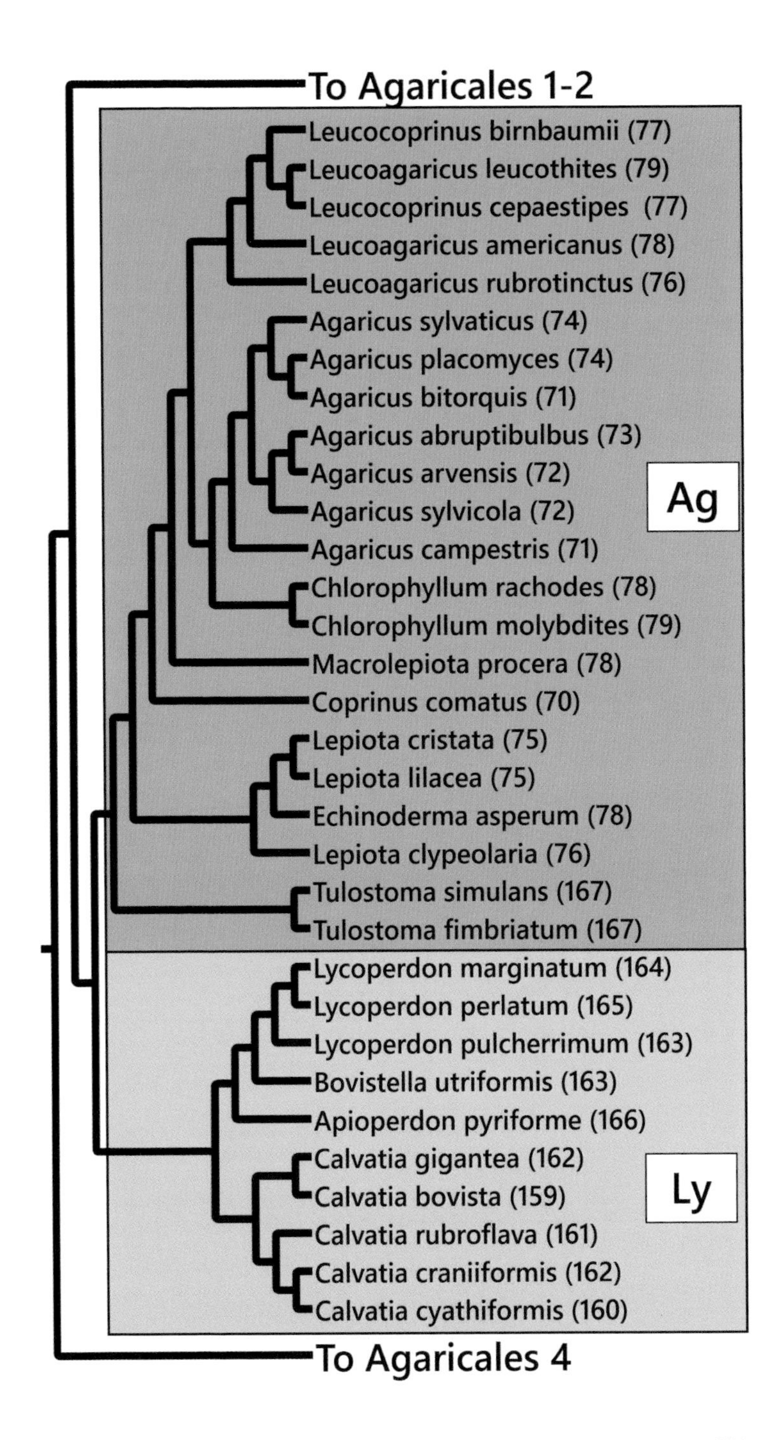
To Agaricales 1-2
Leucocoprinus birnbaumii (77)
Leucoagaricus leucothites (79)
Leucocoprinus cepaestipes (77)
Leucoagaricus americanus (78)
Leucoagaricus rubrotinctus (76)
Agaricus sylvaticus (74)
Agaricus placomyces (74)
Agaricus bitorquis (71)
Agaricus abruptibulbus (73)
Agaricus arvensis (72)
Agaricus sylvicola (72)
Agaricus campestris (71)
Chlorophyllum rachodes (78)
Chlorophyllum molybdites (79)
Macrolepiota procera (78)
Coprinus comatus (70)
Lepiota cristata (75)
Lepiota lilacea (75)
Echinoderma asperum (78)
Lepiota clypeolaria (76)
Tulostoma simulans (167)
Tulostoma fimbriatum (167)
Ag
Lycoperdon marginatum (164)
Lycoperdon perlatum (165)
Lycoperdon pulcherrimum (163)
Bovistella utriformis (163)
Apioperdon pyriforme (166)
Calvatia gigantea (162)
Calvatia bovista (159)
Calvatia rubroflava (161)
Calvatia craniiformis (162)
Calvatia cyathiformis (160)
Ly
To Agaricales 4

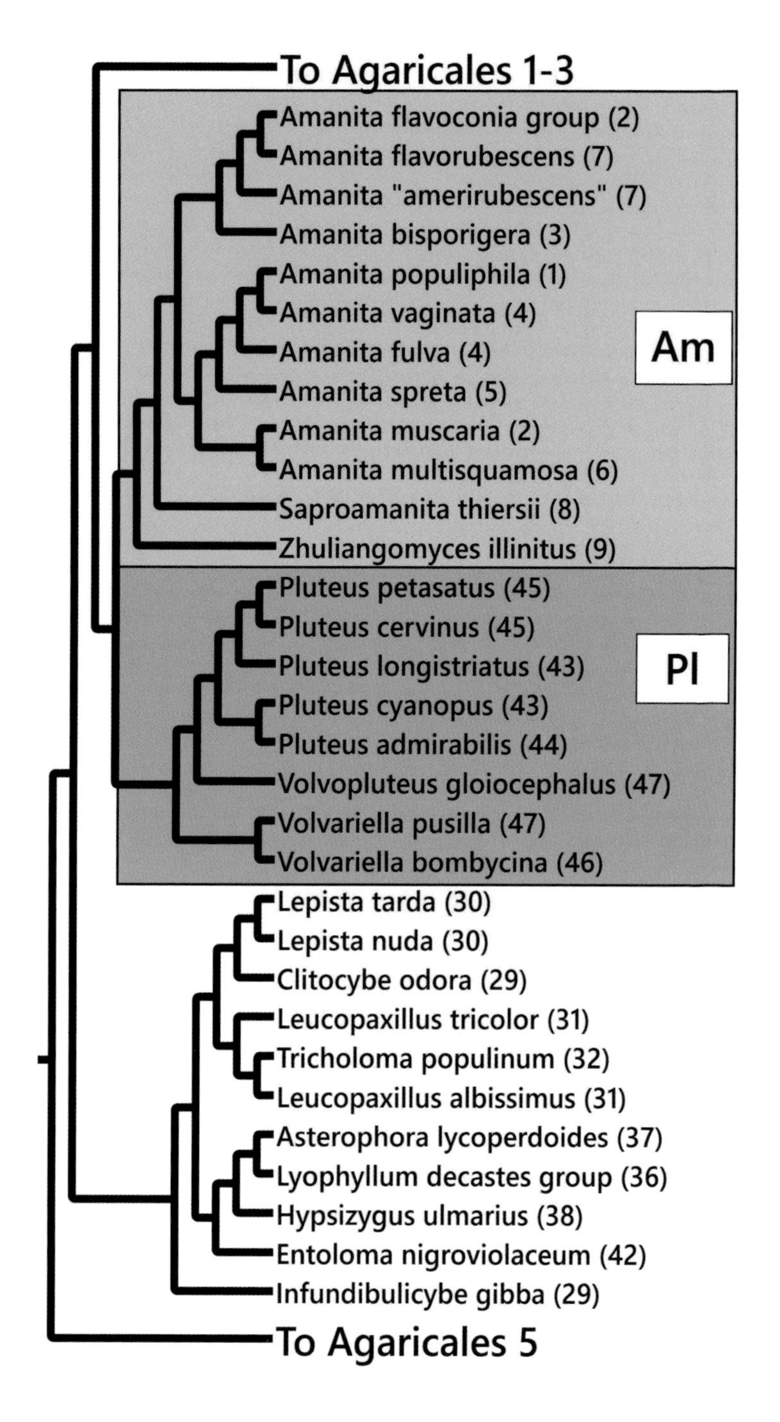
To Agaricales 1-3
Amanita flavoconia group (2)
Amanita flavorubescens (7)
Amanita "amerirubescens" (7)
Amanita bisporigera (3)
Amanita populiphila (1)
Amanita vaginata (4)
Amanita fulva (4)
Amanita spreta (5)
Amanita muscaria (2)
Amanita multisquamosa (6)
Saproamanita thiersii (8)
Zhuliangomyces illinitus (9)
Am
Pluteus petasatus (45)
Pluteus cervinus (45)
Pluteus longistriatus (43)
Pluteus cyanopus (43)
Pluteus admirabilis (44)
Volvopluteus gloiocephalus (47)
Volvariella pusilla (47)
Volvariella bombycina (46)
Pl
Lepista tarda (30)
Lepista nuda (30)
Clitocybe odora (29)
Leucopaxillus tricolor (31)
Tricholoma populinum (32)
Leucopaxillus albissimus (31)
Asterophora lycoperdoides (37)
Lyophyllum decastes group (36)
Hypsizygus ulmarius (38)
Entoloma nigroviolaceum (42)
Infundibulicybe gibba (29)
To Agaricales 5

Agaricales 5

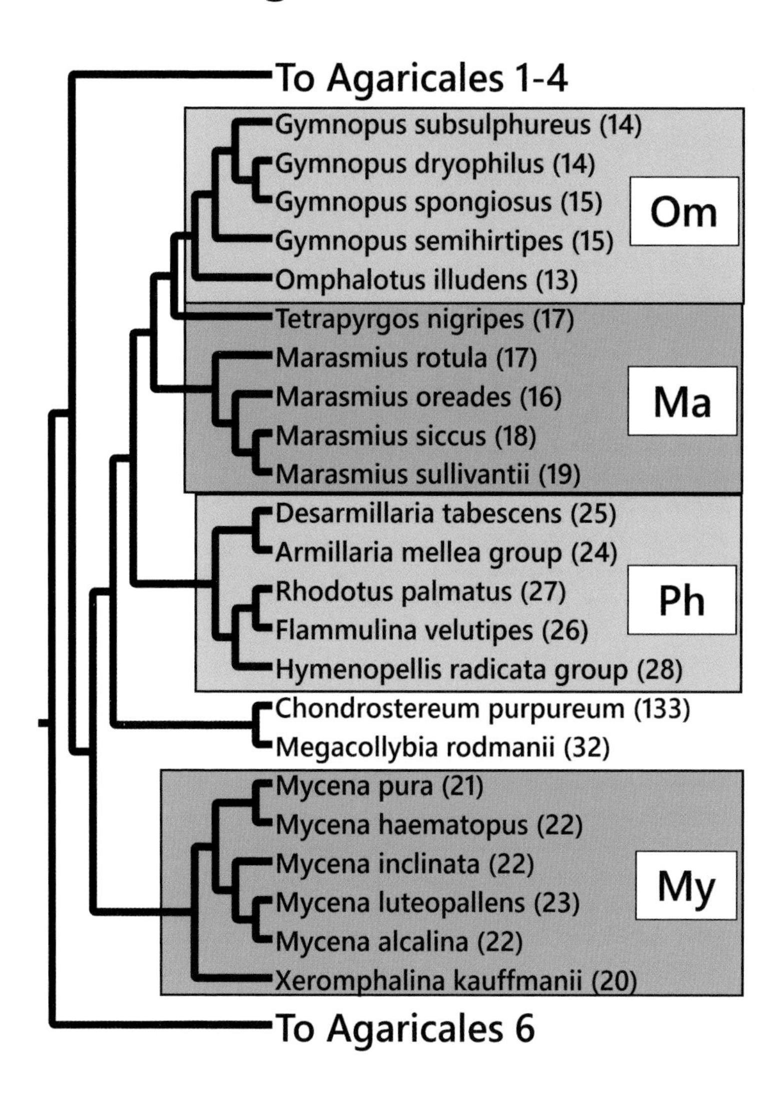

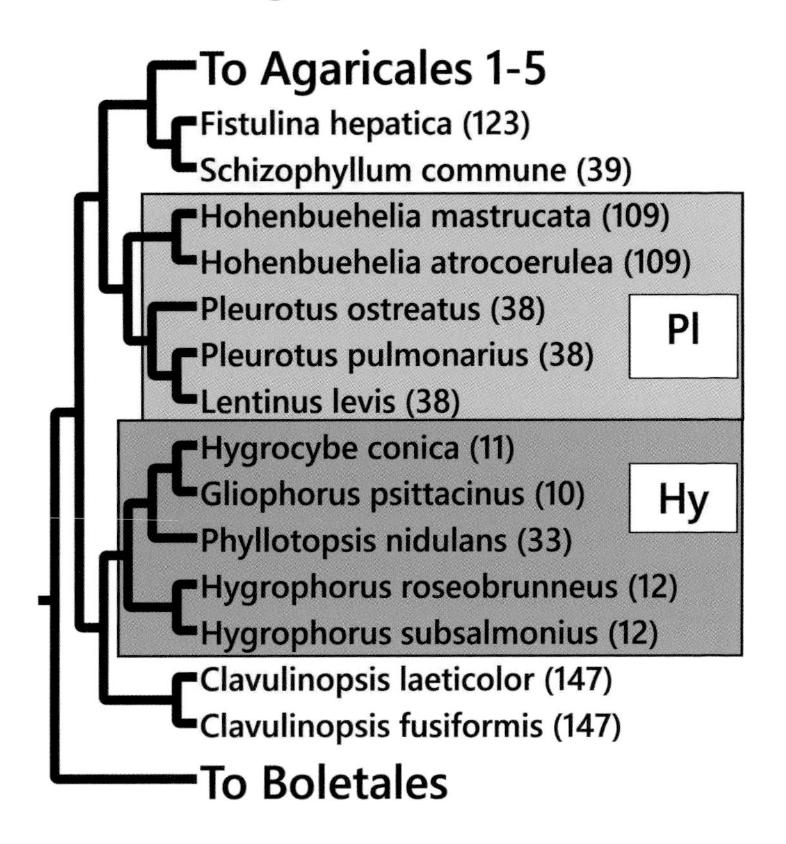
Agaricales 6
To Agaricales 1-5
Fistulina hepatica (123)
Schizophyllum commune (39)
Hohenbuehelia mastrucata (109)
Hohenbuehelia atrocoerulea (109)
Pleurotus ostreatus (38)
Pleurotus pulmonarius (38)
Lentinus levis (38)
Pl
Hygrocybe conica (11)
Gliophorus psittacinus (10)
Phyllotopsis nidulans (33)
Hygrophorus roseobrunneus (12)
Hygrophorus subsalmonius (12)
Hy
Clavulinopsis laeticolor (147)
Clavulinopsis fusiformis (147)
To Boletales

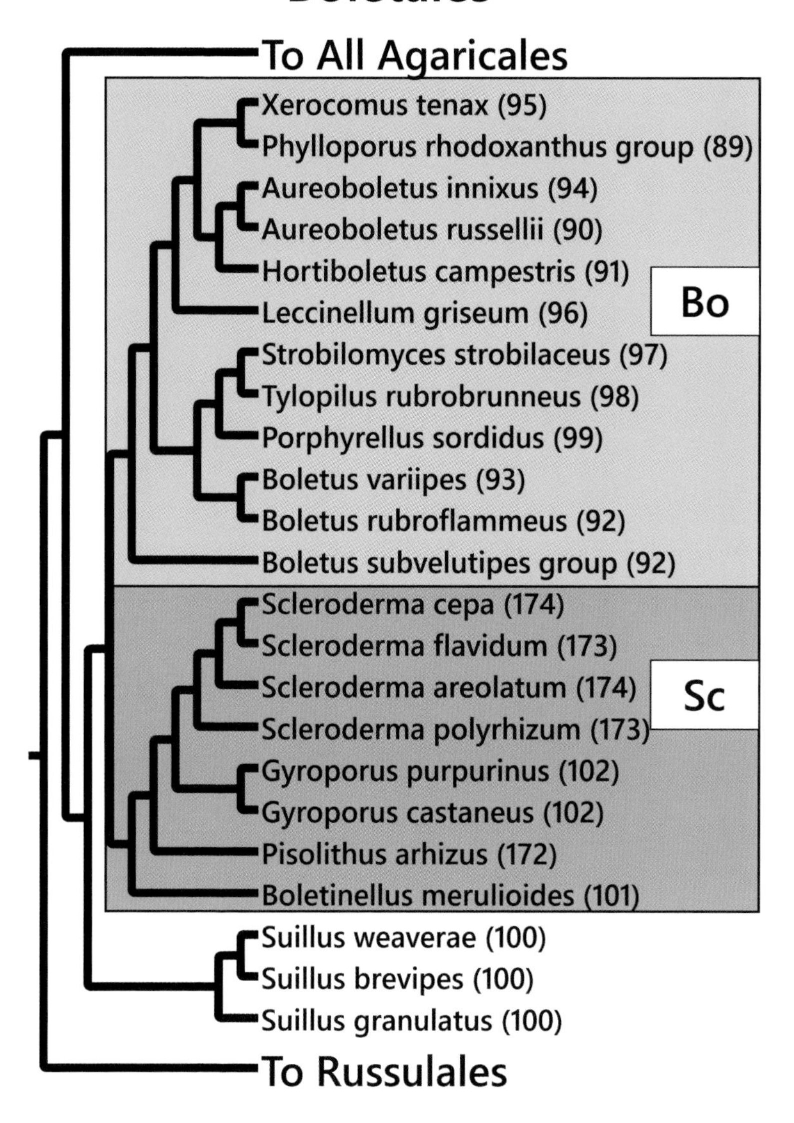
Boletales
To All Agaricales
Xerocomus tenax (95)
Phylloporus rhodoxanthus group (89)
Aureoboletus innixus (94)
Aureoboletus russellii (90)
Hortiboletus campestris (91)
Leccinellum griseum (96)
Bo
Strobilomyces strobilaceus (97)
Tylopilus rubrobrunneus (98)
Porphyrellus sordidus (99)
Boletus variipes (93)
Boletus rubroflammeus (92)
Boletus subvelutipes group (92)
Scleroderma cepa (174)
Scleroderma flavidum (173)
Scleroderma areolatum (174)
Sc
Scleroderma polyrhizum (173)
Gyroporus purpurinus (102)
Gyroporus castaneus (102)
Pisolithus arhizus (172)
Boletinellus merulioides (101)
Suillus weaverae (100)
Suillus brevipes (100)
Suillus granulatus (100)
To Russulales

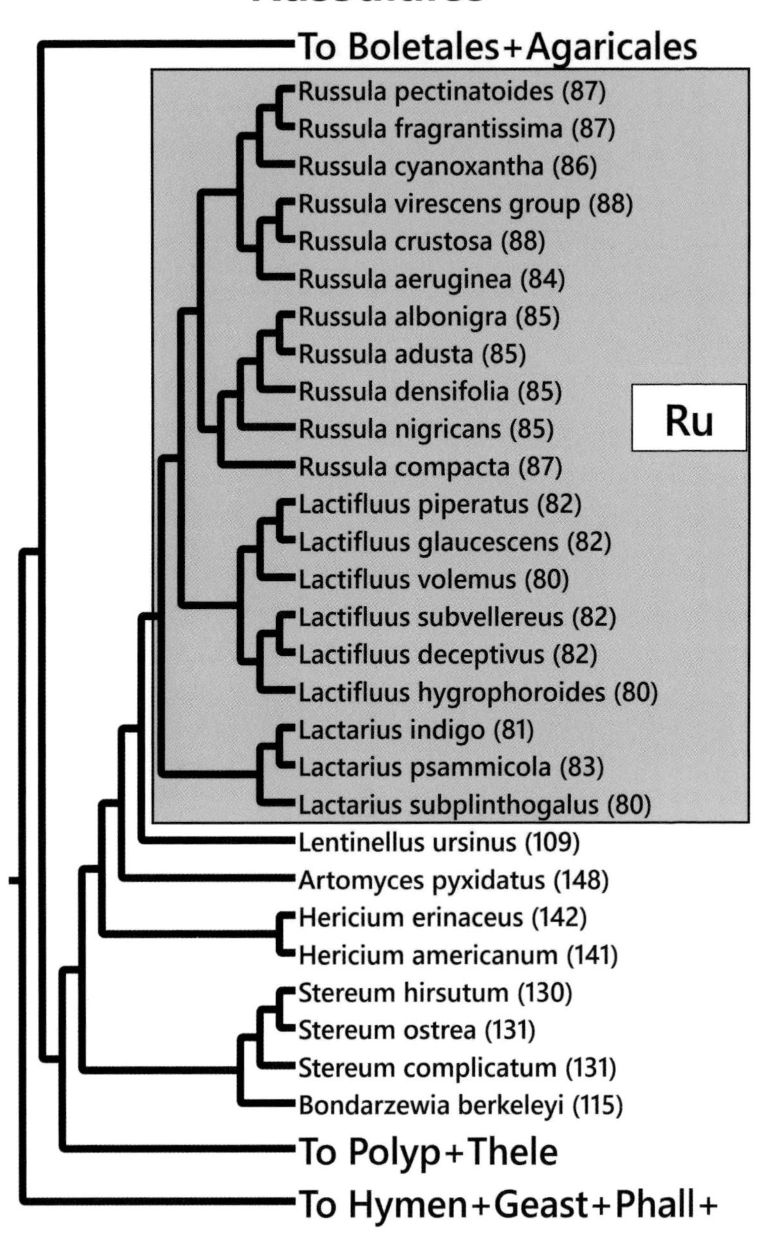
Russulales
To Boletales+Agaricales
Russula pectinatoides (87)
Russula fragrantissima (87)
Russula cyanoxantha (86)
Russula virescens group (88)
Russula crustosa (88)
Russula aeruginea (84)
Russula albonigra (85)
Russula adusta (85)
Russula densifolia (85)
Russula nigricans (85)
Russula compacta (87)
Ru
Lactifluus piperatus (82)
Lactifluus glaucescens (82)
Lactifluus volemus (80)
Lactifluus subvellereus (82)
Lactifluus deceptivus (82)
Lactifluus hygrophoroides (80)
Lactarius indigo (81)
Lactarius psammicola (83)
Lactarius subplinthogalus (80)
Lentinellus ursinus (109)
Artomyces pyxidatus (148)
Hericium erinaceus (142)
Hericium americanum (141)
Stereum hirsutum (130)
Stereum ostrea (131)
Stereum complicatum (131)
Bondarzewia berkeleyi (115)
To Polyp+Thele
To Hymen+Geast+Phall+

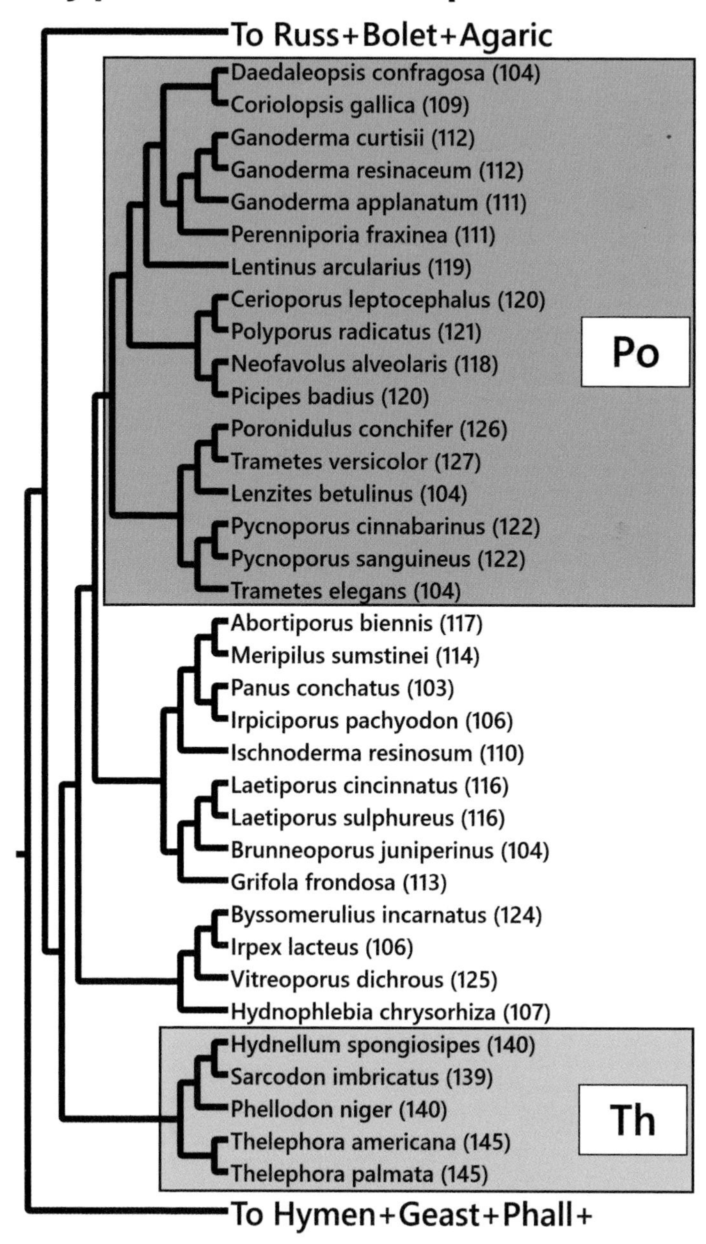
Polyporales + Thelephorales
To Russ+Bolet+Agaric
Daedaleopsis confragosa (104)
Coriolopsis gallica (109)
Ganoderma curtisii (112)
Ganoderma resinaceum (112)
Ganoderma applanatum (111)
Perenniporia fraxinea (111)
Lentinus arcularius (119)
Cerioporus leptocephalus (120)
Polyporus radicatus (121)
Neofavolus alveolaris (118)
Picipes badius (120)
Poronidulus conchifer (126)
Trametes versicolor (127)
Lenzites betulinus (104)
Pycnoporus cinnabarinus (122)
Pycnoporus sanguineus (122)
Trametes elegans (104)
Po
Abortiporus biennis (117)
Meripilus sumstinei (114)
Panus conchatus (103)
Irpiciporus pachyodon (106)
Ischnoderma resinosum (110)
Laetiporus cincinnatus (116)
Laetiporus sulphureus (116)
Brunneoporus juniperinus (104)
Grifola frondosa (113)
Byssomerulius incarnatus (124)
Irpex lacteus (106)
Vitreoporus dichrous (125)
Hydnophlebia chrysorhiza (107)
Hydnellum spongiosipes (140)
Sarcodon imbricatus (139)
Phellodon niger (140)
Thelephora americana (145)
Thelephora palmata (145)
Th
To Hymen+Geast+Phall+

Hymenochaetales+Geastrales +Phallales

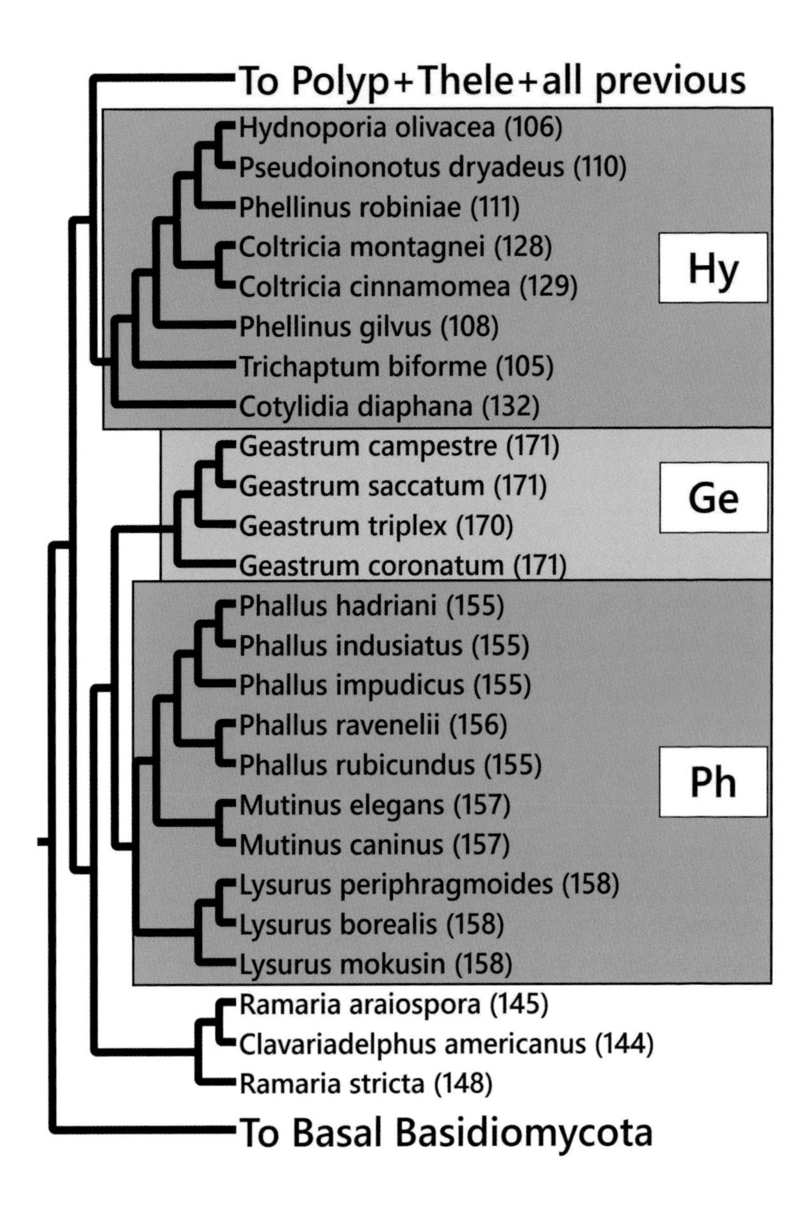

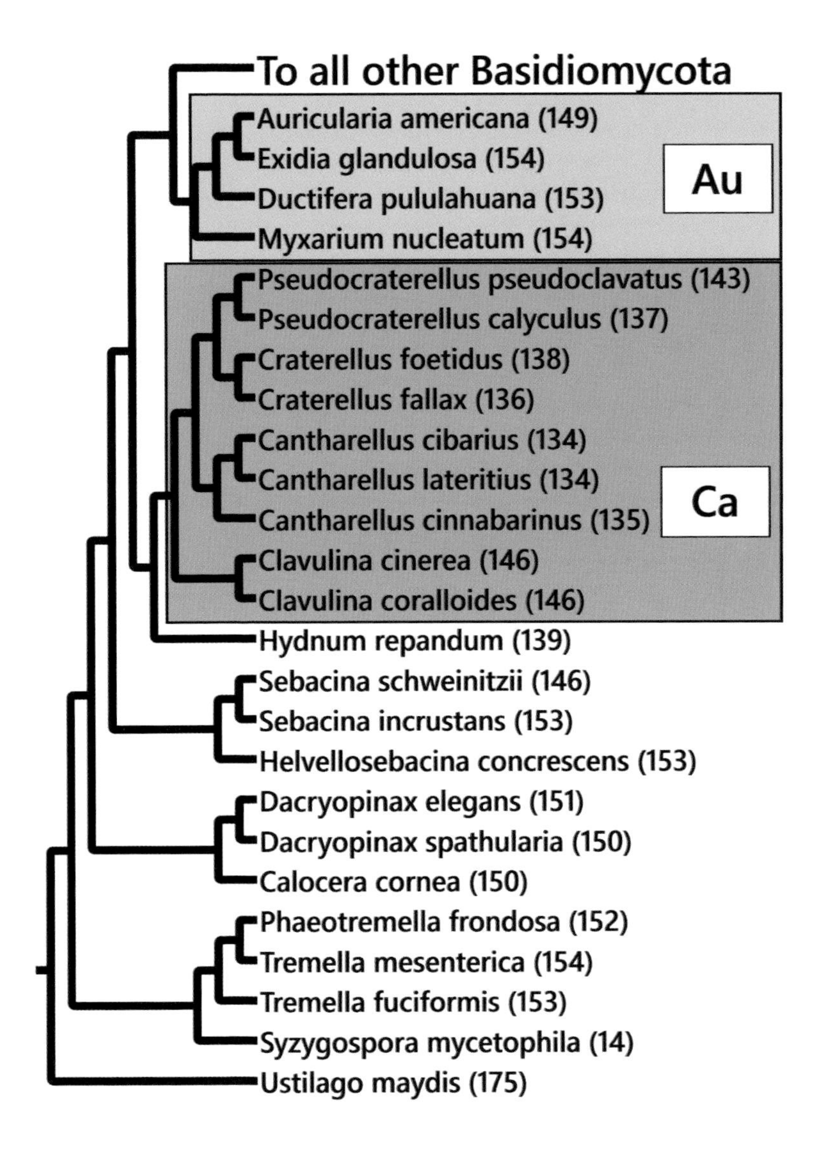
Basal Basidiomycota
To all other Basidiomycota
Auricularia americana (149)
Exidia glandulosa (154)
Ductifera pululahuana (153)
Myxarium nucleatum (154)
Au
Pseudocraterellus pseudoclavatus (143)
Pseudocraterellus calyculus (137)
Craterellus foetidus (138)
Craterellus fallax (136)
Cantharellus cibarius (134)
Cantharellus lateritius (134)
Cantharellus cinnabarinus (135)
Ca
Clavulina cinerea (146)
Clavulina coralloides (146)
Hydnum repandum (139)
Sebacina schweinitzii (146)
Sebacina incrustans (153)
Helvellosebacina concrescens (153)
Dacryopinax elegans (151)
Dacryopinax spathularia (150)
Calocera cornea (150)
Phaeotremella frondosa (152)
Tremella mesenterica (154)
Tremella fuciformis (153)
Syzygospora mycetophila (14)
Ustilago maydis (175)

The relationships depicted here are based on a combination of studies, nearly all of which use multiple genetic markers to map the evolutionary relationships among species. The relationships among the major groups of our species were based on a massive global effort. Within many families/orders, however, we often checked and revised these using recent, group-specific publications for final placement of the individual species. The main bases for the branches in each of these groups (and subgroups) are listed below. We encourage adventuresome fungal systematists to read up on their methods. It's an exciting time for fungal systematics! No doubt new studies move individual species to different areas and continue to improve our understanding of the broader relationships among major groups.

Baseline phylogeny: T. Varga, K. Krizsán, C. Földi, B. Dima, M. Sánchez-García, S. Sánchez-Ramírez, G. J. Szöllősi, J. G. Szarkándi, V. Papp, L. Albert, and W. Andreopoulos, "Megaphylogeny Resolves Global Patterns of Mushroom Evolution," *Nature Ecology & Evolution* 3, no. 4 (April 2019): 668–678.

Additional group-level studies used:

Strophariaceae: E. J. Tian and P. B. Matheny, "A Phylogenetic Assessment of *Pholiota* and the New Genus Pyrrhulomyces," *Mycologia* 113, no. 1 (January 2021): 146–167.

Cortinariaceae: K. Liimatainen, T. Niskanen, B. Dima, J. F. Ammirati, P. M. Kirk, and I. Kytövuori, "Mission Impossible Completed: Unlocking the Nomenclature of the Largest and Most Complicated Subgenus of *Cortinarius, Telamonia*," *Fungal Diversity* 104, no. 1 (September 2020): 291–331.

And: U. Peintner, J. M. Moncalvo, and R. Vilgalys, "Toward a Better Understanding of the Infrageneric Relationships in *Cortinarius* (Agaricales, Basidiomycota)," *Mycologia* 96, no. 5 (September 2004): 1042–1158.

Feedback from Drs. Karen Hughes and Brandon Matheny helped here as well.

Psathyrellaceae: L. G. Nagy, C. Vágvölgyi, and T. Papp, "Morphological Characterization of Clades of the Psathyrellaceae (Agaricales) Inferred from a Multigene Phylogeny," *Mycological Progress* 12, no. 3 (August 2013): 505–517.

Agaricaceae: J. Geml, D. M. Geiser, and D. J. Royse, "Molecular Evolution of *Agaricus* Species Based on ITS and LSU rDNA Sequences," *Mycological Progress* 3, no. 2 (May 2004): 157–176.

And: E. C. Vellinga, P. Sysouphanthong, and K. D. Hyde, "The Family Agaricaceae: Phylogenies and Two New White-Spored Genera," *Mycologia* 103, no. 3 (May 2011): 494–509.

Lycoperdaceae: E. Larsson and M. Jeppson, "Phylogenetic Relationships among Species and Genera of Lycoperdaceae Based on ITS and LSU Sequence Data from North European Taxa," *Mycological Research* 112, no. 1 (January 2008): 4–22.

Amanitaceae: Y. Y. Cui, Q. Cai, L. P. Tang, J. W. Liu, and Z. L. Yang, "The Family Amanitaceae: Molecular Phylogeny, Higher-Rank Taxonomy and the Species in China," *Fungal Diversity* 91, no. 1 (July 2018): 5–230.

Pluteaceae: A. Justo, A. M. Minnis, S. Ghignone, N. Menolli, M. Capelari, O. Rodríguez, E. Malysheva, M. Contu, and A. Vizzini, "Species Recognition in *Pluteus* and *Volvopluteus* (Pluteaceae, Agaricales): Morphology, Geography and Phylogeny," *Mycological Progress* 10, no. 4 (November 2011): 453–479.

Omphalotaceae: J. J. Oliveira, R. Vargas-Isla, T. S. Cabral, D. P. Rodrigues, and N. K. Ishikawa, "Progress on the Phylogeny of the Omphalotaceae: *Gymnopus* s. str., *Marasmiellus* s. str., *Paragymnopus* gen. nov. and *Pusillomyces* gen. nov.," *Mycological Progress* 19, no. 5 (May 2019): 713–739.

Marasmiaceae: J. J. Oliveira, J. M. Moncalvo, S. Margaritescu, and M. Capelari, "A Morphological and Phylogenetic Evaluation of *Marasmius* sect. *Globulares* (Globulares-Sicci complex) with Nine New Taxa from the Neotropical Atlantic Forest," *Persoonia: Molecular Phylogeny and Evolution of Fungi* 44 (June 2020): 240.

Mycenaceae (is a mess and) needed several, including C. B. Harder, T. Læssøe, T. G. Frøslev, F. Ekelund, S. Rosendahl, and R. Kjøller, "A Three-Gene Phylogeny of the *Mycena Pura* Complex Reveals 11 Phylogenetic Species and Shows ITS to Be Unreliable for Species Identification," *Fungal Biology* 117, no. 11–12 (November 2013): 764–775.

And: C. B. Harder, T. Læssøe, R. Kjøller, and T. G. Frøslev, "A Comparison between ITS Phylogenetic Relationships and Morphological Species Recognition within *Mycena* sect. *Calodontes* in Northern Europe," *Mycological Progress* 9, no. 3 (August 2010): 395–405.

Pleurotaceae: G. I. Zervakis, G. Venturella, V. Fryssouli, P. Inglese, E. Polemis, and M. L. Gargano, "Pleurotus Opuntiae Revisited—an Insight to the Phylogeny of Dimitic *Pleurotus* Species with Emphasis on the *P. Djamor* Complex," *Fungal Biology* 123, no. 3 (March 2019): 188–199.

Boletales (including Boletaceae and Sclerodermataceae): M. E. Nuhn, M. Binder, A. F. Taylor, R. E. Halling, and D. S. Hibbett, "Phylogenetic Overview of the Boletineae," *Fungal Biology* 117, no. 7–8 (July 2013): 479–511.

And: N. H. Nguyen, E. C. Vellinga, T. D. Bruns, and P. G. Kennedy, "Phylogenetic Assessment of Global *Suillus* ITS Sequences Supports Morphologically Defined Species and Reveals Synonymous and Undescribed Taxa," *Mycologia* 106, no. 6 (November 2016): 1216–1228.

Russulales: J. M. Vidal, P. Alvarado, M. Loizides, G. Konstantinidis, P. Chachuła, P. Mleczko, G. Moreno, A. Vizzini, M. Krakhmalnyi, A. Paz, and J. Cabero, "A Phylogenetic and Taxonomic Revision of Sequestrate Russulaceae in Mediterranean and Temperate Europe," *Persoonia: Molecular Phylogeny and Evolution of Fungi* 42 (June 2019): 127.

And: R. De Lange, S. Adamčík, K. Adamčíkova, P. Asselman, J. Borovička, L. Delgat, F. Hampe, and A. Verbeken, "From White to Black, from Darkness to Light: Species Delimitation and UNITE Species Hypothesis Testing in the Russula Albonigra Species Complex," *IMA Fungus* (August 2020), doi: 10.21203/rs.3.rs-118250/v1.

And: E. De Crop, J. Nuytinck, K. Van de Putte, K. Wisitrassameewong, J. Hackel, D. Stubbe, K. D. Hyde, M. Roy, R. E. Halling, P. A. Moreau, and U. Eberhardt, "A Multi-Gene Phylogeny of Lactifluus (Basidiomycota, Russulales) Translated into a New Infrageneric Classification of the Genus," *Persoonia: Molecular Phylogeny and Evolution of Fungi* 38 (June 2017): 58.

And: S. G. DeLong-Duhon, and R. K. Bagley, "Phylogeny, Morphology, and Ecology Resurrect Previously Synonymized Species of North American Stereum," *bioRxiv* (January 2020).

Polyporales: M. Binder, A. Justo, R. Riley, A. Salamov, F. Lopez-Giraldez, E. Sjökvist, A. Copeland, B. Foster, H. Sun, E. Larsson, and K. H. Larsson, "Phylogenetic and Phylogenomic Overview of the Polyporales," *Mycologia* 105, no. 6 (November 2013): 1350–1373.

Thelephorales: K. H. Larsson, S. Svantesson, D. Miscevic, U. Kõljalg, and E. Larsson, "Reassessment of the Generic Limits for Hydnellum and Sarcodon (Thelephorales, Basidiomycota)," *MycoKeys* 54 (2019): 31.

Hymenochaetales: K. H. Larsson, E. Parmasto, M. Fischer, E. Langer, K. K. Nakasone, and S. A. Redhead, "Hymenochaetales: A Molecular Phylogeny for the Hymenochaetoid Clade," *Mycologia* 98, no. 6 (November 2006): 926–936.

Geastrales: J. C. Zamora, F. de Diego Calonge, K. Hosaka, and M. P. Martín, "Systematics of the Genus Geastrum (Fungi: Basidiomycota) Revisited," *Taxon* 63, no. 3 (June 2014): 477–497.

Phallales: L. Trierveiler-Pereira, R. M. da Silveira, and K. Hosaka, "Multigene Phylogeny of the Phallales (Phallomycetidae, Agaricomycetes) Focusing on Some Previously Unrepresented Genera," *Mycologia* 106, no. 5 (September 2014): 904–911.

And: T. Li, T. Li, W. Deng, B. Song, C. Deng, and Z. Yang, "Phallus Dongsun and P. Lutescens, Two New Species of Phallaceae (Basidiomycota) from China," *Phytotaxa* 443, no. 1 (May 2020): 19–37.

Auriculariales: V. Malysheva and V. Spirin, "Taxonomy and Phylogeny of the Auriculariales (Agaricomycetes, Basidiomycota) with Stereoid Basidiocarps," *Fungal Biology* 121, no. 8 (August 2017): 689–715.

Cantharellales: E. M. Pine, D. S. Hibbett, and M. J. Donoghue, "Phylogenetic Relationships of Cantharelloid and Clavarioid Homobasidiomycetes Based on Mitochondrial and Nuclear Rdna Sequences," *Mycologia* 91, no. 6 (November 1999): 944–963.

And: B. Buyck, V. Hofstetter, and I. Olariaga, "Setting the Record Straight on North American *Cantharellus*," *Cryptogamie, Mycologie* 37, no. 3 (September 2016): 405–417.

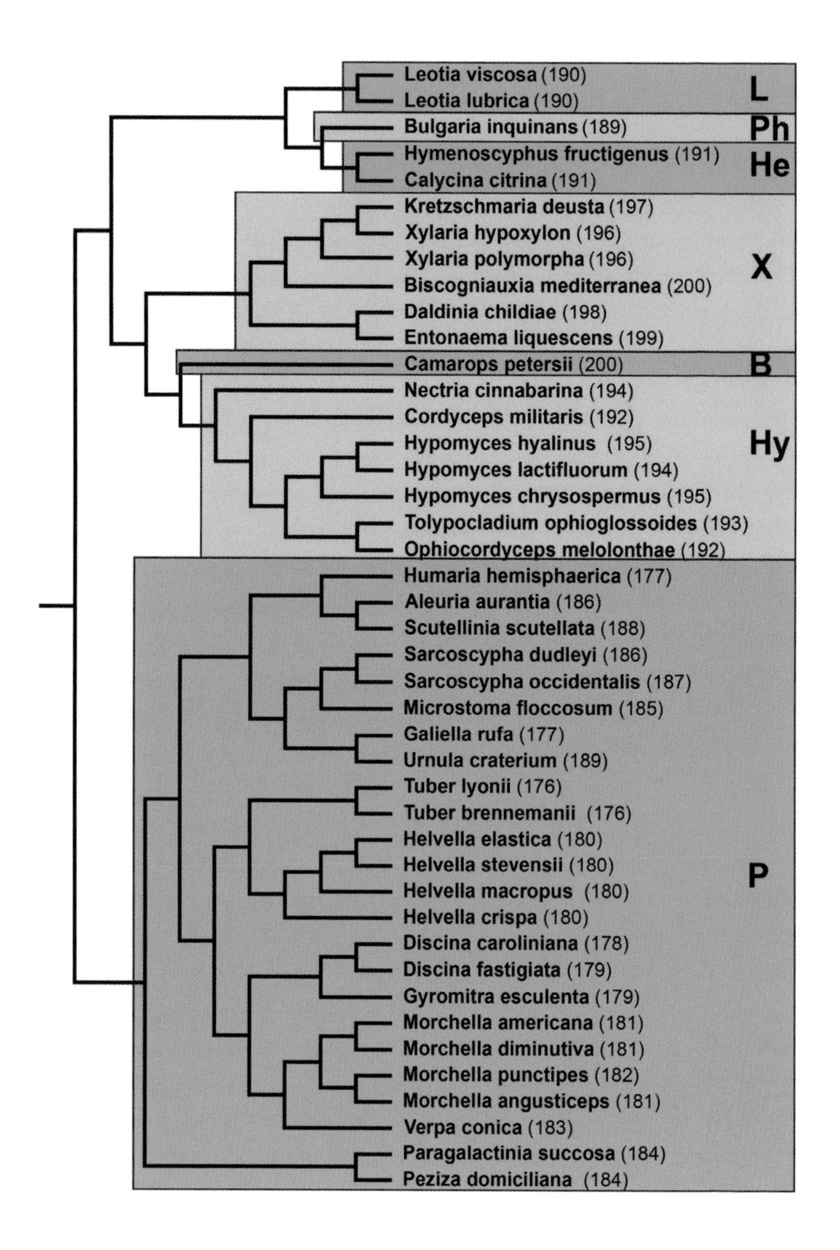

Leotia viscosa (190)
Leotia lubrica (190)
L
Bulgaria inquinans (189)
Ph
Hymenoscyphus fructigenus (191)
Calycina citrina (191)
He
Kretzschmaria deusta (197)
Xylaria hypoxylon (196)
Xylaria polymorpha (196)
Biscogniauxia mediterranea (200)
Daldinia childiae (198)
Entonaema liquescens (199)
X
Camarops petersii (200)
B
Nectria cinnabarina (194)
Cordyceps militaris (192)
Hypomyces hyalinus (195)
Hypomyces lactifluorum (194)
Hypomyces chrysospermus (195)
Tolypocladium ophioglossoides (193)
Ophiocordyceps melolonthae (192)
Hy
Humaria hemisphaerica (177)
Aleuria aurantia (186)
Scutellinia scutellata (188)
Sarcoscypha dudleyi (186)
Sarcoscypha occidentalis (187)
Microstoma floccosum (185)
Galiella rufa (177)
Urnula craterium (189)
Tuber lyonii (176)
Tuber brennemanii (176)
Helvella elastica (180)
Helvella stevensii (180)
Helvella macropus (180)
Helvella crispa (180)
Discina caroliniana (178)
Discina fastigiata (179)
Gyromitra esculenta (179)
Morchella americana (181)
Morchella diminutiva (181)
Morchella punctipes (182)
Morchella angusticeps (181)
Verpa conica (183)
Paragalactinia succosa (184)
Peziza domiciliana (184)
P

Appendix B

Relationships among the Species of Phylum Ascomycota

Like the Basidiomycota cladogram, this figure depicts our current understanding of the relatedness among species in the phylum Ascomycota presented in this book. At the tip of each branch of the tree is the scientific name of the fungus as well as the species account number in which it is described. Although fewer species of Ascomycota than Basidiomycota are covered in this book, this phylum actually represents the greater part of fungal diversity. Each fork of this tree, and each branch tip, may stand in for many (perhaps thousands!) of species. It is probably the case that any two closely related species on this tree actually have even more closely related cousins that are not included in this tree; what is presented in the tree is only the small subset of species we chose for this book.

In the figure, we have labeled the major orders of Ascomycota represented by fungi in the book and colored boxes are used to highlight each. The two groups that arise from the deep fork at the top left of the cladogram represent the Ascomycota classes Leotiomycetes and Sordariomycetes. The Leotiomycetes in the top branch include the jelly babies (genus *Leotia*) in the order Leotiales (L), the button fungus *Bulgaria inquinans* of the Phacidiales (Ph), and the miniscule cups *Calycina citrina* and *Hymenoscyphus fructigena* of the Helotiales (He). The second major branch is the class Sordariomycetes, known as the flask fungi because of the flask-like chambers where they produce their spores. In the book, they are represented by several species of the order Xylariales (X) including the dead man's fingers (*Xylaria polymorpha*); *Camarops petersii*, the sole representative of the Boliniales (B) treated in this book; and the Hypocreales (Hy) which contain important fungal and insect pathogens. Finally, the major branch at the bottom of this cladogram represents the class Pezizomycetes, whose members are all in the single order Pezizales and contain the most Ascomycota species in this book. As in the other two branches, there are several major groups in the Pezizales, but none are currently considered different enough to be distinct orders. If one looks carefully, though, one can clearly see key groups. For example, the branch with *Morchella* species and *Verpa* represents the true morels (the family Morchellaceae).

A final few points are worth making here. First, all of the species of flask fungi covered in this book are more closely related to one another than they are to the cup fungi. While these fungi form two big groups (one deep branch containing members of the Xylariales and the other containing members of the Bolineales and Hypocreales), taxonomists include all of these species in one class, the Sordariomycetes. Both the Leotiomycetes and the Pezizomycetes are considered cup fungi because of how they produce their spores. The Leotiomycetes, however, are actually more closely related to the flask fungi; that is, the Leotiomycetes and Sordariomycetes have an ancestor in common that neither shares with the Pezizomycetes. Notably, then, it appears from this tree that the flask fungi evolved only once—and that their flask-shaped fruiting structure (known as the perithecium) is indicative of evolutionary relationships—but the same cannot be said of the cups of cup fungi. As you might imagine, of course, with a phylum containing some 40,000 species and additional classes, this is not quite so clean as our tree suggests. But if you find a flask fungus not included in this book, you can probably still safely conclude that it belongs in the Sordariomycetes and not one of the other two classes here.

This figure is based on several recently published studies of the Ascomycota, each of which employed multiple genetic markers to map the evolutionary relationships among species. The bases for the branches in each of these groups (and some subgroups) are listed below. We encourage adventurous fungal systematists to read up on their methods.

Leotiomycetes was based on Wendy A. Untereiner, Qun Yue, Li Chen, Yan Li, Gerald F. Bills, Václav Štěpánek, and Martina Réblová, "*Phialophora* Section *Catenulatae* Disassembled: New Genera, Species, and Combinations and a New Family Encompassing Taxa with Cleistothecial Ascomata and Phialidic Asexual States," *Mycologia* 111, no. 6 (2019): 998–1027, doi: 10.1080/00275514.2019.1663106.

Sordariomycetes was overall based on N. Zhang, L. A. Castlebury, A. N. Miller, S. M. Huhndorf, C. L. Schoch, K. A. Seifert, A. Y. Rossman, J. D. Rogers, J. Kohlmeyer, B. Volkmann-Kohlmeyer, and G. H. Sung, "An Overview of the Systematics of the Sordariomycetes Based on a Four-Gene Phylogeny," *Mycologia* 98, no. 6 (November 2006): 1076–1087. Within this,

The **Hypocreales** was based on W. Zhang, X. Zhang, K. Li, C. Wang, L. Cai, W. Zhuang, M. Xiang, and X. Liu, "Introgression and Gene Family Contraction Drive the Evolution of Lifestyle and Host Shifts of Hypocrealean Fungi," *Mycology* 9, no. 3 (July 2018): 176–188.

The **Xylariales** was based on L. Wendt, E. B. Sir, E. Kuhnert, S. Heitkämper, C. Lambert, A. I. Hladki, A. I. Romero, J. J. Luangsa-ard, P. Srikitikulchai, D. Peršoh, and M. Stadler, "Resurrection and Emendation of the Hypoxylaceae, Recognised from a Multigene Phylogeny of the Xylariales," *Mycological Progress* 17, no. 1 (January 2018): 115–154.

Pezizomycetes was overall based on A. H. Ekanayaka, K. D. Hyde, E. G. Jones, and Q. Zhao, "Taxonomy and Phylogeny of Operculate Discomycetes: Pezizomycetes," *Fungal Diversity* 90, no. 1 (May 2018): 161–243. Within this,

Morchellaceae was based on M. Kuo, D. R. Dewsbury, K. O'Donnell, M. C. Carter, S. A. Rehner, J. D. Moore, J. M. Moncalvo, S. A. Canfield, S. L. Stephenson, A. S. Methven, and T. J. Volk, "Taxonomic Revision of True Morels (*Morchella*) in Canada and the United States," *Mycologia* 104, no. 5 (September 2012): 1159–1177.

Helvellaceae was based on I. Skrede, T. Carlsen, and T. Schumacher, "A Synopsis of the Saddle Fungi (*Helvella*: Ascomycota) in Europe—Species Delimitation, Taxonomy and Typification," *Persoonia: Molecular Phylogeny and Evolution of Fungi* 39 (December 2017): 201.

Glossary

Acrid Tastes burning or peppery.

Adnate Gills attached squarely to the stalk (Fig. 3C).

Adnexed Gills attached to the stalk in an upward-curving manner (Fig. 3E).

Amyloid Staining blue-black in Melzer's solution.

Anamorph A form of a fungus that produces asexual spores, rather like clones, not produced by asci or basidia; also called "imperfect" fungi.

Angular Having sides or corners.

Annulus (*pl.* **annuli**) Collapsed partial veil remaining as a ring around the stalk (Fig. 2).

Apiculus (*pl.* **apiculi**) Nipple-like projection on a spore where it was attached to the sterigma of the basidium.

Areolate Broken up into patches, often in evidence on the cap.

Ascomycota The phylum of fungi in which members produce (typically eight) sexual spores inside asci; members are sometimes referred to as ascomycetes.

Ascus (*pl.* **asci**) Sac-like cell that contains sexual spores (Fig. 8A); characteristic of the phylum Ascomycota.

Asexual Not resulting from fertilization and zygote formation—for example, the "spores" of mushroom anamorphs.

Attached Gills joined to the stalk (Fig. 3C–E).

Basidiomycota The phylum of fungi in which members produce (typically four) sexual spores on basidia; members are sometimes referred to as basidiomycetes.

Basidium (*pl.* **basidia**) Club-shaped cell that produces sexual spores externally on the tips of sterigmata (Fig. 8C); characteristic of the phylum Basidiomycota.

Binomial nomenclature Scientific practice of naming species with Latin names, the generic name followed by the specific epithet.

Bioluminescence Emission of light by an organism.

Biotrophic Interacting with living organisms, occurring as a continuum from parasitic to mycorrhizal.

Bulbous Having a bulblike base.

Caespitose Growing very close together in clumps, with stems often touching one another or even fused at the base.

Cap Cap-like structure of a mushroom; its undersurface may support gills, tubes, spines, ridges, or smooth surfaces. (Some examples are depicted in Fig. 4.)

Central Describes a stalk attached at the middle of the cap.

Chlamydospore Thick-walled asexual spore formed directly from hyphal cells.

Concolocous All of one color.

Conical Cone-shaped.

Cortina Cobweb-like partial veil characteristic of the genus *Cortinarius*.

Cup (fungi) Cup-shaped, saucer-shaped or cushion-shaped fruiting body, as in many of the species of the order Pezizales.

Cuticle Outermost tissue layer of the cap.

Cystidium (*pl.* **cystidia**) Distinctive, sterile cell in the hymenium of the phylum Basidiomycota (Fig. 8C).

Decurrent Gills attached downward along the stalk (Fig. 3B).

Deliquesce Liquefy and turn to "ink," as in the gills of the "inkys."

Dextrinoid Staining reddish brown in Melzer's solution.

Dikaryotic Having two genetically distinct nuclei per cell.

Egg Immature fruiting body surrounded by a universal veil or a similar skin-like layer (Fig. 7); spore package of bird's nest fungi.

Epithet Second (specific) part of a Latin binomial.

Eukaryote Organism whose cells contain nuclei and other membrane-bound structures—for example, fungi, plants, and animals.

Fairy ring Circular fruiting of mushrooms (Fig. 5).

Free Gills not attached to the stalk (Fig. 3A).

Fruiting body Spore-producing structure of a fungus.

Fungus (*pl.* **fungi**) Eukaryotic organism that lacks chlorophyll, reproduces by nonmotile spores, has chitinous cell walls, and is generally filamentous.

Gasteroid Having a spore mass enclosed in a tissue sac; usually passively dispersed.

Genus (*pl.* **genera**) Taxonomic grouping of closely related species.

Germ pore Thin region on a spore, usually at its apex (most pointed portion), from which the hypha emerges upon germination (Fig. 9A, H, J).

Gills Soft, vertical plates beneath the cap, radiating out from the center, that bear spores.

Gleba Spore-bearing tissue of the gastroid fungi or stinking slimy part of stinkhorns (order Phallales).

Head Fertile portion of a fruiting body when not on the undersurface of a cap—for example, spore-bearing regions of morels and stinkhorns.

Hygrophanous Changing color depending on the amount of water retained.

Hygroscopic Changing form by absorbing moisture from air (pertaining to a fruiting body).

Hymenium (*pl.* **hymenia**) Spore-producing layer of cells on a fruiting body (Fig. 4).

Hypha (*pl.* **hyphae**) Threadlike filament of fungal cells (Fig. 10).

Kingdom Largest taxonomic grouping of organisms; the six kingdoms are Fungi, Plantae, Animalia, Protista, Archaea, and Bacteria.

Lateral Describes a stalk attached to the edge of the cap.

Latex Fluid exuded by an injured fruiting body, as in the genera *Lactarius* and *Lactifluus*.

Margin The edge, often of a cup or something else.

Melzer's solution Iodine solution used to detect color changes in fungal spores and tissue.

Micrometer Metric unit abbreviated μm (1 millimeter = 1,000 μm); also called a micron.

Morphological Shape related.

Mushroom Fruiting body of a fungus; a term usually applied to the macrofungi of the phyla Ascomycota and Basidiomycota.

Mutualistic Mutually beneficial partnership.

Mycelial cord Relatively undifferentiated rootlike aggregation of hyphae.

Mycelium (*pl.* **mycelia**) Mass of hyphae (Fig. 1).

Mycology The study of fungi.

Mycorrhiza (*pl.* **mycorrhizae**) Mutually beneficial association of fungal hyphae with the root tips of plants.

Mycorrhizal Forming mycorrhizae, typically describing the fungal partner.

Nonamyloid Not reacting in Melzer's solution—that is, staining only yellow (the color of Melzer's).

Notched Gills abruptly indented where they attach to the stalk (Fig. 3D).

Off center Describes a stalk not centrally attached to the cap.

Paraphysis (*pl.* **paraphyses**) Distinctive sterile cell in the hymenium of the phylum Ascomycota (Fig. 8A).

Partial veil Layer of tissue covering the gills or tubes during development (Fig. 2C and D); often forms an annulus after rupturing.

Perithecium (*pl.* **perithecia**) Minute flask-shaped structure containing asci (Fig. 8B), characteristic of the orders Boliniales, Hypocreales, and Xylariales.

Pore Mouth or opening of fertile tubes in the boletes and polypores (see Fig. 4)

Ray Triangular segment from the outer skin of an earthstar.

Reticulate Covered with a netlike pattern of ridges.

Riparian Occurring along a waterway.

Rhizomorph Highly differentiated rootlike aggregation of hyphae.

Saprotrophic Organisms that feed on dead organic matter. Saprotrophic organisms are sometimes called saprophytes.

Scaber Tiny group of hairs.

Sexual Resulting from fertilization and zygote formation—for example, in fungi those spores that develop on basidia or within asci.

Septate Divided into discrete units by the presence of walls called septae.

Species Taxonomic group consisting of one or more populations of organisms that are capable of interbreeding and producing fertile offspring; the determination of fungal species once depended primarily on morphological features, but DNA sequencing has made it possible to better determine species boundaries.

Spine Toothlike structure that bears spores (see Fig. 4); see "Teeth."

Spore One- to many-celled reproductive structure of fungi (Fig. 9).

Spore case Structure containing the spore mass in gastroid fungi.

Spore mass Aggregate of the spores in species of the gastroid fungi.

Spore print Pattern left by spores when deposited from a fruiting body.

Spore slime Stinking, slimy spore mass characteristic of stinkhorns (Phallales).

Stalk Structure that supports the cap or head of a mushroom (Fig. 20).

Sterigma (*pl.* **sterigmata**) Pointed projection on the basidium that bears the spore (Fig. 8C).

Sterile base Sterile tissue at the base of some of the puffballs.

Striate Marked with lines or grooves.

Taxonomy Science of classifying organisms according to their degrees of relatedness.

Teleomorph A form of fungi that produces sexual spores, also called "perfect" fungi.

Teeth Used interchangeably with the term "spine."

Toadstool Popular name for a mushroom.

Tube Fine, tubelike structure whose inner surface bears spores; found in the boletes and some polypores (see Fig. 4).

Umbo Raised area, knob, or hump often in the center of the cap.

Universal veil Layer of tissue surrounding the developing fruiting body of a mushroom (Fig. 2B).

Viscid Sticky or slimy.

Volva (*pl.* **volvae**) Ruptured universal veil or outer membrane remaining as a cup at the base of the stalk (Fig. 2D).

Volval patch Remnant of the universal veil that remains on the cap as a patch (Fig. 2D).

Warts Remnants of the universal veil that have broken into small pieces on the cap.

Zygote Cell resulting from fertilization.

Picture Credits

Dean Abel	78, 101, 112, 148, 149, 158, 183, 193
Felicia Bart	177
Hank Guarisco	1, 42, 43, 49, 52, 61, 94, 95, 96, 106, 124, 140
Sharon Hagen	Figures 2, 3, 7, 8, 9
Bruce Horn	3, 5, 6, 7, 11, 13, 14, 17, 18, 19, 22, 23, 24, 30, 34, 35, 37, 38, 44, 45, 51, 53, 57, 64, 65, 66, 67, 70, 71, 74, 79, 80, 82, 83, 87, 88, 91, 93, 102, 110, 111, 113, 119, 126, 130, 133, 134, 135, 141, 142, 144, 145, 150, 152, 154, 157, 159, 162, 163, 166, 168, 170, 171, 173, 174, 179, 180, 181, 182, 184, 185, 186, 187, 189, 191, 196, 199, 200, Figure 10
Richard Kay	2, 8, 9, 10, 12, 16, 25, 26, 28, 29, 31, 32, 39, 40, 41, 46, 47, 48, 50, 54, 55, 56, 58, 62, 69, 73, 75, 76, 81, 85, 86, 89, 90, 92, 97, 98, 99, 100, 114, 115, 116, 118, 120, 121, 122, 123, 125, 127, 128, 131, 132, 137, 138, 151, 160, 161, 164, 165, 169, 172, 176, 178, 190, 194, 195, 203, 204, 205
Sherry Kay	Figures 1, 6
Sophie Tyler Kaufman Kay	63
Robert Lichtwardt	33, 155, 167
John Little	72 ,77 ,136, 153, 192
Henry Mashburn	84, 104, 188
Ron Meyers	36, Figure 5
Dana Peterson	Figure 11
Bill Roody	60
Kit Scates	4
Walter Sturgeon	139
Carla Wick	15, 20, 21, 27, 59, 68, 103, 105, 107, 108, 109, 117, 129, 143, 146, 147, 156, 175, 198, 201, 202, Figure 4
Katy Willson	197

Index

This index lists all scientific and common names of the mushrooms mentioned in the book, as well as the names of some mushroom families and orders, and a handful of other topics that may be of interest to readers, including habitats, host trees, and toxins. Excluded are most scientific names employed as examples in Mycological Latin (pp. 316–320); names included in the Life List (pp. 329–344); names in the cladograms in Appendices A and B (pp. 348–364); and most terms found in the Glossary (pp. 369–374). Readers should consult the Table of Contents for families and orders not found here. Scientific names, including synonyms, are alphabetized by both genus and specific epithet. Page numbers in italics indicate where a scientific name is found in the keys, while page numbers in boldface indicate a main entry accompanied by a photo.